BLOODY MOHAWK

THE FRENCH AND INDIAN WAR & AMERICAN REVOLUTION
ON NEW YORK'S FRONTIER

Richard Berleth

BLACK·DOME

Published by Black Dome Press Corp.
PO Box 64
Catskill, NY 12414
(518) 577-5238
blackdomepress.com

First Edition Paperback 2010
Copyright © 2009 by Richard Berleth

Library of Congress Cataloging-in-Publication Data:
Berleth, Richard J.
  Bloody mohawk : the French and Indian War & American revolution on New York's frontier
/ Richard Berleth. — 1st ed.
    p. cm.
  Includes bibliographical references and index.
  ISBN 978-1-883789-66-4 (pbk.)
  1. Mohawk River Valley (N.Y.)—History, Military. 2. New York (State)—History—French and
Indian War, 1755–1763. 3. New York (State)—History—Revolution, 1775–1783. I. Title.
  F127.M55B475 2009
  974.7'6—dc22
                                        2009040892

Front cover painting: *The Oneidas at the Battle of Oriskany* (detail),
by Don Troiani.www.historicalimagebank.com.

Maps: Mapping Specialists Ltd., Madison, Wisconsin

Index: J. Naomi Linzer Indexing Services

Design: Toelke Associates   www.toelkeassociates.com

Printed in the USA

25 24 23 22 21

To Emily —

Who was by me on all the roads traveled,

Her presence lovelier than a summer's day.

Contents

FOREWORD

In 2006, Kenneth T. Jackson challenged historians to join together and "convince our fellow citizens that today's America took shape in yesterday's New York." That challenge was based more in hard fact than it was in simple pride. Few states (if any) can claim a past that reflects American history as well as that of the Empire State.

Think simply of the Erie Canal, for example, and you are faced with the realization that, in Jackson's words, no other internal improvement before World War II "had a greater impact on the growth of the nation." The canal was built in the Mohawk Valley through the only low-level breach in the 1,200-mile-long Appalachian Mountains, and it opened settlement and trade between the east coast and the American interior. In so doing, it accelerated the country's economic growth as never before, it transformed upstate New York into one of the most economically and politically vital places in the United States, and it enabled New York City to become the commercial and cultural capital of the world. After the canal opened in 1825, many of the major themes in American history were in fact played out in New York State, often first or most prominently—from the rise of industry, to the growth of cities, to the story of immigrants who traveled to America, many in search of freedom, from countries all over the world. New Yorkers may have helped found a free country in the years before 1825, but as the nation grew and prospered in the years that followed, other New Yorkers helped change the ways in which Americans came to understand their freedom. Think, for example, of the abolition work of Frederick Douglass and Harriet Tubman, the women's rights struggle that found form and substance at Seneca Falls, and the Depression-era leadership of Franklin D. Roosevelt and his "Four Freedoms."

Given this enormously significant history, it is sometimes possible to overlook the fact that earlier events in New York also shaped the course of American history. As you will read in the pages that follow, much of the country's important history had actually taken place in the same valley that would later come to be so closely associated with the Erie Canal—and it happened well before DeWitt Clinton ever imagined the day on which he would pour water from Lake Erie into New York Harbor in celebration of his lifelong dream. Richard Berleth creates an exceptional narrative here that is forever driven by the unique geography of the Mohawk Valley, as well as by the people who settled there—from the powerful Iroquois, to avaricious European fur traders, to the colonials who fought in and ultimately won a series of devastating eighteenth-century wars. New Yorkers may have emerged from this history with a state of their own—and Americans may have won their freedom—but as Berleth shows, these triumphs were achieved at considerable cost, certainly to those on the losing side, but also to the military victors.

The author's decision to present this history in narrative form invites you to use your imagination as you travel along the New York State Thruway or as you encounter historical markers on back roads throughout the region. Readers who accept Berleth's invitation to accompany him on his journey will certainly enjoy the ride—even though his trip travels through time rather than place. With the author's guidance, you will envision the Mohawk Valley as it once was. You will meet prominent historical figures such as Sir William Johnson and Chief Hendrick. You will find yourself appalled by greed, misunderstanding, and intolerance, but uplifted by heroism and courage. And when the trip ends, you will find that you understand yourself and your country just a little bit better than you did when you started. Happy traveling.

Robert Weible
New York State Historian and
Chief Curator, New York State Museum
Albany, New York
September 2009

PREFACE

This book is a narrative history of the Mohawk Valley and region over eight decades of the eighteenth century. The years encompassing the French and Indian Wars and battles of the American Revolution were critical to the foundation of New York State and the creation of a new nation. People of the Mohawk River—Native Americans, colonial settlers, officials of the Crown Colony of New York, great landowners, and patriot leaders—struggled mightily during this period to impose their visions for the future on a wilderness that would some day become the cradle of the new nation's industry and ingenuity.

Between the signing of the Treaty of Utrecht (1713) and the signing of the Treaty of Canandaigua (1794), the boundaries of the Mohawk region took shape. French intrusions were turned back with great loss of blood and treasure, but British triumph proved temporary. In the War of Independence, patriots wrenched the valley from British interests and the Iroquois nations at fearsome cost. At the end, victors inhabited a valley of ashes, while the defeated lost friends, homes, and tribal lands forever.

Bloody Mohawk tells this story through profiles of participants and events set against the defining influences of the land. In order to appreciate the importance of the Mohawk Valley for eighteenth-century America, it is necessary to search beyond the river itself to the surrounding region. Developments along the Montreal-Albany corridor, the Susquehanna Valley of Pennsylvania, and the Oswego-Niagara route are tied inextricably to the Mohawk narrative. As Emerson observed, "Man is a bundle of relations, a knot of roots, whose flower and fruitage is the world." Settlements nourished by the waters of the Mohawk branched outward to Champlain, the St. Lawrence, the Delaware and Hudson valleys.

This book grew from my fascination with upstate New York's long and conflicted history. Wherever one looks are found traces of the past, sometimes well-tended monuments and restorations, other times overgrown foundations in the heart of the woods. The rivers that first opened the state to settlement are constant reminders of how people once lived; the natural splendor of the landscape seems inseparable from human habitation. The wars of the eighteenth century followed the rivers, and as I followed the wars, I was returned time and again to the beautiful Mohawk, to the eastward-flowing river that someday would become the course of the Erie Canal.

For me, as for many downstate residents, the American Revolution was General Washington's war fought on Long Island, in New Jersey, or the vicinity of Philadelphia. What a surprise then to discover the long, bloody guerrilla struggle on the Mohawk and its lasting consequences for Native and immigrant Americans alike. Even more of a surprise it was to meet these people in the historical record and learn of their ordeals.

Out of past accounts, I shape a view of events by connecting episodes of the Mohawk story in chronological order. Early chapters introduce leaders whose influence and actions worked to define the goals of their parties down through the unraveling and destruction of the valley. Later chapters enlarge on the localized history of the conflict and the effect of recurrent military campaigns on ethnic and cultural groups.

This book does not presume to be a definitive analysis of political forces or political outcomes, let alone a comprehensive account of the Iroquoian nations in crisis. Rather it is a synthesis of secondary sources leavened by my research, observations, and interviews. Not least, the book aims to provide visitors to central New York with an introduction to eighteenth-century backgrounds and localities. Where three French wars, a revolution, and numerous Indian raids have superimposed their prints, explorers require a guide to the terrain.

In a sweeping history intended for general readers, there is only so much detail that can be included in narrative before the weight overwhelms. Those who wish to follow an event or figure in fuller perspective are recommended to the works in the bibliography. I have chosen particulars that seem salient to me and by no means imply that these alone are the whole story.

Footnotes, arranged chapter by chapter at the end of the volume, are intended to augment the text as well as elucidate sources. Anecdotal material is found in the notes, along with biographical detail and topographical explanations. The reader is advised to consult these citations as important aids to the main narrative.

Much of this book describes actions occurring over wide tracts of territory. The maps provided therefore are intended to orient readers; they approximate distances and terrain features important for understanding the location of settlements and the direction of forces. To find correspondences with standard road maps, or more exact spatial relationships, consult the notes to the chapters. Obviously, much has changed in central New York over two and a half centuries, yet visitors will be surprised to find how many sites and vistas still remain, connecting them to the people who have gone before.

Finally, let me point out that generations of able historians have written about the founding events of the eighteenth century in numerous ways. Seldom do they all agree on interpretations of fact or motive. In truth, surprisingly little about this vital past is settled and unanimously accepted. I have tried to do justice to diverse points of view, but unavoidably in many cases have had to choose my own reading of events. Where I have erred in comprehension or knowledge, or simply mistaken my texts, the fault is entirely my own and in no way attributable to others.

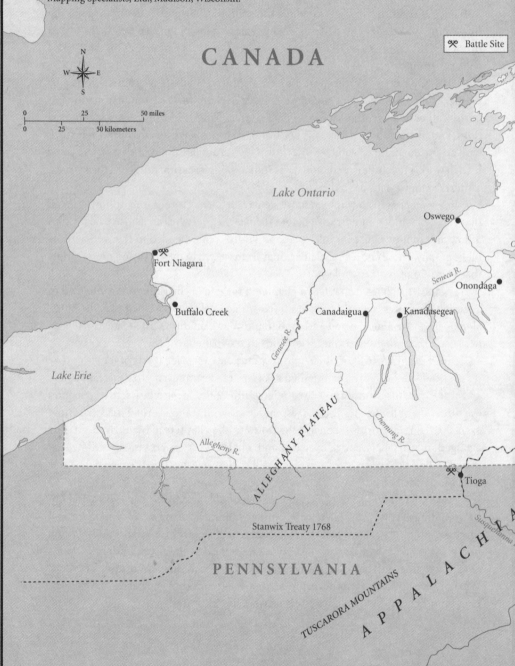

NEW YORK 1713–1794

*The New York frontier would be driven back from the Stanwix Treaty line
to the outskirts of Schenectady by the close of the Revolution.*

Mapping Specialists, Ltd., Madison, Wisconsin.

✂ Battle Site

CANADA

N
W · E
S

| 0 | 25 | 50 miles |

| 0 | 25 | 50 kilometers |

Lake Ontario

Oswego

Fort Niagara

Seneca R.

Onondaga

Buffalo Creek

Canadaigua   Kanadasegea

Genesee R.

Lake Erie

ALLEGHANY PLATEAU

Chemung R.

Allegheny R.

✂ Tioga

Stanwix Treaty 1768

Susquehanna

PENNSYLVANIA

APPALACHIA

TUSCARORA MOUNTAINS

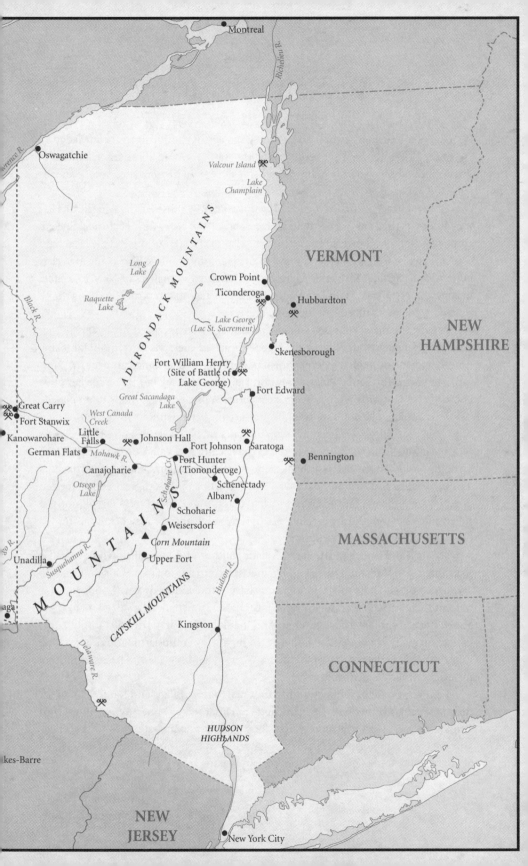

Acknowledgments

In a book based on research begun ten years ago, it is difficult to acknowledge all of the help received from people along the way, including librarians, friends, colleagues, editors, and the many remarkable docents at historic sites, whose knowledge and patience often set me in the right direction.

Of the library staffs I depended on most heavily, those of the American History Room at the New York Public Library and of the New-York Historical Society come first to mind. I owe an immense debt also to the staff of the Everett Needham Case Library of Colgate University and to the Hamilton College library for materials pertaining to Samuel Kirkland. As for anyone engaged in matters of New York State history, the New York State Library at Albany, an essential repository, is ever to be remembered and thanked just for being there.

Among the many curators, guides, and docents who advanced my research, I am especially grateful to Carl Fuller at the Hubbardton battlefield site in Vermont for taking time to walk me through the development of the battle and its significance for the Saratoga campaign. To Bonnie Pulis at Johnson Hall goes nothing but praise for her great knowledge of Johnson's life and the role Catherine Weisenberg and Molly Brant played.

This book could not have been begun or completed without the generous help of St. Francis College. I started my research on a sabbatical leave and over the years received grants from the Dean's Fund and the Faculty Research Committee. To Dean Timothy Houlihan my deepest thanks, and to other colleagues, including Professors Arthur Hughes and Arnold Sparr, who heard me out on this project and suggested directions, abundant gratitude. I also wish to thank Tom Porter, Emily Tarbell, and the Kanatsiohareke community for their warm hospitality and the insights they afforded me into Mohawk life and traditions.

To my old friend, the late Jack Holland, author and journalist, who evinced a great interest in William Johnson and invited my contribution in newsprint, I want to say thank you and how much I miss your sharp mind and ready wit. Thank you also to John Sheldon, who accompanied me into the field and patiently walked many a site at my side as I probed and measured. And thanks above all to my wife, Emily, companion on many long rides, for always encouraging my enthusiasms and contributing immeasurably to the writing of this book. Without her keen eye and persevering gaze my errors would be manyfold more.

I am very grateful to Raymond J. Andrews, Matina Billias and Randy Patten for their many suggestions and criticisms, and I am honored by Robert Weible's foreword and Kathleen Hulser's welcome praise. Their generous contributions of time and talents are greatly appreciated. Finally, my gratitude to Deborah Allen and Steve Hoare at Black Dome for believing in this book and making it finally happen.

Richard Berleth
Brooklyn, New York, November, 23, 2009

Introduction

Before there was an Erie Canal, before New York City could ship goods by water uninterrupted to the shores of Lake Superior or gather the produce of the Midwest for shipment to the world, Native Americans, immigrant settlers, and the soldiers of imperial Europe bled in their generations to control the Mohawk passage. By not holding this inland waterway, America might have lost the Revolution, as well as much or all of the then-poorly-defined province of New York. The first concerted effort of the colonies in the War of Independence began at the confluence of the Mohawk and Hudson. From there, new regiments of the Second Continental Congress launched an ill-fated invasion of Canada, only to be driven back to their point of departure by superior British strength. The battles of Saratoga, Oriskany, Fort Stanwix, and Bennington were fought out on the axis of the Mohawk in subsequent efforts to secure the junction of the rivers. This is a grand story and vital to understanding the birth of the nation, yet it is only a moment in a far more complicated history.

A century before the Revolution, France and Britain contended along the Mohawk frontier for domination of the North American continent. The passage west between the mountains belonged to the powerful Iroquois League and, as European interests maneuvered for advantage, Native America withstood encroachments through diplomacy and war. Even while adversaries negotiated for control, the valley stretching west from Albany filled steadily with settlers of diverse origins and beliefs. Not only was the stage set on the Mohawk for momentous military collisions, but also for ethnic antagonisms that would shape the future of the new Republic and the values for which it stood. These fragments of the past are reasons for knowing more about the region, and we begin by tracing the river's place in time and geography.

The Mohawk River of central New York, *Tenonanatche* to the Iroquois, rises in the western Adirondacks and flows into the Hudson River about thirteen miles above Albany.[1] Over its hundred and thirty mile course, the river merges in places with the Inland Waterway or New York State Barge Canal built on foundations of the historic Erie Canal. For in the beginning, the waters of the river fed the canal, and early attempts to extend water transportation from the Hudson inland centered on schemes for taming the wild Mohawk's falls and rapids.[2]

In an unspoiled state, the Mohawk comprised a great watershed draining the northern Catskill and southern Adirondack ranges. Down the ages, the snow-swollen creeks and streams, plunging into the turbulent, untamed river, carved a deep gorge across the Appalachian Mountain chain. This gorge, over five hundred feet deep at the center of the Mohawk Valley near Little Falls, constricted and propelled waters eastward towards the Hudson River at great velocity. "Had it not been for the cutting of that gorge [one hundred million years ago]," an historian of the Erie Canal writes, "the entire history of the United States would have been different. Without that gorge, Americans might well have grown up split by the Appalachian mountain range into two quite separate nations, or perhaps into even more than two nations."[3]

Today, U.S. 90, the New York State Thruway, runs through this corridor alongside major rail lines linking New York City on the Hudson with Buffalo and Chicago. Canals, railways, highways—traffic through the Mohawk artery flows around the clock, but a traveler's occasional glimpse of the river lined with rusting industrial sites or flowing placidly through flat bottom land hardly suggests its grandeur or dramatic past.[4] The Industrial Revolution in New York was founded on a revolution in transportation made possible by this river. The shells of old factories still stand on the banks, a reminder of technological progress once associated with the Mohawk.[5] The corridor between the mountains carried the agricultural production of young America outward to the world. The wealth generated by this globalization and the opportunities created by the inrush of capital helped earn New York the title of Empire State.

Such achievements were not inevitable; they were the consequence of conflicts undergone many decades before in a bitter struggle for the land and its resources. The river of wealth and progress in the nineteenth century had been a river of blood and distress through much of the eighteenth. This book looks at that earlier time, seeking to trace a way forward from the shocks one population endured to the golden promises a later realized.

During the eighteenth century, many factions competed for living space in the valley; religious, racial, ethnic, and political parties were not above forcing their visions on each other as wars of national determination swept through the region. From the Treaty of Utrecht (1713) until the Treaty of Canandaigua (1794), the Mohawk was tense with strife as immigrant groups and rival powers attempted to dominate the passage through the mountains.[6] In the beginning of the century, the most potent force resisting the reduction of the wilderness to farms and mills was a league of native peoples that had inhabited the land before European invasion. The Iroquois then, even though lacking manufactured goods, tended to surpass the invaders in military prowess, agriculture, and physical wellness.[7] By the end of the century, travelers through the valley found these same people impaired, displaced, and impoverished. The deep bonds they had forged with their tribal lands had been broken by war and devastation, and now the river once called Tenonanatche had become the Mohawk.

For the Iroquois, Tenonanatche was never just a river system defined by a dynamic hydrology; it was the animate earth alive with significance and possibility. Generations before Columbus, or perhaps much earlier, native people used the Mohawk Valley's river roadway to join the Atlantic shore to the Great Lakes and Mississippi.[8] Before the Mohawk became America's corridor to the west, Tenonanatche carried the trade, culture, and warrior might of one of the greatest confederations of native peoples north of the Rio Grande.[9] The river became associated with their symbolic

2

longhouse, the dwelling place of the *Haudenosaunee*, the Five Nations of Iroquoia.[10] One of those five nations lent its name to the white man's river, notwithstanding that Mohawks actually called their valley *Kanyenka*, "the place of the flint," and themselves *Kanyenkehaka*, "people of the place of the flint."[11] For centuries the Mohawks/Kanyenkehaka guarded the easternmost door of the longhouse opening onto the river's gorge. Topography was not for them an obstacle to navigation, a challenge to be removed by engineering; it was an integral part of their identity. Through craft and intimidation, the Iroquois succeeded in holding Tenonanatche against Dutch, French, British, and colonial expansion until the close of the American Revolution.[12] The wartime experiences of the Haudenosaunee and their eventual tragic displacement figures prominently in Part II of this book.

The struggle for the Mohawk Valley began long before 1713, but in that year as the War of the Spanish Succession (Queen Anne's War in the colonies) ground to a halt, British imperial policy turned sharply in a new direction. Instead of seeking European gains, the government settled in victory for North American and Caribbean concessions. As Alan Taylor explains, the meaning was clear for the future: "By giving a new priority to overseas expansion, the English committed their empire to maritime commerce rather than to European territory—a dramatic shift that elevated their American colonies to a new importance."[13] Despite having suffered wilderness defeats in New England and New York, the crown pressed ahead with plans to resettle German-speaking Palatine refugees in the river valleys of the Hudson and Mohawk. These displaced people, victims of religious persecution in their homeland, were intended to form a buffer between the French and Indians and the prospering Atlantic seaboard of the colonies. The Palatines would gravitate to the Mohawk and, thriving among the native people, contest with older Dutch settlers for control of the valley. Driven from the Rhineland by Catholicism, they would also staunchly oppose French inroads into central New York. In Part I of this book, the travails of the Palatines are described in Chapter 4.

The Treaty of Utrecht, signed April 1713, also marked the beginning of three decades of relative peace along the borders of New England, New York, and Pennsylvania. In this period, thousands of immigrants arrived in New York harbor from Europe and Africa. Many sought land thereafter among the Palatine Germans or Dutch settlers in the river valleys of New York. The pressure was growing on the Iroquois to sell or cede large tracts of hunting ground, while at the same time French Canada pursued policies of encirclement and destabilization along the porous boundaries of the crown colony. As so often in this period, the fur trade was at the root of the troubles. Dutch traders, resident at Albany, frequently defrauded native people who trapped and transported pelts in exchange for rum, cloth, and iron implements. The Iroquois countered by playing French interests at Montreal against British interests in New York, but all along the frontier, running approximately north to south through Schenectady on the Mohawk, natives and settlers jostled each other testily.

The Peace of Utrecht was rapidly unraveling when William Johnson, merchant-trader, appeared with twelve Irish families on the river in 1738. No eighteenth-century figure bestrides the Mohawk like Johnson or leaves a greater impression on the conflicts of the time. His legacy is still controversial, and not least of all because the Johnson family in the years following his death helped plunge the valley into bloody civil war. To the Iroquois, Dutch, German, and French influences on the Mohawk, William Johnson brought his own special Irish genius, and eventually the influence of hundreds of Scots-Irish settlers unshakably loyal to the British crown.[14] This book begins with Johnson's arrival in New York, and over several chapters attempts to show how the man and his example affected colonial policy all the way down to the founding of the United States.

That founding is at the heart of this history. It was an excruciating ordeal lasting more than a decade and would forever change the pre-war world of Tenonanatche. Of course the Revolution altered local worlds throughout the colonies, but the social and cultural diversity of the Mohawk corridor and the complex relationships maintained by its inhabitants made the upheavals when they finally came as violent and pitiless as anywhere. Streaming with colonial traffic, the river had become a place where the core ethnic groups of an emerging nation first met in commerce and partnership, only to be wrenched apart by brutal political partisanship. The sides divided sharply over ideas and ideals brought to New York's valleys by New England immigrants. This book examines the impact of the "Great Awakening" on Iroquoia in Chapter 5 and the spread of Whig sentiments in Chapter 6.

When the fighting was over, the valley lay in ruins, as much as two-thirds of its population dead or displaced.[15] To be sure, the struggle was not just neighbor against neighbor. Powerful national adversaries fought by proxy along New York's river waterways. The people of the Mohawk, native and otherwise, were caught in an inferno not entirely of their own making. As we recount the battles of the Revolution in Part II, it is important to note that the greater Mohawk Valley, the Mohawk region, was joined to the Champlain corridor, the upper Hudson, and the Susquehanna and Delaware watersheds by a web of now forgotten byways and tributaries. What happened in one district was quickly reported in others. The borders we tend to take for granted between states were not yet firmly in place, and the differences among New Yorkers, New Englanders, Pennsylvanians, and Jerseymen were more often cultural than geographic.

The highway grids that organize our space had of course not yet been imposed. Like-minded communities, regardless of provincial demarcations, were linked to each other by forest trails and lake portages all but gone today.[16] In 1755, Chief Hendrick led his Mohawk warriors north to Lake George by way of Sacandaga River; in 1777, Nicholas Herkimer sent his Tryon County militia north to Ticonderoga by the same route. General James Clinton, with New York regiments raised in the valley, sailed the East Branch of the Susquehanna River in 1779 all the way from its source at Lake

Otsego into Pennsylvania, then back again into New York. Because the terrain traversed has been greatly altered by time, dams, and public works, these journeys would be difficult to reenact today. In order to trace and understand the wars of the Mohawk Valley, readers require more than a current atlas; they need imagination and attentiveness to features of landscape hiding an older world.

Some jurisdictions simply vanished. In his last years, Sir William Johnson was instrumental in creating a new county at the heart of the colony. Tryon County, named for the royal governor, took as its seat Johnstown on the Mohawk and encompassed much of what is now central New York State. The farms of Tryon, especially those along the Schoharie, provided more food for Washington's army than any other region in North America. Tryon is gone now—swept away in the aftermath of the War of Independence—yet while it lasted, it was called "bloody Tryon" and was known for raids and violence up to and even beyond the cessation of hostilities. Tryon began with great hopes, as described in Chapter 6, but the contradictions inherent in an aristocratic model forced upon a divergent and vulnerable people brought the structure that Johnson labored to build tumbling down around the heads of his successors. The descent of Tryon into civil strife and ruin stands among the colonial period's most sobering spectacles, not just because the destruction was relentless, but because the violence it unleashed broke along fault lines that the United States would revisit—race, class, and religion.

This is the big picture, and like big pictures usually, it tends to obscure the price individuals pay for historic upheavals. The greatest Indian confederation in North America imagined its home as a longhouse stretching the length of Tenonanatche. The crushing of that house and its inhabitants equaled in scope and savagery the genocidal wars perpetrated later against western tribes.[17] Racist assumptions deprived even native people friendly to the American cause of a fair settlement in the wake of hostilities, while black slaves, hoping for freedom under British rule, found their chains swiftly restored under the flag of liberty. Hundreds of the valley's Loyalists, often Catholic or Anglo-Catholic, were uprooted in the wake of the great patriotic war and driven north to Canada destitute of their possessions. From the spotty records, we know such things happened to people who now remain nameless. And yet the victors suffered horribly too and, arguably, won little. Embattled farmers, harried and beaten for their politics before the war, endured years of devastating raids, famine, and epidemic once war came. Their losses were appalling, and they laid their dead in churchyards already filled with graves from four successive French and Indian wars.[18] When it was over, many would rebuild, take pride in their old cause and walk the battlefields with their grandchildren. Washington himself would visit them and purchase a large, lush tract in the valley in 1783.[19] But many others would move on, westward in search of fresh lands without memories or graves.

To tell the story of Tenonanatche is to embrace a river and its people while acknowledging that any such story will depend on a simplifying scheme—you cannot tell it all—and often the narrative will look away from complications, sending readers to notes and bibliography. The historian Patricia Nelson Limerick explains this kind of history: "You can be the world's greatest enthusiast for narrative history, and you can still lose your nerve at the prospect of putting yourself and your readers at the mercy of one of these tales from hell ... loaded with tiresome detail and pointless plot twists that narrative art bends and breaks under their weight."[20] Yet at stake in reviewing the past is the capture of imagined territory on which we all live and depend. Our humanity is challenged in the process and our moral perceptions corrected. What seems right and fitting to us often derives from comparison with what went before. Take for example the statement, "the toll in human suffering along the Mohawk was immense." We recognize this statement as true and argue consequently that the land in some measure be consecrated to uses beyond just commercial development and interstate traffic. To find policies that fit us today, we are continually compelled to recollect, however imperfectly, who we once were and hoped to become. Narrative is the vehicle for negotiating this search through all the twists, plot complications, and detail, and like any story, historic narrative also suppresses the chaos of raw experience in arranging to have a beginning, middle, and end.

As the War of Independence drew to a close—the last of four eighteenth-century conflicts to bloody the waters of the Mohawk—citizens of the United States began to discover the richness of lands thrown open by Britain's defeat and the retreat of the Iroquois people. In Chapters 11 and 12 we trace an order emerging from the desolation as pioneers, the beneficiaries of victory, push aside the old communities of Tenonanatche and by 1790 begin to clear forests for new settlements. The so-called Indian menace had passed because many native people—pro-American, pro-British, or neutral—were driven westward to the Great Lakes and Canada. Their lands, as well as the appropriated lands of the Tories, were often bought for a pittance and resold for huge profits by New York State. Not until the 1794 Treaty of Canandaigua did the federal government step forward to reconcile the Iroquois nations, remove them from state jurisdiction, and finally end the rampant injustices of the postwar land boom. By then, eighty-one years after the Treaty of Utrecht had brought temporary peace to the Mohawk Valley, a new public was emerging from the re-formed townships along the river, and the dream of a great canal, with all that it would mean, only awaited the return of agricultural prosperity and the blessings of peace. The story appears to have a happy ending—at least for those on the winning side. For others, it was stark tragedy as they were left to weep in exile for lost homes and loved ones. Canals, roads, and bridges were bound to come as progress erased the old cultural boundaries of the frontier and states moved aggressively to define their rights. A century of change had given New York its statehood, but in the process, whole communities had been uprooted and cast aside.

Today the state's highways and byways are dotted with blue and gold signs marking places of historic interest. The signs number in the thousands, and could they be assembled together in chronological order, would explain what always has set New York apart.[21] Waves of change in social, political, and economic life rippled outward from here to the rest of the nation. And it happened with great rapidity. After 1794 the feudal, hierarchical society characteristic of upstate New York gave way to a radical modernism in economy and organization. As Gordon Wood contends, "By the early years of the nineteenth century the Revolution had created a society fundamentally different from the colonial society of the eighteenth century. It was in fact a new society unlike any that had ever existed anywhere in the world."[22] Yet a sense of loss also seems to have accompanied the euphoria of freedom, finding expression during the 1820s in James Fenimore Cooper's immensely popular Leather-Stocking Tales, novels nostalgic for the vanished frontiersman, the noble Indian, the brave redcoat guarding the edge of civilization in the wilderness of old New York.[23]

To grasp a transformation of this magnitude is also to perceive how potent were the forces that tore families apart, tested their fortitude and faith, and reassembled them finally in a new nation. The blue and gold signs tell this story as well. New Yorkers bled copiously to embrace or to avoid the new Republic. Their Revolution was different from the one conceived in New England, or the one fought in the Carolinas. The markers come together to explain why this was so, why in this crucial century the colony of New York passed through fires more intense than others endured. To be sure, cultural diversity, geography, and ethnicity set the stage. But greed and ambition played a part as well in challenging the boundaries and moving the borders. It was the drive to vindicate his poor Irish Catholic roots that brought "Handsome Bill" Johnson to an Indian river in the first place.

Part I

River between the Mountains

☙ 1 ❧

ON AN INDIAN RIVER

No colony in eighteenth-century America was entirely secure in its borders. The Crown Colony of New York claimed to own parts of the New Hampshire grants and had designs on slices of Pennsylvania and New Jersey. The Commonwealth of Massachusetts drew its western boundary at the Hudson River, adamant that it had bought the east bank from the Mohawks who, as it turned out, had no right to sell. Tiny Connecticut annexed Long Island, parts of what would someday be Ohio, and joined Virginia in drawing its western boundary at the shores of the Pacific—no matter what peoples lived between New Haven and the western ocean.[1]

Indeed these were grand illusions, especially since British colonies in the early eighteenth century had yet to push over the peaks of the Appalachians. Land conjured up visions of empire and promises of wealth incalculable, and for most of the century land was the raw substance over which people contended—sometimes with writs in courts of law, sometimes with muskets in the dark forests glimpsed briefly today from the Adirondack Northway. The boundaries of New France, Canada, for example, were in places conjectural, because large tracts of New York remained uncharted. No one knew for certain how far Pennsylvania extended westward or who held jurisdiction where the Monongahela met the Alleghany. Representatives of a colonial governor could wander at will through the vast interior, claiming, as young George Washington did for Governor Dinwiddie of Virginia, huge sections of valuable river bottom. The river in question happened to be the Ohio, and near its banks Washington fired shots inadvertently provoking the Seven Years War—the French and Indian War that so bloodied New York's frontiers.[2]

Despite the Old World's visions of the New World as a vast primal emptiness awaiting development, North America in the early eighteenth century was anything but a *tabula rasa*. What seemed wilderness to Europeans was in fact the habitat of native peoples who over several millennia had successfully subdued their environment and maintained extensive lines of commerce and communication. The interior teemed with life. Yet, in the early eighteenth century, the forest ecology was growing fragile, already impaired by human pressures to an extent that many native peoples in the East feared for the eventual degradation of their surroundings. In New York, over a century had passed since white men pressed up the Hudson to found Fort Orange (Albany), and during this time innumerable skirmishes among the Dutch, French, English, and native peoples had left each side wary.[3] The population numbers were small during the seventeenth century, but they were poised to explode as Queen Anne's War came to a close.[4] Between the freewheeling world of near-sovereign provinces prevailing at the opening of the eighteenth century and the imposition of a national state at the close, tens of thousands of immigrants were destined to pour into the New World, displacing Native Americans and altering their natural world beyond recognition. As old boundaries were uprooted, new ones were put down.

In the summer of 1749, the greatest boundary-marking expedition of all pushed off from Montreal. Captain Pierre-Joseph de Céloron de Bienville was under orders to bury lead plates stamped with the French coat of arms at precise locations down the Ohio Valley to the Mississippi. He would affix tin sheets to trees near the site of these monuments, thereby alerting natives and competing interests to the fact that this territory belonged to France by right of La Salle's discovery. Indians who accompanied the expedition watched the first ceremonial planting with growing anxiety.[5] As de Céloron claimed this vast region for his king, they abandoned him, fleeing into the forests. Until this moment, they had believed that they, not the white men, were masters of the land. Now they had reason to wonder. Soon they would have reason to fight.[6]

Certainly, land marks people even as people mark land, for it teaches indwellers new languages, skills, and technologies. Before one can name land, survey and possess it, one has to reach it. This was no small matter in the eighteenth century. If the province of New York was unusually devoid of roads, it was also unusually blessed with navigable rivers.[7] But early settlers had to learn to build craft that could both survive the rushing waters and negotiate the shallow branches opening into the interior valleys. Almost from the beginning, settlers imagined canals fed by river water, but the technology to build such canals did not exist until the next century. In the meantime, bateaux, barges, and canoes carried the province's commerce. Because the rivers froze solid in winter, the newcomers learned to skate; because snow lay several feet deep over trails by the end of autumn, they built sledges and learned to walk on snowshoes. While home in Europe they had once stored oats and grains, they now laid up maize, squash, and beans for the long, dark season. As often as not, they adopted Indian names for places, and in the fashion of the natives, dressed in skins. Many of those who went into the forests for a living married native women.

Despite advantages that would one day make New York rich and populous, the province stayed undefined longer than any other major colony in British America. Survival in undeveloped upstate demanded wrenching adjustments. Spaces were vast, inhabitants often unfriendly, and because the harsh winters came early and lasted long, starvation stalked the interior in most years. Physical danger was ever present. French pressing down from the north collided with Dutch and English pressing up from the south. Along the great rivers moved Native Americans trapping out the wilderness in exchange for trade goods, and frequently at odds with each other. Violence erupted without warning in the forested defiles or along the twisting, treacherous riverbanks. Underpopulated though New York was, it seemed to be succumbing for most of the eighteenth century to an excess of human diversity—too many people, too many disparate cultures, too many national interests jostling each other for advantage.

While New York's plurality of cultures promised great eventual strength, competing groups tended to neutralize each other, allowing power to be concentrated in the hands of a few. The ensuing strife impeded growth that more homogeneous colonies easily achieved. In the early decades of the century, Connecticut, New Jersey, and Rhode Island were more prosperous and secure than New York. The great nineteenth-century American historian Francis Parkman found New York's political mind boggled by an old-fashioned autocracy. "Pennsylvania," he wrote, "was feudal in form, and not in spirit; Virginia in spirit, and not in form; New England in neither; and New York largely in both."[8] How New York managed to shrug off its deeply conservative outlook to achieve a more progressive politic is central to our story. Belligerence, racial strife, and cultural extinction tore the old province apart. By the end of the eighteenth century, no colony had changed more.

Cultural conflict in provincial New York broke along lines of hydrology as well as demography—which is to say that, from one viewpoint, the rivers were to blame. People, seemingly no less than salmon and shad, tend to follow streams inland to their sources, and the waterways of the province early became main highways of communication and commerce. With a few short carries from Lake Champlain to Lac St. Sacrement (Lake George) and from there to the Hudson, a voyageur could travel from Montreal to New York City almost entirely by water. A Seneca making the portage to Tenonanatche at modern Rome could paddle from Niagara on Lake Ontario to the Atlantic Ocean at New York City in under twenty-one days. The problem was that anyone who controlled these water highways also controlled the province, and anyone controlling the province, with its natural gateway to the West, controlled North America. This fact was known in the foreign ministries of Europe, and thus the scene was set along the Tenonanatche and Hudson corridors for world-scale collisions.

As we begin to look at New York's founding century, most of the water network was still in the hands of the Iroquois, but they were increasingly under pressure from floods of settlers pushing inland from the port of New York. Huguenots followed the Hudson and Delaware rivers into the Catskills; Palatine Germans pressed on to the Schoharie; Highland Scots settled on the Hudson north of Albany; Scots-Irish hacked out homesteads along the Mohawk. Everywhere, the New Amsterdam Dutch formed a submerged empire of trade and speculation. West Indians and Africans came north from the great slave *entrepôt* of the city, along with thousands of indentured servants held in seven-years' bondage.[9] All of these river travelers landed in the midst of the Iroquois Confederacy. Not that the Iroquois were implacably hostile; they were far too powerful and politic to squander material advantages on aimless violence against immigrants. But they were notably unhappy at loss of land, depressed fur prices, and the racism of European invaders. Blame this on the city, as has ever been the fashion, but the confluence of the rivers was also responsible.

The port of New York offered one of the best harbors on the stormy Atlantic, and even in 1700 was as tolerant of otherness as any city in the world.[10] Yet, without a river system connecting the port to the heart of the continent, this fine harbor, from the Dutch West India Company's point of view, was just a place to store ships. There had to be a reason to be there, and business soon found it. Down the Hudson, taking into itself the produce of the Mohawk and Champlain valleys, came pelts harvested in the interior by native peoples, fur that would go to make Europe's hats and cloaks. Though it was not the fabled gold of the New World, timber and grain in prodigious quantities also floated down the river on its way outward. Imagine the great harbor as a vast open mouth swallowing resources of the interior for transshipment, and immediately the stark materialism of old New York comes into focus. While it worked, Dutch New Amsterdam was a money machine. All that was needed was a town at the top of the Hudson, Albany, to collect furs, and a city at the bottom, New York, to pack and ship them. Even then, the cities of New York and Albany needed to work together in order to prosper.

But sailing into this mouth from off the Atlantic also came the excess population of Europe, a crowd not always conscience-bound or exile-driven, yet swelling in numbers and hungry for land. From the start, the Dutch knew this meant trouble. The smell of money was in the air, and daring enterprise, with luck, could strike off the shackles of poverty and serfdom. In no time the old comfortable balance was lost. Free, slave, or indentured, the newcomers were destined to collide with native peoples, whose claim to the northern province as tribal land had been repeatedly confirmed by New York's magnates. These promises, once easy to keep, were soon being broken, and as the Crown Colony of New York struggled to placate the providers of its wealth, France vied to exploit the Iroquois' anger and resentment. They had every reason to do so. The six tribes of the Confederation, ranged along the line of Tenonanatche, fielded the most effective fighting force in the wilderness. Whoever won their allegiance would dominate the river highways into the heart of North America.

With all its resources and strategic importance, New York's slow development continued to trouble the Crown. By the middle of the eighteenth century, the province was second in geographic size, but seventh in population among the thirteen colonies. Connecticut and New Jersey had more people than New York and, even including New York City, a higher gross product on the basis of the ratio of people to land. Delaware and Rhode Island were arguably more stable, and Massachusetts, Virginia, and Pennsylvania were rich and prosperous. If New York had a higher rate of immigration, it also had a greater ratio of empty land to inhabitants. In fact, its interior recesses were still largely *terra incognita.*[11] Long Island, New York City, Westchester, and the Hudson Valley remained strongly Dutch, adhering generally to British forms while preserving Dutch language, laws, and customs. Beyond these settled belts, however, where a half-glimpsed land of fertile fields, hardwood forests, lakes and fish-filled streams glimmered, life was extremely harsh. The climate had much to do with it, endemic violence still more. All of present upstate New York was borderland, and along the borders in bloody scrimmages local parties maneuvered for advantage—a scalp taken here, a cabin burned there. A level of aggression persisted such as was found only on the most remote frontiers of Pennsylvania and Virginia.

New York lived next door to French Canada, and from before the turn of the century, governors of New France had pursued a policy of destabilizing British possessions. In 1690 an especially ferocious raid in midwinter seized and burned Schenectady on the Mohawk. Over one hundred men, women, and children were murdered, along with their dogs and cattle. This was during King William's War, and while hostilities in New York were mercifully brief, the ease of French success in destroying Schenectady helped to initiate seventy more years of sporadic incursion and massacre. Queen Anne's War in the first decades of the new century saw attacks down the Champlain corridor almost to the walls of Albany. King George's War in the 1740s resulted in the destruction of Saratoga and the humiliation of New Jersey militia sent to protect New York. And yet for all this uproar, the province might still have eked out a peaceful development were it not for the patriotic wars to come. These were wars of national determination, but their ferocity never compared with the destructiveness of the civil wars New Yorkers endured in the process of being nationalized.

An old map of the Province of New York, one without the Erie Canal and nineteenth-century engineering improvements, shows an interesting anomaly. Almost all of the state's rivers move north or south. Those that flow north, like the Genesee, Oswagatchie, Black, and Ausable, pour into Lake Ontario, the St. Lawrence, and Lake Champlain, while those that flow south, like the Hudson, Delaware, and Susquehanna, empty into the Atlantic at New York, Delaware, and Chesapeake bays. And why should this anomaly matter? Because draining the Appalachian Mountain range as these rivers do, they never pierce the mountain screen from east to west, the most viable direction of pioneer expansion. Neither, for that matter, do the Potomac, Connecticut, or Raritan. The St. Lawrence outflanks the barrier, but flows too far north and is frozen much of the year. Only the Mohawk, running west to east between the Catskills and the Adirondacks, transects the Appalachians and connects the Great Lakes to the Hudson and Atlantic most of the year.

If a Northwest Passage across the American continent existed, and time proved that it did not, the Pacific in all likelihood would have joined the Atlantic at the mouth of the Mohawk, where ocean tides reach farthest inland. The Mohawk then was a loud, full-throated river as it poured over the rocks at Cohoes, tumbled down a hillside at Little Falls, or welcomed the brown Schoharie at Fort Hunter; it was a river that roared and spoke. Out of its source—a trout stream gushing from the western Adirondacks—it seemed at first to lead nowhere. Then, as it turned east and widened at the present site of Rome, New York, the young river brushed a clearing on the bank.

At that clearing, a straight, flat trail ran westward less than a mile to a sluggish creek. The trail was named *Deowainsta* by the Oneida tribe—the "Great Carry" by English settlers—and the swampy creek was Wood Creek, as unprepossessing a water-way as one can imagine. Yet Wood Creek was in fact the Mohawk River's link with the west. Down the creek's twelve meandering miles to Lake Oneida flowed the custom of the eastern seaboard, loaded aboard *bateaux* carted over the carry from river to creek. The creek carried the laden boats to Lake Oneida, twenty-one miles long and famously stormy, from where another river, called the Onondaga, flowed west to empty into Lake Ontario at Oswego. This was hardly a direct connection, but for centuries it had served to move the light cargoes of native people east and west efficiently. After settlement, the route began to bear increasing traffic. Wood Creek, hemmed in by dense overgrowth, still shouts of ambush on a dark afternoon. Indeed, several times in the conflicts of the eighteenth century the creek ran red with blood as contending forces fought for its banks and fortifications.

But this lay far ahead in 1738, when William Johnson first came to the Mohawk Valley to clear and manage land for a rich uncle. We look for a place to begin a history of Tenonanatche, the Mohawk River and its valley, and discover this prototypical hero among the early settlers. Few lives better fulfilled the immigrant promise of America than William Johnson's. But in his person a strange and anomalous fortune also joined for a time the disparate and warring parties of the New World, making him in many crises the unifying figure Britain often sought for her colonies and seldom found.

He sailed from Dublin to Boston, a poor Irishman out of County Meath, pinning his hopes for a better life on his mother's brother, Captain Peter Warren, Royal Navy, *America Station*. Mother and brother were Protestants, yet twelve Catholic families from the neighborhood of Killeen felt sufficiently hopeful to take their chances with young Johnson and risk the voyage to Peter Warren's estate on the Mohawk. At Boston they took ship for New York and, connecting there with a Hudson River sloop, sailed for Albany.[12] Cousin Michael Tyrrell was below, drinking and dicing with the sloop's passengers, as Johnson on deck watched the majestic bluffs rise along the river and sensed for the first time the terrifying sublimity of a wild continent engulfing him.[13] To his uncle and cousin he was simply "Handsome Billy," twenty-three years old, of strong back and pleasant disposition—an immigrant who was lucky enough to have been named manager of a promising enterprise, a frontier store, and 14,000 acres on the south bank of an Indian river.

Uncle Peter Warren had not been there, and never would go, yet nothing kept him from naming the manor after himself, "Warrensburgh," or in the parlance of the valley, "Warrensbush." When the tract on Tenonanatche became available, Warren had just accomplished a brilliant marriage to Susannah DeLancey, daughter of a prominent New York Huguenot merchant and politician and one of the richest men in the colonies. Through Stephen DeLancey's influence, his son-in-law was cut in on the reapportionment of a lapsed land patent. Warren jumped at the chance to found a landed estate in the New World at bargain prices.[14] But since no ambitious sea captain with his eye on prize money from a pending war with France could afford to waste time leveling forests, Peter Warren did what came naturally to Anglo-Irish gentry—he spread the good fortune within the family. To run the new holdings, he summoned his sister's son from impoverished obscurity at home. This nephew could clear the land, divide the grant into small tenant farms, and organize it around a trading post. Billy, to be sure, had been raised Catholic, his father's son, but sister Anne prevailed over Rome, and William Johnson now was solidly Church of England. Yet he stood high among the sort of Irish crofters who might take up tenant leases and put Warrensburgh on the map—thus allowing Peter Warren to go back to sea to capture fat French merchantmen.

William Johnson knew nothing about merchandise. Peter assured him this did not matter, since he, Peter, was a shrewd businessman and could think for both of them. William Johnson also despised absentee landlords, but that was just the point, Peter argued; the beauty was that he, William, would not just milk the tenants. He would be there all of the time, running the store. Peter would send him the right goods and maybe, if the enterprise flourished, cut Billy in for a share of the profits. Of Indians, trappers, and disgruntled German settlers, Peter knew nothing. A deep-water sailor, he had no concept of life on inland rivers.

At Boston, a rather orderly and sanitary city unlike New York, they conferred for several days. Peter spread the map open, marking the route with his finger. In the gap between a mountain range in the north and another in the south, running west from Albany, the river stretched almost to the great interior lakes. It was a highway as yet little traveled. Arrive by sloop at Albany, and then by pack horse around the falls at Cohoes to Schenectady—nearest town of any note to Warrensburgh—and finally home to the loveliest piece of farmland, Peter had been told, anywhere west of the Hudson. What his uncle did not say was that Schenectady, twenty miles east of Warrensburgh, was the frontier border. A few decades earlier, the French had burned it to the ground, murdering half the inhabitants. The shadow of Indian war clung to the place, and down by the river, a ramshackle stockade offered dubious refuge.[15] Townspeople going into the surrounding fields still went armed. Twenty miles west stood another outpost at the edge of Warrensburgh. "You can count on Fort Hunter nearby for society," Peter said. "It's built, they say, next door to a big Indian village, but there's a parson at the chapel named Barclay, to whom I've written; he'll handle your introductions. Set up shop as fast as you can, and get ground cleared for the spring. Winter comes early on the Mohoc, and the snows are deep."[16]

Peter was a fine, fighting sea captain—indeed, one of Britain's best. On his mother's side, he descended from two British admirals—Aymer and Norris—and had been packed off to sea at the age of thirteen. Now thirty-five years old, he was twelve years older than his nephew, with a successful career behind him and an even more promising one ahead. In 1745, Warren was to command British warships in a brilliant capture of Louisbourg, the impregnable fortress guarding approaches to the St. Lawrence River at Cape Breton Island. Before he made admiral he had amassed £126,000 in prize money from seized vessels. He was as flame-headed as his nephew was dark. Both of them were large men, attractive to women, and both attracted to women. The older man saw his broad-shouldered, shambling nephew as slow and hesitant in company. Billy would need looking after, he thought, but was not without a certain native wit, despite his slight schooling. All in all, Peter the gentleman considered that he was gambling on Billy the commoner.[17]

It would turn out the other way around. The rivers of New York linked the Atlantic to the inland lakes and watersheds of the interior, but the rules Peter Warren had grown to live by—the sense of discipline and the deep-water sailor's pride of command—counted for nothing in the bushes lining Wood Creek or the deeply shaded gorges of Tenonanatche.[18] There the game of dynasty was tribal and played by rules the seadog did not understand. To begin with, Peter had encumbered his nephew with the wrong cargo—trade goods that no one in the North Country would want. Nor could Peter imagine the density of the forested land he expected his nephew to clear. To make matters worse, he had acquired his land on the wrong side of the Mohawk River where the sun rarely shown, where the hills lowered over the muddy trail to a nonexistent trading post, and where the soil was rocky and unworkable. To say nothing of the constant companions his nephew would have to keep—angry Mohawk and Oneida Indians, drunken Dutch militiamen, snooty Onondagas, hard-bitten trappers, destitute German farmers. None of this, of course, would matter much if the French raiders got him.

Truth be told, the gamble was all on William Johnson's side, and the first rule he learned as the quintessential New York greenhorn was that no one, absolutely no one, followed orders that disagreed with his interests. The province was not the deck of a man-of-war or a depressed county in Ireland. The national ideal of King and Country lay as far from the average New Yorker's mind as throwing wealth out a window.[19] The rivers of New York might spill out their bounty over the land, but no one until Johnson came to full power ever attempted to make the recipients of these riches accountable to a greater good than themselves.

The New York province that Johnson entered in the spring of 1738 was, as noted, markedly undeveloped. Powerful interests in New York City and Albany liked it that way. Immigrants clashed with Native Americans, and Native Americans accounted for the wealth in furs flowing down the Hudson from the gathering point at Albany. The province's transportation system served the coastal trade and reached no farther up the Hudson (or North River) than Albany. Long Island then was the thriving center of the colony, though it comprised just a tiny fraction of the total land mass.

The cities of Boston, Philadelphia, and Williamsburg were better built, more populous and democratic than caste-ridden, dilapidated, and unruly Manhattan. New York City could decline appallingly into lawlessness. Three years after Johnson sailed into the harbor, fires, allegedly set by rebellious African slaves, resulted in a murderous riot claiming the lives of twenty people of color, many of them burned at the stake in public.

When New York managed to get down to business, often that business was shady. Early in the century, Captain William Kidd kept a splendid house on Pearl Street, maintained with treasure brought from Madagascar and shared out with New York's then governor, Lord Bellamont.[20] How Madagascar, halfway around the world, came to be a favorite destination of the city's merchant seamen, Theodore Roosevelt, future mayor and governor of the state, explains in his history of old Manhattan:

At Madagascar there was a regular fort and station to which some of the New York merchants sent ships for the sole purpose of trading with the pirate vessels who carried their ill-gotten goods thither. Many a daring skipper who obeyed the law fairly well in Atlantic waters, felt free to do as he wished when he neared Madagascar, or cruised through the Red Sea and the Indian Ocean. The rich cargoes of Oriental goods, the spices, perfumes, silks, shawls, rugs, pearls, and golden coin and jewels, were of such value that men did not care to ask too closely how they were acquired.[21]

To call New York City a pirate roost exaggerates only slightly. Piracy went hand-in-hand with slaving, and by 1730 New York had become an *entrepôt* of the West Indian slave trade, a vast depot of cheap labor—some free, some indentured, some shackled—awaiting transportation to the interior. This great, safe harbor on the Atlantic increasingly dominated transoceanic commerce, taking its cut from importations of human flesh as well as mountains of goods entering or leaving the New World. Even in colonial days, New York was a tough place to land. Driven by gain, it was one of the world's fastest growing cities because it was the world's greatest magnet of opportunity. Dutch was still spoken widely in 1738, along with thirty-five other languages. Each passing year saw the city's national and religious diversity increase at the price of growing uneasiness and ethnic strife. From a British point of view, nothing quite worked right in any of the colonies, but Massachusetts, Pennsylvania, and Virginia were at least English.

Into the harbor of New York sailed whole contingents of dispossessed—Sephardic Jews fleeing inquisition in South America, Huguenots escaping persecution in France, Scottish Highlanders driven from their crags, Scots-Irish refugees, whole communities of impoverished German peasants. In 1712 several thousand Palatine Germans, displaced by the war of the Spanish Succession in the Rhineland, arrived in the harbor by way of London. Stricken with typhus and other communicable diseases, they were interned on Governor's Island until the survivors could be shipped up the Hudson as indentured servants of the Crown. William Johnson met survivors of the Palatine immigration on the Mohawk in 1738. He drew Highlanders and Scots-Irish into his retinue, and fell out early with the Huguenot DeLanceys over Indian policies. But most intriguing of all, Catherine Weisenberg, Johnson's future mistress and mother of his three white children, might have been brought from Madagascar as live contraband and sold as a German-speaking indentured servant for £16 at the Phillips manor on the Mohawk.[22] Which is to say that the bizarre history of early New York was not merely a colorful backdrop to Johnson's life, but woven into its very fabric.

Catherine might have been alternatively the widow of a Jewish merchant from Montreal, the daughter of a poor Palatine farmer, or the treasure of a pirate galleon. Mohawk Valley lore—and no corner of the state harbors more legends—holds that she was fair and buxom, exceedingly wholesome, and that Billy loved her to madness. She spoke English with her lover, German with his neighbors and, when tribal guests visited, Mohawk. William Johnson was certainly not uxorious, and Caty, as all called her, came and went much as she pleased over the next twenty years. Her status appears to have never exceeded that of an exalted housekeeper or estate manager in the Johnson family. Yet, while records of her three children's christenings suggest that they were William's illegitimate offspring at birth, reports also suggest that William might have married Catherine before she died sometime in 1759. Until the end of his life, he wore a gold ring belonging to her and inscribed "June 16, 1739."[23] On that date William allegedly liberated her from the Dutch Phillips brothers.

"Johnson, that damned Irishman," one of the Phillipses complained, "came the other day and offered me five pounds for her, threatening to horsewhip me and steal her if I would not sell. I thought five pounds better than a flogging and took it, and he's got the gal."[24] The Phillipses had bought Catherine on the docks of Manhattan, according to this account.

Milton Hamilton offers a less flamboyant explanation: "Catherine Weisenberg was indeed an indentured servant, but she was a runaway from New York who probably joined her friends or relatives among the Palatines in the Mohawk Valley, and she was found there by William Johnson in the summer of 1739."[25] A notice in Peter Zenger's *New York Weekly Journal* for January 22, 1738/9 reads:

Run away from Capt. Langdon of the City of New York a Servant Maid, named Catherine Weissenberg, about 17 Years of Age, Middle stature, Slender,

black ey'd, brown Complexion, speaks good English, although a Palatine
born; had on when she went away, a homespun striped wastcoat and Peti-
coat, blew-stockings and new Shoes, and with her a Calico Wraper, and a
stripe Calamanco Wraper, besides other Cloaths:

Whoever take her up and brings her home, or secures her so that she
may be had again, shall have Twenty Shillings Reward, and all reasonable
Charge; and all Persons are forewarned not to entertain the said Servant at
their Peril.[26]

No one will ever be entirely certain who she was or what she felt, but her children
eventually would do everything in their power to assure that, failing a total Tory victory in New York, British Canada would begin at Poughkeepsie.

This was the world that Handsome Billy entered in 1738, and while his uncle
thought in terms of tidy profits from trade and farming, William Johnson quickly
saw through tidy expectations to the real engine of opportunity. North America's
most precious natural resource was peltry, brought from as far west as Lake Superior, as far north as Hudson's Bay, and funneled down New York's rivers to the
markets of Europe. Fur was to New York what tobacco was to Virginia, codfish to
Massachusetts. The official seal of New York City from 1623 until 1915 displayed
the noble beaver *couchant* on a field of windmills.[27] City residents insisted that
Great Britain seized New Amsterdam only to gain control of its flourishing fur
trade. Otter, mink, muskrat, ermine, fox, wolf, catamount, and bear were trapped
everywhere, but from Pierre Radisson to John Jacob Astor, the staple export of the
industry remained the precious beaver.

Beaver was supplied to the ever-expanding European hatters' trade. It was valued
less for the fineness of its fur than for the peculiar quality of its barbed hair, which
could be torn from the pelt and worked into a felt superior to any other. So long as the
beaver hat prevailed in fashion, the path to quick riches in the New World lay through
trading and transportation from the interior to the coast.

English gentleman that he was, Peter Warren hoped for an imposing manor on
his 14,000 acres. Plantations bequeathed status and afforded aesthetic delight. But
what Warren really needed to make a going concern of his lands, his nephew believed,
was a quick profit in furs garnered by his trading post from Native American consum-
ers. Of course, William Johnson knew nothing about furs, yet he soon concluded that
his prosperity, to say nothing of his safety, depended on knowing Indians more than
knowing how to grade, process, and ship pelts.

Even if Europeans were willing to try, most could not stand the discomforts and
dangers of trapping in the wilderness. Thus, Albany and Montreal relied on Native
Americans to denude their forests of fur-bearing creatures. The rivers of New York
were the arteries of this commerce, and down New York's streams moved forest people
from as far west as the Missouri. In fact, the seemingly empty wastes of North America

were alive with motion and change. The fur commerce was already over a century old in 1738. Fur-bearing animals were depleted in New York and Pennsylvania, and the chase had gone west into the Ohio and Illinois country. Tribes competed fiercely for what was left. They were angry alternately at the rates of exchange offered by Albany and Montreal, the shoddiness of the trade goods, the rudeness of the proprietors. And soon, along these same rivers, empires would be stirring, compounding the native peoples' struggle for existence with a clash of armies.

The approaching disaster was clear to anyone who could read a map. The retreating glaciers of the last ice age had scoured out two vast waterways connecting Hudson's River with the St. Lawrence in the north and the Great Lakes in the west. Down the length of the eastern seaboard, four routes pierced or flanked the barrier of the Appalachians—the soon-to-be national road in Pennsylvania, a rugged and dangerous trek from the plains of the Susquehanna to the Ohio; the wilderness road in Virginia, a narrow, bone-jarring path from deep wilderness into deeper; the Lake Champlain route to the St. Lawrence; and the Mohawk track westward to Lake Ontario. These last two, by far the easiest, found their terminus in the Hudson. In 1738, Europe's two great competing nations were about to battle for their control.

Furthermore, the old Royal Colony that William Johnson entered in 1738 was shaking itself to pieces from within. Albany Dutch were at odds with Palatine Germans, whom they disdained, but also with the Iroquois, whom they cheated with impunity. The province was being chipped away by the French in the north and undermined by rapacious land speculators in the lower counties. Like Peter Warren, many owned vast tracts in New York but had never been to them. It seemed enough to study a chart, draw a line. The problem, William Johnson was about to discover, was that the cartographers were generally wrong.

Throughout his career, territorial disputes claimed a substantial share of Johnson's attention. Tribes were not above selling what belonged to others, and into this confusion rushed land speculators willing to dispossess tribes and pioneer squatters both for huge profits. The great land companies were chartered in London and often underwritten by the realm's most influential people. Johnson's grants alone would eventually total almost 500 square miles of future New York State, but all of this acquisition lay ahead in 1738. At the moment of his arrival, no one clearly perceived the boundaries of someday New York; the forces colliding on the ground were sorting themselves out, and young Johnson's allegiances were unclear. They would not be for long, however, as he wrestled to reconcile the promise of his uncle's "golden opportunity" with the squalid reality of homesteading on the Mohawk.

Fort Hunter on the Mohawk River may have been established at the order of England's Queen Anne, of blessed memory, but this relic from the War of the Spanish Succession in America was by 1738 anything but royal. When Johnson first saw the fort, it could be described as dilapidated, vermin-infested, laughably insecure. The great swinging gate, used to lock up the rectangular enclosure, was unhinged and gaping. Militiamen entrusted with protecting the Mohawk Valley from Indian attack lived in the blockhouses with Mohawk women. The squaws thought themselves the militiamen's wives; they were usually their conveniences. These twenty poorly trained and equipped soldiers served out their three-month enlistments for paltry pay and all the rum they could drink or trade. Hunter stood on the east bank of Schoharie Creek at its juncture with the Mohawk River, where also stood *Tiononderoge*, the lower Mohawk castle and one of the tribe's oldest settlements.

Iroquois "castles" were a prototype of frontier stockades, but Hunter was built by Schenectady Dutch using horizontal timbers; after twenty-seven years, the logs laid lengthwise on the earth were sagging into decay.[28] Everything about the place seemed slipshod and temporary, and if the Mohawk village nearby offended Albanian noses, Fort Hunter, to read reports, smelled worse. Albany funded the post sporadically. Traders stayed a night and passed through; parties of Indians stopped and sought shelter from the weather against the walls, leaving behind their waste and refuse. Locally, the inmates were notorious for foul language, drunkenness, and brawls, yet as long it was not put to the test of war, Hunter did contribute to order on the Mohawk frontier after a New York fashion. At the center of the parade, twenty-four feet square, stood a stone chapel with belfry, then the westernmost outpost of the Church of England on American soil, an installation paid for out of Queen Anne's own pocket. The silver communion service bore her inscription, and in the great trials to come, this plate would be saved by Mohawk Christians at great risk and smuggled to Canada.[29]

In 1738 the rector of Queen Anne's Chapel was the Reverend Henry Barclay, sustained by funds from the Society for the Propagation of the Gospel in Foreign Parts and rewarded for his exile to the edges of the wilderness by lucrative land gifts. Named catechist to the Indians at Fort Hunter, he would marry whom he could, baptize whom he might, and bury Christians of all races until 1745.[30] William Johnson's firstborn son and daughter were christened by Barclay.

Johnson visited Hunter immediately on arriving in the valley because the fort's enclosure marked the westernmost boundary of Warrensburgh. Reaching this point, he was already overwhelmed by his experiences. He had bought his horse in Albany from one of the town's leading citizens, Jeremias Van Rensselaer, paying twice what it was worth. In the streets of Albany, he saw for the first time Native Americans— blanket-wrapped warriors dressed in leggings, breechcloths, and bracelets, their arms tattooed, their feathered headdresses waving above a crowd of beaver hats. He met buckskin-clad frontiersmen and African servants circulating easily among the Dutch farmers and their red-cheeked housewives. Nothing had prepared him for these scenes. The Dutch tongue melded with High German, Mohawk, French, and English in narrow streets overhung by the porches of the houses, but the town was what it had always been—a fortified outpost at civilization's furthest reach, an outpost whose defenses were steadily decaying.[31]

Although Albany's internal contradictions defied reason, the town had managed to survive for over a century. A *frisson* of danger seemed to run through the place, energizing its citizens. Unlike more settled and stratified communities along the coast, Albany, 140 miles into the interior, freely opened its doors to contraries. In fact, this was the town's main ploy—make no stranger an enemy. It was a merchant's response to life lived on the edge. Johnson was given a polite hearing, even some practical advice, but only later would he realize how much Albanian interests were opposed to Uncle Peter's. Buy land, by all means, they said to themselves, but do not develop it, do not compete with us and, above all, do not upset the Iroquois. They sped Johnson on his way, knowing better than anyone that his goods were useless, his land intractable, and his chances of surviving the next winter negligible.

While cousin Tyrrell and his few servants portaged the sloop's cargo around the Mohawk's falls at Cohoes to Schenectady seventeen miles away, Johnson rode ahead to scout the valley. This is a sight no longer to be realized; the pristine river flowing out of the far western Adirondacks was long ago interdicted and redirected. But at that time the majesty of the river was untamed, and the spring floods roaring out of the hills filled travelers with awe. This Mohawk Valley along which Johnson rode may have been the easiest way to the West, but it was never easy. It was dangerous in high water and impassable in low. Even if a boatman caught it right, there were parts of the river no vessel could pass—waterfalls and rock-choked rapids. The drop from Lake Erie to the Hudson was 536 feet, and for most of 130 miles the Mohawk dropped, plunging 150 feet at one point. The beauty of Tenonanatche is what Johnson saw and described—the rich black soil, the fine straight road on the north bank beneath the eaves of the forest, and fish, salmon and trout, leaping in the shining waters. He was on the south bank heading for Warrensburgh, and his trail ran in the shadow of hills through places the spring rains had washed away. To make matters worse, he missed Warrensburgh and rode into Fort Hunter. There was simply nothing at Warrensburgh, not a trace of habitation.[32]

Since the place did not exist, it would have to be built. Like so many other immigrants, Johnson began from scratch. In the fine summer weather of 1738, he threw up a house, a store, a barn, and outbuildings necessary for smoking meat, cooling milk, and shoeing horses. To clear the land, tear out the stumps, and dress timbers for building was backbreaking labor. As he worked, he noticed the Mohawks watching from the edges of the clearing. When he broke open his cargo and put his goods on display, they looked politely at the fineries he had brought and moved on without a word. He had fine Irish linen for trade, parasols to hide the sun, fashionable stockings, and trivets for the tidy pioneer housewife. For the man in the family, there was a

spot of brandy and a twist of Long Island tobacco. But the Mohawks were more interested in Johnson than in his goods. Young women watched him slamming his axe into
trees and whispered. Across the river, where the best road ran straight to Schenectady
and Albany, farmers from German Flats, forty miles upriver, passed regularly. When
they crossed over to inspect his goods, they were not polite. This truck had no value
for the Indians, and not much more for hard-working Germans. The more Johnson
struggled to clear his own land by the sweat of his brow, the more he understood why
this merchandise was rejected. Uncle Peter, back in Boston, had no idea what life on
the American frontier demanded.

Johnson was always a good businessman. The failure of the store, even as the land
clearing continued, bit deeply into his confidence; yet, unlike his stubborn relative, a
person of rank who always knew best, Johnson could admit to failing. His answer was
to consult the Mohawks, try to talk with the Germans, open a keg of rum and act the
neighbor. By September he had resolved to escape Warrensburgh by crossing the river
and buying two square miles of available land directly across from his uncle's grant.
There was the traveled road, the only place for a store and tavern. When Peter learned
of this purchase made out of Johnson's hypothetical earnings, he wrote violently to his
nephew, accusing him of incompetence and disloyalty. Johnson's letter in reply offers
a glimpse of his mind at this point:

> As for the goods which you and Mr. Middleton sent here, they will not
> answer, for when I looked them over, I found all the stockings mostly moth
> eaten, and I fear the rest will be so to, if not already. I have aired them all very
> well, which is the best thing can be done with them. Were they proper goods
> for this country it would be much better. ... As to my moving over to where
> I made the purchase, to live there I never had the least notion in the world
> of it, but what I meant was that it would be the properest place of the whole
> River for a store house and shop in the winter, by reason of all the High Ger-
> mans passing by that way in the Winter, and all the upper Nations of Indians,
> whose trade is pretty valuable.[33]

Peter Warren believed his shiftless nephew had abandoned Warrensburgh and struck
out on his own. William disabused him of this and painted a vivid picture of Fort
Hunter and its Reverend Barclay:

> Moreover there is no likelihood of much vent for rum, if this act passes
> which Mr. Barclay petitions for in the Indians name, the chiefs of whom
> I have asked how they came to sign such a petition, whereas they were so
> well pleased at my settling here, and keeping with necessaries they wanted,
> to which they declared that they never knew one word of the petition, but
> it is all Mr. Barclay's doing which the Indians don't like, rum being the only

thing they mostly trade for. If you could, dear Uncle, dispose of half the white linen, and let me have for it the goods mentioned in the invoice, which are mostly Indian truck, and fit to trade with to a place called Oquago to the southward from here, on the Susquehanna River, towards Philadelphia, there I intend to make a trial this Fall with about £200 worth of goods.[34]

The rector of Queen Anne's Chapel struggled against the endemic drunkenness of the frontier by circulating a petition, purportedly signed by leading sachems, against the trading of rum for peltry. That chiefs might sign their mark to anything in the interest of a general amity occurred to Johnson. The tribes enjoyed the rum, but if it were not available, they would as happily exchange their furs farther north for French brandy. From the beginning of settlement, the politics of alcohol and Indians troubled European consciences. Barclay was following in the footsteps of New France's Jesuits by attempting to restrict the epidemic intoxication of native peoples. Yet, where Indian policy was concerned, clerical qualms gave way to market pressures. As Johnson put it, "rum being the only thing they mostly trade for." Warren wanted to send many more casks of rum forward to the Mohawk, but his nephew urged him to wait, at least until the Barclay petition ran its course. Johnson was never unmindful of the damage alcohol did to the tribes, but he was in no position to dictate what the tribes should want. The missionary impulse grew stronger as the century grew older, and Johnson wrestled with the moral imperatives of Puritan Yankees, Quakers, and his own Anglicans on many occasions. But the basic reality of the frontier—recognized by the Dutch in Albany—was that the Six Nations of the Iroquois Confederacy, planted solidly in the middle of New York province, had the capability of destroying not only Albany, but white settlements everywhere west of the Hudson. Johnson's genius lay in learning to listen to what the Indians wanted.

Thus he learned of a new village hidden on the banks of the Susquehanna and frequented by Mohawks, Oneidas, Tuscaroras, Senecas, and Delawares. Oquaga, present-day Ouaquaga, New York, took shape in deep wilderness, far from encroaching white settlements. Ninety miles as the crow flew from Fort Hunter, Oquaga could only be reached from the north by a rugged trail running over spurs of the Catskills and down the length of the Unadilla River to the junction of the Susquehanna and Chenango. The trail passed through some of the darkest forests Johnson had ever seen, over rocky outcroppings, along the margins of impenetrable bogs. Intermittently, his train of packhorses broke into autumn sunlight as they traversed lush valleys promising great agricultural wealth to pioneers. The route lay to the west of Lake Otsego, over tracts of wilderness that a century later James Fenimore Cooper called "Leatherstocking Country."[35] But Johnson's was an eighteenth-century sensibility, and the forests of Natty Bumppo were for him gloomy and depressing, prowled by hideous bears, filled with howling wolves. *The Last of the Mohicans* is indebted to Johnson for its staging—Fort Edward, Fort William Henry, and the Horican (Lake George) were his to name, and his daughters Anne and Mary possibly were models for Alice and Cora.[36] Yet Johnson was no Romantic. His preference at home was for gentle streams and pastoral prospects; his eventual homes in the Mohawk Valley were well-appointed Georgian houses, and if in time he could strip to a loincloth, paint his body, hunt like a warrior, and dance the war dance in Indian villages, he also never allowed his sheltered daughters to wander in the wilderness.[37]

The journey to Oquaga was his first venture into the deep forests then over-spreading much of North America, and he would never have reached the village without help from the Mohawks. Like Cooper's hero, Johnson learned his forest craft from excellent teachers. They wanted him to find the village, to bring his £200 of trade goods in exchange for pelts, and certainly they wanted to watch him closely

❊ 2 ❊

MUSTER AT ALBANY

When Johnson first saw Oquaga, the village sprawled along the banks of the Susquehanna without the protection of a stockade. Deep in Iroquois territory, Oquaga needed no defense. It was then a community of typical Iroquoian longhouses, twenty-five to a hundred feet long, covered mostly in elm bark. The inhabitants represented diverse tribes living and working together under common governance. Mohawk and Oneida families predominated, but were joined seasonally by Seneca, Cayuga, Onondaga, Tuscarora, and Delaware groups. All but the last were members of the Iroquois League, and the customs and rituals of the league were an important part of village life when Johnson arrived.

Exactly when the Iroquois League was founded is difficult to determine. Daniel K. Richter observes, "it was not a single event but a series of alliances negotiated over a long period" that appears to have accounted for the union.[1] Almost certainly the league predated Columbus, and if over the centuries it helped make the Iroquois a feared presence among their enemies, it also conferred a remarkable level of peace and unanimity on those who lived under its rule. According to the *Haudenosaunee* (the "People of the Long House"), the *Ganonsyoni* ("the Great Union") was forged from the devastation of war and despair by the revered Hiawatha and Deganaweda. Until their arrival, the lands stretching west from the Hudson were infested by "feuds with outer nations, feuds with brother nations, feuds of sister towns and feuds of families and clans."[2] The cure for these ills became a powerful spiritual incantation, a ritual purification, taught to the people of the long house by Hiawatha. Unlike the Iroquois Confederacy, charged with carrying out policies, the league advocated brotherhood based on a religious revelation that intercepted history to change human behavior. Oquaga was a lasting testament to the power of this vision, a place where diverse people met to live in harmony and prosperity. But one group did not belong to the league at all and would remain a difficult partner in the years ahead.

The *Lenni Lenape* (Delawares) had once inhabited the Hudson Valley down to the shores of the Atlantic. They had been pushed back by white invasion, and in the first decades of the eighteenth century were being driven out of northern Pennsylvania and their beloved Delaware River Valley by land speculators. They were denominated "women" by the Iroquois and were a subject people, paying tribute to the league after 1638.[3] Yet there was nothing weak about the Delawares, as British soldiers and settlers in Pennsylvania were to learn. They were furious about their humiliations and had grown difficult for the league to control, all the more so when joined by the Shawnees. Johnson as an Indian agent would eventually find the Delawares a continual source of friction and would argue for the restoration of their rights.[4] The Tuscaroras, admitted to the Iroquois Confederacy in 1722, also had no voting rights on the main council at Onondaga; they had been driven out of North Carolina by the Catawbas and Cherokees and were still held to be under the tutelage of the Oneidas. Yet the Tuscaroras, unlike the Delawares, attended council meetings and received all the benefits and protections of league membership.

Europeans, viewing tribal life through the distorting lens of prejudice, tended only to see the ceremonial and ritual excesses of the assemblies, little suspecting the intricacies of Native American politics or the antiquity of native tradition expressed in florid rhetoric. The Germans on the Schoharie, the Dutch at Albany, the French at Montreal and Quebec—older border communities—had an inkling of how fearsome intertribal conflict could be. They were aware that in some earlier time the Iroquois had annihilated the Eries, decimated the Illini of Illinois, flung the Mahicans back across the Hudson into New England, and were currently chastising the Catawbas of North Carolina. They were also aware that, with much smaller numbers than European invaders commanded, the Iroquois at the beginning of the eighteenth century were capable of expunging frontier settlements the length of the thirteen colonies. So far superior in wilderness warfare were native warriors that only very large and costly expeditions from the coast stood a chance of pressing into the interior without their active support. William Johnson and his Uncle Warren, newly arrived in North America, inclined to believe that baubles and trinkets would buy off Indians and gain their complicity.[5] Both soon discovered that native people knew very well what they wanted and were prepared through war or diplomacy to get it.

Oquaga was a peaceful town even as it lay at the center of a hard-won empire stretching from Canada to the Carolinas and from the Hudson west along the Ohio to the Mississippi.[6] Iroquois conquests resulted from warrior prowess, but also from a political organization that subordinated individuals and tribes under a constitutional order. Ideally, the aims of the confederation were reached by democratic consensus, and once established, all member nations were required to uphold the determinations. The confederacy had long been represented in tribal oratory by the symbol of the longhouse stretching from the Mohawk's confluence with the Hudson to the great falls between lakes Erie and Ontario. In the east, the Mohawks guarded the door of the rising sun; in the west, the Senecas guarded the door of the setting sun; and in the middle of the structure, at Onondaga or modern Syracuse, the Onondagas kept the council fire of Hiawatha burning eternally.[7] Cayugas and Oneidas were arranged along the axis of the house in strategic support. To attack any member nation was to attack them all, but the confederacy could not resolve on war in turn unless all members concurred. Maneuvers to win the league's complicity were to roil colonial politics for over a century—first the Dutch contended with the English; then the English competed with the French; finally the Americans opposed the English in a quest for the confederation's support. As Johnson rode into Oquaga to establish his trading post, he was the guest of the Iroquois League at the pinnacle of its power.

But that power was already endangered by drastic change and dissention overtaking the easternmost nations. Closer to the Europeans geographically than the turbulent Senecas, the Mohawks were already adopting white ways and technology. Some had visited London or Paris, and many were comfortable in European dress and settings. The settler cabin, with hearthstone and chimney, had begun to replace the drafty longhouse with its smoke hole. Iron implements were coming into use for cooking and agricultural work, and literacy was rising. By the mid-eighteenth century, the Anglican Book of Common Prayer, with excerpts of the Bible, had been translated into Mohawk.[8] Once the Iroquoian language was transcribed, a people nurtured in an oral culture using bead-embroidered pictographs as mnemonic devices were suddenly able to translate written documents into their own language for preservation and dissemination.

Despite encroachments and injustices, by midcentury member nations of the league had attained one of the highest standards of living among Native Americans. But this physical well-being came at a cost to culture. Traditionalists among the Iroquois knew that material gain did not reverse the decline of their population or prevent their lands from shrinking. The natives' increasing dependence on trade goods, manufactured commodities, weakened their ability to withstand the alien values thrust on them by Europeans. With trade came disease, and the spread of epidemics during the seventeenth century had done much to send Iroquoian population levels into decline. The strain of tribal warfare also drained communities of young warriors vital to the maintenance of power.

The warrior ethos of the people existed uneasily with the practice of agriculture and industry; Iroquoian men spurned farming and yearned for a life of warfare and hunting. The warrior's lot was generally a celibate one, with late marriage the rule. Tribes accommodated their young men by sending war parties to the far-flung reaches of their territory and shutting their eyes to the troubles they often caused. Iroquoian society was matrilineal, and women continued to elect chieftains and control tribal policy. In the years of ordeal approaching, women would move further to positions of leadership as warriors suffered mounting losses.

The Great Awakening, the eighteenth-century religious revival that swept New England and Virginia, also won converts in the Six Nations. Praying Mohawks, the

Caughnawagas of the St. Lawrence, had been observant Catholics since the mid-seventeenth century. But the Caughnawagas had removed from their homes on Tenonanatche and were increasingly estranged from brethren who remained in the valley. While religion could be deeply felt and could work to mitigate the cruelties of warfare, the missionary activity of the invading Europeans was met less with violent resistance than with reticence and reservation. Intellectually, the forest people were tolerant and forbearing, but Johnson quickly perceived that in religious observance they naturally favored religious rites rich in ritual and symbolization.

In no case, however, did religion trump immemorial ways as a means to power within tribal structures. The forest warrior on the warpath continued to haunt European imaginations throughout the eighteenth century, and little distinction was made between Christian and non-Christian groups. In one terrible instance, a tribe of Christian Delawares, of the pacifist Moravian faith, were attacked and annihilated by settlers just for being Indians. Conestoga Indians, resident outside Philadelphia and long assimilated, were also massacred at the height of the French and Indian War by enraged frontiersmen. [9]

As Johnson entered further into the Mohawk experience, he became increasingly conscious of the underlying reasons for Mohawk policies and practices. Their myths spoke of things he could grasp in terms of impoverished and oppressed Ireland.[10] The Mohawk world did not abstract passion or repress affinities with nature. European records, for example, might speak of a war (King William's) conducted in the Mohawk Valley as an extension of French policy aimed at unseating English power in North America. But Mohawks did not tell time or visualize events in this way; they saw the true story of the conflict in terms not of national entities enacting history, but of individual players caught up in the eternal tragedy of opposing passions.

Here are two versions of the same story. In the English version, a founding father of New France, Count de Frontenac, conducted a bloody incursion along the Mohawk River in 1696, harrowing villages and killing many warriors. During King William's War (1690–1697), the first of the French and Indian wars, Frontenac's forces burned Dover, New Hampshire, Pemaquid, Maine, and Schenectady, New York. To view aggression in this way was to write white man's history. Mohawks saw Frontenac's actions as a father's struggles against the ineluctable laws of nature. They, too, were border raiders who took captives. They believed that the great leader came into the valley searching for his stolen half-breed child, the beautiful Oneta, daughter of a Huron mother. By then, Oneta was the wife of a Fort Hunter warrior named Achawi, who loved her more than life itself. True warriors dream of glory, and Achawi awoke to search through the burning village for his bride. Armed only with a bow and arrow, he seized her from her captors and spirited her away into the hills overlooking the river. There, in the defiles above Konnediega's falls, he defended her against the French invaders, vaulting into his people's annals by slaying with arrows the Chevalier de Grais and Hanyost, a false Dutch guide, along with other French pursuers. Frontenac never got his beloved daughter back; she remained forever a bride of the Mohawks, the beautiful lady of the falls, the peerless lover of Achawi. Fathers must part with their daughters in the end, even the fearless, iron man of the Canadas. For such is the way of nature.[11]

Johnson was left to ponder the meaning of Achawi and Oneta. Son of Ireland, knowing well the heavy hand of the invader, the songs of Tara to be heard no more, he warmed naturally to a heroic people for whom loyalty was honor, and resistance to the oppressor meant rejection of history because the oppressor wrote history. But there was also another point being made for Johnson in the telling of the tale—Mohawks might be able to drive back the French with bows and arrows, but armed with British guns and ample powder, they could clear the frontiers of England's enemies. Treated well, they would even attempt to persuade the rest of the longhouse—Oneidas, Onondagas, Cayugas, and Senecas—to spurn *Onontio*, the French King. Treated badly, on the other hand, they could just as easily decide to sit out a French and Indian attack against New York. Of course, the Mohawks told the same story to the French, extorting comparable promises from Montreal and Quebec.

Johnson realized with sympathy how the Iroquois proposed to survive the growing white pressure; they would play all sides, craftily seeking advantage. To be sure, they wanted the best value for their pelts attainable, but their vision, never fully credited by Europeans, went beyond immediate material advantages. The Indians were sensitive to the racism exhibited against them wherever Europeans achieved majority. In the Mohawk Valley, the native peoples and the Palatine Germans lived equitably enough, but in Albany and New York City, the Palatines were seen as the lowest form of servant because of their easy association with Indians, not just because of their poverty. The shrewd politicians among the Mohawks seemed to apprehend that their valley had become a place of converging cultures—Yankee Protestants, French Catholics, German Lutherans, British Anglicans, Dutch farmers with their African slaves, and now a contingent of Irish and Scotch refugees. Learning and adapting, the Mohawks set out to control as much of their original valley as they could through agreement and solidarity.

Thus, when Johnson arrived, the Mohawk villages might be clamorous and even threatening, but they were also at peace. Tiononderoge balanced Fort Hunter; Canajoharie, the upper Mohawk castle, balanced German Flats. The French moved through the forests in small parties, mapping and surveying, but not unobserved; when it suited their purposes, the Mohawks told Johnson. They were drawing him closer to their world by acting as his eyes and ears. What they wanted in return was for Johnson to become their eyes and ears among the English. Chief King Hendrick—Tiyanoga—was the Irishman's tutor in all these matters concerning Iroquois practices. Tiyanoga never moved without intelligence of his enemy, and while no one read the forest byways better than he, actions in Albany, New York, Boston, and London were difficult for a Mohawk chief to descry. Only as Johnson began to master the Mohawk language did he start to appreciate the political sophistication of the Iroquoian out-look, and also comprehend the role that he was expected to fill. Here was the reason he had been shown the path to Oquaga.

Over the next decade Johnson grew closer to his Mohawk patrons, and as his rela-tionship with them warmed, his relationship with the Albany Dutch and their New York City kinsmen cooled. Johnson did not particularly like cities; he was more at ease fishing and hunting with Tenonanatche denizens than sipping tea in parlors. Thus he gladly accepted Tiyanoga's invitation, extended with the blessing of the Onondaga council, to become an adopted member of the Mohawk tribe. About 1743, Johnson exchanged his name for "Warraghiyagey," translated by him as "a man who undertakes great things."[12] He was thereafter entitled to participate in the councils and assemblies of the Iroquois League. But his new brothers were also entitled to visit his home freely, and while they came to trade and to be entertained, they also studied him closely.

The Mohawks liked what they saw in Handsome Billy. He was faultlessly gener-ous, seemed genuinely to admire their wilderness skills, and enjoyed the warm life of their villages. They in turn grew to trust him, and as his trading post expanded, sent the Northwest fur trade increasingly in his direction. No wonder the Albanians resented the Irishman. Even they, with all their experience, could not communicate with the Iroquois as freely or profitably as Johnson seemed to do. He evidently pos-sessed formidable diplomatic skills and, more to their dismay, his political power was growing. By the early 1740s he had built a large stone house on the north bank of the Mohawk and named it Mount Johnson. Thirty-plus miles from Albany, this new headquarters interposed itself between the merchant city and the eastern door of the Iroquoian longhouse. Tiyanoga, usually at odds with the Dutch magnates and British Crown governors, was enjoying the last laugh.

But there was little enough to laugh at as the 1740s passed. All of the dire predictions about British New York seemed to be approaching culmination. King George's War, in which Johnson served as a colonel of militia, demonstrated how porous and vulnerable the colony's defenses were against French incursions. Under then Governor Clinton's orders, Johnson moved to raise a small army to defend Albany and the Mohawk Valley. On August 8, 1746, he led his Indian allies into Albany by the north road, stripped to his breechcloth with body painted. Mohawk braves moved in single file behind Warraghi-yagey, and as their scalp cries echoed in the streets, they left no doubt in Albanian minds that Irish Billy had accomplished the near impossible—he had created an Iroquois alli-ance that opposed the French and nominally supported the British.[13] But if his success discountenanced Albanians, it also upset the Iroquois Council at Onondaga, where a policy of neutrality between France and Britain had been repeatedly affirmed. The most knowledgeable white man in the forests, Conrad Weiser, disliked Johnson's histrionics and predicted that he would go too far, forcing the sachems to assassinate him.

Yet Johnson somehow survived these turbulent years, with Tiyanoga's help. As King George's War drew to an indecisive close, Johnson was poised to exploit business opportunities opening to him through land companies and trade. This might well have come about if not for a wilderness skirmish in Pennsylvania precipitating the final showdown between France and Britain. There was never any question about Johnson's side; he would always be a loyal British subject and upholder of British imperial interests. But Johnson now was also a Mohawk brother and aware that, for many Iroquois, the French of New France were valued friends.

His loyalty was soon put to the test. In 1754, reacting to Major George Washington's defeat at Fort Necessity and the humiliation of Virginia's militia in the western forests, the British government resolved to end French encroachments without a formal declaration of war. Major General Edward Braddock, with two regiments, the 44th and the 48th Foot, was dispatched to Virginia under orders to take command of all British-American forces necessary to accomplish an aggressive campaign against New France.[14] He would have power to overrule colonial assemblies and governors in mobilizing this campaign. In effect, the home government of the Dukes of Newcastle and Cumberland had resolved to strike first, never apprehending the consequences of a wilderness war in North America.[15] As it turned out, their decision sparked a worldwide conflagration that Europe would call the Seven Years War, and the colonies would know as the French and Indian War. After this upheaval, nothing was ever quite the same again in North America; French Canada became British Canada, and the vast sums expended to achieve victory brought Britain and her American colonies to the brink of bankruptcy. All this lay on the other side of the great divide about to open.

Braddock, apprised of Johnson's relationship with the Iroquois, made certain of his participation in the upcoming campaign by naming him a major general of militia and charging him to capture the French post of Fort St. Frédéric at Crown Point on Lake Champlain.[16] He was to have the support of New York, New Jersey, and New England militia in accomplishing this goal, while Braddock himself marched with his regulars and Virginia militia to capture Fort Duquesne (Pittsburgh). New England protested loudly at the fur trader's elevation to command, and Johnson was put under the command of Governor William Shirley of Massachusetts, who also was instructed to raise a force for capturing Fort Niagara on Lake Ontario by way of Oswego. No one in London appeared to understand in the spring of 1755 how vast were the distances their armies would be required to cover or the difficulties of the terrain to be crossed. The French knew almost immediately that a blow was to be delivered, but they could not tell where. Very soon they would have the answer to that question in hand.

Not long after William Johnson was promoted general of provincial forces, his new commander in chief, Braddock, was climbing the hills of Pennsylvania's Appalachians toward the Monongahela River and Fort Duquesne. Among General Braddock's aides in July 1755 was Colonel Washington, returning with an army of 2,500 British regulars to the scene of his earlier misfortunes. Washington offered Braddock sound advice, the very advice Johnson offered, but Braddock roundly declined to follow any. He rode at the head of the largest military force deployed until that time by Britain in America, and the officers under his command represented the cream of the British army. His supply wagons—mustered with great difficulty at Philadelphia with the help of one Benjamin Franklin—stretched for miles behind his column. His artillery train packed enough firepower to destroy any fortifications within reach of the guns. Braddock found many reasons to dismiss the opinions of provincial minds.

What was curious, however, was how the deep, dense forest through which they had struggled for miles suddenly seemed to open up and grow lighter. Sir John St. Clair, Braddock's quartermaster, observed this change without knowing what it meant. The column, now a short distance from Fort Duquesne, had entered an Indian hunting ground where the forests had been thinned to improve the fodder qualities of its vegetation, reveal game against the light, and allow marksmen to set their sights.[17] Braddock's force of red-coated infantry, without screening scouts, had bungled onto a killing ground where over 900 men—650 Indians, 100 French, and 150 Canadians—under Captain Daniel Beaujeu waited at the ready.[18] The British infantry reeled from their concentrated fire and, hoping to match the accuracy of aimed muskets with blind volleys into the bush, fought until casualties and losses of officers forced them to retreat. "They behaved," Washington reported, "with more cowardice than it is possible to conceive ... they broke and ran as sheep pursued by dogs."[19] In their defense, the British infantry could see nothing to shoot at in the low undergrowth. Colonial militia broke immediately and, firing from behind trees, were mistaken for the enemy by the regulars and shot down. As the powder smoke drifted above the forest tops, the proud British army collapsed and ran for its life. It was a total, bloody catastrophe, and no one had seen it coming. As the columns came apart in panic-stricken flight, crazed survivors, abandoning their weapons and wounded, raced through a gauntlet of warriors wielding hatchets and scalping knives. Washington in the heat of the engagement had had two horses shot from under him, but survived the ordeal unscathed. Braddock and his army did not. And in the debris left behind on the battlefield was found a box containing plans for the military campaigns to be launched against the French in the Province of New York—certainly an embarrassing oversight given that no state of war existed between France and England.[20]

Yet, for all the good this discovery did the victors, the box might well have been Pandora's, on loan to the British Army. Pierre de Contrecoeur, commandant of His French Majesty's fort at Duquesne, had the contents from Charles Langlade, the great French-Indian scout, who gathered up the papers after the Ottawas scattered them in the dust. The braves could not read; they wanted the chest for plunder. The letters, it turned out, belonged to Braddock, who by then lay buried in the middle of a dirt track on the retreat to Fort Cumberland. Aides, on Washington's advice, planted the grave deep where retreating feet could trample and hide it. The general was one of 978 British dead left behind in the wilderness, but his corpse still wore its hair.

As they had loaded the general, shot through the lungs, into the cart, they inadvertently spilled the chest out with other goods to make room. It lay among the bodies of the British dead for two days before the Ottawas found it. From this box, by some malign destiny, would come to those who looked within disgrace, failure, and misery. Down even into the era of the young United States, reflections on Braddock's defeat in the summer of '55 blew like a cold draft into a warm room, reminding everyone how fast the weather could change in North America. The general's last words, recalled by Washington: "Who would have thought it?"[21]

De Contrecoeur was not conversant in English; he had the letters read out loud to him by a prisoner and then translated verbally into French by an illiterate Canadian. The papers' momentous intelligence caused great excitement, especially since the French proceeded by plans and expected that enemy plans would be pursued with the same vigor as their own. De Contrecoeur wrote urgently to his superior, the Marquis de Vaudreuil, Governor of New France at Montreal:

> In separate pages I have prepared for you a full account of our decisive victory yesterday over the English under General Braddock along the River Monongahela not far from this establishment. ... I have now the honor, Sir, to impart to you news of the utmost importance and urgency. The papers enclosed here, written in English, were recovered from a chest on the battlefield. They are complete battle plans for a campaign being launched at this very moment against Fort St. Frederic at Point à la Chevelure [Crown Point]. The English army moving against this installation is under the command of Major General William Johnson. [22]

Hundreds of miles to the east, William Johnson was moving nowhere. As Contrecoeur's courier sped to Montreal, Johnson was stuck at Albany, cobbling together an improbable coalition of New Yorkers, New Englanders, and Mohawks. Implementing plans across the British colonies never ran smoothly. The colonies squabbled over who was to pay and who was to get. The proprietary province of Pennsylvania, for instance, could not pay because the Quakers who controlled the Assembly would not vote money for war. In the aftermath of Braddock's catastrophe, attacks surged against Pennsylvania's frontier communities for lack of men and resources. By the end of 1755, the western counties of Pennsylvania and Virginia were in headlong evacuation.

Massachusetts commanded both men and resources, but only grudgingly shared its bounty with unkempt and irreligious New Yorkers, whose own legislature repeatedly failed to deliver on promises. New Hampshire had lived continually under the threat of French and Indian raids and promised to send militia to Albany. But as Johnson's army prepared to march, they had not yet arrived. Connecticut arrived complaining, and New Jersey sent what it could, but the force at Albany, bound for Fort St. Frédéric on Lake Champlain, was less an army than an itinerant political caucus riven by sectional rivalries, religious antagonisms, and smoldering distrusts.

Historians have sometimes blamed the confusion on Johnson, suggesting that his slack moral fiber allowed troops to mingle too freely with the buxom girls of Albany.[23] Indeed, Johnson kept the rum flowing even as New Englanders sought to imbue the encampment with religious revival. Some of the leading lights of the Great Awakening were bivouacked next to Johnson's wild Mohawks and coarse Germans. Letters home from the New England contingent contain scathing indictments of the superstition and immorality prevailing under the Anglo-Catholic Johnson. "We are a wicked, profane army," Colonel Israel Williams of Massachusetts wrote, "especially the New York and Rhode Island troops. Nothing to be heard among the great part of them but the language of Hell. If Crown Point is taken, it will not be for our sakes, but for those good people left behind."[24]

To the New Yorkers and their Mohawks, the "saints" of New England would never take Crown Point prayerfully or otherwise until they learned to drink, sport, and fight better in the bush. The hostile woods started just north of Albany, above Saratoga, and from there northward to Canada they could expect to meet parties of French Indians and *coureurs de bois*, Canadian woodsmen and itinerant trappers. They would be pressing into the foothills of the eastern Adirondacks where, after the snows melted, black flies would drive soldiers crazy as they sweated to clear a way with axe and saw. Death among the trees crept silently, arriving with the whistle of an arrow or hatchet. Volley fire was useless in the forest. What a soldier aimed at, he needed to hit, and then changing position, reload his musket on the run. Johnson knew what it would be, and his Mohawks drilled the farm boy recruits for a style of warfare no European army practiced. The problem was that they did not have much time. Less time, in fact, than Johnson hoped.

He was not a trained professional himself, but a businessman who had received his major generalship of militia from the King's North American Commander on account of his knowledge of Native Americans. Johnson knew nothing of artillery or logistics and had never led large forces in sustained battle, but he did know how native peoples might be expected to fight in their own forests. Moreover, he knew that one warrior was worth ten infantry in close encounters. In March he wrote to Braddock expressing his doubts about commanding an army:

> You must be convinced that the little experience I have had in military affairs cannot entitle me to this distinction. ... The circumstance that I find has determined your Excellency is the influence I have hitherto maintained with

the Indians whose assistance must be of great advantage on this service, and to obtain it I should have exerted my utmost interest among them if your Excellency had fixed on some other person, which would still be very agreeable to me.[25]

Which was to say, "Find someone else"—but to no avail. The English plan, as Contrecoeur discovered, was a highly ambitious triple thrust at the encircling French positions along the northwest frontier. Braddock would lead a British force from Philadelphia over the Appalachian chain to the junction of the Monongahela and Allegheny rivers, and there capture Fort Duquesne, later Pittsburgh. Meanwhile, General William Shirley, Governor of Massachusetts, would march from Albany up the Mohawk corridor to Oswego on Lake Ontario, and then voyage to Fort Niagara at the ingress to Lake Erie. Johnson would lead his provincial troops north to Crown Point on Lake Champlain, threatening the lake and river approaches to Montreal. And all this mammoth undertaking would transit primal wilderness before reaching its objectives. The requirement for Indians to screen the expeditions was apparent, but only Johnson had actual experience of the wilderness to be crossed. He was to provide the Indians.

The prospect worried him on several counts. Shirley jostled into Albany and bid for services as though the Mohawks were day laborers. Braddock slighted the Indians sent him, and they decamped en masse from his post. No one in command appreciated how ticklish the situation was among the tribes, especially the Six Nations of the Iroquois. Seneca and Cayuga leaned to the French; Onondaga clung to strict neutrality; Mohawk, Oneida, and Tuscarora were willing to bend the policies of the Iroquois League in favor of the British—but only because Johnson, their adopted brother Warraghiyagey, begged them. They had all been let down before by British promises of aggressive action, victory, and plunder, and in their counsels spoke of His Britannic Majesty's lieutenants as "old, indecisive women." British trade goods might be superior to French, but the French delivered on their threats, and so far, the French were winning. Johnson wrote to Braddock in May, before leaving the Mohawk Valley for Albany, with important cautions:

> If the Six Nations should be brought to action in conjunction with us, they will expect not only provisions for such as go but an allowance to support all their aged men, their women & children whom they leave behind. ... They are a begging and insatiable set of people & expect to be denied nothing they ask for, & though a proper moderation must be used towards them in these matters, yet a delicate conduct is necessary till they have heartily entered into hostilities against the French.[26]

Iroquois had to be rewarded for their services, as the French recognized, and any inclination to save at their expense or deny them would result in their desertion, probably to the enemy. What seemed like indulgence to Braddock was nothing less than terms of survival for Native Americans, who in the best of circumstances were hard-pressed to sustain their way of life.

Under no condition, Johnson warned, should Braddock attempt to move without them, no matter how invincible his regiments of regular infantry or extensive his artillery. Johnson suffered with an "uneasy apprehension that the colonials who have engaged themselves to forward and support the attack will not act with that vigorous and generous spirit so very necessary towards its success," and, as usual where it came to money, his fears were justified. Taking upon himself the expense, he sent forward his own Mohawks. As the campaign season began, he wrote again to Braddock:

> The success of wilderness marches such as you will soon be embarked upon depend in great measure upon Indians protection. A party of Mohawks are coming to you soon, representing the Six Nations, and I urge you most strongly, General Braddock, to receive them with courtesy. However do not make the mistake of trying to enlist this delegation. Instead they should be treated well, shown your strength and then sent back with bountiful presents.[27]

By the time Johnson's admonition reached Braddock's headquarters, the general was dead—ambushed by 650 warriors and a handful of French and Canadians on a wilderness trail.

The muster outside Albany received this news from Philadelphia with shocked amazement. If they had doubted they were engaged in mortal combat for their homes, those doubts vanished now along with the lighthearted spirit of their preparations. Braddock's force, they thought, had been the best of the British Army; Braddock himself was one of the Crown's most seasoned commanders. They, on the other hand, were jumped-up farmers from a handful of colonies, their commander an Indian-loving politician with an appetite for rum and women. They did not have uniforms, and some did not even have muskets. A New England regimental surgeon wrote, "I shall be glad if they fight as eagerly as they ate their ox and drank their wine." The party was over, and for the first time ever, though none realized at the time, a purely American army, drawn from across the northern colonies, had taken the field in an hour of supreme crisis. Twenty years later, veterans would remember the run-up to the Battle of Lake George as they formed ranks in Brooklyn or dressed their lines outside Saratoga. Of course, they were not "Americans" at Lake George, but British subjects engaging an ancient opponent, the French, who were aided by a foe hated even more so, the peoples of the forest.

North they marched in August after a long delay, even as the campaign season wound down and word arrived that Shirley, stalled by summer storms at Oswego, would be unable to advance against French Niagara. Johnson waited at Albany for the

New Hampshire regiment still en route, while Phineas Lyman, Colonel of Connecticut forces and sometime lecturer at Yale, led the army two thousand strong forward to the great carry at the top of the Hudson. One hundred Mohawks screened their advance along the forty-mile trail. Behind them, Lyman's men dragged supply carts loaded with flat-bottomed bateaux intended for navigating lakes and rivers. They were bound for a remote trading post owned by John Lydius, an unsavory rum-dealer and land speculator of Johnson's acquaintance. His blockhouse stood at the farthest navigable point on the Hudson, below the falls, at a place where the river divided around a large island. It stood smack against the wilderness, with only Indian trails radiating out toward Lac St. Sacrement (Lake George) and Champlain. And here the weary army rested, waiting for Johnson to catch up and decide its course.

Johnson's choices were perilous. He could widen the carry for carts and cannon to Lac St. Sacrement, fourteen miles away, and from there voyage up the lake to its confluence with Champlain, ten miles below Crown Point. Or he could march over a longer but wetter road to South Bay at the southern tip of Champlain, embark on his bateaux and row north without portage to his objective. This was the choice General Burgoyne would face in reverse twenty-two years later. If Johnson's force had had all its bateaux, the Champlain alternative might have served, in which event he would have collided head-on with the enemy. The presence of the French astride the road to South Bay was brought to Johnson's attention at the last possible moment by his Mohawk scouts. They learned of the enemy's position in conversation with their French cousins, the Caughnawaga Mohawks. To those who knew how to listen, the woods were alive with whispers.

Johnson chose the carry to Lac St. Sacrement, where he planned to build a fort and await more boats. No sooner had he arrived from Albany—still missing the New Hampshire men—he set the army to work raising fortifications. This was a favored tactic in the wilderness—advance, secure a staging point, and defend with a log stockade against surprise attack. The fort thrown up was named Fort Lyman in honor of the Connecticut colonel who would be much a thorn in Johnson's side. The need now was for cooperation among the sections. Later, when the fighting intensified, the fort would be renamed Edward in honor of the Duke of York. The island in the Hudson would be named Rogers Island in the nineteenth century, and legend would hold that Robert Rogers and his Rangers trained there. But as the provincial forces gathered, the redoubtable Rogers still struggled towards Albany with the rest of the lost New Hampshire regiment.

This bivouac in the wilderness has been described down the years as a last occasion for youthful innocence before colonial skies darkened. Much was at stake, yet for a few days while the army organized beside the Hudson, the men seemed drawn together in a mellow, late-summer light. Johnson had believed his men "with very few exceptions not only strangers to military life, but averse to all discipline and regularity." By late August he was willing to concede that his troops "were brave enough, though not regular." Surgeon Williams of Massachusetts conceded on his part that Johnson "is a complete gentleman, and willing to oblige and please all men, familiar and free of access to the lowest sentinel, a gentleman of uncommon smart sense and even temper; never yet saw him ruffle or use any bad language."[28] It helped that Johnson acted the part of a British general, striving to placate grumbling in the ranks by setting a fine table. "The troops will naturally expect to see it," he noted, "the officers to feel it."

Seth Pomeroy, a gunsmith from Northampton and a major in the 4th Massachusetts, kept a journal of these days. For August 27 he enters, "Eat pieces of ham, broken bread, and cheese, drank some fresh lemon punch and the best of wine with General Johnson." The next day, "Dined with General Johnson by a small brook under a tree. Eat a good dinner of cold boiled and roasted venison, drank some fresh lemon punch and wine. We came to the lake about four of the clock."[29]

Pomeroy as an old man would live to fight with revolutionaries at Bunker Hill. His brother Daniel, a captain accompanying him, was shot dead at Lake George a few days later. Israel Putnam, Washington's warhorse at the Battle of Long Island, was a captain in Lyman's regiment. Colonel Moses Titcomb was there for Massachusetts; he had stormed Louisbourg in 1745. Colonel Ephraim Williams also served; he had been a captain under Titcomb in the Louisbourg campaign. Money from Ephraim's estate would someday found Williams College. His cousin Israel Williams was regimental chaplain; his cousin William Thomas Williams was the army's chief surgeon. There were two Hawleys present; one would die, the other would suffer crippling wounds. These names of New England are like a roll call sounding across America's eighteenth-century wars—Pynchons, Newalls, Blodgets, Ruggleses, Whitings, Browns, and more who would fight battles in New York. From his own province Johnson brought Freys and Bradts, Savages, Butlers, Schuylers, Wades, Livingstons, but none of greater eminence than Tiyanoga, King Hendrick to the Dutch, sachem and war chief of the Mohawks.

Tiyanoga was nearly eighty years old when he chose to lead his Mohawks on the Crown Point expedition. He was grossly overweight by then, hardly the champion warrior of his youth. Yet no figure in British North America, European or Native American, grasped as fully as he the totality of transformation being worked on the land and culture of native peoples by the inroads of settlement. By virtue of conquest or agreement, the Iroquois League claimed dominion as far west as the Mississippi, as far south as the borders of Georgia. Over this vast territory little happened that escaped Tiyanoga's attention. Visitors to Canajoharie might find the old man sitting in the sun on the doorstep of his house and never realize the extent of his knowledge and influence. His father had been a Mohegan, his mother a Mohawk of the Wolf clan, and by the matrilineal customs of the Iroquois, he was made eligible for the chieftaincy of his mother's clan.

Tiyanoga understood his people's advantage against the Europeans. They ruled the interior wilderness absolutely. But he also appreciated their great vulnerability. Lacking vital technologies themselves, they had grown dependent on luxury goods acquired by trade, and through these goods, were easily turned against each other. The Indian peoples needed gunpowder and lead, blankets and beads, iron kettles, sharp knives, and rum, and in exchange provided successful traders with a near monopoly of pelts. Tribal wars had already bled away much of the Mohawks' warrior strength in struggles to maintain a North American supremacy. Now their low population growth seemed irreversible against the burgeoning cities and settlements of the colonies. Confronted with all this, some eighteenth-century sachems chose isolation and hostility; Tiyanoga urged his people instead to accommodate change and make a place for themselves.

Critical to their success was timely intelligence about colonial intentions, and this could only flow from constant relationship. On first meeting, Hendrick might deny knowledge of English, but in conversations with Johnson he spoke the language fluently. Tiyanoga treated easily with the great of the colonies, but at heart he was always a Mohawk warrior. On a beech tree behind his house at Canajoharie, he slashed the bark for every enemy killed or captured. A portrait remains of the sachem engraved by I. Faber. It depicts a fine gentleman in laced coat and weskit (waistcoat) who just happens to be holding a string of wampum in his left hand while brandishing a hatchet in his right. A cruel scar from an old tomahawk wound stretches from the corner of his mouth across his left cheek. His expression is sardonic, the mixed dress and posture a parody of European military fashion.

During the Crown Point campaign, Tiyanoga may have tutored a young, promising Mohawk brave in the stratagems of wilderness war; this youngster was Joseph Brant, who in time would know English even better than his mentor. Some accounts state that Brant took his first scalp on this expedition, although in all likelihood he was too young to have been an active combatant.[30] As a war chief of the Mohawks in his own right, he would one day plague Generals Washington, Herkimer, and Sullivan, and contribute to the devastation along Tenonanatche. Conceivably his skills as a guerrilla leader were acquired at the old man's feet, but of course he might have learned his tactics of retreat and counter-ambush from many seasoned warriors. Raised in a Christian family, Brant attended Wheelock's grammar school in Lebanon, Connecticut, at Johnson's expense. In the years before the Revolution, he emulated Tiyanoga by working to bridge the distance between European and native cultures. His translation into the Mohawk language of selections from the Anglican Book of Common Prayer was completed at Fort Hunter in 1772.[31]

To be sure, Tiyanoga also tutored Johnson—but for different reasons. In order to offset Mohawk blindness to white politics and policies, he welcomed this white man into the tribe by adoption. Many Iroquois trusted Johnson, admiring his strong mind and powerful personality, but they also needed him, or someone very like him, to mediate between their interests and the incessant sharp dealings of colonial governors and assemblies. Johnson was unquestionably Tiyanoga's creation. To Europeans who met King Hendrick in negotiations, the aged sachem seemed always to pursue one principle: the greatest possible good for the greatest number of Haudenosaunee, nation of Hiawatha, nation of the Mohawks.

Yet Tiyanoga in his twilight also felt free to gamble the life he owned as he chose. To help the English or the Albany Dutch against the French, he would not lift a finger. This fight was the white man's. Iroquois sachems had learned of Braddock's defeat, probably from Johnson. They shook their heads over what this meant to the British position. They also received news that Braddock's replacement as commander in chief of His Majesty's forces was a sixty-one-year-old Boston lawyer and politician, William Shirley, who had already angered the Iroquois and Johnson by employing the villainous John Lydius to recruit Mohawks. This was not encouraging. Even as Shirley moved to Oswego, he was embroiled in political controversy with New York's governor, James DeLancey. Regrettably, Shirley had also learned that his eldest son, William, Braddock's personal secretary, had been shot through the head and killed at the battle on the Monongahela. Add to this that his expedition, the second of the planned three-part thrust, was hopelessly stalled. Fort Oswego had turned out to be a dilapidated ruin. As he struggled to repair the post, an epidemic broke out among his troops, causing the death of a second son. Shirley, as the sachems predicted, was finished before he had begun, leaving only one tine on London's pitchfork—Johnson.

The Mohawks weighed their position carefully. The majority counseled sitting out the contest between the French and British until one or the other showed signs of prevailing. Native peoples could not afford to back a loser. It was Tiyanoga who turned this advice on its head. A proud father, he declined to abandon his adopted son in the moment of his greatest testing, nor would Johnson's death or failure, he argued, have hurt anyone more than the Mohawks of whom he was a part. Therefore, they and their neighbors the Oneidas would take up the hatchet and move to Warraghiyagey's support at Lac St. Sacrement.

Johnson had hoped for a thousand Iroquois to accompany the army; in the end he was lucky to muster three hundred. Two hundred arrived with Tiyanoga just in the nick of time. Without Mohawk scouts, there would have been no picnic by the river for Major Pomeroy, or even the faintest hint of how close the French had crept to Johnson's green troops.

To his New Englanders, Johnson at the height of his powers was something to write home about. They spied him stripped to the waist, painted for war, dancing wildly to drums with his friends. The word several used to describe their feelings about the half-wild New Yorker was "shuddery." Nothing made the common colonial soldier shudder more than the specter of lurking Indians. James Gilbert of Morton, Massachusetts, saw his first braves on the march. "My pen is not abel," he writes home, "to describe the odiesnes of their dress. They had juels in their noses. Their faces painted with all colouers. They appeared very odious to us also." These Indians, who looked so horrible and smelled even worse to militiamen, had just returned to camp from scouting Lac St. Sacrement to the north.

What Johnson's scouts discovered would amaze anyone visiting Lake George village today. Where the Northway from Albany dumps traffic onto the resort's main street, Johnson's men first beheld New York's most beautiful lake. On any Labor Day weekend now, a succession of events draws thousands of tourists down to the waterside's restaurants, walks, and beaches. Traffic jams the one street through the village, while cruise boats parade up the lake from a pier near the replica of long-ago-destroyed Fort William Henry. Long-time residents consider the village a tourist trap, lined as it is with fast-food joints and brightly painted motels. They like to explain that a terrible history happened here—not once, but several times. Nothing about this vacationland accords with the grim stories told on the historical markers, monuments, and plaques.

Before there was ever a novel called *The Last of the Mohicans*, before Johnson thought of building Fort William Henry or Montcalm of burning it, the dark and hideous forest came right down to the crystal-clear waters. The quality of this water had inspired Father Jogues to name the lake in honor of the baptismal sacrament.[32] But no beach greeted the 4th Massachusetts when they stumbled out of the woods. They had to clear a way to the water with axes, sleeping under the scrub in the rain until they made space to pitch a tent. An oil painting remains by Captain Thomas Davies of this landing at the foot of the lake executed nineteen years after Johnson's expedition; it shows an ample parade ground marred by tree stumps.[33] The army, blind and frightened in the suffocating growth, chopped out the trees as fast as it could. Thirty men mutinied against the duty and, clubbing their rifles over their shoulders, set off back to Albany. Everyone had heard reports of Braddock, of redcoats shot down in rows from ambush, and in the dappled shade surrounding them, Johnson's Indians flitted quietly through the woods on missions the New Englanders could not understand.

Johnson gathered as many hundreds of his men as he could in the small space at lakeside and in a few words renamed Lac St. Sacrement. "This Lake called Lake St. Sacrament by the French," he wrote to Governor DeLancey on September 4, "I have called Lake George not only in honour to his Majesty but to assertain his Dominion here."[34] Of course, it was one thing to rename the lake, another to make the name stick. As his troops cleared fields of fire, he ordered the encampment encircled with rude breastworks and overturned wagons. Where the road back to Fort Lyman bore through the forest, improvements were needed if artillery were to be brought up. Johnson had inveigled the services of a professional artillery officer from Braddock, and to his good fortune Captain William Eyre was detached and sent north to organize the provincial guns and fortifications. Eyre was the only British soldier with the expedition, and quickly became chief of ordinance and quartermaster general. As soon as the woods were dry enough to move artillery and caissons, Johnson ordered Eyre to quit construction of Fort Lyman and come up to the lake with four six-pounder cannon drawn from the arsenal of the Crown Colony of New York. One cannon Eyre mounted on a hill securing the left flank of Johnson's position; the others he sited where the road from Fort Lyman entered the enclosure. Johnson had placed his camp with its back to the lake. The right flank was covered by marsh, and the main line of attack lay from the southwest over level ground just now cleared of trees to beyond musket range.[35]

The general knew that if the French assaulted with artillery before he could construct solid fortifications, his army was lost. The responsibility sat heavily on him as he wrote to Governor DeLancey:

> What with the trouble I have with the Indians & that disorderly management there is among the troops, I am almost distracted. I have neither rest night nor day, nor a comfortable thinking hour to myself. Our sick increase, our men impatient to have the affair ended & most of the officers little better. ... I would exert authority but cannot be sufficiently seconded. ... With the Indian scouts & if the sentries and guards will do their duty I am not afraid of any insult from the enemy—but God help us our sentries I fear are less than diligent. I have ordered patrols every half hour round our whole encampment during the night & if my orders are observed, I do not dread a surprise.[36]

As tensions mounted in the camp, rumors spread through the ranks about the road to Lyman being cut by Indians, about French columns marching on them with hundreds of howling Abenakis, and of their own Indians planning to turn against them. They were trapped with their backs to the lake, rations were low, and the first chill breezes of autumn had begun to blow. They would never see home again. But Braddock, Shirley, and Johnson were not the only chiefs who had looked into Pandora's box. De Contrecoeur and Vaudreuil had peered in as well, and as Johnson's sheep were staked out for slaughter at the bottom of Lake George, the wolves streaking towards them through the forests were experiencing confusions of their own.

3

THE BATTLE OF LAKE GEORGE

The waters of the Gulf of St. Lawrence are clogged with ice in April. This ice, with stormy weather, contrary winds, and thick fog had prevented Admiral Boscawen from finding all the French convoy. In the spring of 1755, Britain was not yet at war with France, but the admiral's orders were to stop all reinforcements landing at Cape Breton Island or entering the St. Lawrence.

The great river, flowing past Montreal and Quebec into the gulf, usually froze in November and thawed in April. Since passage from Le Havre to Canada might take three months in foul weather, shipping followed tight schedules in order to arrive while the St. Lawrence was navigable. Yet Boscawen, intercepting the predicted convoy, caught only two ships transporting ten companies of infantry—about 400 men out of a total embarked force of 3,000. As a consequence, 2,600 infantry of the line appeared at Montreal with their *maréchal de camp*, Baron Jean-Armand de Dieskau, about the time Contrecoeur's courier arrived from Fort Duquesne.[1]

Dieskau, one of the most daring field commanders of his time, was a German officer in the service of King Louis XV of France. He had been a protégé of the great Marshal Arminius Maurice, Comte de Saxe, whose deployment of irregular forces in Flanders during a previous war had much distressed the English. Unlike Braddock, Dieskau would not spurn scouts or march his ranks blindly into ambush. His doctrine called for rapid movement, using Canadian *coureurs de bois*, wilderness trappers, as his eyes, and luring an unsuspecting enemy into range of his Indian allies. The knockout punch arrived on the ships that Boscawen had failed to find—soldiers of the Languedoc and La Reine Regiments, some of the finest infantry in the French Army. Dieskau had plentiful artillery, along with bateaux to float his guns, and in a rare circumstance for New France, ample provisions to carry him beyond Fort St. Frédéric, past the jut of Ticonderoga, and all the way to Albany. This was the kind of body blow Braddock had aimed at Duquesne. The Baron's mission, in fact, was a mirror image of Braddock's. The difference—Dieskau was the better tactician, and his adversaries, as he was assured, were not elusive Indians or infantry of the line, but provincial farmers commanded by a fur trader.

In the war council at Montreal, the Marquis de Vaudreuil, Governor of New France, mapped the French reply to Britain's provocations. Braddock had been destroyed; the remains of his army cowered pitifully in Philadelphia awaiting reorganization, which in all likelihood would not follow quickly.[2] William Shirley's strike at Niagara was deemed most serious of all; it threatened to cut lines of communication through the trans-Appalachian wilderness to the Mississippi and New Orleans. This thrust depended on a line of supply the length of Tenonanatche, over swampy Wood Creek into Lake Oneida, then down the Onondaga River to Oswego. But what if this snake were chopped in half? What if the French took Albany, or at least the mouth of the Mohawk River? Shirley would be cut off in the interior, an easy mark. All that stood in the way was William Johnson with his New York and New England colonials and their Indian allies. In Vaudreuil's opinion, troops of this ilk had never fought effectively in the wilderness. The future of New France hinged therefore on a sharp attack toward the headwaters of the Hudson before the British even recognized the full danger of their position. From Montreal, Dieskau would ascend the Richelieu River into Lake Champlain, navigate the lake to Crown Point, and fall on Johnson's forces wherever he found them.

New France pursued Indian diplomacy assiduously. The Canadian economy was sustained more by the fur trade than appropriations of land, and the fact that Canadian woodsmen frequently married Indian women and lived among the tribes tended to foster mutual understanding. Quebec at this juncture summoned to Dieskau's command displaced Abenakis from New England, Caughnawaga Mohawks from the St. Lawrence, Hurons, Ottawas, Potawatomies from the west, Micmacs from the far north. The marshal would attack with more than 2,000 regulars, 500 Canadians, and a contingent of native peoples over 1,000 strong.

So appointed, Dieskau led his force south to Fort St. Frédéric at Crown Point in early August.[3] Given that he knew Johnson's plans, he might have fortified and awaited his opponent's approach with every advantage. But the marshal always favored aggressive tactics, slashing raids that would peel back the defenses north of Albany. He had also discovered in his journey up Champlain some awkward truths about his allies. The baron's model for irregular warfare called for partisan fighters and, on first impression, the confederated tribes accompanying him gave promise of filling that role. He was soon disabused of the notion, as a report to Vaudreuil in late August indicates:

> They drive us crazy from morning till night. There is no end to their demands. They have already eaten five oxen and many hogs, without counting the kegs of brandy they have drunk. In short, one needs the patience of an angel to get on with these devils; and yet one must always force himself to seem pleased with them.[4]

What the baron was coming to realize, and Johnson had long known, was that Native Americans might associate voluntarily with a military effort, but would seldom submit to martial discipline. They were under the nominal control of a French officer, Legardeur de Saint-Pierre, who after many years of experience on the frontier conversed with them freely. But even Legardeur could not guarantee that they would fight as ordered. What they would have done, had Dieskau decided to sit at St. Frédéric, was to eat his garrison out of house and home, and then, once the inevitable siege had begun, fade away into the forest. Native Americans usually declined to attack or defend fixed fortifications. They only reluctantly joined in pitched battles. These modes of warfare were extremely prodigal of lives, and few tribes could afford steep butcher bills among their warriors and hope to endure. Better, they reasoned, to fight from ambush on their own terms than to throw away the future of their people on forlorn gambles. Moving southward, Dieskau discovered what many eighteenth-century generals learned to their regret—native peoples were not comfortable auxiliaries; they would act in their own best interests, and sometimes those interests could cost their employers victory.

Before embarking at St. Frédéric for Ticonderoga, the marshal issued the following orders to his troops and allies:

> The entire force will prepare and hold itself in readiness for the march which will begin at sunrise tomorrow. In addition to their weapons, officers will take nothing with them but one spare shirt, one spare pair of shoes, a blanket, a bearskin, and provisions for twelve days; the troops will similarly supply themselves. The Indians will continue as they have under Captain Legardeur de Saint-Pierre *and under no circumstances are they to amuse themselves by taking scalps until the enemy is entirely defeated, since they can kill ten men in the time required to scalp one.* The squaws and young Indian boys accompanying the warriors may proceed with the force as far as the point where the army will leave the water and continue afoot, but no farther.[5]

Apparently, the marshal had reconciled himself to the practices of wilderness warfare—torture or burning of prisoners, scalping of the dead. It was not that he condoned these "amusements," but that they seemed an unavoidable consequence to him of employing people he and other Europeans deemed savages. French authorities, both clerical and military, had long ago accepted that the "mourning rites" of native culture were beyond contravening even among Christianized tribes. The French might attempt to buy prisoners, yet invariably some were enslaved, some adopted, some burned at the stake. Occasionally, as Louis Antoine de Bougainville attested, a prisoner might be eaten on a long march when food grew scarce and hunting impossible. These were the terms of struggle for the cruel lands of North America, and the British accepted them as quickly as the French.[6] No one was under any illusions about what would befall either side were they to lose a battle in the forests.

The point of land where the La Chute River empties into Lake Champlain, and Champlain continues south as little more than a river itself, is called Ticonderoga or "meeting of the waters." On this commanding point Vaudreuil ordered Michel de Lotbinière, his engineer, to begin construction of a timbered fort. Dieskau had already detached 500 infantry to garrison Fort St. Frédéric, and now he detached another battalion-sized force to protect the builders of the new Fort Carillon.[7] From here a portage trail could have brought him to the top of Lake George for a move south against Johnson's reported position. Instead, he aimed at Fort Lyman in Johnson's rear, from where he could sever his opponent's lifeline to Albany, trap him against the lake, and bring infantry and artillery forward to annihilate him. Speed was essential, and the marshal decided to leave his artillery train at Ticonderoga in order to reach South Bay and the road to Fort Lyman swiftly. His native scouts reported that Fort Lyman was undermanned and only partially built; he could invest it rapidly with Indians and capture it from the forest with a *coup de main.*

This, of course, except for the fact that Johnson had left 500 men at Lyman to continue construction. Fortunately, Colonel Joseph Blanchard of New Hampshire had just arrived at Lyman with elements of his regiment, but in light of current intelligence, this combined detachment was still too small. The general seized this moment to call a council of war and alert his officers to the impending emergency. If Johnson dispatched additional troops from Lake George, his position there would be exposed; if he called in Blanchard and the Lyman crew, the carry from the Hudson to the lake would be lost, together with all supply from Albany. The war council resolved to send immediately to New England and New York for additional troops, although insufficient supplies were on hand to feed these reinforcements should they arrive.

Johnson's fears are apparent in a letter to Blanchard sent September 6. He urges the colonel to use all resources at his disposal to complete the fort:

> In two or three days at furthest I hope to send you orders to join me here. In the meantime I must desire & expect that your Regiment & the New Yorkers will apply to & finish the Works. ... Pray make use of artillery horses to forward the service. The waggoners I believe to be in general a parcel of rascals & little credit to be given them, few of their complaints are just, you will examine & do as you find needful, but keep them up to their duty & have a strict eye over them. I am afraid of fatal delays for the want of wagons. Good

weather is wearing away fast, and no time must be lost. The moment we can leave this place I will depart.[8]

The place spooked everyone, but no one more than the teamsters who plied the fourteen-mile portage road between Lyman and the lake. This forest stretch had already become one of New York's most murderous avenues. Out of the trees and onto the wagons would leap tomahawk-wielding braves without warning. A team might plod on into camp to deliver a ghastly freight. Understandably, the wagoners wanted out, for there were never enough troops to escort them, and the troops themselves were deserting as fear mounted along the lakeshore.

At Deux Rocher (Two Rocks) on Champlain, Dieskau interrogated one who fell into Indian hands. His companion resisted and was shot, but Andrew Hornsby had surrendered. Camped at Two Rocks on the edge of the Drowned Lands, Dieskau was nearing his destination. His scouts could estimate where Johnson was, but only Hornsby knew the strength of Johnson's force. If he talked, the French would make him prisoner; if he declined, he would be turned over to the Indians. Hornsby decided to lie. Johnson, he explained, had heard that Dieskau had 8,000 troops and had decamped to Albany. Fort Lyman was not finished, and was garrisoned by only 500 men. Hornsby reasoned that Dieskau would attack Lyman and that Johnson would strike him in the rear from Lake George. Hornsby may have survived to tell this story to his grandchildren, playing down the terror that had driven him to desert in the first place.[9]

Armed with this information, Dieskau detached several hundred regulars to guard his base at Deux Rocher. Then, steering for South Bay and Fort Lyman, he pressed on with his Canadians, Indians, and 200 light infantry of the Languedoc and La Reine battalions. The raiding party was just large enough to capture and hold the place, he calculated, until reinforcements and artillery came up from his bases. These were impeccable tactics in the wilderness, but now the size of the marshal's force had dipped significantly below Johnson's—if all of Johnson's troops resolved to fight. The marshal reminded his Canadian officers that they had called Johnson's provincials the worst troops in the world. Now he apprised them, "I do not care how many men Johnson has. The more there are, the more we shall kill." After Mass celebrated by a Jesuit priest, the force embarked in bateaux for the last leg of the journey. Accompanying them were the women and children of the Caughnawagas.

Word reached Johnson at Lake George on Sunday, September 7, that a large party of enemy had passed through the woods near South Bay. This had to be Dieskau, the scouts reasoned, and he was clearly marching on Lyman. While the Reverend Williams observed the Sabbath for his New England congregation with a sermon on Isaiah, the rest of the encampment brooded on this news. Tiyanoga met Johnson in his tent and warned him not to let his men stray from his camp into the woods lest they find themselves in the bellies of the wolves.[10]

Tiyanoga confirmed what Johnson's Mohawks had discovered. Johnson moved quickly now to inform Blanchard of the approaching danger. A volunteer was called for, and a Mohawk Valley teamster named Jakob Adams stepped forward to carry messages to Fort Lyman. Johnson lent him his own horse and warned him to ride all-out and low in the saddle. Tiyanoga's wolves indeed were in the forest. Adams was gone before the Reverend Williams finished his sermon, but his departure was only the first in an epidemic. Several hours later, a dozen wagoners, convinced that they were trapped like rats with the army, decided to follow Adams in a wild dash for Lyman and Albany. They suddenly broke out of the enclosure, whipping their horses forward in a mutiny that threw the whole camp into turmoil.

Yet, as Sunday progressed, Dieskau faced his own mutineers. His Abenakis had finally gotten close to Fort Lyman. They did not like what they saw—strong gates, high walls, signs of artillery behind the embrasures. They would not attack Lyman, and soon were joined in their opinion by the other tribes. Legardeur de Saint-Pierre could do nothing with them. Dieskau's artillery, of course, might have knocked the walls down, but he had left his artillery behind. Now, as it was, his regulars would have to storm the works, and if successful, the Canadians would follow the assault. Only after the gates were breached were the tribes expected to rush in and finish the butchery. Dieskau suppressed his fury at the Indians, and it was well he did, for now another development upset his plans. In late afternoon, the Caughnawagas presented him a blonde scalp and captured dispatch. The courier, Jakob Adams, had been shot off his horse on the Lyman road; the dispatch he carried warned Blanchard of Dieskau's approach, promising support by morning. This was not all the Caughnawagas had to tell. A few hours after they ambushed the courier, they harvested many wagons and drivers fleeing down the same road toward the fort. A few escaped; others were captured and talked. Suddenly, Dieskau understood that Johnson had not retreated to Albany with his 2,000, but lay waiting behind him in the direction of the lake. Fort Lyman was abruptly forgotten as the French party turned to the northwest and struck out on a fresh scent.

Johnson meanwhile had called another council of war. Teamsters from the ill-fated mutiny were straggling back into camp, preferring Johnson's ire to the horrors they had witnessed in the forest. They confirmed that a large body of enemy had infiltrated between the fort and the lake. Under these circumstances, the colonials would have to act. Johnson proposed that, at first light, a column of 500 men fight its way back to Lyman under Ephraim Williams's command. Another column of 500, under Colonel Whiting, would march to South Bay and destroy the French boats. Tiyanoga did not agree. He took a stick in hand and broke it; then, placing the pieces side by side he tried and failed to break them. The point was taken. It was decided not to divide their force, but to send all 1,000 troops to Lyman. Even then Tiyanoga hesitated; "If those thousand are to be killed," he explained, "they are too many. If they are to fight, they are too few." Dieskau commanded upward of 1,500 combatants. But what else were they to do? Tiyanoga finally consented to lead his Mohawks as a vanguard marching ahead of Williams. With any luck they might dissuade their brethren the Caughnawagas from firing on the column. If the force could not engage the French on the way, they were to fort up at Lyman and wait for fresh troops to arrive from Albany. Johnson and Colonel Lyman, with the remaining half of the army, proposed to strengthen fortifications on the lake and repel assaults.

The marshal could not believe the explanation—nor has anyone since.[11] As darkness fell, his army, guided by experts, had become lost in the wilderness. At least, this is what the Caughnawagas told him. Shamefaced, they seemed unable to say exactly where Johnson's bivouac was; the confusing paths and bad light had turned them all around. The marshal swore violently in German, yet he was becoming accustomed to his Indian allies and saw through their ruse.

Of course the Caughnawagas had found Johnson's position, and just as the Abenakis had refused to attack Lyman, they now shied away from assaulting overturned wagons, ready muskets, and cannon. Getting lost served a purpose. But who then, Dieskau might have asked, was really shaping this battle? Not he, not Johnson; rather, it was their Indian auxiliaries determining how and when combat would be joined. At first light, Monday morning, September 8, the French were moving parallel to the Lyman road when word arrived of a large force proceeding in their direction. As the sound of tramping feet grew audible, they moved into a fishhook-shaped ambush on a ridge along the road. At this point, about two and a half miles from the lake, the road climbed through a shallow ravine.[12] Here was what the Indians had wanted from the start—the same conditions that bedeviled and ruined Braddock. Dieskau had the sense to leave the ambush to them and massed his infantry a hundred yards farther up the road. From there, they could deliver a volley and charge with bayonets into the survivors.

Tiyanoga at the head of the column was the only man mounted, as befit his status.[13] Behind him, shuffling in single file, came 200 Mohawk warriors. Colonel Whiting had been slow to push off from the encampment, and Ephraim Williams waited for him to catch up. The colonials marched six abreast in close ranks, and by the time Tiyanoga halted, the nearest formation was fifty yards behind the Mohawks.

It began to look as though the French Indians had lost interest in attacking Mohawks as they entered the ravine. Then a shot sounded in the still forest. "Who are you and what are you doing here?" came a voice in Mohawk. "I am Tiyanoga, principal chief of the Mohawks," was the answer, "supreme voice of the Six Nations and superior of all Indian nations in this land."

"I am Iptowee, chief of the praying Mohawks, now become Caughnawagas," the interrogator replied. "We are here to support our father, the King of France, Onontio, to fight with his soldiers against the English. We wish no quarrel with our brothers, or to trespass against any Indian nations. We ask only that you remove yourselves, lest we are forced to move against you."

"It is you who are in our way," said Tiyanoga. "You were once Mohawks. You know we will not back away from anyone. You should remove yourselves from this way of harm."[14]

The stillness was broken only by the sound of tramping feet and jingling harnesses as Ephraim Williams's colonials closed up. Then a shot sounded and Iptowee was flung back into the bushes. A Mohawk warrior had answered the challenge to Tiyanoga. Seconds later, the ridge exploded in sheets of fire, all order vanishing amid the smoke and shouts of injured men as the companies of Williams's regiment collapsed. Twelve hundred .69-caliber muskets discharged into the ravine, sweeping whole ranks of men into heaps. The momentum of the marching columns pushed up into the rear of the Massachusetts Regiment, and the densely packed men, firing at smoke puffs from the ridge above, made easy targets for hidden assailants. The fog of burnt powder filled the hollow; out of this murk there emerged eventually a New England version, a New York version, and a Mohawk version of what happened on that morning at 10:30 AM.

Tiyanoga was swept out of his saddle at the first fusillade; he was at the head of the column, and his words had precipitated the exchange. His horse was certainly hit; New Yorkers eventually found it dead on the trail and knew it to be one of Johnson's. The chief's corpse, however, did not lie by his mount. For several days, Johnson had no knowledge of his friend's whereabouts. When at last the Mohawks came upon the body, it was sprawled at the edge of a wood many hundreds of yards from the site of the ambush. Francis Parkman relied on New England witnesses when he wrote, "Hendrick's horse was shot down, and the chief was killed with a bayonet as he tried to rise."[15] But were any of Williams's troops, the closest to Tiyanoga, in any condition to observe the chief's demise? New York and Mohawk accounts agree that the body was found to have one small arrow in the chest, one in the leg, and had been run through from front to back, not by a bayonet, but by a fire-hardened lance.[16]

Many discrepancies would occur over the years in reminiscences of the Bloody Morning Scout, as this engagement would forever be known in New England. One region's heroes became another's skulkers, and the truth of that morning would remain unascertainable. In the first blast, probably forty Mohawks fell. At least as many of Williams's men were shot down. Tiyanoga's braves later told Johnson that the green colonials behind them cowered and ran; only the tenacious rearguard action of the Mohawks prevented a massacre. But some of the men the braves saw running were running towards the enemy, not away. Ephraim Williams lost John Bratton, Simeon Wells, and a dozen others from his lead company immediately.

His survivors had to get clear of the road or die where they stood. A volley straight down the road from the French regulars decimated his second company, snatching the lives of Caleb Chapin, Ebenezer Wright, and David Hinkley. Williams led the survivors in a charge up the ridge, hoping to drive the Indians and Canadians raking the 4th Massachusetts back from their cover. As he climbed a boulder, a musket ball smashed his forehead, flinging him off the rock in a shower of blood. His attack fell apart, and the remnants were swept down the road toward the lake in a confused retreat.

Those who fared best often hid behind trees, working their way backward as they fired and reloaded. Daniel Pomeroy stuck to the road, trying to rally the fleeing colonials. He was shot in the back from roadside and scalped as soon as he fell. By now, warriors were dashing out of cover to take trophies of the dead. The wounded left behind in the retreat had small chance; Thomas Whit died under a hatchet; his brother Reuben was killed trying to reach him. Moses Porter and Samuel Livermore fell nearby. Seth Pomeroy rallied a company, ordering them to hold their fire until the first rank of grenadiers came into range. Their discharge withered the first line of French infantry.

Whiting's men, on the other hand, had more time to find cover. Retreating with the Mohawks, they covered Williams's survivors with well-aimed volleys. At this point in the retreat, the pursuers suffered a significant loss. Legardeur de Saint-Pierre broke into the open, directing his Caughnawagas, and was instantly struck by five musket balls—Whiting's men were fighting hard. The colonials were gradually coming under control and beginning to use tactics they had been taught at Albany. Elisha Hawley's company was falling back in good order when the French infantry, closing up on the provincials once again, fired a volley that dropped eight of his soldiers at once. They wavered and broke, but Hawley regrouped and was holding his ground when an arrow flew out of the woods and severed his carotid artery. The Indians and Canadians were hacking at the flanks of the retreating provincials, while the French regulars forced them back bodily down the road.

The Bloody Morning Scout was in no way a victory, but considering that the provincials had taken the fire of several battalions in ambush—more than Braddock's troops received—and still cohered, it was testament to their hardiness and common sense. They were not encumbered with false notions of military discipline. They ran, and because they ran, occasionally turning to fire, saved themselves and their army. What grew out of the wreckage of the Bloody Morning Scout was a myth that provincial troops were crack shots, naturally adept at Indian fighting. This belief lingered through the Seven Years War and recrudesced with the Battle of Concord Bridge, where embattled militia stood and "fired the shot heard round the world." To be sure, as George Washington attests, the subsequent history of militia in battle was less than triumphant. Yet here and there a natural Hawkeye might emerge, a pioneer with the skills of Natty Bumppo. Whiting's men had a strong enclosure to flee to, along with the inestimable aid of over a hundred angry Mohawks. With as many Indian allies, Braddock too might have been saved.

From the swelling volume of gunfire, Johnson heard the retreat draw near. Then, streaming back into the defensive works, poured dozens of provincials from the rear of the column. They knew only that something terrible had befallen the head.[17] Williams's exhausted men tumbled over the barricades next with their wild stories, and Whiting's regiment came into sight at the edge of the clearing, still firing, still running. Squads of men detached from the battle and fled back to the enclosure, while other groups were overtaken and fell to the enemy emerging from the cover of the woods. Although the range was still too great, Johnson urged the defenders to fire. Captain Eyre's cannon opened, spraying shot into the trees. The Monday morning scout was returning winded, wounded, and frightened, but nearly two-thirds had escaped the trap and were beginning to swell the ranks of Johnson's reserve. Yet even then, had Dieskau launched a coordinated attack on the enclosure, the French and Indians would certainly have overwhelmed the defenses.

Dieskau, however, was in trouble. Without Legardeur de Saint-Pierre, he had lost control over his Indians. They and the Canadians were scattered across the battlefield, gathering scalps and prisoners. At the site of the ambush, French officers urged their allies to leave the prisoners and move forward towards the fight. The warriors wasted time tying the captives together and roping them to trees for safekeeping. Their own losses had been slight, and as far as many of them were concerned, the battle was won and over. A nasty dispute erupted between the Abenakis and Caughnawagas over Mohawk prisoners. The Abenakis had collected wood to burn the Mohawks on the spot. The Caughnawagas tried to save their cousins. Dieskau screamed, "Burn them later," as he goaded the disputants to the edge of Johnson's clearing. "The liquor's drawn, now drink it," he ordered, but they refused.[18] Canadians and Indians took cover behind the stumps of trees and kept up a steady fire at a distance. Without his artillery, the marshal had no recourse but to assault the works with grenadiers. The momentum of the morning's victory was being lost as survivors reached Johnson's barricades and rejoined the struggle.

The grenadiers of La Reine and Languedoc formed in three long lines fronting the center of the Lake George position. Bayonets fixed, the first rank knelt and fired, stepped back, and made room for the second and then the third to repeat the action. The precision of these soldiers did more to unnerve the defenders than their volleys of lead, which fell like hail on the logs of the barricade. More terrifying still, hundreds of Canadians and Indians rushed into the clearing shouting insults, gesticulating wildly, and waving scalps taken in the morning. The provincials quailed at the spectacle, and it was all that Johnson and his officers could do to keep them from bolting their posts. He had a strong position—plenty of men, guns, and ammunition. He also had officers who, once the first shock passed, kept the green provincials at their work. Captain Eyre's guns threw most of their shot into the trees, but the thunder and smoke intimidated the Indians on both sides. Johnson's Mohawks were done; they rested in the enclosure, watching the white soldiers fight it out.

Johnson was wounded before Dieskau, a musket ball striking him high on the hip, dangerously close to the spine. He fell, but with the help of his aide, Peter Wraxall, managed to stand and continue directing fire for a time before being led to his tent. The French line by now was disintegrating as grenadiers sought cover behind stumps and fought on alone as musketeers. Nevertheless, Dieskau rallied them and pointed the assault toward the right flank of the enclosure where Moses Titcomb with survivors of Williams's and Ruggles's regiments were holding out. Colonel Titcomb was in front of the barricade, urging his troops to attack the disorganized French, when a shot killed him. Here fell one of the colonies' most respected and valorous soldiers.

For more than an hour, the attack sputtered and flared as the provincials gave fire for fire. Seth Pomeroy wrote to his wife, "The hailstones from heaven were never much thicker than their bullets came, but blessed be God! that did not in the least daunt or disturb us." The log barricade absorbed most of the fire in that quarter. This did not keep Surgeon Williams and Doctor Pynchon from being terrified in their aid tent behind the lines. "It was the most awful day my eyes ever beheld," Williams wrote, "there seemed to be nothing but thunder and lightning and perpetual pillars of smoke. The bullets flew about our ears all the time dressing the wounded; so we thought best to leave our tent and retire a few rods behind the shelter of a log house."[19]

With Johnson in his tent, Lyman took charge and increased the volume of fire, driving the colonials to load and shoot faster. Through the billowing smoke, they could see Indians and Canadians packing up and leaving. The clearing was strewn with bodies. Sensing his battle collapsing, Dieskau rushed across the clearing with his adjutant, Captain Montreuil, to stiffen the attack. He made the mistake of exposing himself within range of the enemy's muskets; instantly, he was hit in the leg. As Montreuil tended the wound with brandy, another ball struck the marshal's leg and a third pierced his thigh, puncturing his bladder as well. Montreuil was hit next in the shoulder, and two Canadians rushing up to help also fell. Dieskau sent Montreuil on to rally the troops and, crawling behind some fallen logs, propped himself against a tree.

The climax came as Johnson's powder-blackened survivors began to sense their enemy retreating. Lyman and Pomeroy could not restrain them; they vaulted the logs and charged into the scattering grenadiers with tomahawks and rifle butts. Scalps were taken now by the rougher types of Johnson's army, as Yorkers and New Englanders scoured the field for prisoners and dead. Dieskau awoke from unconsciousness to see a private of Ruggles's regiment aiming at him. He twisted his torn body as best he could and motioned for the soldier not to fire. But fire he did, the ball passing through both Dieskau's hips. The soldier dove at him then and, shouting in French, ordered him to surrender.

"Why did you fire at me?" the Marshal remembers asking him. "You see a man lying on the ground in his blood, and you fire, eh?"

"How did I know but you had a pistol?" the provincial replied. "Better to kill the devil than let the devil kill me."

"And you are a Frenchman, then?"

"Yes. It is more than ten years since I left Canada."

"Whereupon," Dieskau's account continues, "divers others fell on me and stripped me. I told them to carry me to their general, which they did."[20]

There is about this battle the spirit of border war, of neighbors flailing each other violently out of conflicting loyalties. Iroquois of the Mohawk River fight Catholic Mohawks from the St. Lawrence River; Catholic Abenakis from down east fight Protestant New Hampshire men who have stolen their fields; white Canadians fight on both sides, depending on where they presently find themselves. Formal war had not been declared in Europe when the Battle of Lake George erupted. The European overlay therefore was exceedingly thin. Only Captain Eyre represented the British Army, and Dieskau soon discovered that his life depended not on rules of civilized warfare between nations, but on the control a Mohawk River fur baron exercised over frustrated native people. The Indians for their part could not care less about the commission awarded Warraghiyagey by a then-defunct British commander in chief or a lawyer from Boston. They responded to Johnson's instructions out of an allegiance defined locally along Tenonanatche.

Taken to the general's tent, Dieskau found the wounded Johnson all courtesy as he ordered his own surgeons to dress the marshal's horrible wounds. Johnson doubted that his opponent would survive, yet out of that generous spirit for which he was always commended, he set about comforting the baron and directing his medical treatment. Dieskau floated above the pain for a moment to hear a great commotion in the tent. The Mohawks were glowering at him. When he asked what the argument with the Indians was about, Johnson told him:

> They wished to oblige me to deliver you into their hands, in order to burn you in revenge for the death of their comrades. ... They were going to eat you to avenge the Indians killed here today and to absorb your strength. ... They threatened to abandon me if I did not give you up. Feel no uneasiness. You are safe with me.[21]

Johnson was himself in great pain; the ball stuck in his pelvis could not be dislodged by the surgeons, and the eventual infection would nearly rob him of his eyesight over the next several weeks. Dieskau had another close escape from the Mohawks the following day when they broke into his tent and attempted to carry him away. At last, Johnson resolved to send the baron and several of his wounded officers under heavy guard to a house in Albany that they might recuperate safely before being transported to England.[22] But the Mohawks would not be entirely denied. Johnson allowed them to take away many other prisoners as recompense for their services, while denying that he had ever done so.[23]

The Battle of Lake George did not end in late afternoon with the rout of Dieskau's grenadiers. French losses at this point were only half what the provincials had suffered, but the score soon changed. Indians and Canadians who had survived the attack on the encampment made their way back to the site of the morning's ambush to eat, regroup, and collect their prisoners. The provincials had declined to pursue them vigorously into the afternoon woods. The French were still recovering from their shock and disorder when a new battle thrust itself upon them.

Colonel Blanchard had dispatched Captains McGinnis and Folsom with a company of New York troops to probe the outcome of the battle raging at the lake. The New Yorkers, supported by New Hampshire frontiersmen, moved north over the portage road from Fort Lyman in mid-afternoon. At about five o'clock they came to the morning's ambush site and found the enemy preparing to leave for the boats at South Bay. Their attack was a complete surprise. The Yorkers caught the Caughnawagas and Abenakis going about their work and, disregarding the plight of the bound prisoners, fired massively into them. McGinnis was killed in the ensuing charge and Folsom wounded, but the French force recoiled back and fell apart into pockets of hand-to-hand combat. Most of the French Indians and Canadians who died in the Battle of Lake George fell here—victims of a counter-ambush by a far smaller force of frontiersmen. Unfortunately, besides McGinnis and a few New Yorkers, most of the bound prisoners also perished in the forest's fading light. This was the third and last phase of the battle, and what remained was to discover what it had meant, if anything, and what it had cost.

Over the following days the colonials tidied up the battlefield after the fashion of their region. Outside the camp, New Englanders found and buried the white dead, proudly noting that, unlike the French, who had left Braddock's fallen to the wolves, they interred friend and foe alike with due Christian observance. Ephraim Williams's mangled corpse was sought out and buried with honors beside the rock on which he received his mortal wound. By contrast, they dumped the Indians together in a hole. At the place of McGinnis's victory, New Yorkers labored in the heat of a hot day and grew impatient with the noisome bodies. They separated the French and Indians; then, they simply dumped them all in a nearby pond. Bloody Pond—what else would it be named to this day?—became the resting place for many victims of the battle.[24] One legend holds that Chief Hendrick's body, found nearby, was also heaved into the waters—a most unlikely deed given Johnson's anxiety over the whereabouts of his friend.

But, after springing the ambush of the Bloody Morning Scout, what had really happened to Tiyanoga? James Thomas Flexner discounts Francis Parkman's explanation and offers an answer based on contemporary accounts. The old chief was knocked off his horse by the first burst of fire that morning and thrown to the side of the trail. He was far too crafty to remain there, lightly wounded, waiting to be dispatched. So Tiyanoga crept off into the forest, thinking to circumvent the battle and pop out in the clearing near the encampment. And so he might have, as a young brave. But breathless, losing blood, disoriented in the woods, he stumbled into daylight at an Indian camp. Families of Caughnawaga warriors, brought along on Dieskau's orders, were encamped over the ridge from where the ambush was sprung. The Caughnawaga children played at war with little bows, sharpened stakes, and tiny hatchets. According to one interpretation, they descended now on the struggling chief and struck him several times with their small arrows. Before the squaws could intervene, they had stabbed him fatally with a fire-hardened lance.[25]

Another contemporary interpretation has it that Hendrick was slain by the squaws, not the children, as he blundered into their space. When the body was found, several days after the battle, a patch of Tiyanoga's scalp lock was seen to have been hacked off by small hands. So died the great Mohawk sachem. In his long life he had done as much to shape the Crown Colony of New York as any governor or soldier, and the irony of his end at the hands of noncombatants must have sent unsettling reverberations through the Iroquois world.

Tiyanoga had welcomed the Palatine Germans into his valleys, made room for Johnson and his Irish, and by his influence on the Iroquois League had opened the borders of a vast, ill-defined region to a multitude of people. His passing marked the end of official blindness along the frontier, a time when small government encouraged fluid opportunities for native and immigrant alike. The New York territory had now crashed into Europe's consciousness and, as General Johnson in camp at Lake George reeled from his private hurts and losses, armies mobilized for a war to secure this place of converging lakes and rivers.

Word of Johnson's victory spread down the Hudson and through the colonies with rapidity; here was news everyone wanted to hear—how an American provincial with an army of farmers had humbled the proud forces of France in wilderness battle. Lost amidst the enthusiasm was the truth of the situation. Upward of 330 colonials and auxiliaries were casualties. Over 10 percent of the Mohawk nation's warrior strength had been lost, along with many tribal leaders. The tragedy that befell Northampton, Massachusetts, on that sad day found its counterpart at Canajoharie, New York. Mid-eighteenth-century colonial society was smaller and more fragile than moderns appreciate. Battles on the order of Lake George guaranteed empty farmhouses, failed harvests, widows and orphans thrown onto the charity of their communities. Seth Pomeroy wrote to his brother's wife, Rachel, who had just been delivered of a child:

Dear Sister, this brings heavy tidings; but let not your heart sink at the news, though it be your loss of a dear husband. Monday the eighth instant was a memorable day; and truly you may say, had not the Lord been on our side, we must all have been swallowed up. My brother, being one that went out in the first engagement, received a fatal shot through the middle of the head.[26]

New England's losses in seasoned leadership would not be quickly made good, and recriminations over the management of the "Old French War" would linger until the Revolution.

The French, too, suffered, especially the Caughnawagas whose casualties approximated the Mohawks'. Dieskau lost about 250 combatants, all of his regular officers, half of his grenadiers, and an indeterminate number of Canadians. He lost the battle as well and was taken prisoner. But Johnson had failed to capture Crown Point, had not advanced to the northern end of Lake George, and was nowhere near seizing control of the water corridor between Montreal and Albany. In fact, he was stuck in the wilderness a few dozen miles north of his point of departure. What he had left undone—the capture of Ticonderoga, Crown Point, Fort St. Frédéric—would mean three more years of hard slogging in the New York theater with losses of soldiers in the thousands.

Sick and wounded, riled by the political maneuvers of Shirley and the ceaseless carping of his officers, he wanted to be nowhere else than at home with Caty Weisenberg. Shirley would not hear of his resignation until he had completed his mission. But even as Johnson struggled in misery to raise reinforcements and complete Fort William Henry at the base of the Lake, his fortunes were rising in London. After a season of dismal defeats and discouraging ineptitudes, the Crown had found a North American hero capable of defeating the French. In November, as the first snow fell on the battlefield at Lake George blanketing the half-constructed Fort William Henry, William Johnson became Sir William Johnson, baronet—a hereditary rank only twice awarded to Americans.

In New England, the honor always rankled. "They shot him in the ass," went the refrain, "and he hid in his tent." Connecticut thought Lyman had won the victory, and out of spite, Sir William changed the name of Fort Lyman to Fort Edward.

The Battle of Lake George ended as it had begun, with acrimony and accusation. Colonials of New York and New England proved once again that they could agree on little—not even victory. The lands west of the Hudson might be rich and fertile, but in the eyes of New Englanders they were also wild with strange, dangerous, uncongenial people. Twenty years later, the institutional and cultural otherness of New York would prove a challenge to the patriots, and they would remember with vivid recollection how once before they had gone to Albany and how the adventure had opened their eyes to iniquity.

Baron de Dieskau also had vivid recollections of the New York wilderness, and in Paris several years later shared them with the encyclopedist Denis Diderot. By then his profession had succumbed to his wounds; he never returned to the field again. Like many fine officers of New France, he doubtless deserved better than a blind hazard in the woods. Yet, with other leaders of that year, 1755, he too had looked in Braddock's box. What he found was a plan to intimidate the inhabitants of North America with the might of Europe. The French had only to change the flag to turn this plan to their advantage, never suspecting how foolish it might be from the start. The truth dawned on Dieskau as he watched his glory vanish in the forest mists. Twelve years after being carried into the surgeon's tent, he died of complications arising from his wounds, but not before remembering in his memoirs how Johnson's courage and courtesy saved him.[27] It would be some time, however, before the Mohawks forgave their Warraghiyagey this generosity.

The Battle of Lake George brought Johnson to international notice as a rising force in Britain's North American order. Yet he proved no shooting star consumed in a moment of brilliance. He became a lasting presence in Indian affairs and colonial management. Suffering constant pain from his hip wound, he soldiered on to capture Fort Niagara from the French in 1759 and to negotiate the Treaty of Fort Stanwix among the Six Nations in 1768. Inevitably as his success grew, so did his influence on New York's politics. It was Johnson's special genius to wrap his conservative outlook in practical measures pleasing to the greatest number of people.

Events at Lake George thrust forward a hero desperately needed by the British colonies in their hour of crisis, and during the years immediately following, only Johnson—the lucky amateur—succeeded in distinguishing himself among the Crown's military leaders. As North America's French and Indian War swelled from a localized struggle to a seven-year-long world war, Sir William's public esteem rose higher than that of any other public official.[28] Forgotten were his humble origins. He had been elevated to a baronetcy and within a few years would control one of the largest landed estates in the Colonies. Certainly his influence with the powerful Iroquois had been the key to his success. But Johnson was also a man well placed geographically to capitalize on talent and good fortune.

Sir William built three stately homes on Tenonanatche—Fort Johnson, Johnson Hall, and Guy Park—and all three may be visited today. The houses survive along with several churches, workmen's houses, and town centers planned and erected under Johnson's direction.[29] In those locations where a later industrialization has spared his beloved river, the pastoral splendor that drew him and others shines out from the rolling hills and abundant plains. But the best monument to Johnson's life stares out from the map of New York itself—the shape that he, more than anyone else, imparted to the wilderness province north of the great city.

No public man until DeWitt Clinton better grasped the unique topography, geology, and hydrology of New York. In his long and active career, Johnson built forts and settlements above Albany, helped take the first steps toward opening the Champlain corridor to the St. Lawrence, and pressed for navigational improvements on the Hudson. He governed Oswego on Lake Ontario, and led an expedition to Niagara to seize the shores of Lake Erie. Early in his career he explored the Susquehanna and Delaware Rivers that became in time New York's boundaries with Pennsylvania and New Jersey. What Johnson did not experience firsthand, backwoodsmen in his employ like George Croghan and Andrew Montour experienced on his behalf. Iroquois allies opened his eyes to hidden places beyond the traveled paths. At the height of his affluence, Johnson owned hundreds of square miles of future New York State—including land that the Erie Canal would someday cross, land the New York Central would claim for roadbeds and railroad stations, and land that the New York State Thruway bisects today.

Roosevelt, Rockefeller, DeWitt Clinton, and Robert Moses—New York has a long acquaintance with headstrong builders. But Johnson was the first of the great dynasts whose projects defined not only the physical boundaries of the state, but the social values and civic assumptions of its citizenry. As his fame grew, his influence reached beyond the wilderness of his beginnings until, by the close of his life, he was a benefactor shared by Kings College (Columbia), Queen's College (Rutgers), and the College of New Jersey (Princeton). Johnson believed adamantly in the liberating power of education. He strongly backed Indian schools like Eleazar Wheelock's in Connecticut and the Moravians' in Pennsylvania. This was the side of Johnson that recommends him to modern tastes—his inclusive vision, his tolerance and rejection of narrow sectarianism. These were the highest ideals of British imperialism, and Johnson endorsed and embraced them on behalf of all the people of his province.

That is not to deny that he owned slaves and bought indentured servants, and his sexual mores were those of an eighteenth-century libertine; rather than marry, he kept the two most important women in his life as concubines. Rumors in London about hundreds of illegitimate children fathered by Johnson on Iroquois maidens were doubtless exaggerations, but Johnson did take responsibility for several Indian children. He built his economic base by trading alcohol to Indians for fur, and was not above stomping off into the woods to live or fight with the native peoples. His justice could be swift and hard. Yet, by the sum of all accounts, he was a model eighteenth-century *magnifico*. Which is to say that, while he remained an Irish lord mindful of his privileges, he also aspired to a benevolent paternalism in dealing with neighbors rich or poor. Johnson was never fully at ease in cities, but loved the land and the people who tilled it. They came by the thousands to his funeral in 1774.

As the late century swept in new men and new ideas, was Sir William capable of changing? On the brink of America's creation, he died suddenly of a seizure, and the question remains forever unanswered. At the time of Braddock's catastrophe, Johnson and Washington probably shared comparable outlooks; by 1774, these wealthy men were clearly set on different paths. Sir William's dynasty could find no way to swerve from loyalty to the Crown, its source of power and property. In the aftermath of patriot victory, the Johnsons paid for their Tory sympathies with land, homes, wealth, and citizenship. Sir William's line of influence in New York thus ended abruptly.

In 1911, a fire at Albany destroyed much of the state's archives, and Sir William's voluminous papers were severely damaged. Of the ten volumes surviving, only a small portion reflects his personal activities. Yet, within these documents is hardly a harsh or condemnatory word—for all that Johnson's frustrations are frequently on display. His writings reflect a rational man passionately committed to fulfilling his role in a well-understood social contract.

What he took from the New World he gave back in the spirit of a father spending on his children. Johnson, unlike Peter Warren, did not aim solely to amass riches; he lived where he worked, and the scheme behind what he built was to fashion a practical utopia enshrining material progress as the highest achievement. Warren returned to Ireland and caught his death of cold while visiting the family manor.[30] Had Uncle Peter prevailed, he would doubtless have raised another Anglo-Irish manor on the Mohawk. His nephew was more the true immigrant; he never returned, never looked back. More than two centuries later, the comfortable houses he raised for his workers in Johnstown still stand in tribute to his enlightened view of labor transactions. Johnson's politics did not long survive him, but his example of the master builder, transforming borderlands from wilderness to settlement, set the mark for public figures yet to come.

Ten years after Braddock's defeat and Johnson's victory at Lake George, the western reaches of Tenonanatche were still wild. The French threat was gone, but the dark, impenetrable forests remained as intimidating as ever. North and west from Albany, where armies had trudged to Fort Edward, Fort William Henry, Ticonderoga, Oswego, Niagara, or Montreal, the leafy canopy quickly closed over the clearings and military trails. As often as not, in the first years of the war, British forces had returned vanquished from this wilderness, repelled by the Marquis de Montcalm, or panicked in the deep woods by their own shadows.[31]

On the way from Ticonderoga to Lake George, the shoes of fleeing British soldiers were found in the mud of the roadbed by the French. The drenching rains that followed Abercromby's poorly conceived attack on the fort had sucked the shoes off his routed troops as they escaped through the mire.[32] On that occasion, nothing pursued the provincials but their memories of the 42nd Regiment, the Black Watch, dying on the *abatis* of Montcalm's line. Hostile Native Americans made no appearance in that battle. Yet the charred timbers of Fort William Henry and the moldering bones scattered along forest paths spoke of their ambushes. Abercromby's troops ran because they had been roughly handled, but they left their shoes behind in the ooze because a haunted forest and hostile nature combined to speed them onward.

Frontier shock could extend beyond ordinary soldiers to the respected general officers that led them. Braddock and Abercromby grossly underestimated the hazards of wilderness warfare, but Major General Daniel Webb, commanding at Fort Edward in 1757 as Montcalm invested and besieged Fort William Henry, was stricken by fright at the prospect of advancing fourteen miles with 1,600 men through the forested defiles to Lake George. The very depth and density of the forest seemed to dissuade him from pressing on to save Colonel Monro at the embattled fort.[33] Montcalm had not repeated Dieskau's mistake of leaving his artillery behind. For three nights, Webb listened to those guns thundering as they demolished the wooden ramparts of William Henry. Paralyzed, he did nothing. William Johnson found him, according to Louis Antoine de Bougainville, cowering in his headquarters at Fort Edward. De Bougainville was then with Montcalm, but had the story later from Mohawks of Sault St. Louis who heard it from their New York brethren:

> While we were besieging Fort William Henry, Johnson, Dieskau's conqueror, arrived at Fort Edward at the head of 800 provincials, Mohawks, and Moraigans [Mohegans] a sort of bastard tribe, all in war paint like his troop, tomahawk at his side, halberd in hand. He proposed to General Webb to march at once on the French lines. Webb said he would not, that he did not wish to expose himself to a complete defeat in woods already red with English blood. Johnson replied that these same shores ... would be as fatal to Montcalm as they had been to Dieskau, that French bones would cover this battlefield where, he swore by his halberd and tomahawk, he would conquer or die. General Webb was not moved. Johnson then called to witness the Belgian lion, tore off one of his leggings and hurled it at Webb's feet. "You won't do it?" he said. "No." Tore off the other legging. "You won't?" Hurled a garter. "You won't?" Hurled shirt, tomahawk and halberd down, and galloped off with his troop who had imitated his actions entirely. Where is Homer to paint such scenes more Greek than Greek?[34]

In the fall of 1755, Johnson had ordered Fort William Henry built as he lay half-blind and tossing with fever from an infected wound. Major Eyre sited the fortifications a few hundred yards to the west of the Lake George battleground, and while Johnson recovered at home on the Mohawk, William Henry was progressively improved to withstand French attacks from Ticonderoga just beyond the other end of the lake.[35] It did so in late March 1757, when French forces under Rigaud attacked across the ice and were repelled. Rigaud struck without artillery. The following August, the French moved up the lake by bateaux, 8,000 strong, trailed by siege cannon, mortars, and howitzers for reducing the timbered fortifications. Montcalm also brought 1,800 Indians as scouts and skirmishers, many from the far Northwest. These young warriors, come east for battle, clamored for "broth"—the blood of the English—and they were to have it. Montcalm could no more control his native allies at William Henry than he could at the massacre of Oswego in 1756.[36]

As he raged at Webb's equivocations, Johnson must have realized the consequences of the fort's capitulation. British soldiers and colonials were packed tightly into the entrenched camp east of the fort, fighting desperately to protect their women and children. It was all well and good for one professional military man to trust another under a flag of honorable surrender, but the New York frontier was not Europe. Plunder-hungry warriors were not about to let the garrison depart in peace. At the surrender, they stormed the fort's infirmary and murdered fifty wounded and sick. Pursuing Colonel Monro's withdrawing column, they killed or captured scores of men, women, and children. Sated with rum, they disinterred the dead from the fort cemetery and stripped them of their scalps.[37] No one can tell how many died the morning of August 11, but estimates range as high as 700 killed, wounded, or missing.[38]

Down the years, reflections on the Fort William Henry massacre have terrified imaginations with a nightmare insistence. Seventy years after the fact, Cooper used the occurrence—slaughter in the shadows of the pitiless forest—as a central episode for *The Last of the Mohicans*, and while William Henry was neither the first nor last massacre in America's move to the West, the tale has found continued life in film and fiction as the quintessential frontier disaster. Webb will forever appear as the supercilious British officer incapable of defending the provincials in his charge; Montcalm remains the impeccable European aristocrat with a sinister indifference to claims of humanity. These impressions, of course, are only popular colonial stereotypes, but they had their origin in the palpable horrors of the wilderness wars.[39] During the years immediately following, legends and fables multiplied, until the Hudson and Mohawk corridors lay under a heavy cloud of apprehension.

Yet, gradually the pressures of immigration, the demand for land, outweighed psychological damages, and new settlers began to replace the old along the New York frontier. River traffic north, west, and south of Albany increased dramatically after 1763, while land speculation ran riot through the province's back country as the great landlords, Johnson at their head, realized substantial profits from lands granted or awarded by the Crown. Although the recent conflicts had been costly in colonial lives, the colonies most affected appeared to exercise a collective amnesia. They saw only the opportunities of limitless western expansion over the crest of the Appalachians, forgetting the destructive consequences of the long wilderness struggle on Native America and on the finances of the mother country.

The Johnson family, with retainers and Iroquois allies, were just one force working to shape eighteenth-century New York. German refugees from the Rhineland had arrived on Tenonanatche more than a decade before Johnson. As the century advanced, they were also to become a potent political force in public affairs. Like Johnson, they too had Indian friends, but they had none of the Johnson family's indebtedness to the Crown. In the years following, large-scale migration from New England was added to this already combustible mixture. Scarcity and exhaustion of land sent farming families flocking from New England to the New York frontier. To the Anglo-Catholicism of the Johnsons, the Lutheranism of the Palatines, the Reformed Calvinism of the Dutch, the Animism of the Native Americans, now would be added Baptist and Congregationalist revivalism with a cast of mind more politically independent. In the following chapters, we examine what this movement of peoples meant ultimately in the struggle to hold and possess the way west.

❧ 4 ❧

A Rumored Gift

For a people exiled to travel the world without friends, persecuted, and driven onto strange shores, comparison with the Jews of Exodus came naturally, especially when those exiles were Bible-imbued Protestants of a Reformed or Lutheran persuasion. In their minds they were the new chosen, chastened by adversity, seeking redemption on the road to the promised land. To everyone else they were "Palatines," a generic term in the eighteenth century for German-speaking refugees. "Sick as a Palatine," "poor as a Palatine," "ragged as a Palatine," "ignorant as a Palatine" were epithets commonly applied to any unfortunate group thrown onto the charity of the British Crown.[1]

The Rhineland Palatinate, an area situated roughly within the triangle of Worms, Speyer, and Heidelberg, Germany, had endured thirty years of war, famine, and plague by the end of the first decade of the eighteenth century. The great troubles began in the 1680s, as the armies of Louis XIV swept across the banks of the Rhine and destroyed homes and villages of German-speaking Protestants. The incessant fighting aimed to cleanse the newly secured borders of France of a disruptive and heretical influence. In consequence, tens of thousands perished, while more were left homeless or starving. By the winter of 1709, the survivors of the devastated Palatinate were desperate for hope, and it came in the form of a rumor spreading through the forests and defiles of the countryside into every makeshift hovel where hungry people huddled against the cold. Queen Anne of England would welcome the Palatines to her realm; she would feed and clothe them in London, and she would resettle them on her vast lands in Ireland or the New World.[2] There was a measure of logic to this good news. England's North American holdings were "unpopulated," and these displaced people, some of them French Huguenots, had been among the finest farmers, merchants, and tradesmen in Europe. They had only to follow the Rhine to Holland, where ships waited to carry them to freedom. Thus were the armies of Catholic Louis their Pharaoh's legion, Queen Anne their Moses, and the English Channel their Red Sea. Some who survived the journey would live to resist the French again—on New York's Mohawk River.

Not that New York City welcomed them when they turned up sick and destitute at the port. In fact, the city, alerted by London, did not let them land at all, but shunted them into a camp on Nutten (Governor's) Island. Nine ships filled with Palatines straggled into New York Harbor in the early summer of 1710. They carried over 3,000 men, women, and children—the largest immigrant group to arrive at one time in the city during the colonial era—and many of these were ill with "Palatine fever," or typhus. During the long winter voyage a third of the passengers on the vessels had died, including nearly all the infants and most of the aged.[3] On board the *Lyon*, which came in on June 13, were 400 survivors of a party of 600. Their voyage had lasted six months in the slow, foul-bottomed ship out of Plymouth, and the refugees had been cooped up below decks without adequate food or medical attention. They subsisted on sixpence worth of bread a day per head, bad water, and scant air. Hatches were battened down in storms, and the stench below was unspeakable. The seasickness was dreadful, many remembered, but it was the fever that killed. "I administered aid and Medicines to above 330 persons," Thomas Benton, the *Lyon*'s only physician lamented, "all which were sick at One time in the said passage, and none but myself to assist them."[4]

Of the ten ships that left England in Governor Hunter's convoy, one, the *Herbert*, went aground on eastern Long Island; others buried nearly 1,000 voyagers at sea before reaching New York. More Palatines died at the camp on Nutten Island from illnesses contracted on the ships until, by the time the fever had abated, the island was thronged with widows, widowers, and orphans waiting to learn their fate in the New World. Young children who survived their parents were given away in the city. Older boys and girls were indentured to the city's citizens for terms sometimes as long as fifteen years, the money received going to defray Robert Hunter's costs for maintaining the Palatines on the island. Hunter, the newly named governor of the New York Province, was not a Palatine himself, but a Scottish colonel with impressive credentials and powerful in-laws.[5] His plan for resettling the Palatines inspired the Crown's answer to the London refugee problem—every adult in Hunter's convoy was contracted as an indentured servant to the Crown, with the understanding that only after having paid for their passage and maintenance in tar production for the Royal Navy would they be granted £5 and forty acres of farmland per family. So had Queen Anne's compassionate support of coreligionists been adjusted finally by her Ministry of Trade.

Britain's growing navy needed hemp for cordage, tar for waterproofing, straight timbers for masts and spars. These goods were imported at great cost from Norway, Sweden, and Russia until international tensions disrupted the flow. Swedish tar, processed from pine lumber, was especially vital, and the dream of substituting a New York commodity for this import fired the imagination of the British Board of Trade. New York Province had ample pine timber along the Hudson and Mohawk Rivers— so the board believed—and ready transportation down the rivers to New York Harbor. All that was lacking was an army of laborers available to harvest and render the trees. Enter Robert Hunter with a well-timed proposition. On December 5, 1709, the board made the following recommendation "To the Queen's Most Gracious Majesty." On January 7, 1710, it was approved.

> May It Please Your Majesty: In obedience to your Majesty's commands, signified to us by the Right Honorable the Earl of Sunderland, we have considered the proposals made to us by Colonel Hunter, for settling 3,000 Palatines at New York and Employing them in the Production of Naval Stores, and thereupon humbly Represent to your Majesty—
>
> That the Province of New York being the most advanced Frontier of Your Majesty's Plantations on the Continent of America, the Defence and Preservation of that place is of the utmost importance to the security of all the Rest; and if the said Palatines were seated, they would be an additional strength and security to that Province, not only with regard to the French of Canada, But against any Insurrection of the scattered Nations of Indians upon that Continent, and, therefore, we humbly propose that they be sent thither.
>
> By the best Information we can gett, the most proper Places for the seating them in that Province, so as they may be of benefit to this Kingdom by the Production of Naval Stores, are on the Mohaques River and on the Hudsons River, where are very great numbers of Pines fit for Production of Turpentine and Tar, out of which Rosin and Pitch are made.[6]

Note that the first consideration offered by the board is for the defense and preservation of the province against incursions from the French of Canada and scattered nations of Indians. Turpentine and tar offered practical incentives for the transplantation, but the ulterior motive was to insert a large captive body of settlers between the vulnerable heart of the province and its frontier borders. The Palatines, in other words, were to form a buffer, and possibly, like the French settlers of Canada, marry with and mollify the savages. What made these goals wishful was the simple fact that the Palatines, unlike the French pioneers, brought with them their own wives and children. They were German-speaking peasant farmers, not trappers or *coureurs de bois*, and they had no experience whatever in rendering turpentine from pine chips. Furthermore, the forests of the Hudson and Mohawk were largely hardwood, and in the vicinity of the proposed sites for Palatine settlement, evergreen stands were sparse. The board did do its homework, relying on Hunter's intelligence of the colonial situation, but lacking any experience of the ground, and separated by the Atlantic from those with better knowledge, the recommendation accepted by the Crown was fraught with impracticalities. Yet, by the time wiser heads offered their objections, several thousand refugees had been crammed into transports bound for New York.

What happened on Nutten Island was little different from what happened to indigent immigrants at every port in the colonies. Gotlieb Mittelberger arrived at

Philadelphia in 1750 on a ship as storm-beaten and miserable as the *Lyon*. How the survivors fared, he describes:

> When the ships have landed at Philadelphia after their long voyage, no one is permitted to leave them except those who pay for their passage or can give good security; the others, who cannot pay, must remain on board the ships till they are purchased, and are released from the ships by their purchasers. The sick always fare the worst, for the healthy are naturally preferred and purchased first; and so the sick and wretched must often remain on board in front of the city for 2 or 3 weeks, and frequently die, whereas many a one, if he could pay his debt and were permitted to leave the ship immediately, might recover and remain alive.
>
> The sale of human beings in the market on board the ship is carried on thus: Every day Englishmen, Dutchmen and High-German people come from the city of Philadelphia and other places, and go on board the newly arrived ship that has brought and offers for sale passengers from Europe, and select among the healthy persons such as they deem suitable for their business, and bargain with them how long they will serve for their passage money, which most of them are still in debt for. When they have come to an agreement, it happens that adult persons bind themselves in writing to serve 3, 4, 5 or 6 years for the amount due by them, according to their age and strength. But very young people, from 10 to 15 years, must serve till they are 21 years old.
>
> Many parents must sell and trade away their children like so many head of cattle; for if their children take the debt upon themselves, the parents can leave the ship free and unrestrained; but as the parents often do not know where and to what people their children are going, it often happens that such parents and children, after leaving the ship, do not see each other again for many years, perhaps no more in all their lives. It often happens that whole families, husband, wife, and children, are separated by being sold to different purchasers, especially when they have not paid any part of their passage money.
>
> When a husband or wife has died at sea, when the ship has made more than half of her trip, the survivor must pay or serve not only for himself or herself, but also for the deceased.[7]

John Peter Zenger, who would strike the first and most resounding blow for freedom of the press in the colonies, arrived at New York aboard the *Lyon*. He lost his father in the passage. His mother sold him at age thirteen to the city's only printer, William Bradford, to support her remaining children, and Zenger only completed his indenture eight years later at the age of twenty-one. Seventeen years after that, a printer in his own right and with no love for William Bradford, he launched the *New*

York Weekly Journal to compete with Bradford's *New York Gazette*. When Bradford took the side of venal Governor Cosby, the *New York Weekly Journal* ridiculed the governor and satirized his party. Colonial grievances were frankly and fearlessly discussed in the *Journal* and, stung by its caustic comments, Chief Justice James DeLancey and Justice Philipse ordered Zenger jailed for sedition. As he awaited justice, Zenger's wife continued to publish the paper in the face of threats.

Slowly, New York City warmed to Zenger's side, recognizing Cosby's corrosive corruption. In the most famous trial of eighteenth-century America, Zenger was defended by Andrew Hamilton of Philadelphia and acquitted of all charges in a verdict that won widespread acclamation.[8] Hamilton had argued that to publish the truth, as the truth appeared, could never be seditious. Zenger was guilty only of serving the public's right to know. Zenger never wrote a word in English, but his stubborn resistance to an arrogant plutocracy inspired the *Weekly Journal* to espouse standards of rectitude still fervently defended three centuries later. It was none of Zenger's business how eventually DeLancey and Philipse divided up the late Governor Cosby's parcel of Mohawk land and sold a portion to Peter Warren.

The Palatines, as many feared, would become a potent source for change in the province. Cut off from the mainstream by language and culture, they, like many immigrant groups, turned inward. Zenger's career was not typical; he and a few others of the 1710 immigration were fortunate to make their lives in Manhattan, to become a part of the growing city. The Weisers, on the other hand—Johann Conrad and his twelve-year-old son, Conrad—languished for five months on Nutten Island before Governor Hunter was able to arrange transportation of the remaining Palatines to the interior. Conrad Weiser was a year younger than Zenger, but mortally ill with typhus as the *Lyon* docked. He survived, but was passed over by agents seeking healthy servants, and grew up ultimately near Tiononderoge, the Lower Mohawk Castle on Tenonanatche at the mouth of Schoharie Creek. After Hunter's scheme for manufacturing naval stores had collapsed, Johann Conrad led the Palatines against the governor's wishes into the Schoharie Valley. Like Zenger, both Weisers would do jail time—the elder was arrested for promoting mutiny and mayhem, the younger for inciting Indians to resist Dutch land speculators.

Palatines, as good peasants, made bad slaves and, until the Revolution, could be counted on in central New York to oppose Albany's plutocrats. On several occasions men and women together took up cudgels to beat back government sheriffs trespassing on land they claimed as their own. History shows that Robert Hunter did his best to help his charges, saving them from poverty in London, transporting them at his personal expense to the Hudson, counseling them as governor of New York in what he believed to be their best interests. Yet once the naval stores scheme collapsed, the governor was at a loss over what to do next.[9]

He had trusted Robert Livingston of Livingston Manor to feed and shelter his tar workers. Livingston took the funds, but delivered bad food and leaky tents. The first winter in the tar camps, the Palatines froze and starved. They never forgave the governor for what they took to be his negligence, and on several occasions rioted against his orders. After months of suffering, they decamped en masse from the Hudson, migrating over the mountains into the Schoharie Valley despite Hunter's objections. When the governor tried to make them purchase the land on which they settled for a token of corn, they mobbed his agents, firing on some and beating others. There was no choice but to call out the provincial militia to arrest the ringleaders. All this the Palatines could accept grudgingly, but what earned their everlasting resentment was the invasion of Albany landlords on the coattails of the militia.

Vromans, Van Dams, Livingstons claimed choice parcels of the valley by previous purchase from the Mohawks. The Palatines responded by burning Adam Vroman's house and possibly murdering his bailiff. Hunter had lost control of his difficult, headstrong charges, and what made matters worse was that a new government in London had no interest whatever in naval stores. When he moved to recover his personal fortune, spent to transport and support the Palatines several years earlier, the Palatines refused to corroborate his receipts. Their ingratitude bankrupted and ruined him in the end, but Hunter had already been skinned by the sharp dealings of Livingston and the Albanians.[10]

In fact, as we shall see, the Palatines would always insist that their only genuine benefactors were the Mohawk chiefs, whose providential presence at London in 1709 came to stand in their history as miraculous proof of divine intervention.

Over a long history, voyages to America have scarred many immigrants, the pain of reaching and entering the New World remembered and passed on for generations. The old landing places—Governor's Island, Castle Clinton, Ellis Island—are secular shrines haunted by tales of separation and loss. The voyages of the Palatines are as bad as any on record. They surpass in horror the coffin ships of the Irish immigration, and vie with the worst slave voyages in their bill of mortality. Nor did the Palatines walk off their ships in New York as free people. Queen Anne commiserated with them over the loss of their homes, but her government found the Queen's charity an unwieldy burden and quickly found a way to make profits from the misfortune of these destitute people. The important thing was to get them out of London, out of England, and shoved into the most troublesome corners of the overseas empire.

Most remarkable, and certainly the cause of the Palatines' high mortality rate, was the extreme length of their American voyage. In good weather, a fair sailing ship could make the passage in a month; very bad weather might add one or two more months, but six months was the duration of a voyage from Plymouth to Chile around Cape Horn. In his autobiography Conrad Weiser recalls being in English waters for almost five months before the *Lyon* sailed to the West.[11] The ships lingered off the coast as the government scoured the slums and suburbs of London for the recent immigrants. Few spoke English, but many had heard rumors that they were to be sent to America on signing a contract of service with the Crown. Some came forward voluntarily; others had to be found and brought to the agreement. It took time, as did transporting thousands of people from London to Plymouth, and all the while, ships that filled remained anchored offshore. Over 13,000 refugees had escaped to England from the Rhineland by the time the first consignment of Palatines left for the New World.[12] Londoners came upon them begging in the streets, living in makeshift camps in public spaces, overflowing the rudimentary services available to the indigent. Never before had a European city attempted social rescue on this scale. Sanford Cobb reports the generous measures that the people of London supported:

> It is estimated that the sums, expended by the government and contributed by the people of England for the support and final establishment of the Palatines in Ireland and America, aggregated the enormous amount of £135,000. Much of this generous provision was due to the kindly interest of the Queen, who not only gave of her own purse, and incited her government to similar action, but issued briefs calling for collections throughout the kingdom.[13]

One way or the other, the Palatines had to be moved, and most if asked preferred to be moved to America. Schemes were hatched to settle them in the New Forest of Hampshire or to employ them in Newfoundland fisheries. These proposals came to nothing. In 1709 small parties were sent to Ireland, North Carolina, and the Hudson River at Newburgh. But the largest number awaited transportation to the New York Province for employment in what seemed at first a brilliant stroke for populating New York, satisfying humanitarian impulse, and producing vital resources.

The Palatines' own historians are unanimously charitable towards the British government, understanding that despite the sufferings and losses of the refugees, the Crown did as much as any could in that period for a displaced people. In their proposals the ministries crossed a boundary, visible only in hindsight, between early-modern social practices and modern administration; the surprise is not that they did poorly, but that they did anything at all. Their effort was hugely expensive for the time, but the government's resolve to address humanitarian, economic, and colonial policy in one bold move marks a new realization—a global appreciation of how complex international conditions could impact the welfare of the home island. The board was adamant that the Palatines be rewarded for their services with land and naturalization as British subjects. Where they planned to find this land, however, caused great trouble—not with Indians, but with New York's land barons.

In relation to the Mohaques River: Your Majesty was pleased, by your order in Council of the 26th June, 1708, to confirm an Act, passed at New York, the 2nd of March, 1693 for vacating several Extravagant Grants, whereby large Tracts of Land are returned to your Majesty, and among the rest a tract of Land lying on the Mohaques River, containing About 50 miles in length and four miles in breadth, and a Tract of land lying upon a creek [Schoharie] which runs into the said River, which contains between 24 and 30 miles in Length. This last mentioned Land, of which Your Majesty has the possession, is claimed by the Moheques, but that claim may be satisfyed on very easy terms. ...

We therefore humbly offer that the Governor or Commander in Chief be Directed upon their Arrival to Seat them all, either in a Boddy or in different Settlements, upon those or other Lands as he shall Find most proper and that they be Encouraged to settle and work in Partnership, that is, 5 or more families to unite and work in common.[14]

The British Board of Trade believed that the Palatines would be settled in the Mohawk and Schoharie valleys. Robert Hunter intended to locate his charges far from there, on both sides of the Hudson River in the vicinity of modern Saugerties. But where did the Palatines expect to be put? They claimed a special promise had been made to the Queen on their behalf, and tar, turpentine, or naval stores aside, they would collect on it as soon as their terms of indenture expired.

Shortly before the board met, and before the refugees embarked for Plymouth, all London was excited by the public appearance of four Iroquois sachems. These guests of the Crown were seen everywhere; small pictures depicting them went on sale, and at Court they were received as Indian kings.[15] So Joseph Addison refers to them in *The Spectator*, No. 50 for April 27, 1711:

When the four Indian Kings were in this Country about a Twelvemonth ago, I often mixed with the Rabble, and followed them a whole Day together, being wonderfully struck with the Sight of everything that is new or uncommon. I have, since their Departure, employed a Friend to make many Enquiries of their Landlord the Upholsterer, relating to their Manners and Conversation, as also concerning the Remarks which they made in this Country.[16]

This becomes Addison's pretext for a gentle satire on English mores and customs as seen through the eyes of four "well-upholstered" Indians. It is all fun, especially when Addison falls to quoting King Sa Ga Yean Qua Rash Tow and E Tow O Koam (King of the Rivers), names he certainly invented. But who were these four chiefs in reality? Mohawk Valley tradition holds that one was in fact a Mohican sachem of the Mohawk's Turtle Clan.[17] The connection of the chiefs to the Palatines happened serendipitously, according to a legend the Palatines insisted to be the truth:

> In their walks in the outskirts of London they [the Kings] saw the unenviable condition of the houseless and homeless Germans; and one of them, unsolicited and voluntarily, presented the Queen a tract of his land in Schoharie, New York, for the use and benefit of the distressed Germans.[18]

Conrad Weiser, whose intimate knowledge of Iroquois life should not be discounted, clearly believed in the rumored gift of land. "Five chiefs of the Mohawk Indians," he reports in his autobiography, "saw and pitied the wretched condition of the people, and offered to open to the perishing mass their hunting grounds beyond the sea." Sanford Cobb finds frequent references among the Palatines of this period to "a beautiful valley of scorrie [Schoharie]," their destined promised land. "Certainly," he writes, "the larger portion of these three thousand emigrants left London with Schoharie as the synonym of their hope, and were not satisfied until they looked on its level meadows and lordly hills."[19]

The rumor of the gift is fact, but was there any factual basis to the rumor? Were the chiefs even in London at the time of the Palatines? Addison's "about twelve months ago" would suggest not. The dates remain difficult to reconcile, and Weiser's chronology, constructed years later, contains many inconsistencies. Clearly the Schoharie Valley was the Mohawks to give. The bottomlands along the creek offered fine farming, but game was scarce on the lower reaches, and the Mohawks could easily have ceded the valley without great sacrifice. A settlement there of 3,000 client farmers beholding to the Mohawks could only strengthen the tribe's hand against the Albany Dutch and their rapacious syndicates. Yet while this seems plausible, no evidence of a bequest to Queen Anne or to any Palatine or Crown official has ever been found. Of course, conversation was by way of interpreter, and what might have been said, or believed, or granted by the Mohawk party in London did not necessarily translate into an ironclad accord on the frontiers of New York. It remains that when Johann Conrad Weiser and his son met Tiyanoga at Canajoharie two years later, the sachem, on behalf of the Iroquois League, welcomed the Palatines to the Schoharie. Hunter's enterprise was collapsing beneath the weight of its own contradictions by then, and the elder Weiser brought the survivors of his people over the Catskills and down into the "promised land" of their prayers at Wilder Hook, a sharp bend in the Schoharie Creek below Corn Mountain.[20] They would still have to contest with the Livingstons, DeLanceys, Philipses, Vromans, and Van Dams for every acre, but they would have powerful allies in Tiyanoga, and eventually in William Johnson.

When Johnson sat on the south bank of Tenonanatche in 1738 and watched German farmers riding by on the north to Schenectady, he was meeting the descendants of the 1710 immigration. They had eventually removed to German Flats, forty miles up the river from Warrensburgh between Little Falls and Frankfort. Caty Weisenberg brought them into Johnson's home, and many of them would march with him to Lake George in 1755. Twenty years later, in the time of "the great breaking," the American Revolution, large numbers followed Nicholas Herkimer into the inferno at Oriskany. By then the children of the Palatines had recalibrated their resentments. They had been forced to recognize that if some Mohawks *gave* them land, other Mohawks *sold* the same land legally to Adam Vroman, who did no more than claim his own. The land their grandparents entered on rumor had by now devolved into parcels left to them. In the later eighteenth century, wheat was grown there, and the Schoharie became a breadbasket to the colonies. When the Revolution broke out, these same Palatines bled to defend the strategic valley against invaders with all their customary stubbornness.

Two hunters chased the same deer over the hills behind *Onistagrawa*, or Corn Mountain, and met suddenly in a bend on the trail. From the spot, they could look down on the hamlet of Weisersdorf below in the valley. The white man—short, dark, bearded— was in his late twenties; the Indian was tall, dapper, middle-aged. The buck bounded down the mountainside into the brush, and the younger man put up his rifle and greeted his elder in Mohawk, as was proper. The Indian recognized the white man's accent and returned his greeting. He suggested that the two sit and compose themselves, for surely the deer was fled beyond their reach, and rarely was it that Swatane met a white person conversant in Indian tongues.

In appearance, Swatane was no ordinary brave; his soft, white deerskin dress marked him as an emissary of the Onondaga council fire. In Oneida his name meant "our enlightener," and while the two spoke, the younger realized that he was hearing the mind of a chief of the Oneidas, a peacemaker who marked his descent from Hiawatha and Deganaweda.[21] This was a man entrusted by the league with sensitive missions. Most knew him by his Delaware name, Shickellamy, for he was the sachem appointed by the Haudenosaunee to supervise their subject tribe, the Delawares, or Lenni Lenape. Not an easy task to curb these people, Swatane found, or their friends, the Shawnees. Even now he was preparing to travel down the Susquehanna to Shamokin (modern Sunbury) for a council between Pennsylvania's Indians and the province's white proprietors. What brought him to Onistagrawa at a bend in the river—a prominence called Vroman's Nose by the settlers—was a hunger for venison. Schoharie had been shorn of game, and a hot, droughty summer had shriveled the crops. The young man shared his pouch of parched corn with the elder as they spoke of the valley and its issues.

He, too, bore an Indian name. At sixteen, the Mohawks adopted him and named him Siguras. Shickellamy nodded; he could place the young man now. His name meant "killer," not because he killed, but because he competed violently at sports. He was not above tripping an adversary unfairly in a foot race. His intense striving had won him the name. Indeed, he often spoke with his god, the Mohawks reported, even arguing loudly with him—thinking to barge into heaven behind his fists. This was Conrad Weiser, who had arrived at Nutten Island with typhus in 1710, and after sharing the labors of the Palatines on the Hudson, escaped with his father, Johann Conrad, to Weisersdorf, or Weiser's Village, the current Middleburgh, New York.

With little formal schooling, the boy added English to his native German; then, tutored by immigrant schoolmasters, he acquired a smattering of French and Latin. He early gave signs of being gifted in languages. Life was hard on the Schoharie, and the elder Weiser hoped to provide for each of his eight surviving children. Thus it occurred to him to turn Conrad over to chief Qua y nant, who was then living in a village at the foot of Vroman's Nose and had shown an interest in the boy.[22] Living with him, Conrad could learn Mohawk and come to act as an interpreter between his people and the Iroquois while, in the meantime, Johann would be shut of a hungry mouth and rebellious son at home. A child by Johann's first wife, Conrad despised his stepmother and her brood; nothing pleased him better than to exchange the grinding poverty of a crowded cabin for the freedom and companionship of an Indian village.[23] At this time in life, he had grown to distrust his Protestant god. His story, confided to Shickellamy on the mountainside, was much as Weiser would record it in his great autobiography—one of the most revealing accounts of life in the American interior until Lewis and Clark's journal.[24]

To look at him was to read the hardships of pioneer life in his face and dress. He had just been released from prison in Albany. His young wife, Anna Eve Feck, was pregnant with their first child, and Conrad was immersed in endless wrangling for a small piece of land on Tenonanatche. Shickellamy knew the story; everyone in the valley did. It started after Johann Conrad left for London with other Palatine elders to present their grievances to King George. Governor Hunter received a letter from Adam Vroman alleging that the Weisers were fomenting rebellion against established authority:

> John Conradus Wiser has been the Ring Leader among the Indians and now he is turn'd their Interpreter so that this Wiser and his Son talk with the Indians very often and have made treates for them and have been busy to buy land at many places which is Contrary to your Excellencys Proclamation, and has made the Indians drunk to that degree to go and mark of[f] Land with them.[25]

Old Vroman was a survivor of the Schenectady massacre and no special friend of the Indians. He was a miller by trade, a tight-fisted Dutch businessman, and his accusations might have been nothing more than fox blaming wolf except that he did, indeed, hold legally executed patents to the lands on which the Palatines squatted. Hunter had little choice but to dispatch Albany's Sheriff Adams to investigate the matter. Johann Conrad had already departed Weisersdorf for Europe when his son learned of the sheriff's approach and fled into the hills. Magdalena Zeh, however, a matron of the village, was not to be intimidated. She and others had heard the mockery heaped on Palatine women by Albanians. These large, hardworking farmwomen were ridiculed as "livestock," blamed for their barnyard immodesty, laughed at for facial hair and sunburned arms. Magdalena had every intention of showing the governor of New York the quality of her arms. Taking her cue from Barbara Walch, the legendary heroine of Shorndorf, Württemberg, who once marched a body of women to town hall with brooms to sweep out the town council, Magdalena gathered her forces in the hamlet's byways and awaited the sheriff's arrival.[26]

When Sheriff Adams rode into town, the women of Weisersdorf set on him in a mob, chasing his men away with wooden spoons and kitchen knives; then, dismounting the sheriff, they basted him with mop handles and broomsticks. Connoisseurs of tar, these women covered him with the goo, dumped chicken feathers and manure over him, and tied him to a pole. They carried Adams seven miles down the road to Albany and left him finally to the mercy of the crows. What they had done was to blind the poor man in one eye and break several of his ribs. His servants returned Adams to the governor's residence at Albany, from where he would never serve again. Hunter consoled the sheriff with the observation that at least they had not gelded him, but he also called out the militia to arrest every woman in Weisersdorf. What the troopers found, however, were husbands at home fixing their own dinners, while Magdalena and her girls hid out on Toepath Mountain. The Palatine women had proven every bit as difficult to subdue as their men.

But this could not go on; Palatines needed to trade their crops for the necessities of life in Albany. Conrad was yanked off the streets there and jailed, and even Magdalena Zeh eventually showed herself in town and was arrested. Hunter sent some of the greater ruffians to New York City for trial, but after a few months he relented and let the rest go free on condition that they pledge to pay in corn for the lands they had occupied. The tax was set exceedingly low, but as the culprits signed their release documents, they were in effect conceding their "land of scorrie" forever to the duly constituted authority of the Province of New York.[27] Within a few years many had migrated to Pennsylvania, to the Mohawk settlements at German Flats and Stone Arabia, or westward to the Ohio. Just as he met Shickellamy on Corn Mountain, Conrad Weiser was pondering such a move. The governor of Pennsylvania, acting for the proprietors of the colony, the Penn family, had opened Pennsylvania's Tulpehocken and Swatara valleys to Palatine settlement, and each year more Palatines undertook the perilous journey down the Susquehanna River from Schoharie to the fertile lands in York County between Harrisburg and Reading.[28]

Shickellamy had gone into the mountains to hunt for food, but found in Conrad Weiser a companion and helper who would be with him all of his days. Beyond mere language, the men understood each other perfectly, sharing values and affinities shaped by the clash of cultures along Tenonanatche and Schoharie Creek. In the first half of the eighteenth century, they could have come from nowhere else—these two from New York who bridged the worlds of Indian and settler. Service to the Iroquois League impelled Shickellamy into contact with the power elite of the British colonies. He might return to the Council at Onondaga for instructions, but most of his career as an emissary was spent conveying messages from *Onas* (the governor of Pennsylvania, who spoke for the Penn family) to *Corlaer* (the governor of New York, who was appointed by the Crown) to *Assaryquoa* (the governor of Virginia, who forbade the Iroquois to cross his province). In Native American parlance, such titles of office were independent of individual holders. Like *Onontio*, the name for the governor of New France, they were personifications of political form and function. As a consequence of negotiations, Shickellamy was frequently in Philadelphia, Albany, New York, or Williamsburg, but while he could speak English, he could not write or read English. Plodding through the wilderness of the Endless Mountains, as the Iroquois called the Appalachians, he had frequently wished for a companion to share his lonely journeys and act as an unbiased interpreter and recorder. He was convinced that, without continual mediation, disastrous war was certain between Indian and Indian, and this war embroiling tribal people from New Hampshire to North Carolina would inevitably draw into its vortex the British and French colonies.

Weiser could converse in several Iroquoian dialects, read and write English, French, German, and Latin and, most importantly, was a fiercely moral and independent person. He might decry his brother Mohawks' heathen ways, or lament their wild and drunken behavior, but he had grown to be as much of them as of his European family. Under his anger lay a deep religiosity compounded by a seething resentment of injustice. This was the man Shickellamy had been seeking—a man who could travel the difficult roads, whom he could trust, who would be welcome in either lodges or mansions of power. The trick now was for Shickellamy to persuade Weiser to give up his fruitless life in Weisersdorf, wipe the slate clean, and begin again on the rich and beautiful lands in Pennsylvania. It was a long way to Shamokin, but Shickellamy would welcome Conrad and his young wife to the Palatine settlement at nearby Tulpehocken if only they would come. And, all to the good of colonial history, they eventually did, canoeing down the Susquehanna with their children in the summer of 1729.

The Susquehanna flows placidly enough out of Lake Otsego in central New York, yet by the time its east and west arms come together in Pennsylvania, it is a fierce river, capable in its natural state of terrible floods and destruction. As it snakes through New York, the Susquehanna draws to itself the Unadilla and then drops across the present border into Susquehanna County, Pennsylvania. There, it makes a sharp bend northward and, running back into New York State, picks up the Chenango River before bisecting Binghamton and rushing westward. Where it crosses the border again, the Susquehanna absorbs the Cayuga and Chemung rivers, and then twists southward into central Pennsylvania. The point is that there were many easier ways to reach Tulpehocken in 1729 than by this treacherous flood. But tradition holds that Weiser made the journey with his young family by river despite the dangers.[29] This capable frontiersman would prove his courage on many more occasions as he and Shickellamy voyaged through the Susquehanna country to and from Onondaga.

The border between New York and Pennsylvania was then vaguely defined by the meanderings of the Susquehanna, Delaware, and tributaries. In the shadowy borderlands, roving bands of Delawares and Mohawks responded with ever increasing hostility to the encroachments of powerful land companies and the inequities of colonial trade practices. Weiser saw and recorded the effect of the fur wars on the tribes, and through his vivid descriptions, history glimpses the harsh conditions prevailing among Native Americans in the first half of the eighteenth century. Fifty years later, the great Tory raids of the Revolution, followed by Washington's crushing response, would pass up and down the Susquehanna through channels mapped by Weiser and Shickellamy. Where the two states seemed sewed together by the thread of the river, native villages and pioneer towns sprang up in profusion.

From Unadilla and Oquaga in New York to the Wyoming Valley in Pennsylvania, more than a dozen settlements were founded on the banks of the Susquehanna, only to be destroyed ultimately by the violence of the Revolution. The Hudson, Mohawk, Schoharie, Susquehanna, and Delaware rivers had by then come to signify to immigrants the boundaries of their New World experience. The river valleys that the Weisers helped open to their countrymen had become for German speakers a new *heimatsland*. As crisis followed crisis through the mid-eighteenth century, it also grew apparent that the survivors of New York's Palatine migration were firmly established astride the wilderness nation's interior lines of communication. Thus, how Tenonanatche's Germans, along with their Pennsylvania brethren, interpreted the mounting political conflicts of the century assumed great importance.

By the end of the French and Indian War, many of these communities were fully naturalized and grateful to the Crown for sacrifices on their behalf during the late hostilities. Yet, distaste for local aristocracy and corrupt patronage systems had taken root among the immigrants, and if some would weigh loyalty to the Crown above such resentments when violence erupted, many more chose to support the emerging party of equality and opportunity.

As Conrad Weiser cleared his land and built a homestead for his family, Shickellamy trudged on, stopping by frequently to discuss and advise. In this new environment, far from New York's squabbles, Conrad achieved prominence. Through the offices of Shickellamy, he found a powerful patron in Philadelphia looking for just such a man as he. James Logan, Provincial Secretary of Pennsylvania, remained the colonies' foremost Indian authority throughout the 1730s.[30] He was not an easy man to impress, but Weiser succeeded in winning his confidence. In turn, Logan opened the younger man's eyes to the intricacies of Indian policy. His vision stretched beyond provincial Pennsylvania—from Maine to the Carolinas—encompassing a multitude of tribal leaders and situations bearing directly on the welfare of British America.

At the top of Logan's list of issues was the French problem. New France had made many inroads into the Ohio River Valley, Pennsylvania's westernmost border, and now was consolidating its hold on the disaffected Delawares and Shawnees of the region. As if this were not bad enough, the New York Iroquois Confederation was on the brink of bloody war with the Cherokees and Catawbas of the South; rampages by Iroquois warriors into Virginia risked collision with white settlers, as well as threatening treaties existing between Britain and the southern tribes.[31] Finally, widespread conflict at the confluence of the Delaware branches flowing down from New York and forming Pennsylvania's border with that province and New Jersey, brought potential strife to the doorsteps of Philadelphia and New York City. This was the quality of Logan's perspective—a sweeping appreciation of how fragile was British settlement in the New World.

He needed a dozen hands, as every Indian agent of the Crown did, to act in several directions at once, often over thousands of miles of difficult terrain and across numerous cultural divides. Logan traveled widely, and the farther he fared, the more convinced he became—his Quaker heritage aside—that war was the Crown's worst alternative. He knew well how European armies went awry in the wilderness, how force in the face of Native American provocations always failed. Logan was less a pacifist than a realist, and Weiser confirmed his outlook, sharing his abhorrence of Indian wars. In the interest of peace, they would work together with Shickellamy, Weiser traveling as Logan's interpreter and personal emissary to places Logan could no longer go.

All this was to be if Conrad could tear himself away from Anna Eve and his many children, disembroil himself from the factional struggles of various Lutheran and Baptist sects, and serve a Crown for which he had no intrinsic love. Weiser lived in two worlds. As a man of conscientious faith, he entered the Ephrata Cloister—a monastic foundation of mystical Seventh Day Baptists not far from his home—and there, for a time, persisted in celibacy until brought back to the marriage bed by Anna Eve.

More children followed. But Weiser stayed deeply involved in Baptist, Lutheran, and Moravian matters throughout his life. He did not preach his faith to the Indians, but opened the Bible to any who asked. Rectitude became his testimony, and by the 1740s several Mohawk friends, possibly tongue in cheek, renamed him *Tarachiawagon*, or "Master of Life." Johnson, hearing Weiser so called, forbid Mohawks of his acquaintance to use the title, remonstrating that it was beyond mortal man and blasphemous.[32] Weiser, for his part, competed with Johnson for the attention of the Iroquois. He viewed the newcomer as a wilderness playboy, interested more in carousing with the Mohawks than in instructing them, and Weiser predicted that the Irishman would someday promise more than he could deliver, fall out with his forest friends, and be assassinated.[33]

Nonetheless, Weiser, at the urging of the governor of Pennsylvania, sent a young German immigrant to Fort Johnson in 1749 to learn all that he could about Indian relations. Tenonanatche had become the colonial schoolhouse for studying Native America, and anyone with business in the wilderness could not do better than visit Weiser's home or Johnson's for a crash course in frontier affairs. Daniel Claus was expected to report back to Philadelphia after a decent interval at Johnson's knee. Instead, to Weiser's chagrin, Claus refused to return and stayed on to become one of Sir William Johnson's most trusted assistants. A superb musician and copious diarist, Claus was welcomed into Johnson's family, marrying Sir William's daughter, Anne, in 1762. During the Revolution, he followed the Johnson Tories into the fight and eventually to exile in Canada.

Disagree as they might over policy and decorum, Weiser and Johnson were both blood brothers of the Mohawk nation, and Weiser, like his rival, knew well to swallow his moral and religious compunctions in dealing with his native family. When the great Moravian missionary, Count Zinzendorf, arrived in the colonies from Germany, Weiser introduced him to the leading sachems of the Six Nations. It soon reached him that Zinzendorf was off on the wrong foot, and he wrote to the pastor at Philadelphia about a recent guest, Chief Coxhayion, who had complained:

About the Indian who lodged with you, he is entirely satisfied except that he was given no rum, which if he had been he says he could have joined in with greater heartiness at prayer time, he wondered how people could spend so much time in prayer which surely could have been put off to some future time, when there was nothing else to do, at the moment there were more agreeable things, like rum and such-like entertainments, he spoke very well of you and your company and said he had no doubt that when you came to know more about the nature of Indians, you would never speak to them on weighty matters without treating them to a good trunk rum.[34]

Amid all his activities—farming a large homestead, tending to a growing family, traveling for Logan, attending innumerable councils and treaties—Weiser managed to produce an important treatise on the Six Nations for the benefit of ministries in London and at home. This treatise was published in Philadelphia by Benjamin Franklin, who remained in communication with Weiser over the years on all matters pertaining to Native Americans. Weiser was a prolific writer during his lifetime, producing one journal in English for his employers and another in German for his family and friends. As a rule, the English journal is most complete on matters of negotiation and ritual courtesies offered and received in council, while the German offers the most vividly personal account of travel through the wilderness compiled in eighteenth-century America. A sample follows, drawn by Paul A. W. Wallace from both records, the German translated by Conrad's great-grandson Hiester Muhlenberg.[35]

What occasioned the winter journey described was an urgent embassy called for by Logan in 1736 at the request of Governor Gooch of Virginia. Virginia wished to negotiate a peace treaty between the Six Nations and the Cherokees and Catawbas, and requested that Pennsylvania invite the representatives of the Iroquois Confederacy to Williamsburg for that spring. In a decisive attempt to assure peace along the frontier, Virginia would sponsor the southern tribes, Pennsylvania the northern. This opportunity was too good to miss, and at the end of January, rushing to give the Six Nations as much notice as possible, Logan dispatched Weiser to Onondaga. But to trek from southern Pennsylvania to the location of modern Syracuse along the Onondaga Trail in late winter, to cross the Endless Mountains and ford the ice-choked Susquehanna, was a high-risk mission only a desperate frontiersman would attempt. Weiser's party comprised Shickellamy, an old pioneer named "Stoffel" Stump, and an Onondaga known as Owisgera. Because of heavy snows early in the month, the ambassadors left in late February, expecting to reach their destination by the end of March.

What Weiser counted on was a period of mild weather, which sometimes occurs in late winter. With warm sun and mild air he hoped to reach Onondaga before the rains of April had washed out the trails and swelled the rivers. His party plunged instead into a wintry hell:

> The 25th, after breakfast, we proceeded on our journey. The snow was no deeper [in fact, it was then three feet deep] and before noon we reached a stream which is a branch of the Otzuachtan river, which we had left yesterday. The stream we are now on the Indians call Dia-daclitu, (die berirte, the lost or bewildered) which in fact deserves such a name. We proceeded along this stream between two terrible mountains; the valley being, however, now about half mile in width, and the stream flowed now against this, and then against the other mountain, among the rocks. Here we held a long council as to the best mode of procedure; whether to remain in the valley,

and consequently be obliged to cross the stream repeatedly, or to endeavor to proceed along the sides of the mountains, as we had done yesterday. As it was very cold to wade the creek often, we determined to try the mountain's side.[36]

By now, the party had picked up an Iroquois warrior returning from the warpath in Virginia. They had also met two English traders, who were subsequently drowned when their canoe capsized in Kanasoragu Creek. The rivers were brim full and flowing with cake ice. Note that at this time Shickellamy was past sixty, Weiser over forty.

As we clambered along the mountains, before we had proceeded a quarter mile, Shikelimo [Shickellamy] had an unlucky fall which nearly cost him his life. He had caught hold of a flat stone, sticking in the root of a fallen tree, which came loose, and his feet slipping from under him, he fell at a place which was steeper than the roof of a house. He could not catch hold of anything, but continued slipping on the snow and ice for about three rods, when his pack which he carried in Indian fashion, with a strap around his breast, passed on one side of a sapling and he on the other, so that he remained hanging by the strap until we could give him assistance. If he had slipped half a rod further he would have fallen over a precipice about a hundred feet high, upon the other craggy [*spitzige*] rocks. I was two steps from him when he fell. We were all filled with terror. ... When we reached the valley, Shikelimo looked around at the height of the steep precipice on which he had fallen. We looked at him: he stood still in astonishment, and said: "I thank the great Lord and Creator of the world, that he had mercy on me, and wished me to continue to live longer."[37]

This, of course, is what winter travel meant in the colonies—a grueling struggle through freezing water, across slippery rocks, and down into dark, snow-filled valleys where the sun hardly penetrated. Here is the river fording that follows:

The water reached to the waist, but we crossed safely. We had to suffer the excessive cold, because the hard frozen snow was still eighteen inches deep in the valley, and prevented us from walking rapidly; neither could we warm ourselves by walking, because we had to cross the stream six or seven times. The wood was so thick, that for a mile at a time we could not find a place of the size of a hand, where the sunshine could penetrate, even in the clearest day. This night we prepared a place to sleep in the same manner as last night. During the night it began to storm, and the wind blew terribly, which seemed to me strange. The Indians say that in this whole valley, which is about sixty miles long, it storms in this manner, or snows, every night. It is such a desolate region that I often thought I must die of oppression; I call it the Dismal Wilderness.[38]

None who truly faced it ever made light of the natural wilderness, but along their path Weiser and Shickellamy also found evidence of human wilderness.

The Indians believe that an Otkan (evil spirit) has power in this valley, that some of them could call him by name, and brought him sacrifices by which he could be appeased. I asked if any of our party could do this, or know his name. They answered no, that but few could do this, and they were magicians. ... At noon we reached the summit of the mountain. Before we had quite reached the summit, we saw two skulls fixed on poles, the heads of men who had been killed there a long time before, by their prisoners, who had been taken in South Carolina. The prisoners, who were two resolute men, had found themselves at night untied, which, without doubt, had been done by the Otkan, and having killed their captors and taken possession of their arms, had returned home.[39]

The warfare that drew young Iroquois warriors to the South over many years was resulting in a bloody attrition of Native American strength almost imperceptible to colonists on the Atlantic coast. Cherokee and Catawba prisoners were being sold as slaves in the Carolinas or dragged north into New York as objects of shame by the Iroquois League's war parties. The hope of resolving this useless struggle is what drove Weiser and Shickellamy through the Dismal Wilderness. Even as they endured natural dangers, they found evidence of combat along the Onondaga Trail. Among their party was an Iroquois brave returning from the war. The skulls reminded them again of how long the warfare had persisted. (In the 1740s and 1750s, when Johnson attempted to enlist Mohawks and Oneidas in the wars against the French, he would abruptly realize how deeply native warfare had cut into the tribes' warrior population.)

But the human body could only stand so much exposure to the cruel elements, and as the peacemakers pushed northward, Weiser and the Indians, driven to extremes, started to squabble over where to cross a river:

I said to them, that I had so far followed their advice, but I now required them to follow mine, and to follow the stream downwards until we reached a quiet place, even if we had to go to the Susquehanna River, because on level land the water was not so rapid as among the hills and mountains. Shikelimo answered, that I did not know how far it was; they knew it better than I did; it was impossible. ... Shikelimo retorted, that he was the guide, as being a person who had traveled the route often, while I had never done so; he would cross there; if I refused, I must bear the blame if I lost my life by hunger or any other accident. He would also complain to the Governor, Thomas Penn, and James Logan, of my folly, and excuse himself. The others spoke much to the same purpose, particularly Tawagarat, who was returning from the wars, who said openly, that he was too proud to obey a European.[40]

Weiser sticks to his resolve and, with Stoffel, parts company from the Indians. The break lasts only a moment before the Onondaga and Shikelimo follow, but the warrior persists in building a raft alone to cross the raging river. Ironically, the Palatine turns out to be right. They ford the river in a calm stretch not far below and rescue Tawagarat on his disintegrating raft as he rushes by. There are no hard feelings; hunger now besets them, and they have enough to do in finding a village to feed them.

We reached some Indians living on the Susquehanna river, where we, however, found nothing but hungry people, who sustained life with the juice of the sugar trees. We, however, procured a little weak soup, made of corn meal. I had a quantity of Indian trinkets with me, but could procure no meal. My only comfort this evening was, that whoever labors or is tired will find sleep sweet. ... There are many Indians living here, partly Gaiuckers [Cayugas] partly Mahikanders. We went into several huts to get meat, but they had nothing, they said, for themselves. The men were mostly absent hunting; some of the old mothers asked us for bread. We returned to our quarters with a Mahikander, who directed his old grey-headed mother to cook a soup of Indian corn. She hung a large kettle of it over the fire, and also a smaller one with potash, and them both boil briskly. What she was to do with the potash was a mystery to me, for I soon saw that it was not for the purpose of washing, as some of the Indians are in the practice of doing, by making lye, and washing their foul and dirty clothes. For the skin of her body was not unlike the bark of a tree, from the dirt, which had not been washed off for a long time, and was quite dried and cracked; and her finger nails were like eagles' claws. She finally took the ash kettle off the fire, and put it aside until it had settled, and left a clear liquor on top, which she carefully poured into the kettle of corn. I inquired of my companions why this was done, and they told me it was the practice of these and the Shawanos [Shawnees], when they had neither meat nor grease, to mix their food with lye prepared in this manner, which made it slippery, and pleasant to eat.[41]

This cuisine in time of famine underscored for Weiser the endemic poverty of Native Americans living in the once rich countryside along the Susquehanna. Fur trapping had stripped the forests of small game, and sun-dried produce—beans, squash, and corn—were prone to give out by winter's end. The men of the villages were pulled farther and farther from home in their quest for meat, and between the powder and ball they required and the rum they craved, the villages were stripped bare of everything of value. Most appalling to Weiser was starvation among the children:

> I saw the children here walking up and down the banks of the stream, along the low land, where the high water had washed the wild potatoes, or ground acorns, out of the ground. These grow here on a long stem or root, about the size of a thick straw, and there are frequently from five to ten hanging to such a root, which is often more than six feet long. The richer the soil, the longer they grow, and the greater the quantity in the ground. I thought of the words of Job, Chapter 30, 3–8, while these barbarians were satisfying their hunger with these roots, and rejoicing greatly when they found them in large numbers, and dug them up:
>
> > To dwell in the cliffs of the valleys, in caves of the earth, and in the rocks.
> > Among the bushes they brayed; under the nettles they were gathered together.
> > They were children of fools, yea, children of base men: they were viler than the earth. And now am I their song, yea, I am their byword. [42]

This is only a sample of the Onondaga journal. The sharpness of its detail, the power of its observation and narration are characteristic of Weiser's best prose. The journal notes were prepared at Onondaga after the mission was over, and they go far to qualifying the mythic vision of the American frontiersman, rifle in hand, fighting off assailants to dispense a rudimentary justice. In peacetime, the greatest danger in crossing the wilderness arose from natural conditions and wild beasts. But the villages stretching between Shamokin and Onondaga were also in a process of degradation, and some indeed were dangerous to both Native Americans and Europeans. As often as not, however, people of all races, pitted against the harshness of nature, took compassion on each other. The French and Indian Wars, Pontiac's Rebellion, and the American Revolution still lay ahead; these convulsions would change forever the hospitality and open exchange largely prevailing along New York's borderlands in 1736.

Weiser and Shickellamy could still dream of better conditions for everyone through conscientious negotiation and treaty making. Such was the mythic legacy of Hiawatha and Deganaweda. Yet, for this vision to succeed, the Iroquois League was required to grow stronger, not weaker. The fear that the league's grip on Native

Americans was beginning to falter, that white men and red were approaching the brink of chaos, drove Weiser and Shickellamy onward through their hardships that winter until they arrived exhausted at the council fire of Onondaga.

Descriptions of the Onondaga proceedings are found in the English journal and provide an intimate glimpse into Native American deliberations at the height of the Six Nations' power. Unfortunately, after courtesies were exchanged between the representatives of the governors of Pennsylvania and Virginia, the Iroquois elders declined to visit Williamsburg in the spring. They consented to come as far as Philadelphia to discuss a peace treaty with the governor of Pennsylvania concerning the southern tribes. It would not be until nine years later that peace was finally arranged between the Catawbas and the Six Nations at the Treaty of Lancaster; by then, British America was engaged in a border skirmish with New France that threatened to explode into war.[43] King George's War, as this conflict became known, saw William Johnson immersed in antagonisms between the Tenonanatche tribes of New York and their Caughnawaga cousins of Canada. In Pennsylvania, Weiser and Shickellamy watched their best efforts founder on the mysterious murder of one John Armstrong at the narrows of the Juniata River.[44]

This crime occurred on the eve of the Lancaster conference and was blamed immediately on Delaware troublemakers. John Armstrong might have been a trader of unsavory reputation plying his wares along the frontier, but after he and two of his men turned up missing, the event set off alarms in Philadelphia and New York. Western trade vital to these cities appeared threatened, and hotheads in both legislatures cried out for strong measures. Armstrong's relatives added to the tumult by pledging to prosecute war against the perfidious savages if justice were not served. They mounted an expedition to locate the bodies, and soon did so amidst scenes of unusual horror. The bones were widely scattered and there was suspicion at first of ritual cannibalism. Around campfires people told of a guilty Indian touching one of the bones and then bleeding profusely from nose and mouth. While tales of this sort frightened the settlements, the Iroquois League was drawn into the crisis by imputations of mismanagement among their Lenni Lenape subjects. The peace was unraveling quickly when Shickellamy told Weiser to investigate the murders.

Weiser traveled to the Juniata and found that the Delaware chiefs had arrested two perpetrators and were preparing to surrender them. These braves would be taken to Philadelphia, tried, and if convicted, hanged. The problem Weiser found was that one was clearly innocent but had escaped into hiding, and that the other, his accuser, was certainly guilty. Weiser first needed to persuade the innocent fugitive to return to council in order to testify. According to a letter dated May 2, 1744, he journeyed to Shamokin to meet with Olumapies, the Delaware chief, to help resolve the matter. The transactions he reports are a chilling testimony to how far the relationship between Indian and European had deteriorated.

This day I delivered the Governor's message to Olumapies the Delaware Chief and the rest of Delaware Indians in the presence of Shickellamy and a few more of the Six Nations. The purport of which was that I was sent express by the Governor and Council to demand those that had been concerned with Mussemeelin [the brave still held] in murdering John Armstrong, Woodward Arnold and James Smith. That their bodies might be searched for and decently buried; that the goods be likewise found and restored without fraud. It was delivered to them by me in the Mohawk Language, and interpreted into Delaware by Andrew, Madam Monture's son.

The reply by Olumapies is filled with contrition born as much of policy as sincere regret. He has no intention of bringing down on the Delawares the wrath of the Six Nations over an act of senseless rage.

Brother the Governor. It is true that we the Delaware Indians, by the instigation of the Evil Spirit have murdered John Armstrong and his men; we have transgressed, and we are ashamed to look up. We have taken the murderer and delivered him to the relations of the deceased, to be dealt with according to his works.

But the details of the killings only come out when Weiser confronts Mussemeelin with the innocent brave Mussemeelin had implicated. In front of the entire assembly, the poor man lamented, "Now I am going to die for your wickedness. You have killed all the three whitemen. I never did intend to kill any of them."

Then Mussemeelin in great anger confirms the other's accusation: "It is true I have killed them. I am a man, you are a coward. It is a great satisfaction to me to have killed them. I will die with joy for having killed a great rogue and his companions. ... How will you do to kill Catawbas if you cannot kill a white man?"

The admission is all of killing, of taking up an English axe and hacking apart men separated in the woods and unsuspecting. The crisis passes when Mussemeelin is shackled and led away to Philadelphia for trial. The other brave goes free and returns to his tribe. But the Armstrong incident was a symptom of the powerful anger beginning to sweep through the villages of Native America. Weiser had viewed the ravages of rum and disease firsthand. In his opinion the humiliation of the Delawares by the English and Iroquois stored up dangers for the future. Indeed, ten years after, to young Colonel Washington's amazement, an Indian in his employ suddenly tomahawked a wounded French prisoner without provocation. It was an expression of the same frustration Weiser had found exploding in Mussemeelin. The French prisoner was Joseph Coulon de Villiers de Jumonville, a thirty-five-year-old ensign, and the shedding of his blood by a warrior born a Catawba, raised a Seneca, and made a half-chief among the Delawares was tinder that ignited the Seven Years War in the backcountry of Pennsylvania. As Washington looked on, paralyzed and appalled, Tanaghrisson split open the French nobleman's skull and washed his hands in the man's brains. This wanton cruelty was no different than the cold-blooded murder of Armstrong, though de Jumonville was an innocent soldier and Armstrong a frontier pirate. The ferocity appearing along the wilderness borders of New York, Pennsylvania, and Virginia was about to upset the civilized world, and in the aftermath, whites would shudder at the very mention of red Indians. It should not have been, yet it was, and Conrad Weiser and Shickellamy drank deeply of this bitterness. Not that anyone knew in 1744, but the British colonies were on the road to Braddock's disaster, with worse to follow.

As for Mussemeelin, he remained defiant to the last. Benjamin Franklin's *Gazette* of November 8, 1744, carries the notice: "Monday last, at the Court of Oyer and Terminer held here, the Indian, Mushemelon, who murdered Armstrong the Trader, and his two men, received Sentence of Death, having confessed the fact." On November 15, Mussemeelin was hanged in Philadelphia. The following summer the Six Nations met with representatives of the colonies and southern tribes to sign the peace of Lancaster. It was the fulfillment of all that Weiser and Shickellamy had worked for, yet it was too late to redress the wrongs that western Indians blamed on the Six Nations and the colonies. Treaties would follow that also bore the stamp of Conrad Weiser—the Treaty of Easton in 1758 ended the Indian wars in western Pennsylvania, but that peace was momentary and soon vanished as Pontiac's uprising rippled through the province in bloody waves. Logan, Shickellamy, and Weiser had represented an Indian policy directly opposite Johnson's. New York was committed to winning the Iroquois League to the British cause at all costs, even the destruction of the League. As Johnson put it, he would rather have one warrior in the bush than two sitting around a council fire.

Pennsylvania, under powerful Quaker influence, argued strongly for peace even in the face of violent provocations. To the pious Weiser and the deeply religious Palatines who followed him, the Province of New York was reaping the consequences of greed and profligacy in relationship to the Indians. They preferred dialogue with the tribes to preparedness and war. And they were hugely surprised when, in the midcentury, war with the French and Indians boiled over to within reach of Philadelphia.

The Iroquois League, on which Logan, Weiser, and Shickellamy counted, had grown too old and tired to underwrite more than a fitful and temporary peace. These peacemakers could patch up the league, but as events were to prove, could not save it. If their perspective seemed naïve or idealistic, it was rooted also in an emerging awareness of American identity, in dreams of a new nation in a better land where religion and respect for industry, self-reliance, and material progress flourished in a unity of purpose. While the Royal Colonies bickered endlessly, the Iroquois League offered an admirable model of unified legislative focus. Johnson, drawn always closer to the Crown, embraced the more militant and global European view. For him, the coming war with France would not be to save the Iroquois League, but to build in North

America an unassailable wilderness empire.[45] In the short run this outlook prevailed, as violence swept through the colonies. But over time, it was the wisdom of Philadelphia, of Logan's circle, that came nearer the truth. The English-speaking colonies would not be British much longer, and they would need to find a way to live at peace with themselves and Native America.

Shickellamy died of natural causes in 1748; Logan died three years later. Weiser labored on after Braddock's defeat with the help of Scaroyady, another Oneida sachem, but was drawn increasingly from his service as an interpreter into his role as a colonel of the Pennsylvania militia. Since the provincial legislature could not bring itself to appropriate funds for this militia, Weiser led his Pennsylvania Germans at his own expense, arming them in the early years of the outbreak with axes and pitchforks. The monumental effort of raising forts along the frontiers, recruiting soldiers, and provisioning the British army struggling towards Pittsburgh, eventually told on his health.

Even among the hostiles, the prestige of Tarachiawagon remained high, and his service as a translator was eagerly sought. At Easton he was able to save the conference from descending into aimless blame between the Six Nations and the offending Delawares and Shawnees by abridging the more offensive statements each side directed at the other. Such were the talents that the Great Interpreter acquired on the Tenonanatche forty years before. But by 1760, the Interpreter was gone—dead from a stroke suffered on the road to his home at Tulpehocken. His Indian friends lamented his loss for many seasons, but he was soon forgotten in the colonies. Johnson had edged him out. Weiser was not thought about much until 1776, when the sound of the Iroquois League cracking at last—the old order passing away forever—wakened in his people recollections of frigid winters, scarce food, and the stench of boiling tar. Old Johann Weiser had led them out of hell to the rumored land of "Scorrie," and his son Conrad from the Schoharie to the Tulpehocken. They could not have done this without Iroquois help. The people looked now for new leaders and found them in Brigadier General Nicholas Herkimer and General John Peter Muhlenberg, Conrad Weiser's grandson.

Unlike Johnson, Weiser took nothing from the Crown and everything from his colonial patrons, the proprietors of Pennsylvania. For most of his life, he was part of a radical redistribution of power that would lie at the center of the emerging American cause. The young rebel of 1713 had been submerged, never expunged. John Peter Muhlenberg, his grandson, became one of Washington's most valued generals; Henry Ernest Muhlenberg, another grandson, was a botanist and first president of Franklin and Marshall College; and Frederick Muhlenberg, a third grandson, was a delegate to the Continental Congress and first Speaker of the United States House of Representatives. The rivalry between Weiser and Johnson ran deep. While both had formed their way of life on Tenonanatche, both had come to worship different gods, arrange their households according to different principles, and order their personal lives by different priorities. Johnson owned slaves; Weiser did not. For the benevolent autocrat, Johnson, the Iroquois were to be the clients of a civilizing empire invested in advancing their best interests. For the pious refugee, Weiser, only a league of native peoples, truly united and strong in their own institutions, could negotiate a better future with the expanding forces of Europe in North America. Yet, there remained a third way that neither Indian agent addressed directly. Why not change the way Native Americans lived? Why not bring them out of darkness? Why not educate them in the tools of civilization, and through true religion, also save their souls?

In the years between the wars of empire and revolution, this question was increasingly asked in New England by a public disaffected with the Crown's approach to Indian affairs. According to New England observers, the frontier was in crisis not because the French instigated trouble—they had been defeated—but because the policies of Johnson, Weiser, Croghan and other wilderness entrepreneurs kept Native America locked in darkness. They believed it would take a Great Awakening to defeat savagery, and by saving the souls of the denizens of the forest, open the way for civilized settlement. In the next chapter we look at New England's growing influence along Tenonanatche and the consequences of New England's missionary fervor.

The Missionary

The years between the wars were to see dramatic changes along Tenonanatche as Sir William built on the progress of his own settlers and the industry of neighboring Palatines. Across the frontier, Indian affairs were seldom tranquil, but within the valley, a measure of peace prevailed. Sir William was much to be thanked for this blessing. Yet he would not long have matters all his own way. Expanding westward across the Hudson into New York province, the "saints" of New England increasingly searched for and found fertile lands superior to their stony New England acres, and in the years after Johnson and his Palatine predecessors sank their roots in the Mohawk, this culture, educated and evangelical, empowered by a great religious awakening, sent its missionaries westward into the wilderness to proselytize and educate Indians.

Missionaries were not new to the valley, but the evangelical divines who penetrated the region in the aftermath of the French wars found struggling communities ready to heed their appeals.[1] Publics in Boston and throughout the Northeast were increasingly uneasy with the Crown's Indian agents, their policies of self-interested trade, and their seeming inability to suppress violence. To safeguard settlers and settlements pushing outward from old established lines, a fresh approach seemed warranted, and what better way to assuage savagery, many believed, than to spread the good news of the gospel to Native Americans.

Reports out of the West often appalled the civilized East. How three from Connecticut vanished in the wilderness came to Sir William Johnson's attention years after the event. William and John Pitkin wrote to him March 1766 from Hartford:

> Sir.
> Being (by the Friends of one Isaac Hollister a Young Man taken Captive at Susquehannah in October 1763 Son of Capt Timothy Hollister who with another of his Sons is Supposed to be Killed at the Same time and Place) to Signify the Same to you and Desire your kind Offices to procure his return from his Captivity, they are informed that this Young Man was at the Senick

Castle but the Indians were about to remove him to another Castle but where, they are not informed.

Would therefore in their behalf request your help that he may be returned to his Friends of which the Bearer is one.

He is descended of a Good Family of a Neighboring Town from here.

Your Serving them in the Matter of his return will Oblige Sir your most Obedient and Humble Servants.[2]

Who else could the distraught friends and relatives of those missing on the frontier write to but the Crown's Indian Supervisor? Sooner or later news of shadowy deeds in the forest filtered through to Johnson Hall, and surmises might be made about the fate of people like Isaac. As it turned out, Isaac was captured by a band of renegade Senecas at the height of Pontiac's Rebellion, and these warriors happened to be among the very last to cooperate with Johnson. If the Crown's Indian Supervisor acted quickly enough, a bargain could sometimes be struck and the prisoner returned, but in this instance the appeal was several years too late. Despite Sir William's efforts, young Hollister was never seen again, and the probability remains that he perished in captivity. Mrs. Hollister, back in Connecticut, thus lost her husband and two sons on the banks of the Susquehanna. Her grief is terrible to imagine. Losses of this kind, mounting over the years, had begun to register a powerful effect on public opinion across the colonies. Educated citizens in the flourishing seaboard cities were beginning to wonder whether prevailing Indian policies would ever reduce the disorder of the backcountry.

The tribes were only a part of the problem. Early missionaries to New York and Pennsylvania confronted a virulent hatred of all Indians among the settlers. Fred Anderson describes the attitude of many frontier people towards Native Americans in the aftermath of the wars:

If anything was certain in the aftermath of the great insurrection [Pontiac's Rebellion, 1763–1765], it was that the renewed surge of white settlers into Indian country would once more destabilize the west. For the lessons that backwoods settlers had extracted from the recent conflict and its predecessor, which they knew as the French and Indian War, were the clearest of all. Frontier farmers had suffered by far the heaviest casualties in both conflicts, losing two thousand or more men, women and children killed or taken captive during the first year of the Indian war alone, and literally uncounted thousands in the greater war that had preceded it. The message of all these losses, for the colonists, could be reduced to the syllogism that lay behind the Paxton Boys' plan to exterminate every native person in Pennsylvania: if good Indians did not harm white people, then the best Indians must be those who could do no harm, for all eternity.[3]

This ghastly conclusion, fraught with peril for the future, demanded correction, and while Sir William worked toward a viable treaty line separating white expansion from the core hunting grounds of the tribes, Puritan New England brought forward a radically different proposal.[4] In the light of reason, if not experience, many in New England judged the practices of Johnson, Logan, Weiser, and Croghan corrupt and misguided from inception. Their policies bought the cooperation of the tribes with bribes and concessions, pitting native people against each other, when they ought to have worked to reform the offensive customs of the tribes by virtuous models. Most so-called Indian agents were also fur traders and land speculators, and thus it was in their interests to ply the forest people with rum and send them back into the woods even worse off than they had found them. For many tidewater citizens, without knowledge of the long-standing economic system of the backcountry, the Crown was to blame for the growing butcher bill annually presented to the colonies.

The Native Americans' quality of life depended, Johnson could argue, on acquiring manufactured goods, and the most efficient way to supply those goods was through the mechanism of trade.[5] But the time was also coming, many speculated, when Native Americans would need to change their ways, acquire agricultural skills in addition to material goods, and leave their villages to build towns and churches, schools and factories of their own. In effect, the Native American, confronted by waves of European immigration, would survive only by conforming to Christian culture. From the pulpits of New England, evangelical divines inveighed against the greedy Albany Dutch, the licentious Anglicans surrounding Johnson, the lunatic factionalisms of the Palatine Lutherans. New England was poised now to send its own pure religion into the wilderness to proselytize the savages and bend them, for the good of their souls, to the ways of the Lord.

One of the leading voices of religious awakening in Connecticut belonged to a supremely talented young preacher who had graduated from Yale University in 1733. Eleazar Wheelock received a license to preach in 1734, at the age of twenty-three, and was installed that year as pastor of the Second Congregational Church in Lebanon, Connecticut. He would remain there thirty-five years, at the center of the great revival in Connecticut, before founding Dartmouth College for Indian boys in New Hampshire in 1769. During a long lifetime of service, Wheelock acquired great influence in all matters concerning the education of Native Americans. His personal ministry to the Indians began in 1743 when he took into his home at Lebanon a young, Christianized Mohican, Samson Occom, destined to become a celebrated missionary in his own right. Twenty years later, with the frontiers roiling from the late wars, Wheelock sought to repeat his success with Occom by sending another gifted protégé into the darkness.

He chose as his instrument of outreach a recent graduate of his own Moor's Indian Charity School at Lebanon. This young missionary-to-be was Samuel Kirkland, who had matriculated at Moor's in 1760 as its first white scholar. By 1761, Kirkland had exhausted the Indian School's curriculum, and Wheelock sent him on to the College of New Jersey (Princeton) for further education. Princeton then was the leading center of "New Light" theology in the colonies, and Kirkland was quickly caught up in the growing enthusiasm for spreading the gospel to Native Americans.

He was born at Norwich, Connecticut, 1741, and according to his first biographer, his grandson Samuel Kirkland Lothrop, "His family, for several generations, held influential posts in society and in the Church. Miles Standish was one of his progenitors. Particular mention is also made of Daniel, his father, who was pastor of a church in Norwich, and is recorded as being a devoted minister, an accomplished scholar, a man of fine talents, of a ready wit, and an amiable disposition."[6] Lothrop does not enlarge on the difficulties Samuel's father experienced in holding down several ministries or on the nervous indisposition that led him and his family into near penury.

The elder Kirkland was a great friend of the saintly English evangelist, George Whitefield, and of James Davenport, Connecticut's firebrand answer to Whitefield and to Jonathan Edwards. Highly placed though Kirkland's distant progenitors might have been among Puritan divines, Whitefield, Edwards, and Davenport were the living models young Samuel strove to emulate—all of them principal figures in the colonies' Great Awakening movement. In successive waves during the 1740s and 1750s this spiritual revival crashed against the settled orthodoxies of the principal denominations. A fervent evangelism drove some Protestants to proclaim and demonstrate their salvation loudly—barking like dogs, frothing at the mouth, shouting in tongues—while others, repelled by the emotionalism of the new elect, were driven into the company of Quakers and Anglicans. The net gain across the colonies was a sharp increase in church-going, church-building, and public disputation.

No one professing religion in the years of Kirkland's youth could have escaped the excitement. Old, established authority was turned out by popular outcry as crowds of recent converts sought new vessels to contain their religious experience. Controversy was especially rife among Congregationalists and Presbyterians. Jonathan Edwards, a "New Light" among Presbyterians and an acclaimed preacher of the Awakening, was chased from his pulpit at Northampton, Massachusetts, in 1750 for chastising the frivolities of his congregation. By then, public patience with even this brilliantly original theologian had begun to wear thin. Edwards retreated to a ministry among the Stockbridge Indians where, to his mind, he found converts emerging from the outer darkness of aboriginal sin and waywardness. In 1757 he became Princeton's president, and although he died only a year later, his late mission to the Indians had left a lasting impression on faculty and students.

In emulation, Reverend Dr. Wheelock and others proposed to alleviate the endemic violence and immorality of the frontier by educating Indians in a Bible-centered Christianity. He contracted with the General Assembly of the Province of Massachusetts Bay in 1761 to create a school where he would "teach, clothe and board six children of the Six Nations" for £12 per child per year. The school, established at Lebanon, was to be called Moor's Charity School and undertook to instruct both Indians and white students in courses of study appropriate to an educated eighteenth-century male. Kirkland, from nearby Norwich, studied Latin grammar, Greek, and theology under Wheelock. To help defray the costs of his education, he also assisted in instructing students—most of whom were seventeen or older. Kirkland was already committed to missionary work among the Indians and delighted to meet young Mohawks from Canajoharie who had been sent on to Moor's at Sir William Johnson's expense. Joseph Brant, Molly Brant's brother and protégé of Johnson and Tiyanoga, was instructed in English, Latin, and other matters by Kirkland in exchange for Brant teaching him Mohawk. Thus it happened that the future guerilla leader of the Tory cause in New York studied at Wheelock's under the man who some day would lead the Oneida nation out of the Iroquois League and into alliance with the patriots. But this lay far ahead in 1761, when Kirkland traveled with Brant to Tenonanatche as a guest of Sir William and his Mohawk mistress, Molly.

Johnson, always a staunch Anglican, distrusted New England's Puritan evangelism, but Johnson also fervently supported the education of Native Americans in arts and sciences and had been unable to found a comparable school in the Mohawk Valley. To achieve this second aim, he was willing to compromise the first—that being the independence of New York from Puritan influence. His respectful reply to Wheelock's report on the young men survives:

> Reverend Sir,
> I am pleased to find the lads I sent have merited your good opinion of them. I expect they will return, and hope will make such progress in the English language, and their learning, as may prove to your satisfaction and the benefit of the Indians, who are really much to be pitied.[7]

That the Indians "were much to be pitied" inspired Kirkland's choice of vocation. But what to do about the misery and squalor of the frontier was another matter. Reverend Wheelock's perception of Native Americans could not have been more unlike Sir William's, especially in its unquestioning assumption that his Mohawk pupils were emerging from darkness.

Wheelock's program of study did not offer the standard academic fare that Catherine Weisenberg's children were receiving in New York and Philadelphia; the Wheelock approach required scholars to plant corn, till the earth, and gather its fruits while pursuing their studies. This practical training, so seemingly sensible, infuriated Indian students, who bore the largest share of manual work. Agricultural labor was odious and demeaning to Iroquois warriors. Their tribes relegated planting and harvesting to women. The forest people of North America were hunters and gatherers, and while the men were intended to pursue game for meat and pelts, women were expected to plant and gather the "three sisters"—corn, beans, and squash—feeding and nourishing the family. For Wheelock, the warrior's traditional role seemed a "savage indolence," and every effort was to be made to suppress it in the interest of farming.

Iroquois at Moor's Charity School were thus generally unhappy, and they sent their complaints to Degonwadonti—Molly Brant—their bridge between the two worlds.[8] Yet Molly also realized with Sir William that the forests of New York, Pennsylvania, and Ohio had no more than a century to live at the present rate of settlement. What would become of Indian peoples when game was no longer hunted and land was parceled and enclosed? As an adopted Mohawk, Johnson shared his brothers' passion for a free and unrestrained life, while also apprehending as a colonial leader the growing threat to their survival. What he did not possess—nor did anyone at this time—was a theory for explaining the complex differences between societies at varying stages of industrial development. Where Johnson responded viscerally to the Indians' plight, Wheelock relied on religion to provide a schematic of redemption—native peoples were expected to earn their salvation by the sweat of their brow.

For tasting of the forbidden fruit, Adam receives his condemnation: "Thou shalt eat the herb of the field; in the sweat of thy face shalt thou eat bread, till thou return unto the ground." Genesis ordains that humanity will work the soil, and this judgment in Wheelock's view was processing relentlessly across the globe. As wilderness fell under the axe of civilization, the wild animals sustaining savage life vanished everywhere, for such indeed was the divine plan. Only a shortage of tillers had allowed forests and wild animals to multiply, but a life lived hunting those creatures was doomed to impoverishment and bestiality. Progress meant subduing wild Nature and erecting in its place the towns, factories, and farms of pious industry. When Kirkland taught Joseph Brant the parts of a plough, he was preparing to carry into the wilderness a life-giving program intended to forever change the Indians of Tenonanatche.

Of course, Sir William also knew that the Indians would have to change, but his vision was based more on an appraisal of emerging economic conditions than on insights of revealed religion and divine eschatology. As Jonathan Edwards once said of Johnson, he was "a man of not much religion," but then Johnson did love his neighbor as himself. He could work with Wheelock and Wheelock's disciple, Kirkland, but he was under no illusions about how radically inappropriate their faith would prove on the frontier.

The New Englanders, he complained, tried "to abolish at once the Indians most innocent customs, dances, and rejoicings at marriages." This did nothing to improve Indian manners, but "exchanged natural morality for a set of gloomy ideas." Raised a poor Catholic boy in County Meath, Johnson had felt the stifling discrimination inflicted on Ireland by absentee Protestant landlords. Now he sensed how New England's Indian program denied the intrinsic worthiness of Native Americans in favor of their subordination. Indeed, Johnson could work with Kirkland and help him to survive his first mission to the Indians, but his true views concerning the undertaking he confided to paper, not to the young missionary:

> From these Congregationalists, the Indians imbibe an air of the most enthusiastical cant ... intermixed with the greatest distortion of the features and zealous belchings of the spirit, resembling the most bigoted Puritans, their whole time being spent in singing psalms amongst the country people, whereby they neglect their hunting and most worldly affairs, and are, in short, become very worthless members of society.[9]

What shines through notices of Kirkland's beginnings is a strong conscience combined with pragmatic resourcefulness. His independence of mind and self-reliance enabled him to do what few others could—penetrate the wilderness alone with Bible in hand. "He was trained, like other Puritan boys of the time," Lothrop remembers his grandfather, "to habits of industry and self-dependence. As Cotton Mather wrote of Thomas Hooker, so it may be said of him, that 'he was born of parents that were neither unable nor unwilling to bestow upon him a liberal education; whereunto the early, lively sparkles of wit observed in him did very much encourage them.' His natural temper was cheerful and courteous; but it was accompanied with such a sensible grandeur of mind as caused his friends, without the help of astrology, to prognosticate that he was born to be considerable."[10] His friends little imagined what trials lay ahead for Samuel or how the New York frontier would assault his "sensible grandeur of mind."

Johnson, meeting him for the first time in the early 1760s, sensed that there was something in him to be studied, something new and challenging to the old order of affairs. To be sure, Kirkland's mind was conditioned by an excellent classical education, but much about his outlook derived from the Great Awakening, that potent mass movement just beginning to affect the interior of the colonies. His fervor and determination reached beyond Johnson's experience of sectarian strife and interdenominational rivalry. Indeed, this religious revival of the mid-eighteenth century arguably advanced core values of revolution. By stressing personal salvation over conformity to authority and freeing believers to feel their religion experimentally, the Awakening encouraged a spirit of individualism. This helps to account in part for Kirkland's astonishing self-reliance and inner-directedness. Guided only by his own religious compass, he is able to exist independent of forces surrounding him and to pass unscathed through harrowing ordeals. In some measure he relives the intense dedication of Canada's early Jesuit fathers to the spiritual enlightenment of their charges. In a time of trial, his purity of mind is like theirs, and it is this total devotion to others that saves his life.

To reach the Senecas of west-central New York was to go deep into Indian territory, miles beyond Onondaga or the nearest white settlement on Tenonanatche. This was to be Kirkland's first mission, paid for by the Society in Scotland for Propagating Christian Knowledge and proudly announced by Wheelock to the Countess of Huntingdon, also a sponsor, in 1765:

> A very young English gentleman, Samuel Kirkland, I sent last fall to winter with the numerous and savage tribe of the Senecas, in order to learn their language, and fit him for a mission among them; where no missionary has hitherto dared to venture. This bold adventure of his, which, considered in all the circumstances of it, is the most extraordinary of the kind I have ever known, has been attended with abundant evidence of a divine blessing.[11]

Samuel sensibly approached this long mission in stages by first visiting Johnson Hall and availing himself of Sir William's help. "November 16th. 1764. Arrived at Johnson Hall," he notes, "Kindly and politely received by Sir William, who expressed his approbation of my design & wished me success. When I returned from Onohoghgwage [Oquaga] would have me come to his house, & make it my home till I proceeded to the westward."[12] Inserted in the 1801 reconstruction of his *Journals*, this recollection is wrongly dated by several weeks, but reveals how the missionary prepared for his assignment by first visiting Oquaga over the well-beaten trail from Johnstown.

Traveling with an Indian missionary, a Delaware named Joseph Woolley, Kirkland remembers lodging at Cherry Valley, where he was kindly treated by Captain Wells, and of meeting with Colonel Harper of Schoharie, whom he engaged to pilot them on to Oquaga. Along the way Samuel stops at the home of Good Peter, Peter the Minister, an Oneida chief of the Eel clan famed for his Christian piety and intimate knowledge of Indian ways. Now he hears for the first time reservations about his proposed mission. "It is too long, too far to go," Good Peter advises, "for it is also too soon after wars, and the minds of the Senecas have not yet calmed and put the tumults and troubles behind them."[13] In 1801, Kirkland remembered that Good Peter judged his undertaking "bold if not hazardous," and "he wished God the Father & his son Jesus Christ to be with me and protect me, as I was professedly going to publish the good news of his gospel."

The mission, in fact, alarmed Good Peter, who might have elaborated at length on why it was being mounted at the worst of all possible times. But Johnson, for his own reasons, welcomed Kirkland back from Oquaga and prepared to help him on his way. The missionary was outfitted for winter travel with warm gear, provided with reliable Seneca guides, and armed with letters to leading Iroquois sachems. One in particular recommended that the people of Kanadasegea hearken to Kirkland's message and learn from his words. Yet, elsewhere, Johnson confided his doubts about any missionary activities. "Europeanizing the Indians," he wrote, "should wait until they discover superior advantages in our way of living than in their own, which, as yet they do not. The forest nations do not find reassuring the example of New England's domesticated tribes, who had become Christianized and in some measure civilized. ... They are poor, abject, full of avarice, hypocrisy, and in short have imbibed all our vices without any of our good qualities, and without retaining their former abilities for gaining a subsistence in the only way they conceive that Nature intended they should."[14]

Nonetheless, while Kirkland weathered-over at Johnson Hall, Sir William filled his head with the things he would need to know to succeed among the Senecas. He explained, according to Kirkland, that it was "extremely difficult, if not impossible, to trace their customs to their origin or to discover their explication." He also advised, according to the missionary, "by no means to ridicule any of the traditions of their fathers till I was master of their language, and then I might take them up gently and on rational grounds."[15] Clearly, Johnson did all that he could to prepare Kirkland for his mission. "Extraordinary attentions," is the how the missionary describes his arrival and reception at Johnson's home; "he would have me come to his house and make it my home till I proceeded westward."

Johnson Hall, at present Johnstown on the Mohawk, had only recently been completed—a Georgian-style mansion of wood fashioned to appear as stone. Complete with formal gardens, well-appointed rooms, an impressive library, and lit by rows of windows opening outward from the interior onto prospects of well-manicured grounds, the Hall was like no other structure on the frontier. Nine miles east along the Schenectady road stood Fort Johnson, a stone house also in the Georgian manner, which had been Sir William's previous residence. This house was forted-up with adjacent ramparts and, like Johnson Hall, flanked by defensive positions. Small windows gave onto its beautifully proportioned rooms, but gun loops encircled the heavily timbered attic, permitting a small troop of men to beat back attacks from the surrounding forests.

Fort Johnson had been Catherine Weisenberg's home until her death in 1759. Caty was Johnson's long-time mistress and mother of the children he would claim as legitimate heirs. Johnson Hall, however, was the domain of Molly Brant, sister of Joseph Brant, Degonwadonti to her Mohawk people, and Johnson's aid, comfort, and mistress until his death. She ran the household at Johnson Hall, providing prodigious quantities of food and drink for Sir William's many guests. The scale of the hospitality is described by Judge Thomas Jones, a guest at the Hall who was also Justice of the Supreme Court of the New York Colony:

He [Johnson] had besides his own family, seldom less than ten, sometimes thirty. All were welcome. All sat down together. All was good cheer, mirth, and festivity. Sometimes seven, eight, or ten, of the Indian Sachems joined the festive board. His dinners were plentiful. His liquors were Madeira, ale, strong beer, cider, and punch. Each guest chose what he liked, and drank as he pleased. The company, or at least a part of them, seldom broke up before three in the morning. Every one, however, Sir William included, retired when he pleased. There was no restraint.[16]

"No restraint" was the life Kirkland encountered at Johnson Hall between arriving November 16th and departing with the Seneca guides January 17th. The ever-present Indians overflowed the rooms and passages, camping out in the entry hall to escape the bitter cold. Some were Christians, others not, and many originated in the vast unmapped hinterlands beyond the Ohio River and the sprawl of the frontier. All guests deferred to Molly, who moved gracefully between the gatherings of Europeans and Indians awaiting audiences with Sir William. There was no better place in all British America for a young missionary to meet those who claimed the land by long habitation. But the culture of Johnson Hall—liberal in its frank enjoyment of life's pleasures—must have seemed alien to this son of Norwich, Connecticut, descended from a long line of Congregational ministers. He had the education, determination, and stamina to go among the Indians. But considering his background and his destination, Johnson must have wondered if he would survive the rigors of the journey and the shock of encountering a difficult people.

When Samuel left Johnson Hall, Tenonanatche was blanketed in snow. The party traveled rapidly on snowshoes, each member carrying forty pounds of provisions. Their route lay west along the frozen river toward Fort Stanwix, a crumbling outpost of the French and Indian War. Between Johnson Hall and Kanadasegea (the Seneca castle at the head of Lake Seneca) stretched over 125 miles of icy forest. Tracks were few and Indian villages infrequent. From the moment he turned his back on Johnson Hall, Kirkland entered a primitive world where only the help of his Seneca guides could keep him alive. Years later, he fondly remembered this kindly convoy:

My ankles were swelled not being much accustomed to travel on snow shoes. My convoy were very kind to help me along by going before & making a track for me; this was a considerable relief to me. But if I made a misstep or blundered over a log & fell three or four rods in the rear, they would look back & stop till I came up. ... I presently observed that the second would take the place of the first every three or four miles. I offered to take my turn: no, no, said they, we are to make a path for you not you for us. Sir William Johnson would be very angry if he knew we let you do so.[17]

At Wheelock's urging, the College of New Jersey (Princeton) graduated Kirkland the following spring *in absentia*, but nothing in the curriculum of the divinity school could have prepared their student for the hardship, violence, squalor, poverty, and ignorance that disfigured lives of whites and Indians alike on the New York frontier. Passing through Oneida Castle, many Oneidas expressed their concern for his safety and invited him to come in from the cold and remain with them over the winter. They welcomed missionaries, and any peaceful white men who might teach them crafts of carpentry and iron working. They, too, were a powerful Iroquois nation, but far less hostile than the more remote Senecas. Kirkland's name would eventually be linked indissolubly with the Oneidas, but in 1765 he was determined, so far as his strength permitted, to carry out the mission to Kanadasegea.

Emerging out of the forest in the middle of winter with two Seneca guides and letters from Sir William, Kirkland was welcomed into the large, snow-bound village by a delegation of friendly sachems. His physical comforts were seen to and he was lodged with a respected elder and his family. Kirkland had brought only what he could carry—a few books, his Bible, and a change of clothes. Yet how quickly things turned worse for him, we soon learn:

> Samuel Kirkland knelt and prayed for deliverance by the hut in the woods. The trade musket was flung down at his side, the priming scattered over the sodden leaves. Pursued by the Senecas, he had no chance alone in the forest, and were he to flee, the weapon would be useless to him. Yesterday, the fourth day of his trial, Keneghtaugh led him to the hut, pressed the musket into his hands, and cautioned him to lie still. Now his bag of dried corn was nearly empty, and smoke rose in the damp air over the village of Kanadasegea. On his knees in the rain, the young missionary wondered if the fires kindled were meant for him.

This paraphrase from *Life of Samuel Kirkland*, 1855, written by Samuel K. Lothrop, Kirkland's grandson, dramatizes the critical moments. Forty-seven years had passed since the missionary's death in old age, and the grandson drew on his grandfather's journals as well as family anecdotes to enshrine the experiences of this patriot hero for a new century. Samuel's trial by the Seneca Council at Kanadasegea occurred in February 1765. He was twenty-three years old, and we must assume, despite the measured tones of the 1801 *Journal*, frightened stiff. The charge for which he stood trial was murder by witchcraft.

While Samuel waits, watching the deer trail to the hut for a sign, his trial at Kanadasegea proceeds. First, his accuser interrogates the widow of the deceased.

> "Did he never come to the bedside and whisper in your husband's ear, or puff in his face?"
>
> "No, never," she replies, "he always sat or lay down on his own bunk; and in the evening, after we were in bed, we could see him get down on his knees and talk with a low voice."[18]

The accusation had been occasioned by the sudden death a week before of his host, the elderly sachem. The old man had always been well-disposed to the English, especially to Sir William. He represented a faction, therefore, loudly decried by traditionalist Senecas who tended to favor the French. Yet, were Kirkland to be found guilty of the sachem's death by magic, he would almost certainly burn at the stake for the crime—purging the village thereby of an unwelcome English influence. The Senecas, like other nations of the Iroquois Confederacy, could not conceive of incarcerating malefactors, of depriving even criminals of their freedom. They lived with few punishments, but those few, when inflicted, were severe. They might burn war captives to test their warrior mettle or to revenge harms done; they almost always burned witches to rid tribal lands of doleful influences on crops, weather, and the collective health.

Mary Jemison, in a famous instance, was captured in 1758 by a mixed party of French soldiers and Shawnee and Seneca warriors. While they killed and scalped her family, other settlers taken in the raid on Marsh Creek, Pennsylvania, were burned. "I saw a number of heads, arms, legs, and other fragments of the bodies of some white people who had just been burned," Jemison wrote. "The parts that remained were hanging on a pole, which was supported at each end by a crotch stuck in the ground, and were roasted or burnt black as coal."[19]

But this was not to be Jemison's fate; she was traded at Fort Duquesne (Pittsburgh) to a Seneca band. When she arrived at their village, she entered the real world of the Seneca people. They clothed and nourished her, adopted her into the tribe and renamed her Dehgewanus, "Two Falling Voices." Mary observed that, for all the ferocity of the warriors, Iroquois women exercised decisive power over the conduct of their tribes. In time she would marry a Seneca, lose him to illness, and freely marry a second. She bore her husbands eight children. Jemison was living at Little Beard's Town, present-day Cuylerville, New York, when Kirkland came to Kanadasegea. They did not meet until fourteen years later, when he was chaplain to the army that burned her village.

As credulous and violent as the Senecas could be, they consistently demonstrated a great generosity toward those who came to them weak, hungry, or ill. For they, too, were frequently hungry and often ill from inexplicable diseases that arrived with the white men. After decades of fur trapping and slaughter of forest animals to feed invading armies, game was scarce in central New York. The winter of Kirkland's arrival was unusually severe. Flooding from the abundant snow had swollen the rivers and streams to overflowing, and croplands and orchards were carried away on the brown, rushing waters. Many died at Kanadasegea in the worst of the cold, and the prospects for a spring harvest were poor. Yet, even though he brought nothing but books and a letter from William Johnson, the missionary was welcomed into the village.

For several weeks he lived and ate with the family of the old sachem, opening his books to them, sharing the message of the gospels. As he began to grasp the rudiments of their language and impress on them the sincerity of his purpose, this terrible thing occurred. The old chief, not in the best of health, died abruptly in his sleep. Slowly, Kirkland realized the terrible predicament this left him in. Forty years later the words of his *Journal* recapture the dawning fear:

> The next day by noon, there was a considerable collection of the friends of the deceased & they began their council. I soon found by prudent enquiry, that the circumstances of this man's death had given a general alarm; & that there was a party rather unfriendly to me who intended to charge it upon me.[20]

This was the peril Good Peter had anticipated at Oquaga; Kirkland might not seem a very credible witch, but he had become a symbol of the long English arm intruding into the ancestral ways of the Senecas. To the superstitious, he had been placed at Kanadasegea by the Great Spirit as a warning.

But let's look at Kirkland's actions from another point of view. He had emerged from the forests in midwinter for no practical reason. True, he had a letter of introduction from Warraghiyagey, Sir William Johnson, the Crown's Superintendent of Indian Affairs. He had been brought westward over the Iroquois trail by two Senecas friendly to Johnson. Still, he had no reason to be in Kanadasegea. He had not come to trade. He had not brought gifts. He was not passing through to Niagara or Oswego. He had come out of the snow and bitter cold of the year's long night to stay among them and read his Book. His accuser, Onoingwadekha, speaks before the council:

> Brothers, it is time we were roused up. The late event is a warning to us. We must look about & look forward & see what befalls us, if we don't take seasonable care to prevent approaching evils. This white man we call our brother has come upon a dark design, & employed or he would not have traveled so many hundred miles. He brings with him the white people's book. They call it God's holy book. Brothers, attend! You know this book was never made for Indians. The Great Spirit gave us a book for ourselves. He wrote it in our heads & in our minds & gave us rules about worshipping him. ... Brethren, attend! You may be assured that if we Senecas receive this white man & attend to the Book which was made solely for White people, we shall become a miserable abject people. It has already ruined many Indian tribes by embracing what is contained in this book, although they call it God's Book. How many remnants of tribes to the East are so reduced that they pound sticks to make brooms, to buy a loaf of Bread or may be a shirt. The warriors, which they boasted of, before these foreigners, the white people crossed the great Lake, where are they now? Why their grandsons are all become mere women![21]

Kirkland was not allowed at the council, but learned of this speech later from his adopted Seneca father, the head chief Sagwaenwaraghton. For reasons of safety, he burned the original transcript before leaving Seneca lands. In 1801 he was relying on memory to reconstruct it.

The old Sachem dies, according to Onoingwadekha, because the Great Spirit was angry at the chief's hospitality to Kirkland. The fallacy is apparent—*Post hoc ergo propter hoc* (after this, therefore because of this). Yet who will listen to reason, Onoingwadekha calculates. Those who reject the white man's challenge to the self-sufficient ways of an ancient and valorous people will also reject the missionary. The situation grows grave enough by the third day of the council for a friend, presumably Keneghtaugh, to secrete Kirkland away in the woods. A Dutch trader visiting the village translates the terms of the argument for the young missionary, but does not dare be seen with him in public.

In the end, the widow and family of the deceased save Kirkland by not only rejecting the charge of witchcraft before the council, but by testifying to the young man's grace and earnestness. Coming from one of the leading women of the tribe, the testimony strongly opposes those who would question the sachem's judgment or good sense in welcoming into his lodge a young friend of William Johnson. The trial takes six days, collapses into acquittal, and the question remains forever: why was there a trial in the first place?

That some of the Senecas of Kanadasegea were embarrassed by the affair was soon apparent from a request Kirkland received. After the dispersion of the council, a chief took the missionary aside. "Some of us are afraid of writing," he explained, "as it speaks for many years afterward and does not tell what words have been spoken. It would be good for you, when you write to Sir William, as you inform us that you will, to call several of us together and to interpret the words written. This would please us and make our hearts glad."[22]

It is hard to shake off the suspicion that Kirkland's six days of terror at the hands of the Senecas was not just political theater staged for an absent audience. The witch's magic powder that he did not possess, the spell-casting he had not done, the allegations of a sneaking malignity climaxing in an outcry for his death, all played to the fears of a hundred sullen observers filling the council lodge. But it had little to do with Kirkland himself. The trial was a sham intended from the first to remind Sir William Johnson that the great tribe guarding the western door of the Iroquois longhouse—Niagara, Oswego, the Genesee River and all the Finger Lakes linking to Tenonanatche—was not entirely at Sir William's disposal. Nor why should it be?

Several months earlier, the Senecas clashed with the Crown's Indian Supervisor over their refusal to attend a congress at Niagara. Here was another bead strung on the thread of Kirkland's humiliation. It spoke to Senecas of broken promises, murderous deeds, and the abasement of reproach. Kirkland was learning that the so-called American wilderness was not a desert void of past or culture. Though much had already happened, the story was still in the telling. To interfere in its narration, even for the most selfless reasons, could prove abruptly fatal.

Lothrop—grandson biographer, Harvard doctor of divinity, and a leading Boston abolitionist—looks back on the episode and judges the Seneca way of life as doomed by insupportable superstition. Samuel Kirkland was to be commended, therefore, for bringing light to the darkness.[23] In the midst of the first American Century, sentiments like these belonged to the victors—the people called *Bostonnais* by Joseph Brant—who immigrated to New York in swelling numbers after the Revolution. The idea that the old, corrupt province had only been rescued from lasting ruin by a better virtue, a truer adherence to religion, remained inimical to Sir William Johnson's faction, inimical to the Dutch who had raised Albany before there was a Boston, inimical to the Iroquois who had fought bitterly to hold their lands, and inimical to the citizens of New York who struggled for liberty on the bloody fields of the war. Kirkland had been a part of this as his grandson Lothrop could not be. In his 1801 journal, Kirkland declines to judge or moralize. In fact, he admits to not much liking reminiscence:

> I have neglected journalizing the first two years of my missionary life, which I have frequently contemplated, & from doing which, I have often thought no consideration should prevent me. The reviewing, correcting & transcribing those documents appears to me already to be a work of time; it is certainly an irksome & disagreeable task, as it affords very little intellectual improvement of the understanding or pleasure to the heart: to me, individually, it appears as an exhausted subject. ... Yet I am conscious it is a part of my duty; tho' I had rather preach to the Indians a whole fortnight, than journalise for a day.[24]

Unlike the grandson who celebrates a glorious ancestor at a remove from the discomfort, Kirkland still feels the cold, suffers the hunger, and within the constraints of his nature and creed, loves the manifest goodness of the Senecas. No wonder he delays reliving the ordeal at Kanadasegea. The time is gone and forgotten, with all the other passionate disputes of a vanished frontier.

Yet, one dispute in particular had come close to costing the missionary his life, much as Good Peter at Oquaga feared it might. The background of the bitter conflict between Sir William and the Senecas raises interesting questions about Johnson's support for Kirkland's undertaking in the first place.

The July previous to Kirkland's arrival at Kanadasegea, more than 2,000 Indians from as far west as present-day Minnesota converged on Fort Niagara in response to a summons by Sir William Johnson. Some had been active combatants against the British in Pontiac's Rebellion; others had waited and watched in neutrality. Ottawas, Hurons, Chippewas, Potawatomis, Mississaugi, along with representatives of such far-flung Western tribes as Kickapoos, Kaskaskias, Miamis, Sauks, Winnebagos, Dakota and Lakota came to hear the words of the renowned Warraghiyagey. As expected, the Mohawks, Cayugas, Oneidas, Tuscaroras, and Onondagas of the Six Nations were prominently present, with Abenakis, Caughnawagas, Nipissings, and Algonquins from the far north. They all came at the height of summer, when crops were in and hunting done, to hear what offer of peace the British Crown would make and to receive as downpayment on the promises ample gifts of powder and ball, cloth and iron stuffs, trinkets and baubles and rum—all things they craved and were deprived of while Pontiac's Rebellion raged in the west. Johnson's generosity was renowned; he would not let them down.

Some, however, did not come. The Shawnees and Delawares, raiding the borders of Pennsylvania, Ohio, and New York, sent insolent words in the mouth of a messenger: "Although we have no fear of the English and regard them as old women and hold them in great contempt, yet we feel pity for them and if another invitation should come to us, accompanied by presents, begging us to come, we will then do so and perhaps treat for peace with you."[25]

Johnson shrugged and made no reply. But when a runner arrived with a message from the Senecas—the one Iroquois nation conspicuously absent—a deep silence fell upon the crowds at the council fire. His recitation was brief: "We prefer to go our own way. We find the company of our brother Shawnees and Delawares much more to our liking. We will not come."[26]

Though the Genesee Seneca were the refractory party, their attitudes resonated with the tribe at Canandaigua and Kanadasegea. Too late in the day, they thought, for the tribes of North America to treat with those who would only steal their lands anyway and destroy their way of life. Better to cling together now than to be turned against each other and destroyed in detail later. This had been the message of Pontiac, the great Ottawa, to the tribes of the Northwest Territory: "Awaken your French father, Onontio, with the power of your war cry, and he will deliver New France out from the hands of the English into the hands of his Indian children."[27] Several thousand soldiers and settlers had already died on the frontier beneath the tomahawks of this lost cause when Johnson, responding to the crisis, moved to gather the tribes at Niagara.

He could not escape replying to the Senecas. They were a formidable force in the Six Nations' confederacy, and the confederacy was at the center of British efforts to stem the rampages of the western tribes along the wilderness frontiers of New York, Pennsylvania, and Virginia. Johnson's writings and actions suggest that he understood the anguish and anger prompting the Senecas' response. He knew their leaders, had visited and lived in their towns; he spoke their language. But, by the summer of 1764, equivocation in the face of their challenge was impossible.

> These are my words. Tell your chiefs that it is not my wish but my command that they come immediately to Niagara. Tell them that should they delay, I will put out my council fire and I will gather behind me the three thousand British soldiers you see waiting here, and I will march to the Genesee River. It will be too late for them then, for the anger will blind my eyes and I will be deaf to their pleas, and I will destroy every town and every house, and I will destroy every Seneca. Four days is all they have.[28]

On the evening of the third day, the Senecas arrived at Niagara. They brought "fourteen prisoners, along with several army deserters and a number of runaway Negro slaves whom they had been harboring."[29]

Could Johnson have destroyed them, as the Iroquois once eradicated the Eries? Probably not, for even General Sullivan, assigned twice the number of troops by Washington fourteen years later, did little more than chase the Senecas into the forests and burn their villages. Would Johnson's other Iroquois, notably the Cayugas and Onondagas, have turned on their brother tribe, destroying their centuries-old league? Also unlikely, and Johnson had to remember that five years before, in this very place, he had assumed leadership of a British force from a slain professional soldier and, commanding as an amateur, had captured the vital French fort at Niagara only through the help of the Senecas.

He could not destroy them in July 1764, but he could deeply damage their economy and restrict their capabilities, and the Senecas, knowing Johnson, also knew this to be true. Some of their bands had trespassed in bloody forays against the league and against promises of neutrality made to Warraghiyagey.

During Pontiac's siege of Detroit, Senecas under Kyashuta overwhelmed the frontier outpost of Venango. They killed all the captured British soldiers, tied their commanding lieutenant to a stake inside the fort, and tortured him for several days before burning him. Before Lieutenant Gordon died, he was forced to write a letter on Kyashuta's behalf. This denounced the government of Jeffery Amherst for shorting the Senecas of gunpowder and ball, of denying them rum and trade goods, of refusing to turn over captured French forts, of freeing their lands of white encroachment, and of denying them the prisoners they had themselves captured under British leadership. Indeed, prisoners might be put to death, but just as often the young and healthy went to swell the dwindling tribal population. This meant more Indians, and Jeffery Amherst, commanding Britain's American forces, loathed Indians. Kyashuta's charges were just, if his deeds remorseless.

The Seneca bands repeated their triumph at Forts Le Boeuf and Presque-Isle, along the line of communication between New York, Detroit, and the Ohio Valley, and only a few months before the Congress of Niagara, they conspired to destroy a large British detachment on the portage around Niagara's falls. This well-traveled trail between Little Fort Niagara and Fort Schlosser on Lake Erie was the slender thread connecting Ontario and Tenonanatche with the Great Lakes beyond. Over this nine-mile route, goods from the eastern seaboard flowed west to Detroit, while pelts harvested by the western natives flowed back to New York. General Amherst at his headquarters on Manhattan could hate Indians to his heart's content, but only a remarkably dense strategist would overlook their essential contribution to colonial prosperity and, in the autumn of 1763, the economies of both the American colonies and the mother country were foundering under a mountain of debt incurred in the recent French and Indian War. To permit war to flare up again was the height of irresponsibility.

The Senecas, keepers of the western door of the New York longhouse, also kept the Niagara portage. Normally, they protected freight hauled between the lakes and provided the labor to move it. In mid-September 1763, a mixed band of Senecas and Ottawas, possibly under the leadership of Teantoriance, ambushed a wagon train on the portage, killing upward of fifty teamsters. An army detachment rushing to their aid was similarly ambushed. About eighty soldiers were killed and scalped or flung into the boiling Niagara River above the Devil's Hole whirlpool. The Indians closed the nine-mile portage and cut off all communication between New York and the besieged Fort Detroit. Several weeks would pass before British arms again opened the road, but then only at the cost of another dozen lives. Amherst had failed to realize that an exclusively European force could never hope to permanently subdue disaffected tribes within the forest fastnesses of the Northeast. Concessions and alliances were vital. With a total population never exceeding 4,000, the Senecas had defeated British arms and crippled British trade.

A few days before the attack at the portage, Johnson wrung from the Iroquois council at Onondaga the following concession:

To the Delawares on the Susquehanna River, the nearest tribe at war with you, we will send this message: "Cousins, the Delawares, we have heard that many wild Indians in the West, who have tails like bears, have let fall the chain of friendship, and taken up the hatchet against our brothers, the English. We desire you to hold fast the chain, and shut your ears against their words."[30]

To this lukewarm admonition was appended a warning Johnson could not miss:

We do not like to see the redcoat army march through our country and we will watch it carefully. We will not lift a hand against it, but we will watch to see that it does not lift a hand against us. Your foot is broad and heavy. In your passing through this country, take care that you do not tread on us.

There was no way the council at Onondaga could or would discipline the Senecas, and of this Johnson was aware. He could only play for time, hoping that one side or the other would relent and a semblance of peace be restored. The break came before the end of the year—Jeffery Amherst was recalled to London, and Major General Thomas Gage was named in his place. The Congress at Niagara, planned for the following summer, was endorsed by Gage on Johnson's urging. They were grasping at what might be the last opportunity to placate the tribes. To be sure, British forces won battles and held strong points along the frontiers, but no one was under the illusion that they controlled the wilderness or, for that matter, the increasingly restless towns and cities of the seaboard. Here was the reason that Johnson landed hard on the Senecas. They were divisive and dangerous. Among the Iroquois, they had been most swayed by the French. The Seneca towns contained more warriors than all the Iroquois nations combined, and many of these warriors had taken white scalps. Shawnees and Delawares were denizens of the deep western forests; they could be ignored for the time being. But the Senecas on the Genesee River were astride the northern colonies' gateway to the west, perilously close to New York's vital Hudson Valley. They had to be wrenched back to neutrality, and as the congress proceeded to divide and conquer the gathered tribes with special concessions, the Senecas bowed to Johnson's threats. They never forgot them, however, or forgave them. It was in the wake of these events that the not-yet-ordained, twenty-three-year-old missionary Samuel Kirkland arrived at Kanadasegea.

Why did Johnson advance Kirkland's mission knowing full well the troubled disposition of the Senecas? In all likelihood Johnson believed that his name and prestige would protect the young, inexperienced New Englander, and that Kirkland's progress would draw the Senecas back into the English fold. On the other hand, if Kirkland failed, his demise might go far toward dissuading New England's missionaries and divines from meddling further in New York. As it turned out, Kirkland worked his own salvation and, in the end, emerged from his long mission as a brother of the Iroquois League.

He survived the trial for his life in February only to be bushwhacked in April. The snows had abated and the search for food begun along the shores of Lake Seneca. Corn supplies were exhausted, game was scarce, and the tribe was reduced to scrounging nuts and roots from under the snow. "Wild potatoes" they called the bitter black tubers, an inch or so in diameter, dug out of the frozen sides of the riverbanks. On these morsels the young and sick were fed, while the warrior braves ranged far into the forests on snowshoes hunting meat. At the height of the desperation, Kirkland led an expedition back to Tenonanatche begging grain and dried corn, forage for horses, a wagonload of real potatoes from settlers. Returning through melted snow, axle-deep in mud, the party barely reached Kanadasegea as the last food reserves gave out and the village faced imminent starvation. Kirkland was making himself useful in the ways that he knew best, but the antagonistic Senecas were not convinced. Who could say that his preaching and psalm-singing did not bring the famine, that his presence where he did not belong chased the game from the forests? There were dreams; the spirits of the land were uneasy, and some thought the demon missionary was to blame.

When the weather improved, Kirkland liked to ride around the lake on his favorite pony visiting Seneca villages. On one especially fine day he seems to have forgotten where he was, or who he was. Sauntering along alone, talking to the pony, humming hymns, he heard the click of a hammer being cocked behind the trees. Sosone—old and vindictive, implacable in his hatred of white men, a warrior of renowned prowess—lay in ambush for the missionary. Kirkland turns his mount to escape the trap. "Wait. Missionary!" he hears behind him as the pony gains its footing. Glancing back he sees Sosone in the middle of the trail with a musket pointed at his back. The hammer strikes, but the flint fails to spark. Sosone picks at the flint, resets the lock and, aiming once more, cries, "Stop. Stop." Kirkland is gathering speed. He pretends to misunderstand. "Just going around the lake," he shouts back, refusing to spur the pony or hunker down in the saddle—but also expecting at any moment to feel the ball slam between his shoulders. But again the musket fails to fire. Sosone shakes it and flings it into the bushes. The flint was new, the powder dry; the ball should have flown to the victim. In silence he stands watching Kirkland amble around a bend into the woods.

More theater, to be sure, but this time Kirkland is the actor-director. He has faced death like a man three times and refused to cower, refused to run. There is no pure chance in the Seneca view of life; every happening unfolds meaning, and the most dreamlike events unfold the most meaning. The failed ambush is a turning point in the missionary's relationship with the tribe. His would-be killer searches him out in Kanadasegea hours later. He takes the shaken missionary in his arms and, weeping, begs forgiveness. The scales have fallen from the old warrior's eyes; he sees at last how the Great Spirit holds Kirkland under its protection, and he, Sosone, will evermore stand by the missionary's side. Kirkland had found an ally, if not a convert, and thenceforth during his stay with the tribe, he was welcomed into the counsels of the community.

For a year and a half Kirkland lived among the Senecas sharing their hardships, giving back what could be given out of hard work and application. Something about the missionary clearly endeared him to his hosts, for they tested his human qualities in ways that Johnson knew they would. They searched out and found the strength of the man's heart. Kirkland was initiated into the tribe at Kanadasegea becoming, as other white people had before him, a brother of the Senecas. Henceforth, he was to be treated as a citizen of the Six Nations. He had been given a key to Tenonanatche and the Iroquois lands beyond. But what these rites entailed, Kirkland never revealed. "Speak only of them to Warraghiyagey," the chiefs had counseled, "and if questions occur to you about Iroquois matters, also speak only of this to your white brother."[31]

The strain on the missionary had been severe. For eighteen months he lived entirely as the Seneca did, seldom seeing or speaking with outsiders. What he needed to grasp, and soon did, was how essential the harvesting of the forests were to the Native Americans of the Northeast. Food was not the only issue; trading furs with the French Canadians, the Dutch, or the English in exchange for manufactured goods continued to be essential to Indian peoples. This lucrative trade, like any other of long standing, had grown devious and corrupt. Senecas might trade for pelts at Niagara with impoverished western tribes, then trade these pelts for higher profits with the Dutch at Albany, with Sir William on the Mohawk or, at the right price, with the French at Montreal, from where the pelts might still reach Dutch hands, smuggled up Lake Champlain to be exchanged for superior English manufactured goods. No Europeans could reach deeper into the interior than the French, and inland these English goods gave traders a marked advantage. Sharp dealing had not ended with British General Wolfe's capture of Quebec in the French and Indian War; if anything, the trade wars of the interior had grown more intense. This was the background, not the substance, of Kirkland's concern. Trade was Sir William's lookout. Families destroyed by alcohol, torn apart by the endemic violence of the frontier, sunk in poverty and illness became Kirkland's. The Senecas found that they could believe him. That is, they believed in him, because he took nothing from them even in their weakest hours.

What they had to offer, without his having to ask, was sex. Jesuits, decades before Kirkland, had also been greeted eagerly by the young women of the tribes. How they managed these attentions is not mentioned in *The Jesuit Relations*. Missionaries found the situation tricky. The "dusky ladies" of eighteenth-century erotic imagination were often as not Iroquois women permitted by the community to share their bodies with visitors. Johnson must have explained these realities to Kirkland. The Iroquois were not a promiscuous people; rape was infrequent among them, and however cruel they might be to their prisoners, they did not abuse them sexually as white soldiers often did. An Iroquois warrior did not take a wife, indeed could not, until about his thirtieth year. Celibacy, it was believed, enhanced strength, and only after men had passed their physical peak as fighters and acquired a modicum of wealth would they decline into matrimony. The young women of the village in the meantime were free. There was no stigma attached to pregnancy out of wedlock, for tribal membership descended in the matrilineal line. A child born would belong to its mother's clan—Wolf, Turtle, Bear—whether the father was an Iroquois or a white. Births among Native American populations barely kept pace with deaths.

Traders, trappers, French *coureurs de bois* who went among the tribes of the *pays d'en haut*, the interior, usually took Indian wives as a matter of course. To do otherwise, whatever the dismay of outraged Christians in the settlements, was to draw suspicion on oneself. All along the Mohawk the colliding cultures mingled, and so quite naturally did people. A dense network of kinship resulted from the relationships and would someday turn a rebellion-grown-civil-war into a brutal family fight. But how, in 1765, did Kirkland manage this challenge? His journal does not tell. Lothrop, a clergyman in Boston a century later, seems unable to grasp the situation. For him, as he tells his grandfather's glorious story, the Indians are skulkers, vicious villains, heathens or savages—epithets his grandfather would never have used. By Lothrop's time, the forest Indians' dignity had vanished with the forests. But one relevant item does appear in the tissue of the account. When Samuel returned as a missionary to the Oneidas a few years later, he made it his business to order up a suitable wife from Wheelock. He did not go into the wilderness alone again.

Here is how Johnson saw the long mission end. In the early summer of 1766, a party of three appeared on the road from the west—two men walking beside a woman on a tired horse. All three were gray with dust, unrecognizable until he met them at the door to the Hall. "My God, Mr. Kirkland," he exclaimed, "you look like a whipping post, scarred all over and thin as a rail."[32] The missionary arrived with an adopted Seneca brother and the brother's sister-in-law, who was suffering the last stages of consumption. They had come to Johnson Hall to find her help. Kirkland was clad in shreds of clothing, half-naked under the dust. Johnson rushed to wrap him in a new blanket, warning him, "Don't give it away! And don't give it back after you're done."[33]

The sick woman was brought into the Hall and a physician sent for, even though one look told Sir William that there was little chance of arresting the disease. Tuberculosis was grown epidemic among the Iroquois in the aftermath of the starvation winter. He saw that the men were fed and the woman made comfortable, and through his couriers sent word requesting that the woman's husband come to Johnson Hall. He did not arrive in time. She died in the drawing room attended by Molly, Kirkland, the brother-in-law, and Johnson's physician. At a point, Johnson was compelled to leave the room, tears coursing down his cheeks. "I have never seen anything so sad," he confided to his journal, "as this pitiful death."

What a strange interlude Kirkland's return provides. Nothing explains why the death of the young woman so strongly affects Johnson. He had lived on the frontier through savage wars, witnessed great suffering, and himself was no stranger to death. Yet, by the time Kirkland comes out of the woods, the ground is beginning to shift under Johnson's feet. He was fifty-four and a battered survivor. He suffered from a multitude of maladies, while the musket ball still in his hip from the Battle of Lake George continued to cripple him in cold, damp weather. The more surprising it is then that this deathbed scene moves him to flee the room. The relationship between

Kirkland and the sister-in-law, or between the missionary and his Seneca brother, is never made clear. Johnson provided the Seneca brother-in-law and the woman's husband and family with mourning garments and paid for the woman's obsequies. As for Samuel, Johnson put the young man up at the Hall until he was strong enough to continue home to Connecticut.

Not long after, in the uproar caused by the Stamp Act, the Crown received a charge brought by the Reverend Samuel Kirkland, missionary resident among the Oneida tribe, that Sir William Johnson had prejudiced Indians against New England's Congregationalists by alleging that they had killed their king. The king in question was Charles I, beheaded in 1649, and Johnson, Kirkland alleged, well knew with what indignation Indians viewed regicide and other crimes committed against the natural order. Sir William replied in a hearing held before the Board of Trade that he always suppressed references to disunity and division among the king's subjects when treating with the forest peoples. He worried lest they "interest themselves in the affair, or fall upon the inhabitants in revenge for old frauds." Kirkland withdrew his accusation, and the matter sank out of sight by 1771 as a petty squabble between Anglicans and Congregationalists. In truth, however, the lines had been drawn, and Kirkland and Johnson would never again be on the same side.

Divisions among the king's subjects in the Mohawk Valley were already dividing Johnson's Scots-Irish, Herkimer's Palatine Germans, Kirkland's New England settlers, and Tryon County's Albany Dutch. The Iroquois watched all closely, and then, in the most traumatic moment of their history, also split apart as an angry Mohawk chieftain kicked apart the eternal council fire at Onondaga. Because of Samuel Kirkland's successful ministry among the Oneidas during the 1760s and 1770s, that tribe, with its cadet branch, the Tuscaroras, largely supported the patriots during the Revolution. In an address to Congress in 1775, Washington recognized Kirkland's contribution: "I cannot but intimate my sense of the importance of Mr. Kirkland's station, and of the great advantages which have and may result to the united colonies from his situation being made respectable. All accounts agree that much of the favorable disposition shown by the Indians may be ascribed to his labor and influence." The respectability of which Washington spoke was Kirkland's appointment to head of the Oneida Scouts in the Continental Service. He would become brigade chaplain to General John Sullivan by 1779 and accompany him on the Susquehanna campaign.

Kirkland, as Johnson probably supposed, had proved a harbinger of the revolutionary spirit. Certainly, New York politics were sufficiently corrupt, Johnson had reason to know, but whether independence served the Indians better than loyalty to Britain, he hotly disputed.

As for the Oneidas, they did indeed provide a slender edge for the Americans in the decisive battles of 1777. But in the Tory warfare that followed, they suffered terribly for breaking the unity of the Iroquois League. Other Iroquois followed Joseph and Molly Brant, the family of Sir William Johnson, and Anglo-Catholic settlers on

Tenonanatche into alliance with the Crown. These Tories would invade the new state repeatedly from Canada to exact revenge on patriot neighbors who had confiscated their property. By the end of the Revolutionary period, two-thirds of Tenonanatche's homesteads lay destroyed or abandoned, and three-quarters of the population had fled from the violence or died in the raiding.

New York, the state with more Revolutionary War battle sites than any other, became the scene of the Revolution's most copious and tragic bloodletting. Nowhere else in the colonies did an array of antagonistic factions align themselves against each other with such ferocity. Beyond the politics of national and regional allegiances, upstate New Yorkers fought a war of cultural boundaries determined by ethnicity, religion, and tribe. At moments in the War for Independence, New York's strife coincided with the greater effort of the united colonies; at other moments, it was a blind and savage slugfest between families and neighbors.

The presence of the Iroquois nations in the middle of the future state also contributed to the fierce racism of both sides. Tory rangers, white children of the Mohawk Valley, painted themselves as Indians and punished their rebellious neighbors just as the real Indian warriors did—they took scalps. Thus, when the valley's patriots marched with General Sullivan into the heart of Iroquois country on a campaign of extirpation, they flayed their fallen enemies in one instance and made leggings from human skin. Violent retribution continued longer in New York than elsewhere in the colonies, extending beyond the War for Independence even to the War of 1812. Nor would outbursts cease until all sides were exhausted. By then, the old province was gone and a new place discovered unlike anything Tiyanoga and Johnson, Weiser and Kirkland, the Brants or the Butlers had ever known.

In hindsight, the dress rehearsal for the Battle of Oriskany was Johnson's Battle of Lake George. At that time, the decisive power in the forests clearly belonged to the tribes. After Oriskany and Saratoga, that power was broken forever. Iroquois could raid New York, but increasingly could not live in New York. This came to pass in a single generation and is the story of the next section.

Sauvage Iroquois. Throughout the seventeenth century, the Iroquois were a constant torment to French settlers in New Canada. Note this warrior's tomahawk, pipe hatchet, and war club. *Courtesy of Ron Toelke.*

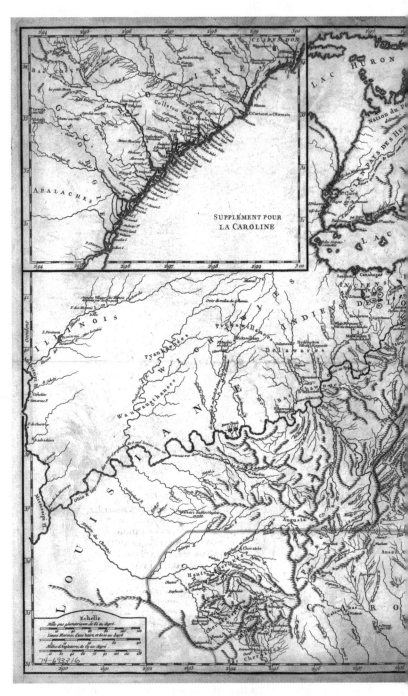

A French map from 1755 shows New France, the English colonies and the

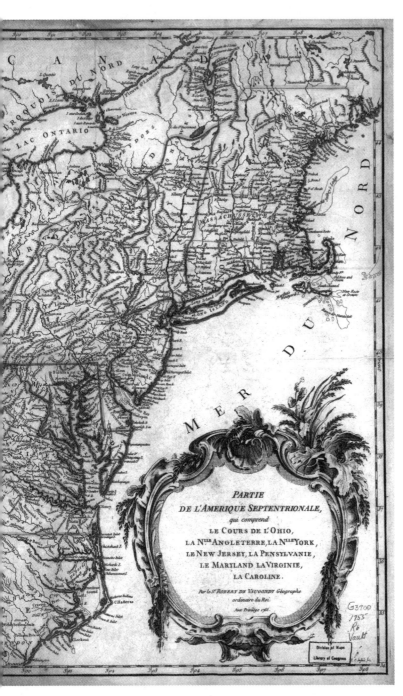

Ohio country at the start of the French and Indian War. *Library of Congress.*

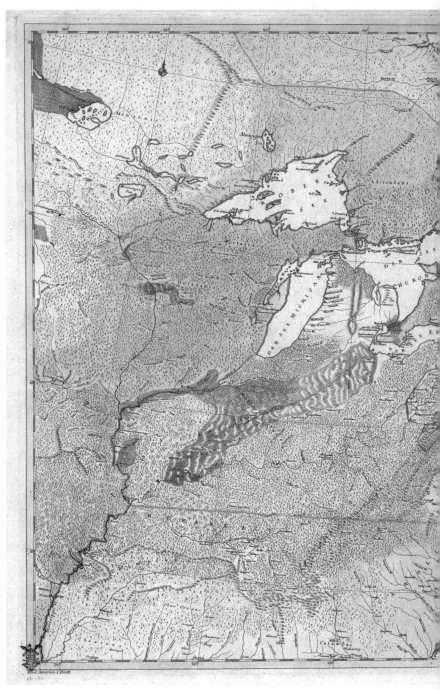

Mid-eighteenth-century German map of the northern and mid-Atlantic

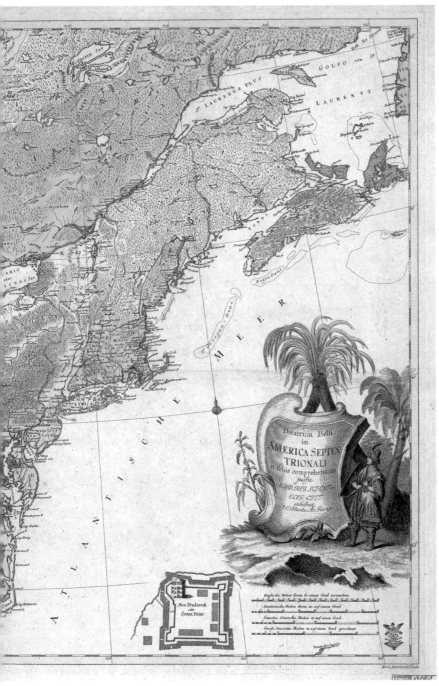

colonies, New France, and the western regions. *Courtesy Randy Patten.*

Sir William Johnson. Copy by Edward L. Mooney, 1838, of the lost original by Thomas McIlworth, painted at Johnson Hall in 1763 at the height of Sir William's power and influence. *Collection of the New-York Historical Society. Negative #6871.*

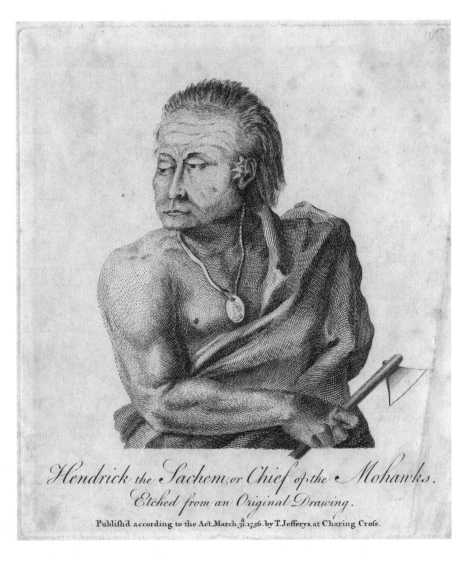

Chief Hendrick (Tiyanoga). The great Mohawk sachem as Sir William Johnson knew him, etched from an original drawing, published by Thomas Jefferys, 1756. *Collection of the New-York Historical Society.*

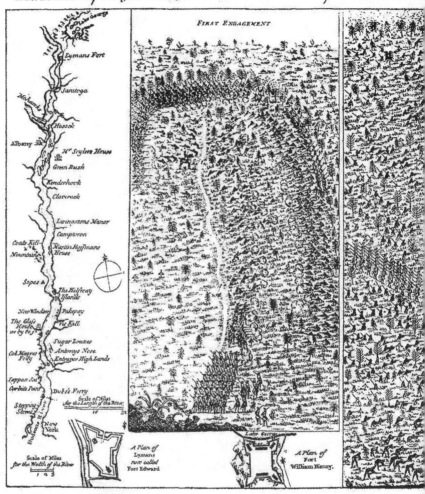

A Prospective View of the BATTLE fought near Lake
under the command of GEN. JOHNSON: 2500 French & Indians under the command of GEN. DIESKAU in which

FIRST ENGAGEMENT

Lymans Fort
Saratoga
Mohawks
Hosock
Albany
Mr. Scylers House
Green Bush
Kenderhock
Clovernck
Livingstons Manor
Camptoron
Coats Kill & Martin Hoffmans
Mountains House
Sopas
The Halfway Islands
New Windsor Pokepsy
The Glass Vis Kill
House 100 by 60
Sugar Loaves
Col. Moores Antonys Nose
Folly Entrance High Lands
Tappan Sea
Corlairs Point Dub's Ferry
Scale of Miles
for the Length of the River
Stepping 10
Stones
New
York
Hudsons River
Scale of Miles
for the Width of the River
1 2 3

Lake George

A Plan of
Lymans
now called
Fort Edward

A Plan of
Fort
William Henry,

KEY TO FIGURES. — First Engagement: 1. The road. 2. French and Indians. 3. Hendrick on horseback.
4. Provincials. 5. Mohawks. Second Engagement: 6. Canadians and Indians. 7. French regulars attacking the
centre. 8. The road. 9. Provincials in action, posted in front. 10. The trees felled for the breastworks. 11. Cannon. 12. A cannon posted "advantageously" on the eminence. 13. Place where Dieskau fell. 14, 15. Canadian's
attack. 16. The man that shot Dieskau. 17. Reserves. 18. Woods and swamp. 19. Morass. 20. Cannon defending
flank. 21. Baggage wagons. 22, 23, 24. Stores and ammunition. 25. Mortars. 26. Road to the lake. 27. Boats. 28.
29. Store houses. 30. Mohawks. 31. Maj. Gen. Johnson's tent. 32. Maj. Gen. Phinehas Lyman's Regiment. 33. Col.
[Christopher] Harris' Company. 34. Col. William Cockroft. 35. Col. Ephriam Williams. 36. Col. Timothy Ruggles. 37. Col. Moses Titcomb. 38. Col. Guttridge [Ellsur Goodrich.] 39. Officers.

A Prospective View of the Battle fought near Lake George on the 8th of September.
Samuel Blodget, a civilian who provisioned military forces, was present at the Battle of
Lake George in 1755 and afterwards prepared these drawings of the Bloody Morning
Scout (left) and defense of the main encampment (right) from his observations. Note

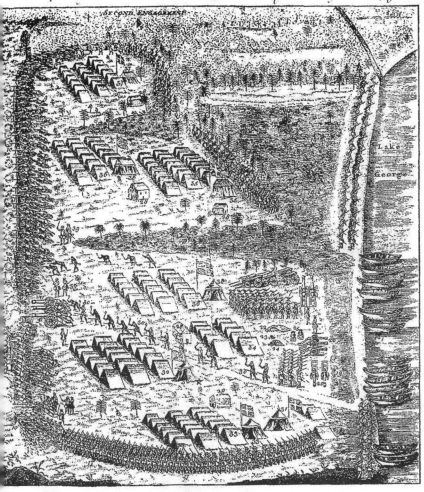

the 8th of Sept. 1755, between 2000 English, with 250 Mohawks.
... torious captivating the French Genl. with a Number of his Men, killing 700 & putting the rest to flight.

★ MONUMENT COMMEMORATING BATTLE ERECTED BY SOCIETY OF COLONIAL WARS IN THE STATE OF NEW YORK, SEPTEMBER 6, 1900

the fishhook shape of the ambush. At far left is a map of the Hudson River from New York City to Lake George, with inset maps of Fort William Henry and Fort Edward. *Courtesy Ron Toelke.*

Samuel Kirkland. Augustus Rockwell's portrait. *Courtesy of the Emerson Gallery, Hamilton College.*

"Good Peter"—Chief of the Oneida Indians (c. 1717–1793). John Trumbull's 1792 portrait of the venerable Oneida sage. *Collection of the Yale University Art Gallery, Trumbull Collection.*

Joseph Brant. This 1786 painting by Gilbert Stuart was commissioned in London by Lord Rawdon. Mrs. Catharine Johns, Brant's youngest daughter, claimed that the portrait was the best likeness of her father. At the time, he was forty-three years old with ten years of warfare behind him. *Collection of the Fenimore Art Museum, Cooperstown, New York. Gift of Stephen C. Clark.*

Johnson Hall (Sir William Johnson Presenting Medals to the Indian Chiefs of the Six Nations at Johnstown, N.Y., 1772). Painted by Edward Lamson Henry in 1903, this dramatic scene of Johnson Hall, the fortified storehouses, and council grounds is an

accurate representation of the many tribal gatherings called by Sir William during the mounting crises of the early 1770s. *Collection of the Albany Institute of History and Art, Albany, New York.*

Sir John Johnson. This portrait by John Mare, a colonial artist active at Albany during the 1760s and 1770s, shows Sir John as a young gentleman. Johnson was thirty-two years old when he acceded to his father's estates several months before the First Continental Congress convened in Philadelphia. *Courtesy of New York State Office of Parks, Recreation and Historic Preservation, Johnson Hall State Historic Site.*

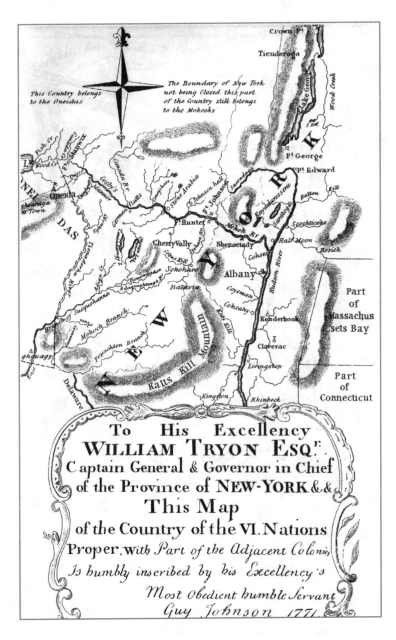

Guy Johnson's 1771 map, presented to Governor William Tryon, shows the vast extent of the newly created Tryon County, with disposition of Iroquois nations relative to settlements much as they were at the outbreak of the Revolution. *Documentary History of the State of New York*, vol. IV.

General Philip Schuyler. Contemporary engraving. A brilliant logistician, the general was often handicapped in the field by chronic rheumatism. *Courtesy of American Antiquarian Society, Worcester, Massachusetts.*

General Peter Gansevoort. Painting by Gilbert Stuart, c. 1794, oil on canvas, 30 1/8" × 25". Gansevoort, age twenty-eight, heroically defended Fort Stanwix during the siege of 1777. He went on to lead New York State levies in defense of Albany during the raids of 1780 and 1781. *Courtesy of the Munson-Williams-Proctor Arts Institute, Museum of Art, Utica, New York. 54.88.*

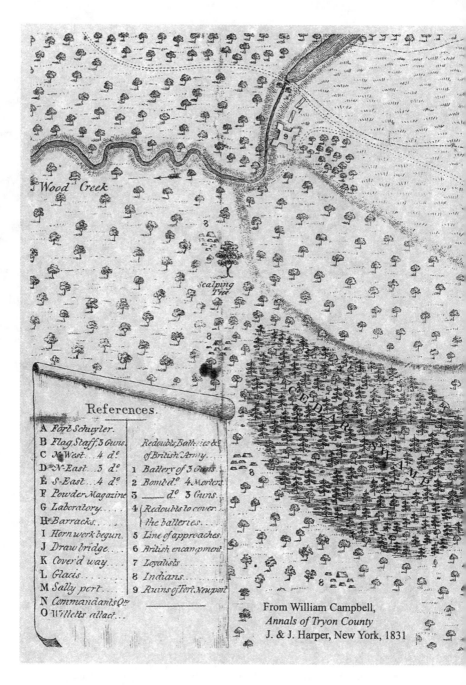

Wood Creek

scalping
Tree

CEDAR
SWAMP

References.

A	*Fort Schuyler.*		*Redoubts Batteries &c.*
B	*Flag Staff 5 Guns.*		*of British Army.*
C	*N. West . . 4 d.º*	1	*Battery of 3 Guns.*
D	*N. East . . 3 d.º*	2	*Bomb d.º 4 Mortars*
E	*S. East . . 4 d.º*	3	*___ d.º 3 Guns.*
F	*Powder Magazine*	4	*Redoubts to cover*
G	*Laboratory . . . .*		*the batteries . . .*
H	*Barracks . . . .*	5	*Line of approaches.*
I	*Horn work begun.*	6	*British encampment*
J	*Draw bridge . . .*	7	*Loyalists*
K	*Cover'd way . . .*	8	*Indians . . . .*
L	*Glacis . . . .*	9	*Ruins of Fort Newport*
M	*Sally port . . . .*		
N	*Commandants Qr*		
O	*Willetts attack . . .*		

From William Campbell,
Annals of Tryon County
J. & J. Harper, New York, 1831

A Sketch of the Siege of Fort Schuyler from Campbell's Annals of Tryon County, 1831.
The location of Fort Schuyler (Fort Stanwix) beside the Mohawk made this west-ernmost defense vital to the protection of the Mohawk Valley. Note the Great Carry

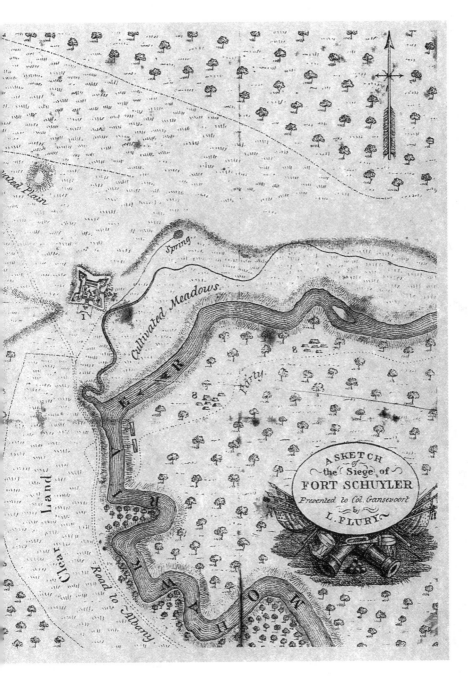

(*Deowainsta*) between the river and Wood Creek directly under the fort's guns. *From* Defenders of Liberty *by Alan E. Sterling (Fort Whitesboro, N.Y.: Mohawk Valley History Project, 2005).*

The Oneidas at the Battle of Oriskany, by Don Troiani. Honyery Tewahangaraghkan receives a loaded musket from his wife, Senagena (Two Kettles Together) in the des-

perate struggle at Oriskany. Behind him, Honyery's son engages the loyalists at his father's back. *Courtesy of Don Troiani, www.historicalimagebank.com.*

Wyoming Massacre. Painted by Alonzo Chappel in 1858, this scene depicts Butler's raiders running amok amid surviving Wyoming Valley militia. The lone Native American is front and center, scalping a fallen patriot. Nineteenth-century viewers took this Indian to be Joseph Brant. Today it is certain that Brant was nowhere

near Wyoming during the July 1778 raid. Of the 232 men captured in arms after the battle, 227 were subsequently killed by the Indians. Total deaths in this frontier disaster may have run as high as 1,000. *Collection of Chicago History Museum. P&S-X.0038.*

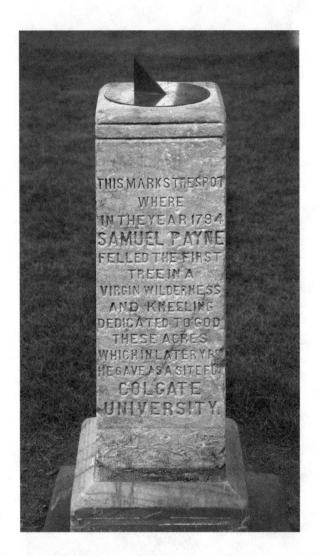

Samuel Payne's Plinth. The plinth stands in front of the Colgate University chapel on College Hill. It is said that Payne knelt in prayer at this spot before felling the first tree of the clearing that would become Colgate's main quad. Payne journeyed to the Chenango Valley in the wake of the Revolution accompanied by numerous families of devout Baptists from Lebanon, Connecticut. *Courtesy of Colgate University.*

Part II

Vale of Nettles

✣ 6 ✣

A Revolutionary Idea

June is usually a beautiful month in the Mohawk Valley, and the June of 1772 was no exception. Late in the month, on a bright Sunday at Johnstown, a long-anticipated public event occurred, bringing together for possibly the last time in one place the principal figures of colonial New York. To the roll of drums beneath waving Union Jacks, the gathered dignitaries of the province laid the cornerstones of a county courthouse and an adjacent jail.[1]

What made these simple acts momentous was the recognition that Johnstown, Sir William Johnson's town, had now become the seat of a new jurisdiction, established the previous March and named in honor of William Tryon, Royal Governor of New York. Tryon County was torn from old Albany County in a move that dramatically shifted the balance of political power. With Tryon's creation, Johnson finally wrested control of New York's northern districts from the hands of the Hudson Valley Dutch. He was content to contribute heavily to the future courthouse out of his own pocket, and was already planning for roads and bridges.

To Tenonanatche was come at last the civic respectability conveyed by public buildings, public works, and established seats in the New York Assembly. Sir William, to be sure, would control these seats; he nominated Guy Johnson, his son-in-law and nephew, for one and Hendrick Frey, a long-time family retainer, for the other. Johnson Hall's nominees invariably were elected in Tryon County.[2]

Johnson did not have to concern himself with votes. In 1770 the New York Assembly had one representative for every 1,065 white adult males, making that body notably less representative than any other colonial legislature.[3] While the colony's population had more than doubled between 1761 and 1771—from 80,000 to over 168,000—suffrage as a percentage of population had actually declined. Only 400 men out of 10,000 adults enjoyed the right to vote on the Mohawk in 1773. In an election for five constables, fourteen electors voted, and all fourteen were allied by interest or patronage to Sir William Johnson. Not surprisingly, all voted for the same candidates.[4] Two years before Lexington, Tenonanatche was sharply divided between those who enjoyed the franchise and those who did not.

New York State has known political bosses down the centuries, but these opera-
tors usually built patronage machines to reward voter turnout. As an appointed official of the Crown and a peer of the realm, Johnson did not answer to an electorate.
Yet, it was in his nature to help his neighbors where he could, and this very generosity tended to focus his vision more on local matters than on the political storms
approaching the colonies. As James Flexner observes, "What the Johnsons were swinging their big stick to achieve were provisions for public buildings in Tryon County,
improved roads and controlled ferry service, curbed 'filthy' swine, exterminated 'hungry' wolves and panthers. Sir William was still using colonial politics altogether for
local ends."[5]

This indeed was a risky course to pursue, considering the vast area Tryon County
encompassed—today's Delaware, Otsego, Herkimer, St. Lawrence, Jefferson, Franklin,
Hamilton, Fulton, Montgomery, and Schoharie counties. Here were a lot of neighbors
to be helped, and many were bound to feel slighted by the great man's attention to
his Indians or support for districts closer to extensive Johnson holdings.[6] If he was
unable to establish a true feudal manor in the interest of his heirs, skeptics quipped,
Johnson had at least found a way to create and control a county larger than the Colony
of New Jersey.

Though Johnson Hall was arguably storing up troubles for the future, little of
this seemed to matter in the high summer of 1772. British flags and a detachment of
redcoats at the site of the new courthouse might have soured the day for proto-patri-
ots, but most guests needed no reminders that only a few short years before, Pontiac's Rebellion had sent them scurrying for cover behind the Crown's defenses. The
colonial frontier then ran through the heart of New York—hundreds of miles west of
Boston's angry citizens. Johnson had negotiated the frontier's location at Fort Stanwix in 1768, and he remained, at least for the western tribes, a visible guarantor protecting Indian lands from white encroachment.[7] As the population of the Mohawk
Valley swelled toward 20,000, white inhabitants and civic institutions took hold in
the more developed districts of the valley, and no merchant, mechanic, farmer, dray-
man, bargeman, or tradesman required to be told that the worst calamity that could
befall burgeoning New York was another Indian war. In comparison, controversies
over taxes and stamps seemed minor issues.[8]

That was then, of course. Sir William was alive, and if a bit old-fashioned in his
political views and scandalous in his moral conduct, still a symbol of King and country to the comfort of his neighbors.[9] They attended his party at Johnstown on June 26
to honor him. Who came and who did not augured much about the future. Samuel
Kirkland and Chief Hanyerry of the Oneida nation were not present, nor was the
Stockbridge sachem, Jehoiakim Mothskin. The aged chief of the Mohawks, Steyawa,
brother to Tiyanoga (King Hendrick), stood proudly at Sir William's side. Gucinge of
the Senecas and Ghalto of the Cayugas came with families, and Rozinoghyata, principal speaker of the Six Nations, arrived with an Onondaga delegation. Several hundred

Native Americans were on hand at Johnson Hall to witness the birth of Tryon County, and to eat and drink at Sir William's expense.

Not least, of course, came William Tryon himself, Royal Governor of the Colony, accompanied by a detachment of officers on leave from General Gage's headquarters in New York City. Livingstons, Van Cortlandts, Van Rensselaers, and Van Schaicks arrived from Albany County to pay their respects. Eminent citizens the length of the valley appeared—Nicholas and Yost Herkimer from German Flats, John and Walter Butler from Johnstown, Anthony van Vechten and Christopher Fox from Canajoharie. Johnson had supported Phillip Schuyler as an assemblyman from Albany, and now Schuyler returned the favor by journeying to Johnstown from his summer home at Saratoga. Such local tradesmen as Jelles Fonda, Peter Bellinger, and Frederick Visscher were invited and came. George Klock was not invited but came anyway, just to heckle the speakers. For more than a decade this old reprobate squatted illegally on lands belonging to the Mohawks. He appears never to have met an Indian he would not cheat or a legal judgment he could not evade. In the following years, Klock and his large family became prominent members of the Tryon County Committee of Safety and persistent agitators for the patriot cause.

But on this summer day, as if by common consent, most visitors put by their discontents and turned from troubling issues. "Regretfully it must be said that the Mohawk was not the place to look for heroes," Isabel Kelsay remarks of that moment. "Its people were wholly absorbed in their small daily ordinariness. It was enough just to make a living, to raise children, to work in the fields, to drink flip in the taverns and sit close by the fire in the long, cold winters."[10] Whatever excitement aroused the valley in 1772 was usually associated more with the founding family gathered on the dais in front of the crowd than with distant rumblings in Boston or New York.[11] The Johnson dynasty seldom gathered in one place, but on this occasion they appeared for all to see.

Sir John Johnson attended the festivities out of filial duty. Catherine Weisenberg's only son, he had become heir to the Johnson title with Sir William's late marriage to his mother. Yet, assuming the baronetcy and family fortune was as far in the great man's footsteps as John was prepared to walk. He had been educated at Philadelphia in the pursuits of a cultured life, and like many young heirs of the century, celebrated his majority with a grand tour of the Continent. In 1768, George III knighted him in his own right, and he returned from London soon after to take up residence at Fort Johnson, the original family homestead. By 1772, John was courting Mary Watts, daughter of a prominent New York family, while also living at Fort Johnson with his mistress, Clarissa Putman, daughter of a local minister. The valley would be scandalized when he packed Clarissa and her two illegitimate children off in 1773 and married Mary. To his father's chagrin, Sir John showed no interest in politics or Mohawk affairs; he rather resented his Indian in-laws and affected the life of a hunting squire. He turned thirty the year of the Johnstown celebration, and if many viewed him as a slender reed on which to rest the Johnson legacy, they underestimated his deep attachment to the valley of his birth. Sir John would prove far more resilient in war than anyone expected.

Guy Johnson, Sir William's nephew from Ireland, had arrived on Tenonanatche at age sixteen. Under his uncle's guidance he rose to civic prominence through hard work and perseverance. Clearly he deserved a place on the dais. By the time of the celebration, he was thirty-two, held a lieutenancy in the British Army, and had already been appointed Deputy Superintendent in the Indian Department by his uncle. As a member of the New York Assembly, he would soon represent Tryon County in Governor Tryon's administration. Guy spoke several Iroquoian dialects and was well received in villages of the Six Nations, where he often represented Sir William in tribal councils. In 1763 he married Sir William's youngest daughter by Catherine Weisenberg, Mary, and took up residence at Guy Park, built especially for the newlyweds on the Schenectady Road.[12]

Sir William obviously had weighed the realities; Guy, not his son John, possessed the training and ability, the winning personality and interest, to replace the Crown's Chief Indian Superintendent. Declining health was much on Sir William's mind in 1772 as his vigor faded and aggravations of his office mounted. Whig agitation, in his view, tended to fuel violations of treaty. The tribes regularly complained to the Indian Superintendent that the Fort Stanwix line was being broken in numerous places by arrogant invaders.[13] Johnson wrote to Lord Shelburne, Secretary of State for the Colonies, that the sachems had warned him sternly "because settlers are not fighting people but traders who would do anything for money ... the tribes well knew their own present strength and capacity to ravage the frontiers ... whilst we can distress them very little."[14] So frightening was the prospect of a patriot rebellion abrogating Indian agreements and igniting an Indian war that the ailing Johnson felt pressed to name a successor who could react quickly to crises.

Among the leading candidates, George Croghan conversed freely with native peoples, but proved too rough-hewn to impress colonial leaders or legislators. Daniel Claus had talent and ability, but his heavy German accent counted against him. Sir John was at home in colonial society, but spoke only halting Mohawk. Guy, who met all the requirements, was a better businessman than leader; he was exceptionally personable, but lacking the political instincts required by an Indian agent in wartime. With the stakes high as they were, and no perfect fit to be found, Sir William resolved that John would have his money, and Guy his mantle. Uneasy though he may have been with this choice, he wrote to Lord Dartmouth of the Board of Trade advising that Guy be confirmed as Chief Indian Superintendent in the event of his own incapacity. One purpose of the Tryon celebration was to introduce Guy in the best of all possible lights to influential New Yorkers.

Playing a supportive role to Guy, and prominent on the platform, was his brother-in-law Daniel Claus. Conrad Weiser had sent the immigrant Claus to Johnson many years before, and through Claus's intelligence and application he had advanced in the Indian Department to become the Canadian Deputy of Indian Affairs. Claus married Nancy, Sir William's oldest daughter by Catherine Weisenberg, and lived in a well-appointed home located between Fort Johnson and Guy Park. He journeyed frequently to Niagara on official business and from conversations with Crown officials knew that if trouble were to come, his Canadian tribes might be called on to open the door for British forces into New England. With no significant British forces across interior New York or New England, and only a few hundred troops in all of Canada, General Gage envisioned such a contingency. He was prepared to use the Crown's Indian allies to suppress civil unrest—a desperate, drastic measure that Sir William would never countenance. But who could be certain about Sir William's successor? No wonder the citizens of the valley watched the Johnson party with the greatest of interest.

They also watched the "brown" Johnsons with fascination. Molly Brant, Degonwadonti to the Mohawks, hovered near Sir William's side. By 1772, Molly knew better than anyone the great man's infirmities, and she worried that the bright June sunlight might be too much for him. Recently they had visited together several curative springs, and she had nursed him with remedies that seemed to bring relief.[15] At Johnson Hall, Sir William's nephew and physician, Dr. John Dease, treated him with exotic imported potions, but the sufferer felt a special regard for Molly's herbs. "There are," he wrote, "many simples in this country which are, I believe, unknown to the learned, notwithstanding the surprising success with which they are administered by the Indians."[16] His need for her had never been greater, and she, having borne him seven children and managed his home for over a decade, was totally devoted. Yet Molly was mindful always of her own people, and they reciprocated her affection by honoring her as the leading matron of the Six Nations. In fact, her fame spread far beyond the Iroquois to western tribes. They were aware how this native woman moved at ease through circles of colonial officials, and many turned to her as an intermediate or advocate. Native Americans viewed Molly as truly married to Sir William by Indian custom; indeed, most whites in the valley thought of her in the same way. She was "Lady" Johnson, not some live-in nurse-mistress. In her own right, she commanded more prestige among the disparate tribes than Guy Johnson, Daniel Claus, or Governor Tryon together.[17]

Joseph Brant (Thayendanegea), Molly's brother, had also turned thirty by the time of the Johnstown celebration and attended the festivities as part of the family. Sir William's protégé, he had been educated at Wheelock's school along with Samuel Kirkland and other soon-to-be missionaries. Like his sister, Joseph moved freely between native and white societies. The closing years of the French and Indian War had schooled him in forest warfare, where in several sharp engagements he had earned the commendation of respected warriors. Yet, while he might take up musket or bow to hunt in the ways of his people, he was usually content to farm his acres in the vicinity of Canajoharie, raise his children, and enjoy the attentions of his wife. He was a devout Anglican during this period, laboring with the Reverend John Stuart at Fort Hunter to translate the Book of Common Prayer into Mohawk, and worshipping at the tiny Indian Church built by Sir William on acres Joseph himself had donated to the parish. By 1772, however, he was at odds with the Reverend Stuart. Early that year his wife, Peggy, had died of consumption, and following Mohawk custom, Brant proposed marrying Peggy's sister—the loving aunt of his children—in services Christian and Mohawk. Stuart objected that, according to the laws of the Church of England, wedding a deceased wife's sister was not permissible; he declined to bless the union. Joseph journeyed upriver to German Flats, found a Baptist minister to perform the service, and married Peggy's sister anyway. He was not one to be easily thwarted in his desires.[18]

At home in the vicinity of Canajoharie, Joseph was known and liked by neighbors of both races; he was thought of as a gentle, courteous man, helpful to all. But where George Klock defrauded and swindled Indians, Brant could lose his temper. Sir William used his influence as Warraghiyagey to see Joseph named "war chief," the highest honor attainable by merit in Mohawk society. In July 1772, Joseph was invited to Johnson Hall as "war chief" to present the Indians' case against Klock to the visiting Governor Tryon. Accompanied by Johannes Tekarihoga, king of the Mohawks, Joseph spoke forcefully against Klock's land schemes and theft. Tryon promised to do all in his power to bring the forces of law down on the culprit, but in a land where Indians could be murdered with impunity and scammed of money due, Tryon's powers, indeed the Crown's powers, were decidedly limited.

Tryon had come to Johnstown to review the Tryon County militia, a force of about 1,400 volunteers notably indifferent to military discipline. Yet, looming even larger than the issue of the militia's poor performance was the question of their loyalty. The treatment of Indians rankled in Joseph's mind, but he foresaw a time when the Crown would need its proven Indian friends and, come that moment, the main bargaining chip in Mohawk hands would be New York's overthrow of Klock and his ilk.

Close by Joseph in the family entourage stood a large, silent, unsmiling man. Joseph and Molly were Mohawk commoners of great intelligence and ability. William of Canajoharie (Tagcheunto), Sir William's son by Caroline, niece of King Hendrick, stood higher in Mohawk society than they and yet was less fortunate. Although recognized by his father and amply provided for, he was often dour, surly, inclined to violence when drinking. At Wheelock's school in 1765, he was required to saddle the horse of Wheelock's son. He refused on the grounds that his father was a gentleman. When asked if he knew what a gentleman even was, he replied that he did—"a gentleman is a person who keeps race horses and drinks Madeira wine, and that is what neither you nor your father do. Therefore, saddle the horse yourself."[19] In time, William was expelled and sent on by his father to Lancaster, Pennsylvania, where he studied in the household of Thomas Barton. There, at local taverns he met buckskinned frontiersmen who boasted of killing Indians. His reply was to break their heads, until at last Barton was forced to send him home again. Back in the valley, William did little but drink. His father threatened to disown him, but never did. Sir William had come to realize that Tagcheunto, unlike his other children, would never reconcile the strands of his lineage; he would always hate whites. At the Johnstown celebration, William of Canajoharie appeared noticeably disinterested in the proceedings.

Towards the end of what had been otherwise a pleasant year, a deep political chill seemed to descend on Tryon County with the onset of winter. Local officials were instructed to require that all free citizens sign a pledge of allegiance to George III and Protestantism by December 8, 1772. The oath began: "I do sincerely promise and swear, that I will be faithful and bear true allegiance to his Majesty King George the Third so help me God." The document rambled on to extract promises never to support Stuart pretensions to the throne, and to uphold the Church of England in America.[20] Ostensibly, this loyalty test had nothing to do with Whigs or republicans and everything to do with the Hanoverian succession. No one was fooled. The Johnson party was acting through the oath to augment its hold on the Mohawk Valley in a time of great economic uncertainty and political turmoil. Many settlers resented the arrogance of the Johnsons, but in 1772 few doubted that they were loyal subjects and true Protestants.

As 1773 dawned, however, the population of the valley was changing. New Englanders, pushing across the Hudson in growing numbers, tended to strengthen the Whig faction and provide fertile ground for radical patriotism. If New Yorkers resented New Englanders, they were even more resentful of the Tory answer to the Puritan invasion. Scottish Highlanders, refugees from persecution by British authorities, had flocked to the valley during the previous decades. Though often Catholic, and once strong supporters of the Stuart cause, the impoverished immigrants were offered homesteads on Sir William's extensive lands. Highland Scots saw eye to eye with Johnson's Irish, and time had shown that they could be loyal subjects to a Hanoverian monarch and no friend to rebels. The problem was that, as 1773 turned into 1774, Highland "ruffians," heavily armed, seemed to appear as if on signal in public spaces where crowds gathered.[21] The Johnson party viewed them as their defense against mob violence, an answer to incessant political brawling in the local taverns. But to valley people, these Highlanders often seemed hired henchmen intent on intimidating any who would speak his mind. In one respect they succeeded. Never during Sir William's lifetime was a liberty pole raised on the banks of the Mohawk.

What brought about the political chill of 1773, impelling Sir William to tighten his grip, was evidence of mounting chaos and anarchy in the colonies. Fred Anderson examines the correspondence of General Gage, commander in chief of His Majesty's forces in North America during this period. Before September 23, 1765, he writes:

> Gage's reports had focused on the west and the problems of imposing order there. After it, his letters thickened with news of riots in the cities and towns of the east—descriptions of what seemed a flood tide of anarchy. This change reflected Gage's amazement at the violence of colonial reactions against what he (like Grenville) saw as incremental additions to the imperial reform program.[22]

Gage indeed was on the horns of a dilemma. He could not afford to garrison the west, maintaining trading posts advantageous to native peoples, without tax revenues raised in the east. Yet these taxes were the very cause of disorder in the cities. Consequently, Anderson writes, "To keep up a symbolic presence in the trans-Appalachian interior was all that Thomas Gage could hope to do after 1765."[23] The Crown's Indian Supervisor would increasingly face the crisis of the frontier alone and without British troops.

Behind Gage's impotence lay the stark fact that Britain's Seven Years War had come near to bankrupting the mother country. As after all wars, those who bled the most only asked that those who prospered the most—rich merchants of Boston, New York City, and Philadelphia—pay their fair share. Taxes would follow undoubtedly, Sir William Johnson assumed, and not merely to recoup expenditures, but to solidify the dependency of the colonies on the Crown. In January 1766 he wrote to Cadwallader Colden, New York's maladroit lieutenant governor, about the colonies' opposition to the new Stamp Act:

> I have not heard anything lately from England, so that I cannot form any Judgement of their Sentiments on the late Affairs here, other than by supposing that they must be greatly enraged, how far this may operate on America, time must Shew. Indeed I am apprehensive that the Scheme here is to stir up the Commonality of England by representing their grievance as equally affecting them, hopeing thereby to effect a Repeal [of the Stamp Act], which from the unsettled State of Affairs at Home they may possibly obtain. I heartily wish the Government may well consider the Point before they give up an Article on which the Dependency of America depends, for that, and not the Stamp Act is now the Struggle, and if England Lets Slip this opportunity they may never meet with such another.[24]

The letter is intriguing for its focus on the "dependence" or "independence" of "America" a decade before the Declaration. What Johnson heard on all sides of the frontier was a clamor for repayment and restitution; not only was he owed a personal fortune by the Crown for expenses incurred among the Indians, but George Croghan and other Indian agents were also begging for reimbursement. Placating Native America was a costly venture, yet skimping on gifts and subsidies had proved costlier still. Jeffery Amherst's stingy policies in the aftermath of the Seven Years War had provoked Pontiac's Rebellion, the frightfulness of which reached deep into New York and Pennsylvania. Raise taxes from the wealthy of Boston and New York City, Johnson believed, or lack the means to govern "America" effectively.

Ten years before, at the close of the French war, Johnson had ridden west on the Schenectady Road to see what had become of German Flats. French raids by M. de Belletre in 1757 and again in 1758 had leveled the villages of Herkimer and Palatine Bridge. Farms on both sides of Tenonanatche had been burned; two hundred settlers had been murdered and at least as many dragged away to Canada. The forts that defended the Mohawk settlements were down, while the forts stretching west to Oswego along Woods Creek, Lake Oneida, and the Onondaga River had been destroyed with great loss of life. Only the Crown could guarantee the security of the New York frontier. As financial ruin forced the discharge of regular soldiers and the abandonment of posts, the restive Native Americans, also impoverished by the war, loomed even larger as a menace to resettlement.

Left without monitors, the mounting pressure of colonial expansion would inexorably lead to bloodier wars, yet the Crown's policing powers were fiscally exhausted. What to do? Help England pay for the prodigious expenses of the Seven Years War and at home shoulder part of the burden of self-defense. But that was unlikely to happen, Johnson apprised Colden in March 1766:

> People here oppose all who differ with the Majority, tho all this Springs from an interested few, yet the many headed Populace Supporting it, neither Governours or anyone else that I can find chuse to enter into the Affair, but rather incline to remain quiet & leave it to time than incur the Trouble & Abuse, with which every Man that differs from the rest is loaded.[25]

The event that sparked this correspondence occurred at Albany in January. A mob, assembled outside the house of Post Master Vanschack, accused him of sending to England for excise stamps. In the ensuing riot, Vanschack was beaten and his house pillaged. The growing anger seemed beyond the power of any governor of New York to address or curb. So far had civil authority fallen in the province that Johnson could joke: "When Doctor Shuckburgh was asked by an Acquaintance if he knew the name of the then appointed Governour 'No faith (says he) nor do I give myself any concern about it, as I shall hear him called Names enough before he is here long.'"[26]

Indeed, the Crown would have its taxes one way or another, and during the next ten years the colonies would move steadily toward independence. The outcome was that, at home on Tenonanatche, Johnson was left to wrestle with ways of preserving tribal hunting grounds with diminishing support from government.

London's so-called Halifax Plan of 1763 had forbidden settlers from crossing the Appalachian barrier into Indian Territory. Lord Halifax hoped thereby to assure peace with the Indians by locking down colonial expansion and guaranteeing the integrity of tribal lands. Nothing would go further toward averting Indian wars than controlling the encroachment of pioneers. Yet the Crown's drastic economies soon dismantled the very garrisons that would be required to enforce the plan. The vast scope of the frontier boggled the minds of planners, for where they saw impenetrable mountains on charts, pioneers on the ground soon uncovered narrow passes through wooded defiles into Ohio and Kentucky.[27] Understandably, the tribes felt betrayed, and again, black smoke from burning homesteads appeared on the horizons. The Halifax Plan was born toothless, but managed to bite everyone.

The Fort Stanwix Treaty of 1768 was Sir William's answer to the containment problem, but even as he hammered out terms with representatives of the Six Nations, the sheer scale of colonial immigration guaranteed a human wave breaking against the boundaries before the ink dried on the document. "People moved," Gordon S. Wood describes, "from village to village, from colony to colony, over distances of ten, a hundred, even a thousand miles. The movement was neither smooth nor orderly, nor was it directed simply into empty or sparsely settled spaces. New people poured into settled areas as others moved out."[28] The quest for cheap land had become a right no government now seemed able to abridge without facing armed resistance. To some, a new nation was forming on the ruins of the old imperial order. In the valley, not everyone saw the logic of this argument, and they bickered over its terms.

Some of the Johnson party just did not get it. "Sir John," Isabel Kelsay writes, "was genuinely bewildered to hear all that talk about liberty. He said he had liberty. Didn't everybody have liberty? Daniel Claus was another man who knew exactly what he stood for. He thought the rebels 'stupid,' and he suggested as early as October 1774 that his Indian charges 'might easily be brought to fall out with them.'"[29] This was almost a full year after the Boston Tea Party had warned alert conservatives everywhere in the colonies that serious trouble was brewing.

While the colonies dissolved into disorder and rebellion, Sir William was preoccupied with conflicts hundreds of miles west of settled American life. Messengers appeared at his door from the banks of the Ohio River with alarming accounts of war between the Shawnee and frontiersmen. Not only was the Treaty of Fort Stanwix in tatters, but Indians traveling along the Ohio were being murdered without cause by white desperadoes. The details of these massacres equaled in savagery any perpetrated against whites, and in reaction the Shawnee now sent to the Iroquois for aid in their war against the settlers. Peace along the frontier was unraveling quickly, Gilbert Simpson informed his employer, George Washington, in early May 1774:

> The country at this time is in great confusion, the Indians declaring war against us. I suppose there have been broken up and gone off at least 500 families within one week past, but I am determined to stand to the last or lose my life with what I have. There have been two or three skirmishes with whites and Indians. There have been 19 Indians killed and one white man killed and one wounded—all between the Mingo Town and Pittsburgh, & I believe it has been the white people's fault altogether.[30]

As Lord Dunmore, Governor of Virginia, set about raising an army to fight the Indians of the Ohio, word also spread to New York of martial law established in Massachusetts. Henceforth, General Gage might quarter soldiers where he pleased, and Gage had begun to concentrate troops in Boston. To placate French Canadians, Britain's Parliament had also passed the Quebec Act, extending the boundary of British Canada to the Ohio and Mississippi Rivers, cutting off colonial land claims in the west. What rankled most in New England and New York, where many had sacrificed during the French and Indian Wars, was the restoration of Catholicism and class privilege in Canada—virtually a return to the status quo of New France. Johnson, who had struggled mightily against this very enemy, must have winced, and yet refused to be broken by bad news. On April 17, 1774—exactly a year and a day before the Battle of Lexington—he wrote that "tumults and disorders have given place to tranquility," and that "the troubles in Boston are not so formidable at bottom as is, I believe, imagined by some people in England."

All this before Michael Cresap killed three peaceable Indians near the Ohio. This inspired his neighbors to invite some Mingos in for a drink, and when the Indians were too drunk to defend themselves, chop mortal holes in the guests, who included a brother and sister of the great Cayuga chief, Logan."[31] It just did not get any worse. In response, Sir William called for a grand council to be held at Johnson Hall on July 11, 1774, inviting all injured parties and advocates, even Mohawks seeking redress for the wrongs done by George Klock.

Actually, the Mohawks had tried to settle the Klock provocations in their own way. A few weeks before, a delegation of twenty braves had visited Klock's house, confronted him over the theft of money from a hapless Indian, and beat him soundly. Joseph Brant was their leader, and before they were done they had threatened to kill Klock and his sons, seized back the money and goods stolen, and shot several sheep belonging to the family by way of making their point. All this would need to be explained in council, and Joseph Brant was at Sir William's side when, on that hot

July day behind Johnson Hall, several hundred Native Americans convened to listen and argue over the events in motion.

Sir William had been speaking at length against the proposed alliance of the Iroquois and Shawnee, when the heat seemed to overwhelm him and he was helped to a chair beneath a shady arbor. His last utterance, as reported, was an injunction to the tribes: "Whatever may happen, you must not be shaken out of your shoes." Whether Sir William meant shaken by white incursions like those on the Ohio, by injustices like Klock's, or by rumors of war between Americans and British is unclear. He complained about a tightening and compression in his stomach, and moments later Joseph and Molly realized that he had lost consciousness. In his bedroom on the ground floor of the Hall, he appeared to revive and even called for a glass of wine. To Joseph he said, "Joseph control your people," then, his chin sinking onto his chest, William Johnson died. The loose ends he had tried to tie down in the rising storm were snapping wildly in the wind. When the valley recovered from the shock of his passing, the loss of his unifying presence, the people of Tenonanatche understood at last how deeply divided they were. Nine weeks later, the First Continental Congress met at Philadelphia.

Precisely how the plan was hatched, or by whom, is not clear. When the First Continental Congress met at Carpenters' Hall, versions were already under discussion among the delegates. It was John Jay, chief representative from New York, who made explicit what others only thought by urging Congress to confront the problem of Canada. He expressed his indignation in the "Bill of Rights and Grievances," ratified by the First Congress and bequeathed to the Second on the brink of war. "The following acts of Parliament," the petition begins, "are infringements and violations of the rights of the colonists," and inserted in the list just before the Act of Quartering is Jay's contribution:

> Also the act passed the same session for establishing the Roman Catholic Religion in the province of Quebec, abolishing the equitable system of English laws, and erecting a tyranny there, to the great danger, from so great a dissimilarity of Religion, law, and government, of the neighboring British colonies by the assistance of whose blood and treasure the said country was conquered from France."

Those "neighboring British colonies" were, of course, the provinces of New York, New Hampshire, Massachusetts, Maine and Connecticut. They, more than the others, had stood the cost of the Seven Years War in blood and treasure, and Parliament's

Quebec Act offended them deeply, not least because it opened western boundaries to Canadian expansion while blocking colonial access. Despite the possibility that French Catholic citizens might remain neutral, New York's patriots on the eve of revolution—John Jay, Philip Schuyler, Philip and Robert Livingston, George Clinton—suspected that an armed Canada aggressively commanded by British officers posed a substantial threat to New York and to Whig hopes of negotiating a satisfactory settlement with His Majesty's government.[32]

Jay could read his map; the great cities of New York and Philadelphia were terminals on a watery line connecting Quebec and Montreal with Lake Champlain and the Hudson.[33] The Canada card easily could trump efforts of the northern colonies to stand united in their demands. A thrust from Canada would isolate New England from the others, while laying open New York and Philadelphia to land attacks. Although these trepidations were apparent to Jay and others in late 1774, no responsible leader thought to address the issue by means other than negotiation with Canadians, a few hundred of whom seemed sympathetic to the American cause. It was left to the wartime Second Continental Congress to grasp the danger and void it by calling for the plan: *The invasion of Canada by armed forces from the United Colonies.* Though the plan had no known parent, it found many stepfathers. Benjamin Franklin, Samuel Chase, Charles Carroll, George Washington, John Adams, and Roger Sherman would all embrace it.

The moderates' hope for peaceful solidarity with Canadian Whigs gave way before the radicals' call for decisive action. Plant liberty in Canada, join hands across the border, and in a final repudiation of British perfidy, sweep aside the threat of incursions by redcoats and Indians. Whether this program was practicable, given Congress's limited military resources, or feasible, given Canada's overwhelmingly French Catholic population, posed a question too impolitic to be entertained in the excitement of the moment. The Dickinson faction in Congress, desirous of reconciliation with the Mother Country—the view shared by most New York delegates—was fast losing ground to radicals who believed reconciliation impossible.[34]

The First Congress adjourned over the winter months, agreeing to meet again in 1775. By the time the Second convened, blood had been shed at Lexington and Concord, and the number of delegates attending had more than doubled. To represent New York, John Jay was joined now by Philip Schuyler, Robert Livingston, Francis Lewis, George Clinton, and Lewis Morris, all firm in their opposition to Parliament's abuses, yet hardly firebrands for independence.[35] At this point John Ferling writes: "Congress was waging war for reconciliation, but on its terms. During the first fifteen months of hostilities, America fought to reconstitute the British empire into a confederation of sovereign states united under a common king, but one in which Parliament's authority, if it existed at all, was severely circumscribed."[36] Little did anyone know that the Canadian question bearing on the direction of hostilities was about to be answered by events in the field.

On the day the Second Continental Congress met at Philadelphia's State House, a strange fruit fell from the liberty tree—revolutionary forces led by Ethan Allen and Benedict Arnold seized Fort Ticonderoga in a bloodless assault. By the time word of the deed reached Congress on May 18, ad hoc companies had also captured Crown Point and raided St. Johns at the head of the Richelieu River in the Province of Quebec. Now, if Americans could only capture St. Johns and Chambly, the way would be open down the Richelieu to Sorel, a point halfway between Quebec and Montreal on the St. Lawrence River. At the end of May 1775, New England militia looked to be well on their way to wresting Canada from Royal control without Congressional authority.

Yet, the actions that delivered Ticonderoga, the "Gibraltar of the North," into patriot hands had more to do with *opera buffa* than revolutionary élan. Congress at first was overwhelmed with pride and joy as the news broke, but then, as the picture cleared, many delegates began to fear that a handful of fanatical patriots had prematurely scuttled all efforts of Congress to negotiate a neutral Canada.

Here is the story behind the triumph. Ethan Allen arrived at Hand's Cove, two miles from the fort, with 230 Green Mountain Boys and no boats to cross the lake. He planned to capture a notorious loyalist, Major Philip Skene of nearby Skenesboro (modern Whitehall), and appropriate his boats in the name of liberty.[37] Suddenly, to everyone's amazement, a full colonel in fine new dress uniform appeared in camp to take charge of the proposed attack. This was Benedict Arnold, dispatched to Lake Champlain by the Massachusetts Committee of Safety with orders to capture Ticonderoga's guns and haul them back to Boston. The plan was Arnold's, and a good one, but Arnold also had no men and no credibility among Allen's frontiersmen. The first battle of Lake Champlain was fought in the camp at Hand's Cove where Arnold, arguably the finest tactical commander of the American Revolution, faced down Allen, the loudest mouth of the American Revolution, and came away joint commander of an untrained, inept, and largely intoxicated assault force.

They are seen at one another's side racing towards the gap in the east wall of the fort. Allen wears his self-designed uniform of yellow breeches and green coat with gold epaulets, while Arnold is decked out in finery becoming a naval captain. Behind them come 83 men wearing an assortment of forest animals on their heads—skunks and raccoons, otters, and squirrels. They have not a bayonet to their name, no artillery, and no siege train, but they have surprise. The frosts of winter have done their work, toppling the stones of the old wall into a pile, and as they charge the decayed gate, only a lone British sentry opposes them. His musket sputters, misfires, and he runs into the *place d'Armes* sounding the alarm. Now another sentry steps up and wounds an American in the leg with his bayonet. Allen hits the man over the head with the flat of his sword and charges into the guardroom, where he finds British Lieutenant Jocelyn Feltham pulling on his drawers. "By what authority do you intrude?" Feltham is said to ask. Allen replies with resounding bombast, "In the name of the Great Jehovah and the Continental Congress"—though, of the two, Congress was certainly the last to learn of the attack.[38]

The fort's commandant, Captain William Delaplace, surrendered promptly, delivering into American hands "two officers, two artillerymen, several sergeants, and forty-four privates, many of them invalids, also twenty four women and children."[39] More important, Arnold achieved his aim; over eighty artillery pieces, some of substantial caliber, were taken at Ticonderoga and transported, thanks to Colonel Henry Knox, to Boston by the end of the year. They would be used by Washington to force the British evacuation of that city.[40] Arnold, a sea captain in civilian life, then took charge of one of Skene's captured sloops and sailed up the lake to raid St. Johns, while Seth Warner, one of Allen's energetic lieutenants, seized Crown Point. Allen himself had begun to plan for an assault on Montreal as a first strike in what he believed to be his destined conquest of Canada. It all seemed too good to be true, and in many ways, it was. Nowhere in their rampage to the Canadian border had the Americans confronted an alert and organized enemy.

Yet, by the end of May, John Jay was inviting support from Canadians as a "fourteenth colony." He appealed to them in full knowledge that the ad hoc army thrusting towards them from Lake Champlain had every intention of proceeding with or without the consent of Congress. "The taking of the fort and military stores at Ticonderoga and Crown Point was dictated by the great law of self-preservation," he explained, "you may rely on our assurances that these colonies will pursue no measures whatsoever but such as friendship and regard for our mutual safety may suggest. ... We yet entertain hopes of your uniting with us in the defense of our common liberty."[41] To be sure, Jay addressed only Protestant Canadians, who might be won over to the American cause. In private he could be as bigoted as his New England adversaries. He predicted that a swelling tide of Catholic immigrants from either Europe or French Canada would "reduce the ancient free Protestant colonies to a state of slavery."[42] A true New Yorker nonetheless, Jay was conflicted on the Canada question, and never more so than when he deferred to other New Yorkers more knowledgeable than he about the wilderness and waterways lying between the two countries.

Myths about Ticonderoga, Lake Champlain and Lake George were fixed in New England's consciousness. The region had paid exorbitantly in lives for William Johnson's

Bloody Morning Scout, for the massacre at Fort William Henry, for Abercromby's blunders at Ticonderoga. Generations had grown up in the dreadful shadow of raiding French and Indians. Thus, the people of the northern colonies breathed easily only when Ticonderoga, Crown Point, St. Johns and Sorel were in their hands. Fort Ti was the bastion at their backs that had to be defended and held at all cost.

Not so, Philip Schuyler tried to reason. He had served as a supply officer under Johnson and Bradstreet during the French Wars and, as a quartermaster, understood the brutal logistics of wilderness warfare better than most. A wealthy Dutch patrician from Albany, Schuyler maintained a fine home in Saratoga (today's Schuylerville), where he also ran one of the largest timber mills in the province. His sloops sailed the Hudson in trade with New York and Montreal, and over years of business dealings he had grown familiar with the ways and byways of the North Country. Schuyler could say with perfect candor that Ticonderoga was a broken-down relic of bygone wars, difficult to supply and sited in the worst place possible to command the narrows of Champlain.[43] That the British even bothered to garrison the fort was surprising; that they had failed to secure its artillery was incomprehensible. Indeed, the cannons helped to drive the British out of Boston, but did anyone expect that the British, commanding the greatest navy afloat, would not come back—to New York City next time, a far more vital port to the American cause than Boston. No sooner had Washington winkled the British out of Boston than he and his army rushed headlong to Manhattan, and with good reason.

As for Ethan Allen and his Green Mountain Boys, they were, in Schuyler's opinion, a gang of frontier hooligans who not only invaded New York's sovereign soil without consultation, but long resisted New York's lawful claims to the New Hampshire grants with mayhem and manslaughter.[44] Schuyler did not think they would make a promising army; they, for their part, did not think the Dutch Yorker would make a promising general. As it turned out, on June 16, a day before the Battle of Bunker Hill, Congress appointed Schuyler one of its four major generals reporting to George Washington, and in consideration of his wide experience in New York, named him commander of the Northern Department, an area comprising all of upstate New York and as much of Canada as the patriots could seize. The Department did not encompass New England, where Schuyler's appointment was much derided. Schuyler's background is described by John Ferling: "Similar in many ways to that of Washington and essentially the same age, Schuyler came from the New York aristocracy, lived on a large country estate, speculated heavily in frontier land, was a conservative assemblyman, had soldiered for five years in the French and Indian War, and was a member of Congress. The New York delegates spoke admiringly of his courage, prudence, perceptivity, thoughtfulness, and attention to detail. They said that he possessed some engineering skills, and they mentioned that he was habitually well prepared."[45] Yet no one, in New York or New England, viewed Schuyler as a decisive field commander.

Resentments against New York, sowed twenty years before in the run-up to the Battle of Lake George and the aftermath of Johnson's victory, still rankled in New England and contributed to strained relations between the regions. Through no fault of his own, the tall, commanding patrician from Albany became a lightning rod for class jealousies and insinuations. The fact that he was wealthy and did not suffer fools gladly seemed enough in certain minds to disqualify him as a loyal revolutionary. To be sure, Schuyler was no leveler, but the personal sacrifices he made in order to keep American forces in the field were as impressive as any demonstrated during the Revolution. His singular weakness as commander had nothing to do with his Dutch ethnicity or wealthy origins and everything to do with poor health. He was a year younger than Washington, with chronic rheumatism that precluded active campaigning in the harsh conditions of the northern corridor. But Schuyler's worth and genius lay most in supply and support from the rear, and so long as his efforts were teamed with those of Richard Montgomery or Benedict Arnold, both fine battlefield leaders, the army of the Northern Department fared better than its slender experience warranted. His New England critics claimed that he avoided the guns and lined his pockets with contracts, never appreciating how much Schuyler's personal credit underwrote Congress's army or how often he rode into danger clearing obstructions to his army's advance. Seemingly before there even was an American army, army politics and Congressional chicanery were enough to bring down worthy commanders. Washington, Arnold, and Schuyler all spent precious time and energy defending their decisions in the face of malicious and baseless charges.

Schuyler was right about the Green Mountain Boys. As an outfit under orders, with a requirement to stand up in all manner of adversity, the Boys lacked discipline and leadership. This did not keep Allen and Seth Warner from presenting themselves on the floor of Congress in Philadelphia on June 23, 1775, and requesting that the Boys be enrolled in Continental service. Six days after the Battle of Bunker Hill, Congress could find no reason to deny the Green Mountain Boys regimental status and pay. Allen's appearance, to be sure, hardened Congress's growing resolve to finally settle the Canadian question.[46] Now it formally directed General Schuyler to proceed to Ticonderoga and Crown Point, and "if he finds it practicable and that it will not be disagreeable to the Canadians, he do immediately take possession of St. Johns, Montreal, and any other parts of the country."[47]

But Schuyler knew he would need regiments of better stuff than Allen's to reach Montreal and hold the city against General Guy Carleton's counterattacks. Carleton was also Governor of Canada, a British officer with much military service in North America and a principal architect of the Quebec Act. He could be counted on to fight back with the small number of troops available to him while waiting for reinforcements. Only with highly professional soldiers, well-supplied and restrained from plundering, could Schuyler ever hope to invade Canada, hold off Carleton, and still foster friendship with Canadians. Given the raw state of Schuyler's regiments, the assignment was virtually impossible. The Boys' frontier exuberance, for example, suited them to chasing New York land speculators; it did not help them meet the demands of siege warfare or eighteenth-century infantry tactics. Allen might move his men over rough country at great speed; he could not, however, move them wisely or hold them together in combat. Nor could he keep them from looting and pillaging targets of opportunity. Unfortunately, these failings were typical of most militia regiments early in the war, and militia would be the mainstay of the Northern Department from the Battle for Quebec to Saratoga.

To their credit, the old farmers of the New Hampshire Grants recognized the wartime shortcomings of their firebrand leader. When they met in July to nominate the officers of their new regiment, they ignored Allen and elected Seth Warner lieutenant colonel, leaving the colonelcy vacant.[48] The Boys would eventually fall into sorry condition after heavy losses during the invasion of Canada, but Seth Warner would reorganize and lead them to victory two years later at the Battle of Bennington. As for Allen, he rushed alone to Ticonderoga and placed himself at the service of General Schuyler. "I am apprehensive of disagreeable consequences arising from Mr. Allen's imprudence ... his impatience of subordination," Schuyler admitted, but Allen made "a solemn promise ... that he would demean himself properly." He was attached to headquarters thereafter. Politics dictated the decision. Schuyler could not afford a rabble-rouser, with ready access to Congress, troubling his already fractious regiments. Yet Allen would soon prove to be his own worst enemy. No sooner did an opportunity for glory and fame offer than he broke his word to Schuyler and, in an example of flagrant insubordination, lost both his command and his freedom.

By the end of summer, Schuyler and New York's Richard Montgomery had landed regiments on Ile aux Noix at the northern end of Lake Champlain, preparatory to an attack on St. Johns. Schuyler fell ill with a bout of rheumatism and, leaving Brigadier General Montgomery in command, returned to Ticonderoga. The 1st New York and 5th Connecticut regiments mustered about 1,000 effectives. Soon they were reinforced by James Easton's Massachusetts regiment and Seth Warner's Green Mountain Boys, bringing the total American invasion force to near 1,400. As Montgomery moved to besiege St. Johns, he ordered Allen with a small force to swing wide around the town and seize Chambly to the north. Allen was there to make contact with friendly Canadians recruited by Captain John Brown, and to organize this party in support of the main effort against St. Johns.

Allen and Brown, however, hatched plans of their own. Once combined, they agreed to march on Montreal and capture the city in a *coup de main*. Not for them the slow, slogging advances of professional soldiers like Montgomery, or the tedious attention to logistics of Schuyler. To mount their attack, they chose two columns converging on Montreal simultaneously from across the St. Lawrence River—one of the most difficult of all military maneuvers.

And predictably, their timing was off; Allen in three crossings by canoe assembled his volunteers at the eastern gate, but Brown failed to arrive at the western gate at all. Now Allen, back to the river, was faced by the need to retreat. The alarm bells of Montreal were ringing, and the populace had been alerted that "Ethan Allen, the Notorious New Hampshire Incendiary" was about to attack. Allen could not withdraw his men one-third at a time without fatally weakening his front; besides, his volunteer Canadians were fading away into the woods as 200 British soldiers, Indians, and citizens ventured out of the city to repel him. Some of his men escaped in canoes, but Allen, backed to the water's edge and surrounded, was forced to surrender along with forty of his survivors. His bravery was never in question, just his common sense. By jumping at what he took to be a golden opportunity, he placed his neck and those of his men in a tactical noose. While their loss was regrettable, it did not compare with the damage done the Colonial cause in Canada. Canadians of all persuasions now saw the American adventure as a poorly organized, badly led, under-subsidized bid for conquest. More than ever now they were inclined to support General Guy Carleton and his handful of British regulars, or to remain neutral, as cold and hungry Americans struggled towards them over swamps and wooded ravines.

To make matters worse, the hero of the action at Montreal was one Peter Warren Johnson, a young cadet and eldest son of Molly Brant by Sir William Johnson. Allen, flailing about to avoid capture, chose the most gentlemanly assailant to receive his sword of surrender. Young Peter, only sixteen, received that sword, and from it eventually a commission as ensign in His Majesty's forces from Governor Tryon.[49] Nor was this the last Allen would see of Molly Brant's relations. Manacled and down in the hold of the HMS *Adamant* for transport to London, Allen was taunted by the ship's passengers. These happened to be Guy Johnson's party, furious at the rebellion and bound for London to confer with the Crown's ministers for favors and advancements. Joseph Brant stared through the barred door at Allen and the thirty-four other prisoners taken in the fighting. Walter Butler, who was on board, Daniel Claus, and Guy all visited the chained Allen, and of these leading Tories, only Claus, according to Allen's own account, refrained from railing at him. When the *Adamant* reached Falmouth, a great crowd was on hand to see this conqueror of Ticonderoga, famous throughout Europe, led forth in chains. "People lined the wharf and gaped at him from windows and climbed to roofs to watch."[50] Most expected Allen would be tried as a traitor and hanged; Allen himself expected as much, but the capture of English officers as the conflict continued argued against such treatment. Allen would be exchanged for a British officer later in the war.

At St. Johns, meanwhile, the siege continued. Montgomery wrestled not only with the stubborn British defenders, but also with the inadequacies of his troops.

What had seemed a few months before *fait accompli*, now devolved into inconclusive wilderness warfare. On September 5, within sight of St. Johns, the 5th Connecticut was crossing Bernier's Brook, a deep, muddy, winding stream, "when they were met by a surprising blast of fire. A hundred Indians led by Captain Tice, a New York Tory, had ambushed them. Several of the Americans fell, but the rest fired on the unseen enemy, then wheeled smartly to the left into dense thickets and for half an hour or so there was irregular bush fighting before the Indians retreated."[51] Eight men were killed in this exchange and eight, including the regiment's officers, severely wounded. Tice, who had managed a tavern in Johnstown a few months before, was also wounded; he would convalesce and travel as a passenger on the *Adamant* a few weeks later as a guest of the Johnson party. The Indians, like Tice, were from Tenonanatche.

In this instance Montgomery's troops did their job; not so when he ordered Lieutenant Colonel Ritzema's New Yorkers to flank St. Johns from the riverbank through the swampy woods. "It was dark in that forest," some later reported, "and the flankers, remembering the ambush on the former expedition, were nervous and apprehensive."[52] As they veered toward the riverbank in the dark, they accidentally collided with the head of their own main force. Not a shot was fired, but Ritzema's 500 Yorkers broke and fled back through the woods convinced that they were ambushed. Montgomery rallied them with patriotic speeches and led them back toward the trenches they were intended to capture. Once again, half fled at the first shot; the remainder held the ground, but declined to advance. The American army was in need of learning, as it had been under Johnson two decades before, that steadiness of nerves in wilderness combat was everything. Schuyler himself was panicked into withdrawing from St. Johns by bogus intelligence reports overestimating the enemy's forces; he retreated, saw that he had been made a fool, countermarched and returned to the siege. Eventually Montgomery managed to place artillery on the heights overlooking St. Johns and captured the place. Next, with superior numbers and guns, he seized Chambly and Montreal. Carleton simply did not have sufficient troops to defend both Montreal and Quebec. He counterattacked fiercely at St. Johns, but Ritzema's Yorkers and Warner's Green Mountain Boys managed to beat back his assault. Green troops, Montgomery discovered, would defend positions they often could not be brought to attack.

As the seesaw campaign for lower Canada continued, New York, Connecticut, and Massachusetts regiments experienced increasing desertion rates. Some blamed the situation on the worsening weather, the poor supplies, or bungled orders issued by incompetent, political appointees. General David Wooster of Connecticut declined to obey orders originating from New York. Montgomery railed at the leveling tendencies of the Yankees, who seemed to think that the lowest ranks were equal in judgment to the highest. "Were I not afraid," he wrote, "the example would be too generally followed, and that the public service might suffer, I would not stay an hour at the head of troops whose operations I cannot direct." Yet he did not forget how poorly the troops of his own province performed; "the first regiment of Yorkers," he observed, "are indeed the sweeping of the York Streets." Disgust extended up the chain of command all the way to Schuyler, who admitted that he had only himself to blame. Back at Ticonderoga, he saw "a scandalous want of subordination and inattention to my orders." He had relied on officers who could not be trusted.

The conditions at the front were best characterized by Montgomery: "We have been like half drowned rats crawling through a swamp." The men were falling sick. Supplies of all sorts were missing. Late in September the men were on half-allowances of pork, and the flour was giving out. Powder, as always, was scarce.[53] Schuyler took charge himself and in six days pushed as much supply northward as would have been carried in three weeks. But the farther his army advanced into Canada, the longer this supply chain stretched. As Montgomery rushed to meet Benedict Arnold, who had climbed Maine's wild rivers to the gates of Quebec, the line reached over 300 miles across wilderness. At a number of depots on the way, thieves hijacked vitally needed stores. The Canadian winter was beginning; the lakes had begun to ice over, and American forces would either batter their way into Quebec quickly or freeze in the snow.

Schuyler pushed supplies and reinforcements from Albany and the Hudson Valley to Ticonderoga and St. Johns by every available vessel, but few men and even fewer supplies seemed to arrive. At the close of November, on evidence that Carleton was reinforcing Quebec, Arnold fell back to Pointe aux Trembles, twenty miles above the city. The 675 survivors of his wilderness *anabasis* were without artillery, food, or winter clothing.[54] On arriving at the Plains of Abraham, Arnold's ragamuffins had called for Quebec's surrender; the inhabitants on the walls noted the soldiers' wretched condition and laughed. Yet their mockery would soon turn to alarm. Washington, without notifying Congress, had ordered Arnold north to Quebec with every intention of striking a deathblow against British possession of Canada. With Arnold marched some of the most redoubtable figures of the Revolutionary War—Daniel Morgan, Henry Dearborn, the young firebrand Aaron Burr. The best riflemen in Washington's army were aligned outside the city gates. More formidable than it looked, this force was hardly ready to give up. Montgomery had liberated military provisions in Montreal along with a supply of winter coats. He floated down the St. Lawrence to Arnold's position now with 300 men of Schuyler's original force and New York's available artillery. Arnold recognized Montgomery as his superior officer and accepted joint command of the siege. Yet both men knew a siege was impractical. Carleton's garrison outnumbered the Americans. Many local Canadians favored the garrison, and the besiegers were unable to close off all of the city's portals. Only a desperate, all-out attack could save the campaign, and Montgomery weighed this option against his very personal knowledge of Guy Carleton.

New York and the American cause had found a leader of surpassing quality in Richard Montgomery. One of Arnold's men, John Joseph Henry, described Montgomery as "noticeably pock-marked, but well-limbed, tall and handsome, with an air and manner that designated the real soldier." He was the son of an Irish baronet and Member of Parliament, and from his seventeenth year had been raised a soldier in the British Army. Montgomery fought in Amherst's 1759 expedition to capture Ticonderoga and Crown Point. He knew the New York wilderness, the corridor north from Albany, as well as any general officer and appreciated the strengths and weaknesses of provincial troops.

Between the wars, Montgomery left the British Army to resettle in New York City. An eighteenth-century intellectual inspired by enlightenment ideals, he envisioned a revolutionary order based on the promises of the New World. In 1772 he resigned his commission to pursue law and politics. It certainly benefited him to marry a Livingston heiress, and once in the orbit of that patrician family, to espouse the patriot cause championed by Livingstons, Schuylers, Van Cortlands, and Rensselaers. But he was no mere opportunist, and Arnold, Morgan, Schuyler, and Washington knew him as a fervent believer in the rights of man and an accomplished officer, this last a rarity among newly commissioned officers. During his British service, Montgomery had served with Guy Carleton. He acknowledged the governor of Canada as a friend, if not a fellow, and could promise Arnold that Carleton would never surrender to a siege. Moreover, the New England forces' term of enlistment expired at the end of the month. It had to be all or nothing—a night attack on the gates while he and Arnold could muster men, or a long retreat to Montreal.

They attacked in a blinding blizzard on the last day of 1775 just as the militia prepared to depart. General Montgomery hoped for surprise in the storm, but an American deserter had alerted Carleton to the assault, and Quebec's defenders were awake at their posts. Montgomery's wing of the attack charged up a treacherous pathway toward a portal into the Lower City, and there received a blast of grapeshot that unhinged the attack. The brigadier, leading the charge, was shot in several places and fell sprawled on his back in the snow. His New York troops, shocked and confused by the sudden ambush, ran away without retrieving their general. It would fall to Carleton to bury his old comrade's body with military honors.[55]

Meanwhile, Arnold led his 675 men in a spirited assault on the north of the city through the Palace Gate. All went well until a ricocheting bullet struck him in his left leg below the knee and, tearing along the leg bone, lodged in his Achilles tendon. Arnold hobbled forward in pain, propped on a musket, but the attack soon lost headway. Morgan was given command. Driving his force through the mounting drifts, "the old Waggoner," as his men called the towering Virginian, managed to scale the icy walls and drop down into the city streets. At this point the Americans were behind the only defenses capable of denying them success. Unfortunately, the officers chose this moment to pause and regroup, and during the delay, Carleton was able to rush forward enough reinforcements to barricade the streets and alleys. The penetration, so close to success, was boxed in and squeezed off until Morgan's force was surrounded and made to surrender. Morgan and Dearborn both were led into captivity with more than half their men; Arnold, crippled and weak from loss of blood, managed to escape into the city's suburbs, while Montgomery's troops cowered leaderless in their start position.

No American military thrust would ever pierce deeper into Canada than the attack on Quebec, and no American defeat in the Revolution, with the exception of the Battle of Long Island, would ever precipitate a longer or more arduous retreat. This lay ahead in 1776, when all concerned had finally grasped just how far Congress's Canadian plan had wandered from reality. Now it fell to Schuyler to make good the damages and find a way to parry the inexorable counterthrust already preparing.

On April 7, 1776, at 7:30 in the morning, a Hudson River sloop tied up at a dock in Albany. General Schuyler with his two young daughters welcomed the sloop's passengers ashore and directed them to carriages for the short ride to the Schuyler mansion on Catherine Street. The general's guests had arrived after a frigid voyage north from New York City. They were delighted to reach the warmth and hospitality of Schuyler House overlooking the river, rather than spend another night cramped below decks on the icy sloop.[56]

For Doctor Franklin, seventy years old, the trip had already proved exhausting and still was nowhere near its end. He wondered if he would survive the wintry journey over the lakes to Montreal and home again.[57] Benjamin Franklin, Samuel Chase, and Charles Carroll had been dispatched to Canada by Congress early in March to negotiate a secret peace treaty. Unknown to them, they were arriving too late, with too little to offer. As Schuyler met the men at the dock, he realized that they also had been sent to his Northern Department on a mission of inquiry. Word of the defeat at Quebec spread quickly through New England, and members of Congress were demanding explanations. Schuyler was expected to facilitate the Congressional party, arrange their transportation to Montreal, and answer all questions as might arise over the deployment and condition of American forces.

On January 19, as winter closed down movement across the northern front, Congress had voted to reinforce the army in Canada "with all possible dispatch."[58] Militia regiments from New Jersey and Pennsylvania were prepared to move north with spring as General David Wooster replaced Arnold and readied forces to renew the siege of Quebec. What someone needed to tell Congress was that on April 2, with Wooster arrived in the trenches outside Quebec, the entire American army numbered 2,000 effectives confronting a city of 5,000 inhabitants, 146 artillery pieces, and a well-rested defense force of 1,600—a large portion of whom were angry Mohawk Valley Loyalists and Highland Scots. Loyalist bands in New York interdicted food shipments from the Schoharie Valley to the famished Americans outside Quebec. The poorly clothed and nourished Americans were already down with smallpox. Inoculations had placed more than 200 in hospitals, while among Arnold's survivors over 400 had contracted the disease. Men and officers alike were dying of the affliction. Between April and June, an open burial pit on Ile aux Noix received more than 1,000 bodies— the remains of soldiers fleeing Canada. Spring was certain to see British forces arriving at Quebec from Halifax, Nova Scotia's main port for staging British reinforcements into North America. To support the siege of Quebec, New England might have used its maritime strength to reduce Halifax, but New England had not, and the consequences were about to be felt.[59]

All of this Schuyler doubtless told his visitors before they resumed their mission. We can imagine these four eminent patriots gathered over Madeira in Schuyler's study. The walls are lined with volumes containing maps and travel accounts, surveys and engineering reports. History and mathematics predominate in the Schuyler library; he is an amateur mathematician.[60] Thus, he triangulates New York's great rivers for the visiting congressmen, opening before them a forecast for the summer and fall. In his thinking, Quebec is lost with Montgomery, Arnold, Morgan, and their soldiers. The campaign for Canada has ended; the battle for New York—the city and the province—is about to begin, and to lose both will surely mean to lose the war. Albany, Montreal, and Oswego on Lake Ontario form a rough right triangle. The triangle's easternmost vertical member follows the course of Lake Champlain and the Richelieu River 90° north from Albany to an apex at Montreal. Who controls a triangle's apex also contests its hypotenuse, the 200-mile line west along the St. Lawrence River to Lake Ontario and Fort Oswego. There, the third angle forms the base line, 200 miles long, from Oswego down Tenonanatche to Albany. Allowing that the north is lost, Schuyler plans to fall back to Ticonderoga and contest the upper waters of Champlain. Yet, none of this will save the American cause unless he can also contest the base line of the triangle. Which leads directly to a critical question—in what condition is Fort Oswego? So far as Schuyler can tell, the fort, deep in Indian country, is a total ruin. If Washington can find him the men, he plans to rebuild and garrison Fort Stanwix instead, and doing so, shield the upper Mohawk Valley from invasion.

The congressmen and their companions are appalled at what they hear, and will be more so at what they are soon to witness. In the contagious optimism of 1775, Schuyler had been charged not only with conquering Canada *peacefully*, but also with forging alliances throughout the Six Nations and suppressing loyalist agitation.

In New York City, June 1775, Washington instructed him "to keep a sharp eye on Governor Tryon and neither to delay the occupation of the northern posts nor to fail to observe Guy Johnson's dealings with the Indians lest they be incited against the colonists."[61] It helped that Schuyler was fluent in several Iroquois dialects, and because of honest trading with the Six Nations, was a trusted agent. He nevertheless was no William Johnson, and his associations with Samuel Kirkland and the Oneida tribe had outraged Guy Johnson and Joseph Brant. No one could see the pieces of the American Revolution coming together in New York quite as Schuyler could, but as Franklin and his party were forced to admit, his orders sent him in contrary directions, while an overreaching Congress provided none of the means necessary for his success. In fact, the New England faction in Congress was already pressing for his replacement by Horatio Gates. Franklin met Gates at Ticonderoga and recognized at a glance that he possessed none of Schuyler's stature or ability.[62] Washington would loyally defend his major general against detractors, but whether he could reinforce him in time to meet converging pressures from Champlain and the Mohawk would depend on how his own defense of New York City fared.

In early May 1776, as Washington arrived at the head of his army in New York City, fifteen British transports pushed up the icy St. Lawrence to land at Quebec seven Irish regiments, one English regiment, and 4,300 German mercenaries. This vanguard of a larger army to come was General John Burgoyne's answer to the invasion of Canada. By then American troops were commanded by General John Thomas. Thomas immediately abandoned Quebec and fell back on Sorel. At a post below Montreal, 400 Americans confronted 600 British redcoats and surrendered without a fight. The army of the Northern Department streamed into Sorel at the mouth of the Richelieu from every direction. Their condition is described by John Adams from reports he received:

> Our army is an object of wretchedness enough to fill a human mind with horror: disgraced, defeated, discontented, dispirited, diseased, naked, undisciplined, eaten up with vermin, no clothes, beds, blankets; no medicines, no victuals but salt, pork & flour.[63]

Schuyler, meeting them as they tumbled back out of Canada to Crown Point, admitted as much:

> The fragmented regiments from New Jersey, and Pennsylvania, New York, and New England were not an army but a mob ... the shattered remains of twelve or fifteen very fine battalions, ruined by sickness, fatigue, and desertion, and void of every idea of discipline or subordination ... the very acme of human misery.[64]

It had not helped that General Thomas himself had contracted smallpox, gone blind from the disease, and died miserably in camp at Sorel.

Franklin sensed the end of the tragedy approaching at Montreal and departed for home with Schuyler's help ahead of the other emissaries. Chase and Carroll were caught up in the disastrous retreat, experiencing fully the misery Congress had helped to loose. They arrived home sobered by the cost of the war and shaken by a realization that the real war had only just begun. New York's vast scale and scenic grandeur had impressed them on the trip north. Now, fleeing south through the forest and lakes with men desperate to escape, had taught them what war in the Northern Department was going to demand of the American cause.

Schuyler had weeks, not months, to forge a new plan before the British crushed Albany between an attack from Canada and a loyalist uprising on Tenonanatche. In the face of this he would have to rely on Ticonderoga's defenses, the remnants of his Northern Army, and the torturous terrain north of Albany to delay one arm of the attack while he sought high and low for means to meet the other.

⚜ 7 ⚜

Estranged Neighbors

O n the morning of May 31, 1775, a startling sight greeted inhabitants of the
Mohawk Valley as they woke to a bright spring day. Passing upriver in stately
procession, a flotilla of bateaux stretched back as far as eye could see. Swift
canoes darted in and out among the slow craft with shouts of greeting and snatches
of conversation thrown shoreward on the light breeze. To sharp observers watching
from the banks, Guy Johnson, acting Indian superintendent, appeared to be leaving
Guy Park in full force, accompanied by at least 120 white retainers, 90 Native Americans, and his pregnant wife, Mary, the youngest daughter of Sir William Johnson.[1]
Guy was due at Oswego for a tribal council beginning the next month. Ostensibly, he
wished to remain close to his expectant wife during this time, providing her with all
the comforts of home.

But, shielded from the sun beneath a canvas awning, Mary and her sister, the
wife of Daniel Claus, knew as they watched the valley of their birth vanish behind
them that they might never again see Johnson Hall or Guy Park Manor. A few days
ago their instructions had been to pack everything needed for a long wilderness journey, including cold-weather clothing and personal effects. Thirty armed Highlanders
accompanied their party as bodyguards, and under no circumstance were the women
to be allowed ashore. These were dangerous times, and should Mary or Nancy fall into
the hands of enemies, Guy believed, they could be used as pawns. The carefree river
scene only masked the Tory party's growing paranoia.

Some who watched the flotilla's progress waved at the bateaux and the familiar
valley celebrities accompanying Guy—Joseph Brant, Daniel Claus, John and Walter
Butler, the Johnson sisters, and Molly's son, Peter. Others, scanning the mile-long
watery parade, had darker suspicions. They surmised that the Johnsons were steal-
ing a march, decamping from the valley for reasons of their own. Anxiety came later
when rumor spread that Guy meant to join hands with Indian allies in the west and
descend on the valley's patriots in a surprise attack. Clearly, numerous patriots lived
along the Mohawk, though from the sparse and confused records of the period it is

difficult to determine how many.[2] Following Lexington and Concord, and before the grave events at Breed's Hill (Bunker Hill), tensions in the valley had become palpable. Frequent agitations brought people thronging into the streets, where talk was often of a document called the "Palatine Petition," drawn up weeks before at Adam Louck's tavern in Stone Arabia.

To be sure, this petition contained the customary protestations of loyalty to King and Parliament, but in a closing section appeared the sentence: "we think it is our undeniable privilege to be taxed only with our own consent ... we will join and unite with our brethren of the rest of this country in anything tending to support and defend our rights and liberties."[3] The petition laments the blockade of Boston and declares the solidarity of Mohawk farmers with their embattled brethren in New England. By degrees the inhabitants of Tenonanatche were edging toward action, and when action came at last, Johnsons and Palatines would be at the center.

Near Caughnawaga (Fonda) on May 11, a party of patriots attempted to raise a Liberty Pole on the King's Highway in response to news from Boston. They were loud but unarmed, and as the pole fell into place, the celebration was interrupted abruptly by John Johnson, Guy Johnson, Daniel Claus, and a party of Highlanders. Guy climbed the porch of John Veeder's house nearby and proceeded to laud the virtues of George III to the gathering crowd. In the midst of his harangue, young Jacob Sammons cried out that Johnson was a liar and a villain. Guy vaulted off the porch, pushed through the crowd, and grabbed Sammons by the throat. As they scuffled, one of Guy's men struck Sammons with a bullwhip, knocking him unconscious. Sammons woke to find a henchman seated on his chest. He rolled the man off, struggled to his feet, and found that he was alone facing the bodyguards. Sammons's Palatine neighbors, threatened with brandished swords and pistols, had vanished. His assailants needed no time to make an object lesson of him, leaving him sprawled in the dust of the road with broken ribs. This was the first blood to be shed on the Mohawk in defense of "liberty," and accounts of the event were still circulating when locals witnessed Guy's departure.[4]

Struggles with errant villagers troubled Guy not at all; more serious was the spreading allegation that he was fomenting an Indian uprising. Indeed, this allegation was true, yet as patriotic fervor mounted, hiding the truth became more important than ever. A party of Oneidas spoiled Guy's subterfuge. Earlier in the year, the superintendent had forbidden Samuel Kirkland and other Presbyterian missionaries access to Indian Territory. Kirkland was detained during April at Guy Park Manor on grounds that he was actively engaged in promoting the American cause to the Indians. Guy clearly was within his rights to restrain Samuel Kirkland, James Dean, and Samson Occum from moving among the tribes as missionaries while also spreading sedition.[5] But what many Oneidas objected to was Guy's arrogant muzzling of men whom the Oneida, Stockbridge, Tuscarora, and Caughnawaga faithful trusted to speak the truth. Thus, when Guy wrote to the Oneidas, informing them that his life was in danger and that in memory of Warraghiyagey they should move to defend him from the Yankees, the Oneidas closest to Kirkland conveniently arranged for Guy's letter to reach the Palatine Committee of Safety, from where it was forwarded to the New York Provincial Congress at Albany.[6] To be sure, Guy, through the agency of Joseph Brant, was actively lobbying the Iroquois. On the other hand, Kirkland, Dean, and Occum were doing no less for the American cause when they recited the minutes of Congress from their pulpits.[7]

What frightened Guy most was the negative publicity his maneuvers generated in Albany and Philadelphia. He had convinced himself that an army of patriots, raised in New England, was about to force the valley and take him hostage. In truth, only over the next few months, as Schuyler prepared for the invasion of Canada on Washington's orders, was the situation on the Mohawk even discussed. Schuyler was instructed to keep an eye on Guy Johnson, and then to do everything in his power to win the support of the Indians through negotiations and gifts. Yet, so bellicose was the rhetoric in Congress during May that a British spy in Philadelphia thought well to warn Guy that a force was coming from New England to detain him. The Whigs in the valley denied any knowledge of this and were angered when Guy fortified Guy Park and barricaded the King's Highway west of Schenectady.[8] In exchange, they commenced intercepting couriers riding west from the superintendent's headquarters.

The last straw for Guy came in an encoded message from British General Thomas Gage in Boston. According to a letter from Guy to Lord Dartmouth in London, Gage ordered him to leave the valley before the rebels moved to take him. Guy was to make his way to Canada, where he and his Indians would join Governor Carleton and plot to invade New England.[9] Surely this was an old plan and bore little resemblance to reality in the spring of 1775. Yet it was also a measure of how desperate Gage had become. He knew that Guy was working strenuously to put the hatchet in Indian hands and, assuming that the Whigs knew as much, he feared for Guy's safety. The Whigs, however, were working just as strenuously to bury the hatchet and encourage neutrality; the last thing they thought to do was arrest the Indian Superintendent, Uraghquadirha to his Mohawk friends, provoking a frontier crisis. Whatever his Tory beliefs, Guy was still his uncle's appointee and the guarantor to the tribes of gifts, trade concessions, and treaty enforcement. Not even the Oneidas would stand for his removal, to say nothing of Mohawks, Senecas, Onondagas, and Cayugas, where Guy's support was strongest. The Whigs might push Guy, but they would no more eliminate him than Guy would eliminate Kirkland and other New England missionaries—at least not at this point in the conflict.

Why, then, the precipitous flight in May? The only answer is that Guy lost his nerve and, surrendering to Gage's panic, fled the valley for Oswego and Canada before necessary. The Tryon County Committee of Safety, successor to the Palatine Committee, had no notion of pursuing him and no suspicion that he was abandoning the Mohawk. To further negotiations, they sent Colonel Nicholas Herkimer and Edward

Wall to find him and deliver a conciliatory message.[10] The two emissaries caught up with the Johnson party at Cosby's Manor, on the edge of the frontier, and handed Guy the Tryon County letter. The committee wished to inform the Indian Superintendent that a mass meeting of Tryon County's citizens had been held, and for the first time ever, representatives to the Congress in Albany had been freely elected from each district. Guy, as a member of the old State Assembly, bitterly opposed these doings. The letter, nonetheless, was courteous, even deferential, as it sought common ground between the sides:

> We beg of you to use your endeavors with the Indians to dissuade them from interfering in the dispute with the mother country and the colonies. We cannot think that, as you and your family possess very large estates in this county, you are unfavorable to American freedom, although you may differ with us in the mode of obtaining redress of grievances.[11]

Suppressing his anger with difficulty, Guy turned his back on Herkimer and Wall and stomped off to pen a reply to the committee. He charged therein that certain people in Albany and Philadelphia were known to be plotting his capture, and that any such act would have disastrous effects on Indian relations. His advice to the committee was that they lay their grievances before their king and trust to the Crown's promises of redress. As for fomenting trouble among the tribes, he wrote:

> I am very sorry that such idle and injurious reports meet with any encouragement. I rely on you, gentlemen, to exert yourselves in discountenancing them, and am happy in this opportunity of assuring the people of a country I regard, that they have nothing to apprehend from my endeavors, but I shall always be glad to promote their true interests.[12]

Indeed what those "true interests" might be was left to the imagination. Herkimer and Wall, receiving Guy's letter from Joseph Brant's hand, sensed a deep estrangement. They had all been neighbors, affable and accommodating before the troubles began, and though they could still shake hands, their friendship was clearly strained.[13] To the emissaries, Guy's entourage seemed too numerous and too heavily armed to be just a treaty delegation; the Tories apparently were moving to a war footing even as the patriots equivocated and sought negotiations. Herkimer knew the wilderness stretching west beyond the Mohawk; he was under no illusions about what Guy could do once out of sight and communicating directly with Canada. The problem was that under Guy's pressure the sides were being drawn too quickly and rigidly for many settlers and natives to comprehend or accept. Herkimer's own brother, George, could not make up his mind; another brother, Yon Yost, called himself an American, but leaned British. Chiefs like Little Abraham (Tigoransera) at Fort Hunter begged their people to remain neutral even as other sachems grew uneasy at being rushed into war with white neighbors at Brant's urgings.

By abruptly quitting the valley, Guy as well as admitted his hostile intentions toward elected officials of Tryon County, signaling to all concerned that there could be no compromise, no neutrality in the looming clash with the mother country. What had been only rumored until now was confirmed as fact, and not many weeks would pass before the shock of Guy's actions registered fully on the inhabitants of Tenonanatche. About the time Herkimer was delivering his letter to the Committee of Safety, Guy's party was leaving Fort Stanwix by Wood Creek for Lake Oneida. They moved swiftly through the wilderness in drenching rains and yet, despite the weather, dozens of Indian families flocked to them. Guy never hesitated to tell these inhabitants of the forest that enemies of their king were hounding him out of the Mohawk Valley. Backed by the powerful presence of Joseph Brant (Thayendanegea), Guy called for their support, inviting them to the great council at Fort Ontario (Oswego).[14]

Between late June and early July, as word reached central New York of the fighting at Breed's Hill, Guy's Indian council met at last. Out of the bateaux, rowed and portaged from the east with great effort, poured the trade goods and gifts intended for the western tribes. With their rum, powder and ball, the tribes also imbibed the Johnson message of how their king would soon call them to defend their homes and lands against encroaching rebels. In the time-honored rhetoric of the Six Nations, the Iroquois peoples were urged to hold fast to the chain of friendship binding them to their British father, and to receive the black wampum of war for the sake of their people and his. More than 1,400 Native Americans attended Guy's council, and among those were several hundred who said they would heed Brant's call to arms.[15] The oratory at the tumbledown fort was neither more nor less strident than either side could expect under the circumstances, but as Guy's recruiting efforts moved down the St. Lawrence later in the month, the call to action grew increasingly shrill. Barbara Graymont, quoting the Claus papers, describes a council near Montreal, attended by 1,700 Caughnawagas:

> The Indians were then invited "to feast on a Bostonian and drink his Blood." The old ritual cannibalism had now been transformed into more humane outlets, however, and the British, while using the traditionalist rhetoric, provided a roast ox and a pipe of wine to take the place of the Bostonian, as the rebel Americans were called. The Indians also sang their war songs for the occasion.[16]

Guy's activities did not go unnoticed by authorities in Schenectady and Albany. On July 13, Ebenezer Cox informed the Tryon County Committee that according to reliable sources (read disaffected Indians): "Colonel Johnson was ready with 800 or 900 Indians to make an invasion of this County, that the same Indians were to be under the command of Joseph Brant and Walter Butler, and that they were to fall on the inhabitants below Little Falls, in order to divide the people in two parts, and were to march yesterday, or the day before."[17] This was precisely the campaign that the Johnson party had in mind, with their strength in Indians approximating Cox's numbers. What they were soon to discover, however, was that Governor Carleton in Canada, though desperate for help, wanted no part of Indian war.[18] He removed Claus as Canadian superintendent and challenged Guy's authority. Two years were to pass before Carleton's replacement, General Burgoyne, empowered an invasion of Tryon County spearheaded by Brant's warriors.

In the meantime, patriots in the Mohawk Valley moved heaven and earth to prepare for the anticipated attack. Schuyler, arriving at Ticonderoga to ready the push into Canada, resolved to hold an "American" Indian council at Albany in August. Congress acted quickly to create three Indian departments according to geography, the northern department to be headed by Schuyler. On July 18, Congress voted Samuel Kirkland $300 to cover travel from Oneida to Philadelphia or to be spent on appropriate Indian affairs.[19] Of troops to protect the Mohawk Valley, there would be none; the siege of Boston, where Washington had just taken command, was the foremost effort, and in New York all available men were being rushed to Lake Champlain for the invasion of Canada. Guy had played the Indian card prematurely, with the consequence that the Mohawk and Schoharie valleys knew now that they would be on their own against the most fearsome type of warfare. In the months to follow, patriots would impound Loyalist property, detain and imprison Loyalist suspects, and by their harsh actions remove any hope that the contest might be settled in a manner short of war.

Perhaps, given his mercurial temper and the situation in which he found himself, Guy's misjudgments are understandable. The Crown's acting superintendent had everything to gain by negotiating with opponents and nothing to gain by fueling their fears, but the temptation to wield the force of the Indian Department against class adversaries clearly overwhelmed Guy's better sense. Both he and his charges were to pay a high price for this rush to arms. Among the Iroquois, a deep and dangerous chasm opened between those who favored neutrality or the Americans, and those who supported the British. At risk was the survival of the ancient Iroquois League, and indeed, before the crisis passed, that venerable league would be sadly broken. Guy lost his beautiful home on the Mohawk and all of his property, but this was nothing compared with what the precipitous flight through the wilderness cost him in family. On July 12, as he prepared to leave Oswego for Canada, Mary Johnson, Sir William's youngest daughter, died while giving birth in a drafty, dilapidated barrack at the fort. The journey and the weather had proven too much for her.

One Johnson remained in the valley, unheeding of Guy's call. Sir John, a baronet in his own right and the largest landholder in the region, saw no reason to abandon Johnson Hall while his wife Mary was pregnant. At this point John's only public duties involved his office as colonel of the Tryon County horse, a meaningless post given the attachment of Tryon County forces to General Schuyler's Northern Department. In John's estimation, however, Philip Schuyler was just another wealthy fellow who could be counted on to protect private property no matter what political winds blew. Thus he felt he had nothing to fear from Albany so long as he remained quietly at Johnson Hall immersed in his own business. Sir John made no secret of his complete loyalty to King George or his belief that Whig agitation advanced a treasonous agenda. Nor did he see any reason why he should not, ensconced at the heart of his own property, collect munitions and armed retainers to protect his interests in a troubled time.

No one was fooled; word spread rapidly through the valley that John was fortifying a base on the Mohawk against the day of Guy's return with British troops. Yet, neither was anyone in authority disposed to act forcefully against a Johnson in Johnson Hall. During the last half of 1775, on the Mohawk as elsewhere, antagonists moved in a curious dance. The Tryon County Committee of Safety (Ebenezer Cox, James McMaster, and John Klock) offered the noble patron of Johnstown an intriguing proposal:

> We wish to know whether you will allow the inhabitants of Johnstown and Kingsborough to form themselves into companies, according to the regulations of the Continental Congress, for the defense of our country's cause; and whether your Honour would be ready himself to give his personal assistance to the same purpose; also whether you pretend a prerogative to our county courthouse and jail, and would hinder or interrupt the Committee making use of the same to our want and service in the common cause.[20]

This communication, flying in the face of all that Sir John was known to avow, contained the Tryon Committee's bid to appropriate the courthouse and county jail in Johnstown. They proposed to use Sir William's civic bequests as places to try and jail many of John Johnson's Loyalist friends. The reply was prompt and bitter. John considered his father's courthouse and jail to be his property and would not part with them for anything less than a large sum: "Concerning myself, sooner than lift my hand against my King, or sign any association with those who would, I should suffer my own head to be cut off. As to the court-house and jail, I would not deny the use of it for the purpose for which it was built, but they are my property until I shall be refunded seven hundred pounds"[21]

This was a bold response indeed considering that Congress was advising local authorities to arrest "all persons who might endanger the liberties of Americans," and that New York's Royal Governor, William Tryon, had been recently driven to seek refuge aboard a British warship in New York harbor. The infant Revolution had gobbled up Chambly in the Province of Quebec and was about to capture Fort St. John's. In late October the Tryon County Committee wrote to the Provincial Congress in Albany seeking advice. In a reply dated early December they were told rather archly that no request need be made of Sir John for raising companies among his tenants and that, furthermore, his father had donated the courthouse and jail to Tryon County. Nonetheless, the Tryon Committee was advised not to use the premises as a jail for Tories, since such actions might further inflame a combustible situation. More startling still, the Provincial Congress warned Tryon County to keep its hands off Sir John:

> We give you our advice not to molest Sir John as long as he shall continue inactive and not impede the measures necessary to be carried into execution from being completed.[22]

What Schuyler thought of this decision to leave in his rear a dangerous enemy, possessed of a private army, ample munitions, Mohawk support, and a network of agents and spies bent on undoing the patriot invasion of Canada, can only be imagined. At the present, his attention was focused entirely on the capture of Montreal and Quebec, even as rumors persisted of Sir John's involvement in plots. How duplicitous in fact was Sir John? In early December, Isaac Paris, chairman of the Tryon Committee, informed the general that "inimical preparations are taken against the Friends of the American Cause in Johnstown," by which he meant that 600 or 700 men were already under arms and provided with cannon.[23] Also on record is the secret mission of Johnson's trusted retainer, Captain McDonnell, to William Tryon in New York. McDonnell told Tryon verbally that Sir John and his Tory neighbors had raised a battalion, appointed officers, enlisted the support of about 500 Indians, and were ready to take back the forts along Tenonanatche. A large cache of arms at Johnstown included light artillery and numerous stands of muskets with powder and ball to sustain 300 men in the field.[24] Sir John in the waning days of 1775 was assuredly not going about his business quietly; everything indicated that he was up to his ears in subversion.

The outbreak of revolution had taken the Mohawk Valley loyalists by surprise, and they found nothing more urgent now than to arm, organize, and open lines of communication to British Canada. In order to buy time, Sir John had no compunctions about misleading rebels, whom he considered in any case inimical to the moral order. The rebels, for their part, found his dissembling ways condescending and dishonorable, and as fighting intensified along the Canadian border, suspected him of sneaking supplies and warriors through the Adirondack wilderness to Captains Tice and Brant.

Some opponents viewed Sir John as the spoiled child of a rich man, more nuisance than military threat. Forgotten was the son's service beside the father in the French and Indian War. From navigating the great boreal waste between Tenonanatche and the St. Lawrence, John knew the forests and rivers of the North Country. How the lakes lay from north to south, how they were linked by portages to the Sacandaga, Oswagatchie, West Canada, Black, and Ausable rivers had been learned in his youth from Sir William's Iroquois guides. Now, as war erupted, the porous nature of New York's northern borders worked against the patriots; rivers and lakes of the Adirondack wilderness provided highways from Canada into the heart of New York's fertile valleys.[25] If the British could only hold on to Canada, Sir John and his confederates would swing open the back door to General Washington's granary by controlling Indian trails running north to south across the great farming regions. Counting as much as arms and men in a guerilla war for the back country were the quality of intelligence and level of complicity Sir John could expect from a wide network of friends, family, and associates. Typical of this group on whom he depended was the family of Sarah Kast McGinnis, positioned on the north of Tenonanatche near the western outskirts of German Flats.

Sarah Kast McGinnis enters the Johnson family story in the aftermath of the French and Indian struggle. She was the fifty-year-old widow of Captain Timothy McGinnis who, with Michael Tyrrell, Patrick Flood, and James Rogers, had followed William Johnson from Ireland to the New World in 1738.[26] Timothy McGinnis, called Teady Magin by associates, had run a farm and trading post under Johnson's patronage along the trail to Oswego. He and Sarah made a great success of it until he was killed in the Battle of Lake George. McGinnis led the Yorkers who charged the French and Canadians at Bloody Pond. He perished of wounds in this action and was buried with other casualties beside the lake. Sarah's eldest son was an invalid, her surviving daughters were grown and married, and her other sons were too young to manage the trading post and farmstead. Thus, she appears in 1764 at Johnson Hall not for a handout, but for a helping hand. She needed credit and several strong young servants to help repair her property. The neighborhood was destitute and depopulated from the late war.

Daniel Claus, the young man Conrad Weiser had sent to Johnson Hall for training, befriended Sarah. To him she told her story. She was born on the Hudson among the Palatine survivors of the 1710 immigration, and she had grown up in a tar camp. After her father died in the camp, his widow moved the family up the Mohawk River to German Flats, where they subsisted until allotted a portion of land comprising the westernmost farm in the Province of New York. Like Weiser, she was taken in by a Mohawk family and adopted. Claus recommends her to a busy Sir William:

> She from her childhood was much beloved by the 6 Nations, so far that they prevailed upon her parents to let her live among them, and adopted her as one of themselves, whereby she acquired the language perfectly, and after her riper years was so far capable as to render many a signal service to Government.[27]

Of course Sir William would help the widow of one of his Irish tenants, a man killed in his service alongside his own brother-in-law, Matthew Ferrall.[28] But, beyond the great man's charity, lay policy. Sarah Kast McGinnis would not only thrive as a farm manager and fur trader, but would become the Indian Commissioner's ears and eyes on the Onondaga (Oswego) River. She had all the requisite skills of a frontierswoman—familiarity with Native Americans, a command of the Mohawk language, a business sense sharpened by hard times, and the tempered judgment of one inured to danger. How well Johnson read character. Sarah turned out to be hugely successful on her own terms, and when war came, she returned Sir William's favor, remaining loyal to his family and the Crown. The Kast house on the upper Mohawk became a safe house for Tory agents, and Sarah, now in her sixties, an interpreter between the Iroquois and the British.[29] Her son George, now grown to manhood, would serve throughout the war in Butler's rangers.[30]

Sarah Kast McGinnis was one of many Mohawk inhabitants who clung to the skirts of Johnson Hall as Revolution arrived. Just as she declared her loyalty, so also did her daughters Elizabeth and Dorothy Thompson, married to Thompson brothers. Kinship ties figured importantly in the valley, not only for the Kast-McGinnis-Thompsons, but for the Klocks, Sammonses, Fondas and Freys. One matriarch or patriarch deciding for a faction could sway an extended family, and while women did not bear arms, they could spy on their neighborhoods, reporting all that they saw. Molly Brant, residing at *Kanatsiohareke* (Canajoharie) watched the roads and the rivers, communicating regularly with Sir John and her brother, Thayendanegea. Prying eyes proliferated across central New York. As suspected Tories were detained and arrested, or patriots ambushed and intimidated, the mounting wrongs done by hidden agents far outweighed claims to justice made by either side.

This situation was tolerable and containable from Schuyler's point of view so long as the American cause prospered in Canada. Troublemakers in the Mohawk Valley were unable to seriously impede Washington's efforts at Boston or affect the security of New York City. But, should the Canadian enterprise fail and were the British to reinforce Quebec from Halifax, the political position of central New York would change drastically. Native Americans located on the Mohawk or St. Lawrence Rivers were understandably confused by this sudden, sharp division of the white world. As many did during the French and Indian wars, they equivocated and waited to see which side emerged victorious. At Onondaga, the Six Nations leadership worried that Americans would ally themselves with Delawares for a march on Detroit across Iroquois lands. Everyone waited nervously during November and December for some resolution to the intensifying conflict.[31]

Finally, on the last day of 1775 at the walls of Quebec, the American invasion of Canada ground to a halt with Brigadier General Montgomery dead in action, Colonel Arnold severely wounded, and many leaders of the Kennebec march made prisoners. Word of the defeat reached Schuyler shortly after the HMS *Adamant* docked, landing Guy Johnson, Joseph Brant, and the manacled Ethan Allen in Falmouth, England. Weeks would pass before the good news from Quebec reached the Johnson party in London. Congress meanwhile persisted in viewing the repulse at Quebec as only a momentary setback in an otherwise commendable campaign. American forces, after all, had liberated Montreal, St. Johns, and Chambly. Schuyler knew better. One glance at the casualty lists showed that he had lost his fighting edge at the brink of victory. Now, as winter shut down Canadian operations, Carleton had time to reinforce and reorganize his regulars. When spring came round again, breaking up the ice in the St. Lawrence, a fresh British army would arrive at Quebec to confront Arnold and Montgomery's survivors. Schuyler could no more plumb to the bottom the disasters the American cause would suffer during 1776 than anyone else, but he did see clearly at the beginning of the year that the Northern Department no longer had time to play Sir John's game. With a retreat from Canada a distinct possibility, central New York stood to become the Revolution's decisive theater.

Yet, to march on Johnson Hall at Johnstown required a substantial force detached from the Canadian effort. Sir John could be counted on to raise several hundred armed Highlanders and a band of Mohawks to defend his property, and any force large enough to disarm this party would need to pass through Fort Hunter and *Tion-onderoge*, the lower Mohawk castle on the south bank of Tenonanatche. To do so without the explicit permission of Chief Tigoransera (Little Abraham) would be a violation of the peace treaty Schuyler himself had negotiated with the lower castle in August. While he scratched together enough Continentals to capture Sir John, he dispatched a delegation to seek Tigoransera's approval. The Mohawk's reaction was swift, predictable, and correct. An army marching across their lands to seize the respected son of their late and revered superintendent was not just a treaty infraction, but an unforgivable trampling of Mohawk sentiment and protocol. "Why not send a few men, accompanied by impartial and well-meaning Mohawk elders, to settle matters peacefully with Sir John? Let the issues be laid out for all to see. Let those who wished peace be heard." The fundamental policy of the Six Nations was to discourage the march of armies through their lands. Behind white armies came squatters who invariably abused Native Americans and appropriated their property. Moreover, "the proposed route of the intruding force was not through wilderness but through farms and settlements more than a century old where inhabitants native and white were often friends and relatives. This was not the way Christians treated each other."[32]

Tigoransera wasted no time pushing on to Albany with a delegation of his own to confront Schuyler. It was not that he favored one side or the other; he only knew that his people were being gripped in a vise that would continue to squeeze them until patriots and loyalists came to agreement. Unfortunately, he was too late. At Schenectady he walked head-on into Schuyler's forces. Militia had poured out of Albany County to join the general's Continentals, and Schuyler rode west at the head of almost 1,000 men, artillery, and a mile-long supply train. Marching east on the same river road came Nicholas Herkimer from German Flats with the entire Tryon County Militia. When the two forces joined, Schuyler had over 3,000 soldiers to present at Johnson Hall. What shook Little Abraham was not just the size of this army, but the visible proof that Tenonanatche had risen for the American side. Sir John and his followers believed that the majority of the settlers would turn out for the Crown. Herkimer's numerous battalions gave the lie to that theory.

Schuyler, however, had no wish to provoke or intimidate the Mohawks, whose neutrality was critical. Face to face with Little Abraham, he admitted to being wrong in his actions, if well-intentioned in his pursuit of peace—a song Native Americans had heard before. The main sticking point was Schuyler's contention that Sir John was fortifying Johnson Hall. Little Abraham argued that if this allegation were true, the Mohawks would have learned of it. All that Schuyler could do to assuage Little Abraham's displeasure was to include a party of Mohawk elders in his entourage to act as advocates and negotiators. Together they would march on the Hall to see what Sir John was really up to.[33]

The river that carried Guy Johnson's bateaux in late spring was now frozen solid, and on the hard surface south of the village of Fonda, Schuyler and Herkimer drew up their troops for review. It was a scene valley dwellers would not soon forget—3,000 men in uniforms, with regimental banners waving, presenting arms on the glittering ice.[34] The purpose of the display was to dissuade Sir John's followers from indulging in any foolish resistance. On word arriving of the patriots' approach, the Hall roused itself quickly, calling in armed retainers. Sir John, surprised by Schuyler's sudden strike, set to burying his valuable possessions behind the mansion and burning his papers. But if he thought of flight or resistance, the size of the force encircling the Hall soon dissuaded him. American officers disarmed his few dozen Highlanders and, breaking into the storerooms of the Hall, confiscated arms and munitions. Ingenuous as ever, Tigoransera remarked that Johnson Hall had always been flanked by stone blockhouses and stocked with arms for trade purposes; finding powder and ball proved nothing. His was not a voice raised on behalf of King George III, but on behalf of the Johnson family for whom Little Abraham and his people felt an undying affection. The general acknowledged the worthiness of their sentiments, for he too was a part of the prewar society of Tenonanatche.

Could Tigoransera forget that King Hendrick and his fabled Iroquois chieftains had been transported to the court of Queen Anne in 1710 at the expense of Schuyler's grandfather?[35] No, the Albany Dutch were hardly newcomers to the valley or strangers to loyalty. Yet, something precious and different was at stake now, Schuyler insisted. A new nation struggled to be born from the ruins of an old, and as a general officer of that new nation, he was held to deal with the last Johnson at Johnson Hall not as a neighbor, but as a threat to the greater idea.

His terms were severe, and Sir John received them in shocked amazement that any power in the land could dare to so deal with his family. Deliver up all "cannon, arms, and military stores," Schuyler demanded, "cause all Scotch inhabitants to deliver up their arms and turn over six of their number as hostages," and order "all loyalists in Tryon County to surrender their arms while also surrendering all Indian goods belonging to the Crown." Finally, Sir John was to consider himself under arrest. He would be sent to a place of safekeeping in Tryon County, unless Congress agreed to allow him to depart the Province of New York for another colony. His wife and child were to be held in Albany as guarantors of his compliance. Accept these terms, Schuyler's note promised, and he would receive the protection of the thirteen colonies.[36]

Of course Sir John balked at Schuyler's terms, but the general was not to be put off. Either John Johnson accepted the stipulations, or the Army of the Northern Department would arrest and imprison everyone at Johnson Hall, hunt down the Hall's associates, and as necessary, arrest and detain them. To these debasements the Mohawks objected strenuously, but they were brushed aside. John was left no alternative but to enter custody and be escorted by a mounted detachment to temporary confinement at Fishkill. Mary, with her newborn son, was to be removed to Albany, where she would be held comfortably but anonymously pending Congress's pleasure. The Johnson hold on Tenonanatche was at an end. Or so everyone thought on January 20, 1776. What followed during the ensuing weeks was a wholesale confiscation of loyalist property, arrest of sympathizers, and suppression of public opinion favoring the King. In reality, those who had bet on the Whigs now felt licensed to turn over their loyalist neighbors to the nearest lockup. In the vicinity of Johnstown, this place of tribulation became the county jail Sir William had donated to Tryon County, renamed Fort Johnstown and soon filled with Tory suspects.

But the great idea for which the colonies took up arms was not about to be realized in 1776. The British left Boston in late March, but their withdrawal went no farther than Halifax. Far from evacuating North America, Sir William Howe's forces merely positioned themselves to be redeployed. Thus, on April 13, Washington arrived in New York City, losing no time to move the main American army south behind him. By late April, outside the walls of Quebec, word spread among General Thomas's troops that a British fleet was in the St. Lawrence. On May 6, 1776, that fleet arrived, delivering General John Burgoyne with seven Irish regiments, one English, and 4,300 German mercenaries under Baron Friedrich von Riedesel to the defense of Quebec. The siege was over; the Americans were forced to retreat.[37]

On June 29, off Sandy Hook, New Jersey, a huge British fleet suddenly materialized out of the mist, beating to landward like "a fleet of pine trees trimmed" on the broad sea.[38] General Howe's army, 10,000 strong, had arrived from Halifax and would make itself at home on Staten Island in New York Bay awaiting the arrival of a far larger troop fleet sailing from British ports. As the war shrugged off its winter doldrums and gathered to begin in earnest, John Johnson was once again at Johnson Hall and up to his old tricks.

In the excitement of that spring, he had been allowed to give his parole and continue residing at the Hall with his wife. And there, while patriot attention turned to the collapsing Canadian effort and the swelling threat to New York City, Johnson busied himself establishing communication with the British fort at Niagara, 160 miles west of Johnstown. John Butler, acting Indian Supervisor in the absence of Guy Johnson, labored at Niagara to bring the Iroquois League to unanimous support of the crown. "Could you not make it so that you are one, as at the time when Sir William Johnson was alive," were his plaintive words to the league's councils.[39] But Butler, an old confederate of Sir William's and a longtime Mohawk neighbor, knew how to back up his pleas with substantial gifts of food, clothing, and rum during the hard winter of 1776.

As he roused the Indians to action, he also organized a company of rangers for frontier duty, and here John Johnson was of inestimable help. Displaced loyalists, harried out of the valley, were sent west to Niagara with his connivance, while Indian couriers came and went between Johnson Hall and Niagara carrying vital intelligence about American intentions.

From *Kanowarohare*, the principal Oneida castle, Schuyler's friends watched this traffic and sensed the rising threat from Oswego and Niagara. They were positioned south and west of old Fort Stanwix on the trail to Onondaga, and urged Schuyler to close the door to the valley before it was too late by repairing the dilapidated fortifications.[40] This Schuyler would do when he could, but for the moment he chose to confront Johnson for one last time. Sir John was summoned to Albany to answer charges of disloyalty brought against him by undisclosed informers. No one truly doubted that he was implicated in seditious activities, but witnesses called to testify at the tribunal on March 20 somehow managed not to appear. The case against Johnson folded, and Schuyler ordered him back to Johnson Hall with the usual adjurations—refrain from spreading seditious rumors, avoid meddling in matters of state, and desist from aiding the enemies of your country. If Schuyler felt let down by his no-show informers, he was not about to let Sir John know, and in the weeks to come surveillance of Johnson Hall tightened. By the beginning of May, Schuyler had the hard evidence he needed to take Johnson into custody, and this time he intended to make the arrest stick.

The 3rd New Jersey Regiment had arrived in Albany on its way north to Canada, where reinforcements were desperately needed to replace losses from desertion and smallpox. Now, on Schuyler's orders, a detachment of 350 Continentals, the cream of the regiment, was detailed under Colonel Elias Dayton to proceed to Johnson Hall and arrest John Johnson. On the way, Dayton was instructed to stop at the lower Mohawk castle and inform Little Abraham of his intentions. A special commission would arrive in advance of the regiment to negotiate the soldiers' passage over the river. And, if this were not difficult enough, Dayton was also to be alert to the presence of armed bands in the vicinity of Johnstown and the possibility of attack by hostile warriors.

Sir John, meanwhile, was well-informed of Schuyler's plan. Captain John McDonnell, passing through Albany in May, heard gossip about Dayton's intended mission and sent the news to Johnson Hall. From there, John Deserontyon, an educated Mohawk, was dispatched to Albany to discover the date of the expedition's departure, a mission accomplished easily by circulating through the taverns of the town. Barbara Graymont describes the outcome of Deserontyon's mission:

> Upon arriving in Albany, he learned that Dayton was to leave with his force three days hence. The trusty Mohawk then left Albany in the evening with a loyalist who had come from Governor Tryon with letters for Sir John and the commander of Niagara. They slipped through the guard around the city, and the Tory entrusted the letters to Deserontyon, who arrived with his message at Johnstown at 10:00 the next morning.[41]

This delivery occurred on May 18. The next day Joseph Bloomfield, captain in the 3rd New Jersey, takes up the account:

> Sunday the 19th of May. Proceeded on our March early this Morning. At 8 passed by the elegant Buildings of Col. Guy Johnson & Col. Claus, Son in Laws of Sr. Wm. Johnson, & now in England doing America all the Mischief in their Power. At xi passed by the very Neat and Elegant Buildings that the late Sr. Wm. Johnson lived in, generally called Fort or Castle William on the east side of the Mohawk river and within four Miles of the lower castle of the Mohawk Indians called Fort Hunter, which we passed by 12 O'Clock alarming the Indians along this delightful Country not a little & who appeared at a distance to be collecting. ... At 4 P.M. arrived at Johnstown, pitched our Tents at the upper End of the Town, our Troops being greatly fatigued with their march & heavy Burden of Provisions.[42]

Bloomfield studied hard to be a model officer during his first field assignment, hefting the same weight in packs as his men and marching at their head. The men, on the other hand, were anything but finished soldiers. Just before breaking camp at Albany, this entry from the captain:

> Last Night Seeley Simkins, Benjn. Simkins, Ebenezer Woodruff, Lewis Thompson, Uriah Maul & James Logan Deserted from me after Stealing a Watch & sundry other Things from the Company. ... Engaged on a Court Martial. Tried John Brewer of Col. Dayton's Regmt., Capn. Sharp's Compy.

For Desertion. Sentenced to receive 25 Lashes & return to his duty. Robert Barry for Drunkeness & Disobedience of Orders Sentd. To receive 25 Lashes. Michael Calen for Theft, Embezzlement & Selling the Publik Stores Sentenced to be carried to the Post with a Halter about his Neck & to receive 39 Lashes for Theft, also 39 Lashes for making way with the Congress Stores, be carried back with a Halter about his Neck to the Guardhouse & be confined 8 Days on Bread & Water & return to his duty. Spent the Eveng. & Supped with Mr. Caldwell our Chaplain at Mr. Henry's.[43]

Bloomfield was an observant New Jersey Presbyterian, recently admitted to the bar, and assiduous in his pursuit of the arts of war. He would succeed in many respects, rising to major before he was wounded at Brandywine, and eventually becoming a brigadier general in the War of 1812. With time he would be elected governor of New Jersey and also serve several terms in Congress. These honors lay ahead as he led his soldiers into Tenonanatche. What they thought of him, a fellow officer, Lieutenant Elmer, recorded in his diary: "Capt. Bloomfield is active, unsteady, fond of show, and a great admirer of his own abilities; quick passions, but easily pacified." Bloomfield was twenty-three years old, and this verdict might have been worse. He was learning, as they all were, and war would change him, hardening him to his duty before he retired as a wounded veteran. Thankfully, he was a prolific writer, appreciative of social nuances. Through his eyes, history has been left a vivid picture of Tenonanatche on the brink of hostilities. Arriving finally at Johnstown, they learned the following:

Sr. John Johnson had left John's Town with most of the Male Inhabitants & all the Highlanders, Dutch & Irish about it with 50 Indians, that they were embodied Armed and intended to Attack us Very probably this Evening.

Indeed, Sir John was gone, tipped off well in advance, but no one would say where or why. That night, according to Bloomfield:

being in a strange Country surrounded with woods added greatly to our apprehensions of being attacked which made our Centeries as Watchful as Night-Owls. Though the Officers and Soldiers were anxious to engage the Enemys of their Country, yet they wished for the Daylight for such bloody business. The latter part of the Night all quietness, no alarms or Accident happening in the Camp."[44]

The 3rd New Jersey had never been in a fight, and their apprehension was intensified by rumors and sounds. "The forepart of the Night," Bloomfield writes, "we could frequently hear the Indian Warriors yell the War-hoop or Alarum in a most hideous manner and this added to the Darkness of the Night." They were in no danger, but the inhabitants of the lower castle at Fort Hunter also had no intention of allowing them a peaceful night's sleep.

The next morning they were treated to a council in Johnstown. Little Abraham's warriors had arrived in war paint, stern and haughty, demanding an explanation for Colonel Dayton's invasion of their lands. The colonel and the commissioners sent forward by Schuyler assured the Mohawks that they wished them no harm as brothers, but were compelled to find and arrest enemies of Congress known to be in the neighborhood. All this was as expected. Then, bursting into the tense assembly, a Mohawk brave railed at the colonel and the emissaries as treaty breakers whom the Mohawks would crush as they willed. This also was as expected. Novices at Native American negotiations quailed at the surliness of the gathered braves, only to find the colonel standing up in the charged atmosphere, delivering the anticipated answer:

> Dayton threatened to break the covenant chain, to burn the upper and lower castles on the Mohawk, to burn the houses and homes of the Mohawks, destroy all of their towns, and cast them with their wives and children off the face of the earth. This to happen if they persisted in coming between the estranged factions of the white family.[45]

Of course this would not and could not be accomplished. But bellicosity was expected from both sides, and their flamboyant rhetorical exchanges signaled the end of the beginning as the parties now settled down to serious discussion.

While Dayton lost the day in endless reiterations of Schuyler's intentions and the friendship felt by all Americans toward the Mohawk people, Bloomfield was ordered to approach Johnson Hall with a letter to Lady Johnson, still residing at the house:

> I was early this Morning directed by Col. Dayton to take a file of Men & go to Johnson Hall with my side arms only & wait on Lady Johnson with a Letter, The substance of which was to demand the key of the Hall & drawers in the Rooms with direction for her immediately to Pack up her own apparel only and go to Albany. ... I asked for her Ladyship who was then a Bed and after waiting an hour she came into the Parlour. I gave her the Letter with assuring her Ladyship it gave me Pain that I was under the disagreeable necessity of delivering her a letter that must give her Ladyship a great deal of uneasiness. She hastily broke open the Letter & immediately burst into a flood of Tears, which affected me, so that I thought proper to leave her alone. After some time she sent for me, composed herself, ordered the Keys of the Hall to be brought in & given to me ... after which I breakfasted with her Ladyship.[46]

But while the lower castle negotiations continued, and as Mary played on Bloomfield's finer sentiments, where was Sir John? He was then approaching ten-mile-long Indian Lake in the heart of the Adirondacks with a party of 170 men and three Mohawk guides from the lower castle.[47] On May 19, traveling as light as possible, he had raced out of the valley just as Dayton's troops were arriving at Fort Johnson on the Schenectady road. Over the next three days the lower castle Mohawks and Lady Johnson did all in their power to hinder Dayton's pursuit—alarming the troops with intimations of ambush, confounding their command with long-winded negotiations, resorting to tears and even breakfast as a delaying tactic. John Johnson was gone to Canada on the straightest line his guides could contrive, and once there, angry to his core, he meant to throw off subterfuge, turn, and fight.

Of course, he had to get there first, and the Johnson escape through the forested mountains, at the beginning of spring as the snows began to melt and the black flies to swarm, remains a famous wilderness adventure. Game was scarce, and in many valleys the snow lay six feet deep. The party had brought little food, moving as fast and unencumbered as it could. The trek would last nineteen days, the last nine in Sir John's own words, "being nine days without any thing to subsist upon but Wild onion Roots and the leaves of the Beech Trees."[48] And which way did they go? No one quite knows. Eckert's theory that the flight led to Crown Point and north up Champlain is unlikely, given the heavy traffic of American troops over this route.[49] Another theory advanced by Adirondack historians has John moving north up West Canada Creek to Racquet Lake, from there through the present Seven Ponds Wilderness to the head-waters of the Oswegatchie, and at the rapids above Wanakena onto an Indian trail running to old Fort La Présentation at present-day Ogdensburg. Racquet Lake is said to have gotten its name from a pile of moldering snowshoes found at the lakeside where the Johnson party abandoned them during a sudden thaw.[50] No doubt Tories did move in and out of central New York by way of the Racquet and West Canada rivers, but a more likely escape route, given that Sir John eventually met Mohawk scouts from Akwesasne, were the trails passing west of Indian Lake, Long Lake, and skirting north around Tupper Lake into the Racquet River.[51] The point remains that in the years of the Revolution, because of active Mohawk support, the Adirondacks virtually belonged to the loyalists. From this fastness, raiding parties could descend east and west along the length of Tenonanatche with near total surprise.

Sir John emerged from the mountains with his party intact and, once fed on corn mush and maple syrup, the starvelings were quick to recover. They had man-aged to arrive on the British St. Lawrence, and during the following weeks, as General Carleton moved to recapture Montreal, they received arms and uniforms at Sir John's expense as the first battalion of the King's Royal Regiment of New York—Johnson's Royal Greens. Some were Highlanders or Palatine Germans loyal to the Johnson family, some descendants of the Irish tenants who had come into the country with Sir William in 1737. What would hold them together over the coming years was a mutual hatred for the rebels of the Mohawk Valley and an everlasting resentment of the injustices done them by what they took to be a hypocritical people forward in pleading their own rights while violating those of their neighbors. The patriots first saw them in action at Chambly on June 16, 1776, as Arnold's rearguard abandoned the town and fort in its flight southward. They were a motley force then, 500 strong and armed indifferently, but their leader would turn them into one of the finest ranger forces of the war.

Gavin Watt paints a romantic picture of John Johnson emerging from his nineteen-day trek:

> Sir John Johnson dressed like a frontiersman in a wide brimmed round hat adorned with a rattlesnake band and a fringed deerskin jacket and trousers. A scalping knife hung round his throat, and in his belt was a tomahawk. Sir John was thirty-four, erect and square shouldered with a long bridged nose set in an oval face and a thin, well-formed mouth. His dark, intense eyes were framed by natural brown hair swept into a queue.[52]

This was a man more like his father than many realized. He was brimming with energy and, having surrendered wife and home to his enemies, thought of nothing so much as the long road back. That road would lead through Oriskany, Cherry Valley, Wyoming, and Stone Arabia. Joseph Bloomfield mused on the differences between the father and the son:

> I'll say that we saw all Sr. William's Papers of all the Treaties He made with the different Indian-Nations ... all which placed Sr. William Johnson's Character in a Very important station of life and greatly merited the warmest thanks of his Country. But when we reflected on Sr. John's (his Son's) Conduct, it afforded a contrast not to be equaled. ... We could but detest and discommend the foolish imprudent, treacherous & base Conduct of the son, who, instead of Walking in the Paths of his good old Father in supporting the Liberty of America & thereby Merit the applause of his Country, He has basely endeavored and still is endeavoring to destroy the Libertys & Propertys of his Native Country.[53]

Captain Bloomfield had no idea of the forces that had driven Johnson and his followers into opposition to the grand American scheme. As Bloomfield struggled to master war on a European model, he also had no idea how much closer New York Tories would adhere to Native American tactics in turning their smaller, more maneuverable forces against the Continental Army. Schuyler had allowed a very dangerous enemy to escape his grasp. His vociferous critics would hold him accountable.

Three days after the Continental Congress accepted a final draft of the Declaration of Independence, July 4, 1776, the army of the Northern Department, under General Sullivan and Colonel Arnold, reached safety at Crown Point. Ten months earlier, under the command of General Montgomery, they had attempted the conquest of Canada. Over 13,000 Americans had been sent north to that war; now, 8,000 returned, and of those, more than 3,000 were in hospital. Schuyler and Gates watched the last of them come ashore at Crown Point, rowing hard and looking behind constantly for signs of British pursuit. Carleton and Burgoyne were moving schooners to the lake with sailors to crew them.[54] It would not take long to build flatboats to transport several thousand regulars south to Crown Point. Schuyler ordered the American survivors back to Ticonderoga.[55] Like it or not, he would have to hold there for as long as possible with exhausted, ragged, and demoralized troops.

Washington could not expect much help from the Northern Army as his own soldiers labored day and night on the defenses of New York City. But Schuyler also could expect little help from the hard-pressed Continental Army. On July 12, Admiral Richard Howe arrived outside the New York Narrows with 150 ships transporting 11,000 fresh troops—these to join his brother's force of 10,000 that had arrived in June. Two weeks later, Generals Clinton and Cornwallis appeared off Staten Island from Charleston with another 2,500 veterans. The odds against Washington were growing steeper.

Also coming ashore at Staten Island on July 12 were two travelers in civilian clothes returning from London. Guy Johnson and Joseph Brant had come home at last. They were brimful of new ideas for recapturing New York and splitting the rebellion in half. Colonel Johnson was to be attached to General William Howe's headquarters in New York City, while Captain Brant was to make for Niagara by way of Oquaga. This would free John Butler and his loyal Senecas to move to Oswego, from where they would be in constant communication with Sir John Johnson at Montreal. The noose was tightening on the patriots of the Mohawk Valley. Lady Mary, interned in the vicinity of Fishkill and moved constantly to new locations, slipped free of the American grasp in a daring escape. Disguised, and aided by a Johnson servant who provided horses, she managed to reach her family's home in Paulus Hook, New Jersey.[56] There, she lay hidden until Howe succeeded in capturing Manhattan in early August, freeing Mary at last to rejoin other Johnson exiles. Legend holds that Sir John visited his wife and family in the city, then smuggled them back to Canada through the help of ubiquitous Mohawk guides.

By the close of 1776, the Johnson party was positioned north, south, and west of Tenonanatche, prepared to squeeze their old neighbors in coordinated attacks. With Indian allies, they would provide the westernmost thrust into the valley, Howe the southernmost, Burgoyne and Carleton the northernmost. Mary could anticipate residing again at her aunt's spacious house in a loyalist Albany. That autumn, with the early onset of winter, all signs pointed to a quick demise of the American cause.

Washington's tatterdemalions, shivering in the unseasonable chill, fought again at White Plains, Mamaroneck, and Fort Washington, only to fall back to New Jersey in disarray. By late November a young captain of artillery, Alexander Hamilton, sited his pair of six-pounders on advancing British troops fording the Raritan River at New Brunswick. Hamilton was the rearguard of a battered, demoralized, and disintegrating army. Lord Stirling had arrived on the 29th with 1,200 fatigued troops to reinforce Washington, but as they shuffled into New Brunswick, 2,000 New Jersey and Maryland volunteers, whose enlistments had expired, took the opportunity to return home. Water was pouring out of the bucket faster than the bucket could be filled. By December 8, Washington's troops had been driven from New Jersey altogether and were holding a thin line on the Pennsylvania side of the Delaware River.

In the Northern Department, autumn 1776 brought even colder temperatures and equally appalling patriot conditions. Schuyler was facing calamity as he and Gates struggled to salvage a few hundred serviceable troops from the Canadian debacle. The generals in the north had soldiers who would fight and commanders who would lead, but they could not live through the winter on promises. As never before, Schuyler would dig into his own resources to feed and equip them. Ticonderoga was at stake, and New England responded mightily to the threat with fresh levies of militia. But the enemy approaching in his magnificence was not to be stopped by farm boys and ragged Continentals. Only an act of Nature could forestall Ticonderoga's capture and the loss of Albany before the end of 1776. Yet, in this moment of decision, to everyone's astonishment, Schuyler was busiest sending saws, axes, and men to a forlorn lumber mill at Skenesboro, where Arnold's survivors had been detailed to fell timber. If they could not stop the British on land, they might just stop them on water, at least long enough for Nature's icy grip to do the rest.

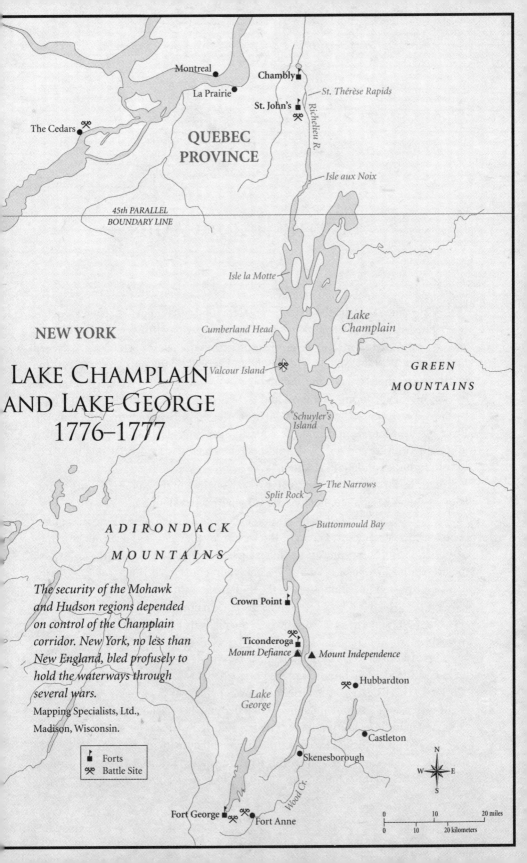

Montreal

La Prairie

Chambly

St. Thérèse Rapids

St. John's

The Cedars

QUEBEC
PROVINCE

Richelieu R.

Isle aux Noix

45th PARALLEL
BOUNDARY LINE

Isle la Motte

NEW YORK

Cumberland Head

Lake
Champlain

LAKE CHAMPLAIN
AND LAKE GEORGE
1776–1777

Valcour Island

GREEN
MOUNTAINS

Schuyler's
Island

The Narrows

Split Rock

ADIRONDACK

MOUNTAINS

Buttonmould Bay

The security of the Mohawk
and Hudson regions depended
on control of the Champlain
corridor. New York, no less than
New England, bled profusely to
hold the waterways through
several wars.

Mapping Specialists, Ltd.,
Madison, Wisconsin.

Crown Point

Ticonderoga
Mount Defiance   Mount Independence

Hubbardton

Lake
George

Castleton

Skenesborough

Forts
Battle Site

Fort George
Fort Anne

Wood Cr.

N
W   E
S

0   10   20 miles
0   10   20 kilometers

8

AT THE BARRICADES

How much time did they have before Carleton, with Burgoyne's reinforcements, sailed up Lake Champlain to the battlements of Ticonderoga? It was early summer, and on this determination rested the fate of Schuyler's Northern Department, Washington's lines of supply, and very likely the American cause. If the British, many thousands strong and amply supplied with artillery, arrived at the fort by summer's end, nothing Schuyler and Gates had at hand could save Ticonderoga. By the end of autumn, the British could be in Albany, with the mouth of the Mohawk River and the Mohawk's deep, fertile valley in their control. Should Washington then lose New York City and the lower Hudson, rebellious New England would be all but cut off from the contiguous colonies.

Some historians challenge this classic appreciation of the colonies' strategic situation at the close of 1776. Despite the Crown's overwhelming numerical superiority and material advantages, they question whether Britain ever had the strength to secure such vast wilderness areas in the face of an energetic and determined opponent.[1] Yet, in those desperate days, soldiers on both sides believed that Britain did have the power and that possession of the Champlain/Hudson corridor would settle the issue. Foremost in their thinking was the impact a British victory in the north would have on the growth of Tory formations. A rebel majority could hinder British success, but in the summer of 1776, who held the majority across the colonies remained in doubt.[2]

Out of a dozen well-equipped regiments Schuyler had rushed north to Canada, he had salvaged a few hundred ragged but reliable troops to man the defenses of Ticonderoga. His garrison had neither powder nor ball for muskets and cannon, slight rations, and almost no shoes. They had not been paid for several months. For every man fit for duty, another was hospitalized with camp fever. The dispensary stocked no medicines except simple herbs and homemade remedies. Men were dying in summer at a rate exceeding reinforcements. Schuyler had sent word to New England and the Schoharie and Mohawk valleys pleading for men, and gradually New England and New York responded. Josiah Bartlett of the New Hampshire Committee of Safety sent forth an impassioned appeal to militia colonels: "Supose your House in Flames, your wife, your Daughters Ravished, your Sons, your Neighbors Weltering in their Blood," would it not be time to wake up and man the walls of Ticonderoga?[3] From his home in the Mohawk Valley, Brigadier General Nicholas Herkimer sent Tryon County militiamen to Schuyler's service with orders written in the region's Palatine patois:

> Ser yu will orter your bodellyen do merchs Immiedietlih do ford edward weid for das brofiesen and amonieschen fled for on betell. Dis yu will disben yur berrell from frind Nicolas herchheimer. To Carnell pieder bellinger, ad de plats, oehdober 18, 1776.[4] [Sir: You will order your battalion to march immediately to Fort Edward, with four days' provisions and ammunition fit for one battle. This you will disobey at your peril. From your friend, Nicholas Herkimer. To Colonel Peter Bellinger, at the Flats, October 18, 1776.]

The threat to Bellinger is clear—Herkimer expects a battle in the neighborhood of Ticonderoga and he is rushing 300 men to the fort's defense with one battle's worth of ammunition. Either Bellinger will come to Schuyler's aid in time, or the Tryon County militia and the patriot organization in the Mohawk Valley will be in peril, which in turn will be Peter Bellinger's peril.

Miraculously, however, by late October the immediate danger to Ticonderoga had passed. The marriage of Philip Schuyler's logistics and Benedict Arnold's tactical brilliance had forced a delay in the British advance. From a late victory on Lake Champlain, General Carleton seized only a postponement of operations for the balance of 1776, and hard-pressed patriots on Tenonanatche and the upper Hudson gained six more months to prepare for invasion. Peter Bellinger had much to be thankful for, but many patriots who fought to buy him time would not be home at Christmas.

Their achievement in delaying Carleton went largely unnoticed as defeat after defeat seemed to plunge the American cause closer to extinction. No one in Congress was satisfied by skirmishes and strategic withdrawals, and yet these tactics practiced by the disparaged partnership of Schuyler and Arnold were laying the groundwork for recovery. What would succeed in 1777 by a slender thread could not have succeeded in the autumn of 1776 following devastating reversals. The strange sea battle at Valcour Island, fought off the shores of New York's Adirondack Mountains in October, would give Schuyler the months he needed to reinforce his barricades and ready an army for the coming year.

Once Carleton and Burgoyne had cleared St. Johns of American troops and laid open the lower waters of Champlain to British traffic, they needed to consider how next to move their regiments to Crown Point and Ticonderoga. Their combined forces numbered over 10,000, and even had roads been hacked through the wilderness to their objectives—and they had not—many more men would be required to secure those roads than Carleton or Burgoyne deployed. Reasonably, they could traverse the 100-mile-long lake by water. This was feasible, except that the Americans maintained a small flotilla on Champlain left over from their glory days in 1775. The schooner *Royal Savage*, twelve guns, had been captured by Montgomery at St. Johns; the sloop *Enterprise*, twelve guns, had been seized by Arnold at Ticonderoga; the schooner *Liberty*, six guns, was taken from Skenesboro by Captain Eleazer Oswald and Captain John Brown; and the schooner *Revenge*, six guns, had been built at Ticonderoga under Schuyler's direction. The vessels' two-, four-, and six-pound ordnance was sufficient to rake and sink a fleet of bateaux ascending the lake with British soldiers. The flotilla was not capable, however, of fighting back frigates and armed schooners manned by British sailors.

Thus, in the early days of summer 1776, Carleton attempted to drag several seagoing schooners from the St. Lawrence River past the Richelieu rapids above Chambly. The logs used as rollers for the ships sank in the mud of the unimproved roadway, and the plan was abandoned.[5] Desperate to make progress while fair weather lasted, Carleton ordered the vessels dismantled and carried piecemeal over the portage for reassembly. While British soldiers and sailors labored to move the schooners, carpenters and shipwrights from the British fleet parked in the St. Lawrence worked to build seaworthy vessels at St. Johns. Carleton had little notion what Schuyler and Arnold were up to, but he did realize that his window of opportunity was closing quickly. As governor of Canada, Carleton was familiar with northern winters and under no illusions about what would befall a campaigning army after a splendid New England autumn drew to a close.

Schuyler, too, knew what winter meant; he had thrown an army into Canada across the ice and snow. He gambled now that the British Army, used to a cessation of hostilities during inclement weather, would go to camp rather than pursue the ragged American forces. What he and Arnold contrived in the summer of 1776 was a blocking action that could delay the British advance until it was too late for Carleton and Burgoyne to exploit their advantages.[6] The first sign that Americans intended to fight for Champlain appeared in shipments of axes sent up winding Wood Creek to Skenesboro (Whitehall), New York. In Albany, Schuyler bought every axe available, begged more from local farmers, and managed to transport 1,500 to the solitary sawmill at Skenesboro. Governor Trumbull of Connecticut found another 1,000 and shipped them north.[7] What followed the axes were the men to wield them—shipwrights and carpenters from New England, laborers from the valleys of New York, lumbermen and farmers from Vermont. Schuyler paid riggers and chandlers top wages to make the dangerous trek into the wilderness. As his laborers and woodsmen felled the majestic trees at the head of the lake, and as lumbermen cut the timber into green boards, shipwrights and riggers fashioned the boards into gondolas—square-rigged vessels with short masts and flat bottoms, modeled on Spanish design. These awkward craft were meant to carry twelve- and eighteen-pound bow guns, with deck armament of three- and six-pound cannon.[8] They would be manned, ideally, by eighty to ninety men. American sailors, profitably employed by the thriving privateer trade, were everywhere in short supply; therefore, farmers from New York, New England, and Vermont would not only have to build these vessels, but also sail and fight them.[9]

Schuyler and Arnold were aware of Carleton's efforts at St. Johns to create a first-class naval force armed and manned from the British fleet, and equipped with gun platforms and giant *radeau* for transporting heavy artillery and mortars south against Ticonderoga. What they did not know until mid-September, when American scouts returned, was that the enemy also had under construction a frigate of twenty guns, the *Inflexible*, capable of destroying all of their vessels.[10] Yet Carleton, despite the efficiency of British intelligence, had little idea how extensive the American fleet was until he spied Arnold flaunting his new command in the southern waters of the lake. Carleton had seriously considered attacking in September without the *Inflexible*; now he resolved to wait into October for the completion of the frigate. The fatal delays, on which the Americans counted, had begun.

The idea of stopping the British on the lake was successfully sold to the governors of the northern colonies, and before long men and equipment poured in from Connecticut, Rhode Island, Massachusetts, Pennsylvania, and New Jersey. Brigadier General David Waterbury arrived at Skenesboro with elements of a Connecticut regiment; they would sail the *Washington* into battle. Colonel Edward Wigglesworth appeared with Massachusetts's militia; they would build and fight the *Trumbull*. The existing American flotilla was commanded by a Schuyler appointee, an irascible Dutch Albanian named Jacobus Wynkoop, who in a jealous, choleric fit over who had title to be called commodore of Lake Champlain, fired on Arnold's vessels. Wynkoop was arrested by Gates, and when brought to the attention of Schuyler, found a steely response from his fellow Albanian. The "commodore" was clapped in irons; Schuyler was more intent on winning the war than in assuaging the pride of ethnic groups, even his own. As the fleet at Skenesboro grew, the endless bickering and sectional rivalry that characterized the war in the north continued unabated. The general could never be sure when word might arrive from Congress dismissing him from command.[11]

Difficult as the construction of a battle fleet proved, the selling of Arnold's brainstorm to common soldiers was even more so. The whole plan terrified the simple farmers who had turned out after harvest to save Ticonderoga. For one thing, many of them could not swim; few had ever sailed a boat larger than a bateaux. And for another, all of them knew that green planks would quickly warp and leak on the stormy lake. Firing an eighteen-pounder from the bow of a cockleshell also did not recommend itself, especially since few of Arnold's conscripts knew how to lay a gun at sea. They would be up against some of the finest sailors in the world, who would also be aboard real vessels and heavily armed. If ever a force looked like a "forlorn hope," it was the 800 amateur seamen training now at Skenesboro and Ticonderoga to deny the British Lake Champlain.

But time was the worst enemy, and it seemed to be passing that summer faster than Schuyler could act. He had no time to order up seasoned lumber for shipbuilding; his men would have to fell standing timber and saw it into lumber on the spot. Schuyler, aided by the hard work of his secretary Richard Varick, rushed cordage, nails, and hardware for ships to Skenesboro, along with kegs of tar and bales of oakum to plug leaks in the green planking.[12] The fleet had to be ready to sail for Ticonderoga in September, where it would be fitted with ordnance and supplied with powder and ball.[13] Arnold wanted oars and lateen sails for maneuvering in the tight waters of Champlain, and he argued for galleys, keel-laid vessels, even if they took longer to build than flat-bottomed gondolas.[14] His novice sailors would be safer hauling sheets on an efficient hull than trying to tack unwieldy gondolas about in the wind. Arnold had been a ship's captain before the war, and his plan had much to do with the prevailing Champlain winds. The British, he knew, would not come south, that is, up the lake, except on a strong northerly blow. And they would come fast. If he could hide his fleet along the shoreline until they passed, he would have them beating back and tacking towards his position against the wind. Slowed and struggling for seaway, the British would face the broadsides of Arnold's vessels. Too many ifs, some might argue, but the hour was late and the situation of the patriots desperate.

By early October the British were on the move. Generals Burgoyne and Fraser reached the New York State line with six British regiments, one Hessian regiment, and a battery of Hanau artillery. On Ile aux Noix they left the 20th and 61st regiments as a rear guard and moved into the lake to meet Carleton's fleet. Four hundred Native Americans accompanied the British infantry in canoes. Flanking out to either side of the flotilla were a hundred Canadian rangers in bateaux. By then Carleton had over 13,000 troops under his command and adequate shipping to bring at least half that number immediately to the walls of Ticonderoga. In mid-September, Gates mustered 5,000 troops fit for duty, mostly Pennsylvanians who had recently come north. The good news was that Congress had finally succeeded in supplying his garrison with requested quantities of flint, powder, and ball.[15] For food, uniforms, and pay, however, they would continue to wait.

Arnold came into the lake on August 20 with the schooners *Royal Savage* and *Revenge*, the sloops *Enterprise* and *Liberty*, the gondolas *Boston, New Haven, Providence,* and *Connecticut,* and the gunboats *New York, Philadelphia,* and *Spitfire.* The fleet scouted north as far as Windmill Point, where it challenged the British to come out and meet it. Instead, a storm lashed the ungainly vessels and forced them to shelter in a secluded bay for several days.[16] Arnold ordered spruce trees felled to fashion fascines for the sides of the galleys and gondolas. These would obstruct boarding parties and deflect small shot. Ashore, his work detail was surprised by Indians and three men killed before they could return to the boats. Britain's wilderness allies were scouting the shores of Champlain, moving south in advance of Carleton's fleet.[17]

The Americans escaped, heading south along the New York side of the lake. They were joined as they rounded Cumberland Head by the newly completed galleys *Washington*, *Trumbull*, and *Congress*. The gunboats *Jersey* and *Success* (*New York*) also arrived, and Arnold now set course for Valcour Island aboard the *Congress*. Between Valcour and the New York shore lay a strait about half a mile wide and two miles long. The island was heavily forested and towered in places 180 feet over the water. Anchoring his vessels close together in a curved line across the strait, Arnold had lines rigged to swing the galleys broadside to the channel's southern approaches, uncovering their guns. As the British raced past Valcour, they were expected not to see the Americans. When alerted that the enemy fleet was behind them, they would beat back into the channel, snag on obstacles prepared in their way, and come under the combined firepower of the opposing fleet. Such was the plan, and Arnold's sailors now had days to think about the impending battle as they lay hidden in their leaky, camouflaged tubs.

Their general sent a continual stream of messages to Gates at Ticonderoga. The high hills around Valcour were painted with all the colors of a peak autumnal season, but the temperatures at night were frigid, and Arnold's men were dressed only in summer rags. No one could risk going ashore or lighting fires. Arnold begged for watch coats, breeches, blankets, caps, and shoes.[18] None arrived. He begged even harder for more men—sailors if Gates could find them. "We have a wretched, motley crew in the fleet," he wrote, "the marines, the refuse of every regiment and the seamen few of them ever wet with salt water, indifferent men in general and the great part of those who shipped for seamen know very little of the matter."[19] Schuyler's cash incentives had delivered many sorry specimens, and officers in the Northern Department tended to forward their greatest troublemakers when pressed for volunteers. Thus Arnold, like Washington, had his share of poorly disciplined summer soldiers. On the eve of battle, word arrived from Gates that Washington had been forced to evacuate Long Island and New York City. Arnold was stunned. "The Being in whose hands are all human events, will doubtless turn the scale in favor of the just and oppressed," he replied, and with a furious determination resolved to turn back the British invasion at any cost.[20]

Carleton sailed from St. Johns on October 4 with a fleet consisting of the square-rigged ship *Inflexible*, the schooners *Maria* and *Carleton*, the radeau *Thunderer*, the gondola *Loyal Convert*, twenty gunboats, and twenty-eight long boats lightly armed and stocked with supplies. His fleet was manned by 670 seamen from the British Navy, and each of the four larger vessels carried a company of the 29th Regiment acting as marines. The British brought forty-two guns to the battle compared with the Americans' thirty-two; in weight of fire, the British discharged 500 pounds against the Americans' 265.[21] As the enemy was spotted rounding Cumberland Head, Waterbury urged Arnold "to come to sail and fight them on a retreat in the main lake as they were so much superior to us in number and strength and we being in such a disadvantageous harbour."[22] One look at Carleton's vessels tacking towards Valcour was enough to convince Arnold that his clumsy force stood no chance of out-sailing them. The Americans hunkered down for a slugfest.

As Arnold expected, once the British spotted their foe, they came about into the wind and immediately found maneuvering difficult. But so too did the *Royal Savage*, returning to the anchorage from having roused the enemy. The American schooner, Arnold's best, was hit three times by gunboats, partly dismasted, and ran aground on the southern tip of Valcour Island. Its crew continued to man the guns even while the *Inflexible* swept the schooner's decks with gunfire. Meanwhile, the *Carleton*, with total disregard for American naval prowess, sailed smack into the middle of the curving line and was promptly shot to pieces by the bow guns of the gondolas and galleys. The *Carleton* was sinking, most of its crew dead or wounded when, with skill and daring, British sailors managed to bring the schooner off and out of range. Like ravening wolves, the gunboats flocked to the slab-sided gondolas and pummeled them with twelve-pound shot. The *Philadelphia* was holed below the waterline and was soon sinking; the *Washington* and *Congress* were shipping water and beginning to wallow when a lucky shot from the *Congress* exploded a British gunboat in a fountain of timber, smoke, and debris. Body parts splashed onto the blood-slicked deck of the galley, and a cheer went up from the crew for their powder-blackened demon gunner—Arnold himself, the only member of the crew who knew how to fire a cannon. He ran from gun to gun laying it on target, priming, and firing.

Several times British boarding parties tried to capture the stranded *Royal Savage*, only to be driven back by soldier sailors wielding muskets and bayonets. Fire from shore was intense; Indians and Canadians on both the island and the mainland crept as close to the vessels as possible, but the Americans' spruce branch fascines deflected their flaming arrows. Slowly, inexorably, as the battle continued through the afternoon of October 11, the mighty *Inflexible* drew closer to the inner channel. With her broadsides she should be able to shatter the American line, and now the British small boats, sensing their opportunity, pressed in for the kill. They met a nasty surprise. Grapeshot on top of cannonballs would sweep a boat of crew while the shot smashed through its bottom. The American fleet was battered, in some instances sinking, yet fighting back amidst a sea of floating spars, bobbing bodies, and tangled cables when at last the *Inflexible* closed the range and loosed its first broadside.

Probably most of the casualties suffered by the American side in the battle occurred during the five broadsides fired by the *Inflexible*. The anchorage was swallowed in flame-stabbed clouds of smoke; the sun was setting and the air darkening, but through the failing light, gunners made out shot bouncing off the *Inflexible* while her artillery sheered away the rigging of the *Washington*, swept the deck of the *Congress* with a deadly hail of iron and splintered wood, sank the *Philadelphia*, and blew men off the decks of the *Trumbull* into the blood-stained waters of the lake. But the frigate could come no closer, and the Americans winched their wrecks farther up into the channel. Aboard the gunboat *New York*, Lieutenant Thomas Rogers touched his linstock to the firing hole of a six-pounder and the cannon exploded. Rogers was torn apart by flying fragments, his gun crew blown over the side, and all officers but the captain of the *New York* were killed by the blast.[23] Yet somehow the gunboat stayed afloat, and this saved the life of Sergeant Jonas Holden, whose right side had been severely burned and lacerated. Trapped beneath falling rigging or pinned under overturned gun carriages, men drowned as their vessels slipped under the surface of Valcour strait. But Holden, who had fought at Concord and would live to witness Yorktown, was in luck. The *New York* extricated itself from its fallen rigging and went to oars; it would be one of the few gunboats to survive the battle and arrive at Ticonderoga.[24]

The arrival of early darkness saved the Americans from further harm, but with 10 percent of crews dead or wounded, most of the vessels holed and leaking, and ammunition largely expended, the prospects for morning were hardly encouraging. The *Royal Savage* had been set afire by British boarders and was burning brightly, illuminating the anchorage. Indeed, the enemy had suffered heavy damage as well, but many of his vessels had never engaged. British gunboats bore the brunt of the American fury, while Arnold's galleys and gondolas were severely mauled. During the night Arnold could count on the British plugging both ends of the strait, landing marines on both shores, and wrestling guns onto the island. To stay where they were was almost certain to cost the Americans their fleet. Carleton knew from past experience that Arnold favored night actions, and the British flotilla at the southern opening of the strait was put on alert against the enemy's escape.[25] What Carleton did not reckon with was the dense autumnal mist that often rises over Champlain as air temperatures drop. In the dense fog of early morning, the American fleet slipped anchor and, relying on muffled oars, followed the *Trumbull* unseen through the British pickets into the lake.

By the time the British awoke to discover the anchorage empty, Arnold's fleet was eight miles south of Valcour at Schuyler Island. The most heavily damaged vessels were run ashore for repairs. Two badly hit galleys were towed off the beach, abandoned, and sunk. By mid-afternoon of October 13, American survivors were rowing south on Champlain toward Crown Point with the furious Carleton in hot pursuit. No one doubted who would win this race, and when at 11 AM the *Inflexible* drew within gun range of the fleeing flotilla, Arnold ordered the *Congress* to come about, signaling the *Washington* to accompany him. Over the next two and a half hours these two galleys occupied the enemy's attention, buying time for the smaller gondolas and gunboats to escape. General Waterbury, the only officer left alive aboard the *Washington*, fought the *Maria* and several other assailants before surrendering his shattered hulk. Aboard the *Congress*, Arnold stood off the *Inflexible* until he spotted a gap between his adversaries and rowed upwind. Slipping clear of the desperately tacking British, he opened distance, driving the *Congress* into the opposite shore. Arnold led his soldiers into the woods with their small arms, leaving the *Congress* to burn to the waterline.

The following day most of the scattered small fry of the American fleet turned up at Crown Point. They proved handy in evacuating the old ruined fort and ferrying Arnold and his survivors south to Ticonderoga. The mood of the defeated Americans was somber as they salvaged what could be saved from their encampment at Crown Point and rushed out just ahead of the British. On October 14, Carleton informed Lord Germain that "the Rebel fleet upon Lake Champlain has been entirely defeated." Following this news came the concession for which Arnold had fought: "Yet the season is so far advanced that I cannot yet pretend to Your Lordship whether anything further can be done this year." Burgoyne, second in command, was furious with the decision. His chance to make fast work of the Americans with his infantry and artillery had been postponed until the following year.

Few fully appreciated at the time what Schuyler and Arnold had accomplished with their leaky boats and farmer sailors. Colonel William Maxwell, commander of a New Jersey regiment, wrote to Governor Livingston, "General Arnold, our evil genius to the north, has, with a good deal of industry, got us clear of all our fine fleet ... a pretty piece of admiralship."[26] Maxwell's sarcasm spoke of the bitter disappointment many felt at the string of defeats presided over by Arnold and Schuyler from the gates of Quebec to the walls of Ticonderoga. Only much later did the Battle of Valcour Island come into focus as a decisive action leading to American victory in 1777. Admiral Alfred Mahan, the nineteenth-century naval strategist, inscribed for posterity the meaning of those splintered and bloodied galleys: "The little American navy on Champlain was wiped out: but never had any force, big or small, lived to better purpose nor died more gloriously, for it had saved the Lake for that year."

Indeed, the year to come would be full of ordinary men making extraordinary sacrifices, but beyond all the grand strategies lay the irreducible realities of war. Sergeant Jonas Holden came home to tell his story of what happened on the *New York* that late afternoon, October 11. He, or someone else who knew, explained to Lieutenant Thomas Rogers's widow in Westford, Massachusetts, that her young husband had been killed and his torn body thrown overboard. The body would never be found. Mrs. Rogers was nine months pregnant, and in Westford's Fairview Cemetery she raised in time a memorial to the dead father of her child. The inscription reads:

This Monument is Erected to the memory of Lieut Thomas Rogers by Mrs Molly his Sorowfull widow He was Killed by the splitting of a Cannon on the Lake Champlain on the 11th day of Oct 1776 in the Continental Army in the serves of his Country and in the caus of Liberty Aged 26 years and 9 months.[27]

As General Carleton huddled in his cloak on the landing at Crown Point, the icy wind sealing his decision, 100 air miles to the southwest an Oneida blacksmith defied the weather wrapped in a blanket. Thomas Spencer—Ahnyero to his people—was a watcher. From his vantage point on the edge of a wood, he could see the desultory repairs going forward at Fort Stanwix under Colonel Elmore. Elmore and his Connecticut line had just replaced Colonel Dayton and his 3rd New Jersey. In Thomas's opinion, the Connecticut men were too few and too late; winter would soon be upon them, shutting down all work beneath a blanket of ice and snow. If the bad news reaching the Oneidas that fall were any indication, the patriots of Tenonanatche would need a defensible redoubt come spring. Yet, from the look of the gap-toothed palings and sagging casemates, Stanwix, recently renamed Fort Schuyler, would not be ready.[28]

News of Washington's defeats came to Ahnyero from his spiritual guide, the Reverend Samuel Kirkland, who often preached in the vicinity of Stanwix and Oneida castle twelve miles away. With many others at old Kanowarohare, Thomas supported the American cause out of a fervent piety and a growing resentment at British coercion. On his mother's side he was Oneida, and through her, a warrior of the Wolf Clan. From his English father he inherited the blacksmith's trade, along with a tidy farm in Cherry Valley in the southern highlands of Tenonanatche. Because his occupation took him through the Mohawk districts, mending ploughs, shoeing horses, repairing gunlocks, Ahnyero was the perfect scout—a keen listener and sharp observer in the villages he visited.[29] Thus, by the end of the year, he was aware that Thayendanegea, Joseph Brant, had returned from London and was resident at Oquaga.[30] Commissioned and charged by the King, Brant was raising recruits among the tribes for war on the New York frontiers.

From the elderly war chief of the Wolf Clan, Skenando, came a warning to Colonel Dayton in early September that Sir John Johnson was reported landing at Oswego with several hundred Tories. This rumor proved unfounded, but not before another arrived claiming that John and Walter Butler were at Oswagatchie with a large party of marauders. In each instance Thomas was sent deep into the wilderness to confirm stories that often were only garbled tales of hysterical sightings. Hostiles, villagers insisted, were spying on Cherry Valley from nearby mountaintops; the village had sent all its militia to Washington or Schuyler. Who would protect them? Thomas Spencer tracked the lurkers westward along trails to Niagara and confirmed that unknown braves were paying inordinate attention to a small, out-of-the-way hamlet. This particular sighting *was* a cause for alarm. Cherry Valley was added to a long list of villages requiring protection. Fear was everywhere as 1776 faded into 1777, and the Oneidas were not alone in looking to the old blockhouses and fortifications of the French War as places of refuge. Spencer screened and confirmed what reports reached him, passing them on to Kirkland, who sent them forward to Schuyler. In late September, Kirkland wrote to Schuyler from Fort Stanwix:

> Tuesday received some account from the Indians which were in favor to our Cause & Col. Elmore requested my tarrying a few days longer & not to leave this post till Mr. Spencer might be procured to tarry here during my absence. This evening informed that the Oneidas refused to send any of their young men in quest of three tory deserters from German Flats. Viz. Col. Tinbrook, Honyost Harkimer, & Honyost Schuyler.[31]

Well-disposed as many Oneidas were to the American cause, they outright refused to be used for tracking fugitives from patriot justice. Nor would they raise a weapon against fellow Iroquois except in self-defense. Neighbors judging neighbors, hunting them down, confiscating their property, abusing wives, children, and servants did not square with the gospel principles of Kirkland's flock or the deep politic of the Oneida sages. Neither Schuyler nor Kirkland pushed them. Schuyler had his own watcher among the Mohawks—a young, attractive Mohawk woman named Mary Hill whom many took to be his mistress. The allegation survives, yet to imagine Mary as a spy for the Americans or, as is more likely, a double agent in Molly Brant's employ, adds another intriguing plot to the twisted relationships in the Mohawk Valley.[32] She did travel to the general at Albany many times during these troubled months to report on the Mohawk dispositions at Fort Hunter and Canajoharie, and from Mary, Schuyler certainly had confirmation of the strain being placed on the Iroquois League by committed adversaries—Brant and Butler for the Crown, Kirkland and Skenando for Congress.

Poor Little Abraham at Fort Hunter was trapped between these forces and lived in constant anticipation that one side or another would uproot his people and send them off to Albany or Niagara, the opposite poles of the growing struggle. Schuyler was fluent in Mohawk, conversant in Iroquois dialects and, with the Johnson party in exile, received many Native American delegations. He and the Dutch families of the upper Hudson were under no illusions about what might happen if the Iroquois League collapsed. The council at Onondaga acted as a brake on the downhill rush of league members to one side or the other. Release that brake and there would be no control over murderous war in the Province of New York. To the farsighted, this likely outcome spelled an end to two centuries of political engagement protecting native and immigrant alike. Only a fool would press an advantage so morally perilous, but by now the British Crown was calling in its markers with a total disregard for consequences.

The old year had passed to a cold grave when, on January 19, a party of Oneidas braved a snowstorm to bring Colonel Elmore shattering news: "The Oneidas declared that the Central Council fire of the Iroquois at Onondaga had been extinguished and that henceforth the tradition of unanimity of the Six Nations would no longer exist.

Each nation would now act on its own behalf. That unity, so long a major factor in the strength of the League, was now dead."[33] The Onondagas gave out that "a devastating pestilence of unknown origin had swept through their settlement, leaving disaster in its wake and disrupting the normal relations of the tribe. Such a sudden and great tragedy caused the extinguishing of the great council fire."[34] Stories were told of how the fire was extinguished by angry partisans, but the Onondagas' transparent allegory of a great sickness disrupting normal human relations contained the essential truth. Accommodation had grown impossible between firebrands urging war and neutralists counseling caution, between clans leaning British and clans leaning American. A middle ground was nowhere to be found. The Iroquois dependence on British bounty and imperial policy, encouraged by Sir William and a long line of colonial secretaries, had resulted at last in the political paralysis Conrad Weiser and Shickellamy had long ago predicted.

At a council in late January, General Schuyler announced to an assembly of sachems that to help combat the devastating "pestilence," he was sending aid to Onondaga. Along with blankets and medical supplies this aid took the form also of news. He told them of General Washington's stunning victories at Trenton and Princeton far to the south. The assembly cheered. But the only league members attending Schuyler's council fire were Oneidas; the rest of the Iroquois either stayed away or had left for Niagara in the west, where supplies and provisions were given freely in exchange for a commitment to raise the hatchet against rebels.

On the frontier, the harsh reality of daily life usually trumped matters of politics or party. Carleton restrained his Indians from raiding patriot settlements in order to preserve the fur trade vital to Canada's economy.[35] Senecas, with memories of humiliation at British hands, still required trade goods, and thus were thrown onto the detested British at Niagara for barest survival. Schuyler, bankrupted by war, ill-supplied by Congress, had terribly little to offer them. They had kept the peace as promised, but now in a hard winter when they were in need, American doors seemed shut to them. Schuyler lamented to Congress in January 1777, "My house is daily crowded with them, and I have next to nothing wherewith to relieve their distress."[36] His slender trade goods were reserved for Indians committed to the patriot cause. Isabel Kelsay explains the dilemma:

In February 1777 Philip Schuyler not only had no ammunition for the Indians; he had none for the northern army which he commanded, and he did not even know where the Continental magazines were, if any! It was a stern fact of life that the rebels had to supply the Oneidas or give up the frontier and the great granary that was the Mohawk valley. For the people of Oquaga and the rest of the Indians along the Susquehanna they had scarcely anything left. The latter were being pushed, inexorably, toward the British at Niagara.[37]

But the people of Oquaga were not without a daring and resourceful leader, and Joseph Brant had no intention of watching his neighbors and in-laws starve. From Oquaga, he had journeyed the "Forbidden Path" into Seneca country and on to Niagara.[38] Along the route through the Finger Lake country, he pleaded the Crown's cause to a desperately confused people, who often as not met his offers to clothe, feed, and arm them with surprising silence and skepticism. Thayendanegea might bring hope of restoring the largess of Sir William's time, the peace and prosperity of empire, which Americans, he argued, sought to overthrow for their own gain. Yet, who indeed was this Thayendanegea, people asked, to tell Senecas when to raise the hatchet. The sell also proved harder than expected because John Butler, Carleton's Indian Supervisor at Niagara, had no intention of releasing his war bands piecemeal and worked against Thayendanegea's mission in every possible way. Behind Butler's calculations lay a stratagem of preserving Indian strength until it could be combined in support of British troops invading New York. Disappointed, Brant returned to Oquaga to find fresh avenues of attack. What he had not realized was that Schuyler, informed by Ahnyero, had been following his every move.

No sooner was Brant off to Niagara than Colonel John Harper, militia commander at the Schoharie forts, rode into Oquaga with a company of scouts to ascertain whether local hostiles were indeed preparing for war. Harper interrogated villagers, contributed a roast steer to the community supper, and concluded that if the Oquaga Iroquois were sullen, they were certainly not spoiling for a fight. Yet there were pieces missing. Harper noticed that most of the young braves were gone; they were said to be hunting far away. Game was sparse that February, and the chase led deep into the upper Delaware mountains. All very well, Harper concluded, betting that many of these warriors were actually rustling cattle and other livestock along the Mohawk. No, no, he was assured, they went east to the mountains, not north to the river.

Harper on the trail home was not surprised to spot fifteen warriors returning towards Oquaga from the south banks of the Mohawk. They skirted his party and vanished into the forests. He tracked them with a company of Schoharie militia all day and into the night and found them at last asleep beside a roaring fire on Schenevus Creek. All fifteen were arrested on suspicion of raiding, and in the morning taken to Albany and jailed. Harper contended that they were heading to Unadilla to plunder isolated farmsteads; the Mohawks replied that they were hungry and scouring the countryside for food or game. Either or both could have been true. No shot was fired in this confrontation, but a sense of mortal threat hung over apprehended and apprehender alike. Tenonanatche's fuse was lit and smoldering.

Brant answered Harper's provocation, once he learned of it, by raising eighty warriors and storming into the tiny hamlet of Unadilla, five miles downstream from where the Unadilla River leaves its picturesque valley to flow into the Susquehanna.

Thirty or so houses comprised the Unadilla settlement then, and Brant's sudden appearance found most of the inhabitants at home. They were dragged from their houses into the village square and told that the Mohawks were appropriating their livestock and grain. The reasons given: 1) the rebellion against the King had driven loyal Mohawks from their rightful fields and gardens; 2) the people of Unadilla supported the said rebellion and had helped to confiscate Mohawk property; 3) the loyalist Mohawks were only reclaiming their own in time of severe need. The villagers protested that they had nothing to do with rebellion yet, surrounded by dozens of armed warriors, they had no choice except to watch their goods loaded into wagons and carted away. On a flagpole in the center of town, Brant hoisted the Union Jack. It flapped in the raw wind as the villagers stood by silently. This time, there would be no further retribution, he announced, but rebellion would not be tolerated beneath the flag. Any who could not accept the law of the King, had best leave Unadilla and the surrounding country before too late.[39]

Harper's arrest of fifteen Mohawks had inadvertently unleashed a concerted effort by loyalists to cleanse settlements along the Susquehanna of patriot influence. In the town of Oquaga, Oneidas, such as Brant's in-laws, clung more firmly to neutrality, while across the southern tier of the province, Whig-leaning settlers pulled up stakes and moved closer to the Mohawk and Schoharie forts. Indeed, people seemed to be in motion everywhere across central New York as sides took shape and communities came together for mutual safety.

Schuyler would have to reply to the Oquaga provocation, but in February he could not risk adding to his troubles by precipitating a frontier war. One glance at the map makes his precarious position clear. The Northern Army of Congress, at the head of the Hudson, was virtually encircled. Around the province's peripheries the British controlled powerful, interlocking positions. In New York City to the south, Howe commanded a force capable of ascending the Hudson along New York's borders with New England or fanning out across New Jersey to seize Philadelphia. At St. Johns, on the northern end of Lake Champlain, a fleet was in readiness to carry fresh British troops south to Ticonderoga and beyond. Along the Susquehanna, near the headwaters of the Delaware, Oquaga loomed as a base of operations from where raiders could ascend to Lake Otsego in the center of the province, penetrate the Catskills, or break into the Schoharie and Mohawk valleys. Across Indian country to the west stood formidable Fort Niagara, linking Montreal and Quebec with Lake Erie and Detroit. On the shores of Lake Ontario, Fort Oswego threatened the western end of the Mohawk, while down the St. Lawrence, at an intersection of trails crossing New York's Adirondacks, Oswagatchie was to become a magazine for raids south into the Mohawk and Schoharie regions.

To his dismay, Schuyler presided over a principality of ruined forts. Ticonderoga and Independence soaked up the resources of New York and New England while contributing little to the security of the region. At the top of Lake George, Fort George, largely dismantled, guarded the road from moldering Fort Edward to the cinder-strewn site of old Fort William Henry. Schuyler wrote to Washington that so little defensive value remained to Fort Edward that he had jumped his horse over the sagging walls. Fort Miller, closer to Albany, was nothing more than a stockaded enclosure, and Fort Anne, screening the east bank of the Hudson above Albany, had long been a pile of mildewed logs. Fort Herkimer, like Fort Schoharie, was a barricaded stone church surrounded by outer works, and Fort Dayton, the Tryon County militia headquarters at Herkimer, was nothing more than a log-enclosed parade ground without cannon. Faced with the enemy's numerous infantry and artillery, Schuyler was a prince without clothes, even while Congress persisted in thinking him well-dressed.

Lacking defenses, men, and guns, Schuyler knew he would have to fight in the woods. Once again the axe might prove mightier than the musket. But one place in his defensive cordon was startlingly devoid of trees, and here he needed stopping power more than anywhere else. The Great Oneida Carry, located between the Mohawk River and Wood Creek, lay on a flat, swampy plain. The roads approaching the mile-long portage ran on either side of the river through flat, sandy fields, and while the terrain was intersected by numerous small watercourses, these offered little obstacle to invasion. For just this reason, Brigadier General John Stanwix built his fort at the Carry in 1758 to replace three smaller British forts destroyed during the French and Indian War. He built ingeniously low to the ground in a rising meadow with heavy logs laid lengthwise and piled high with cut sod. An attacker would not see the depth of the defensive ditch outside the palisades or the long slope of the *glacis* until almost to the fort's escarpment. In fact, looking into Stanwix from outside revealed almost nothing about its condition. The deep embrasures were designed to mask light artillery suitable for wilderness defense, while the bomb-proofed bastions provided firing platforms ample enough for companies of infantry. Stanwix could neither be reduced easily by small artillery nor burned by fire arrows. It closed Tenonanatche in the west like a cork in a bottle, and was the principal fort in Schuyler's domain that needed to be repaired and held.

By April 1777 the general suspected that the main attack in his theater would be mounted in early summer against Ticonderoga. From preparations underway at Oswego, and reported by Thomas Spencer, Schuyler also expected a flanking attack into the Mohawk Valley coordinated with the main advance on Albany from Canada. By no means was there agreement in the Continental camp about the impending attack. John Hancock thought that the British troops in Canada would be sailed to New York City and employed against Philadelphia. General Horatio Gates doubted that the British would try the wilderness route from the north again, and told General Arthur St. Clair, Ticonderoga's fifth commandant in a year, that his post would remain a quiet one.[40] St. Clair trusted these assurances and brought his young son with him from Philadelphia. Only months later, on the brink of assault, did Gates think to remind St. Clair of the heights looming over his position that were accessible to enemy artillery.[41]

The detailed contents of Burgoyne's plan, "Thoughts for Conducting the War from the Side of Canada," unveiled to King George and his ministers in early 1777, could not have been known to Schuyler as he resolved to reinforce Fort Stanwix with his best troops and most energetic officers. His prescience made sense only after Colonel Barry St. Leger, with a mixed force of regulars and Indians, slipped up Wood Creek in July and seized the Carry. By then Fort Stanwix's bastions contained 600 Continentals of the New York and Massachusetts line, supported by Oneida scouts and equipped with ample small arms and light artillery. St. Leger, brevetted a brigadier general for the campaign, arrived at the head of a rapid, hard-hitting infantry thrust 2,000 strong, and marched headlong into a siege for which he and his force were not prepared. How Schuyler managed this sleight of hand, while also reinforcing doomed Ticonderoga and preparing for guerilla warfare above Albany, was just one of the surprising accomplishments of the great, sprawling Saratoga campaign.

There was good news amidst the bad as American forces moved into action with the spring thaw. Two years of war, bitter losses and retreats, had tested the patriots, and now a corps of junior officers increasingly able to lead in the field had begun to emerge. Schuyler noted this evolution, and in late April called Colonel Peter Gansevoort to his headquarters at Stillwater. Gansevoort commanded the Northern Army's supply depot at Fort George, a tedious assignment from which little glory flowed. Gansevoort was twenty-eight, an ardent patriot, and a veteran of the Canadian campaign. He was Princeton-educated, the scion of a well-to-do Dutch Albanian family, and presently the commanding officer of the 3rd New York. Under his stern but benevolent leadership, that troubled regiment had finally begun to cohere. On April 17, as ice cracked along the Mohawk freeing the river for barges, Schuyler dispatched the 3rd to Stanwix. A few weeks later, Gansevoort was transferred to the post with instructions to repair the rotten palings, build barracks, and block Wood Creek with fallen timber. In support, Schuyler assigned a French engineer, Captain B. La Marquisie, recently arrived and commissioned by Congress. Gansevoort was to work his men twelve hours a day, with only short breaks for lunch and dinner, until the fort's lines of approach were defensible.[42] Schuyler, meanwhile, would ram through supply boats to fill the fort's magazines and find additional troops to bolster the garrison. What he also needed at Gansevoort's right hand was a field officer with proven ability to train and lead infantry.

If he meant to fight at this barricade, the general could not have done better than assign Lieutenant Colonel Marinus Willett, late of the 4th New York, to Gansevoort as second in command. Willett was the fighter Schuyler sought, a street brawler in the early days of the Revolution who had led a party of New York City ruffians in an attack on British stores. The muskets Willett liberated went to arm the 1ˢᵗ New York, the regiment Montgomery led to the walls of Quebec. Willett was a tradesman's son from Jamaica, Long Island, thirty-seven years old and no stranger to hard campaigning. He had enlisted in His Majesty's Colonial Provincials at age seventeen, been present at Abercromby's disastrous assault on Ticonderoga in 1758, and served under Bradstreet at the capture of Fort Frontenac the same year. The harrowing wilderness march back from Frontenac had nearly cost him his young life, but Willett survived the ordeal to return through the Mohawk Valley to New York City.[43] He participated in the fighting around St. Johns in 1775 and took command of the fort after Montgomery moved north to Montreal. Everything that war on the frontiers had taught him was about to be applied at Stanwix, where rough men under hard taskmasters were laboring through the lengthening days to seal off Tenonanatche.

Gansevoort arrived at the fort on May 3; Willett followed with the remainder of the regiment on May 10. Schuyler got them up just in time. Ahnyero reported braves from Oswego probing the tributaries east of Lake Oneida. Ice had broken up in the St. Lawrence, and on May 5, General Burgoyne sailed past the rock of Quebec to join his gathering expedition. He carried with him from London orders placing him over General Carleton as senior field officer of Britain's northern army. Carleton was relegated to a secondary role, and with his demotion, word spread along the circumferences of New York that Carleton's modest use of Native Americans was about to change. In the future, the new commander instructed his subordinates, Indians were to be used aggressively. Within a month, Burgoyne was at St. Johns; a month later, he was at the gates of Ticonderoga. The diversionary attack up Wood Creek into the Mohawk Valley was also preparing, and at Oswego, Native American scouts in war paint slipped silently into the forests.

Fort Stanwix was hardly an ideal post for withstanding large-scale assaults. It had been designed to fend off raids, not lengthy sieges. The enclosed parade ground was small, and the barrack space, storage, and magazines accommodated only a few companies. Schuyler judged that Gansevoort would need at least two regiments to stand a chance. He packed 500 men of the 3ʳᵈ into the fort and was still sending up detachments of the Massachusetts line over and above these.[44] Where was the room to live, the food to eat for 750 soldiers? Gansevoort's force seemed too small to maneuver and too large to defend. Water was a serious concern; the fort tapped a small stream running under a covered way. Once hostilities commenced, this brook would certainly be cut off. The garrison's latrines also were built over the brook, just below the water supply. Under fire, the latrines would be unreachable and noisome pits would have to be dug within the enclosure.

The answer to these problems, according to Engineer La Marquisie, was to locate troop barracks outside the walls of the fort. One structure was even completed before Gansevoort and Willett managed to persuade Schuyler to recall the French captain and place Lieutenant Hubbard, a practical American, in charge of Stanwix's works. Both knew that the Indians would strike the soft exterior targets first and, using their burnt-out shells for cover, press closer to the walls. Captain La Marquisie, like his countryman at Ticonderoga, Matthias Alexis Roche de Fermoy, brigadier general by act of Congress, demonstrated a lamentable lack of frontier sense.[45]

But most urgently, what was Schuyler to do for a maneuvering force beyond the escarpments? Even if he could hold the post, he was faced with the necessity of preventing a larger enemy force from bypassing the fortifications and storming into the valley. The only troops available to meet this contingency—and none of them regular—were from the Mohawk and Schoharie valleys. Most of these men served as volunteers in the Tryon County militia battalions commanded by Brigadier General Nicholas Herkimer. They were reputed to be poor soldiers—badly disciplined, slow marchers, indifferent marksmen. Worst of all, they seemed to lack the aggressiveness that won battles. Their detractors did not doubt their patriotic ardor, only their aptitude for war. They were good farmers, the best in America, but they had never fought Indians to win their land or taken their share of the New World as conquest.[46] Now they were expected to fight the Iroquois, the King's regulars, and mercenaries with axe, pitchfork, and hand-me-down muskets.

Albany tried everything to persuade Tryon County to repair and man Stanwix, thereby freeing Schuyler's Continentals to deepen the valley's defenses. At every turn local politics, mutual distrust, and the recalcitrant nature of the valley volunteers frustrated attempts to integrate militia into the battle order. Tryon County officials did authorize the use of Tryon militia at Stanwix—but only for seventeen days. The farmer soldiers could not spare a day more. They would meet to drill, gossip and drink, but hard training and long service were not part of their bargain with the county. They could be called out to face an emergency, but few of them were old enough to remember what a frontier emergency looked like. Accounts of French and Indian raids of twenty years before were now tales told to frighten children. Tryon County militia, who had not run off to join the loyalists, were by and large steady patriots; most were willing to fight for the American cause, but few among them imagined what "fighting" in this kind of conflict meant.

At the root of Tryon's turmoil lay the multicultural composition of the county's institutions. General Herkimer preferred to speak German; some junior officers favored Dutch. In fact, even Peter Gansevoort spoke English with a Dutch accent. When Willett came into the valley, inhabitants thought he smelled Yankee; only after they placed his downstate accent and sensed his resolution did they accept him as one of their own. Among the militia might be heard French and Gaelic as well as Dutch, German, English, and Native American dialects. More or less everyone agreed to communicate in a form of pidginized English, but to the disgust of ardent New England patriots, New Yorkers hardly ever surrendered prerogatives to any but members of their own caste or group.

The dominant faction in the Tryon organization was Palatine German, mostly grandsons of original settlers, conversant with the language and faith of their fathers. They followed Herkimer gladly and spelled his patronymic "Horcheimer," "Ergheimer," "Hark'mer." His childhood nickname, Honnikol, was affectionately retained and used by everyone. Honnikol was forty-nine years old, a successful businessman whose wealth flowed largely from the barge trade on the Mohawk River. At the outbreak of the Revolution, he was probably the wealthiest man in the valley after Sir John Johnson; his stately Georgian home on the river, completed about the same time as Johnson Hall, vied with the Johnsons' seat for elegance and luxury. The Herkimers might be working class, but they were never *parvenu*. Survivors of the first Palatine migration, the family inhabited the valley before William Johnson arrived. They joined with the young, aggressive Colonel Johnson during the French wars for the common good, and Nicholas remembered watching his father fortify the family's tavern near Little Falls as a way station between Fort Johnson and German Flats. A few years later the Herkimers helped build a fort around the old stone church across the river from German Flats where they worshiped. To this day it bears their name. No residue of resentment divided the Herkimer and Johnson families; they were neighbors who could meet over a tankard of beer, advance a loan, or share a joke. Nicholas thought Joseph Brant the most remarkable Native American he had ever met, and Brant treated Nicholas and his in-laws as his neighbors.

Given the Herkimer wealth in land and capital, Honnikol's early and continued support of the patriot cause raised eyebrows along Tenonanatche. His brother Hon Yost started out a Whig and ended up defecting to the Tories; he would serve in St. Leger's force against his brother. Another brother, Edward, would stick to the patriots and march with Nicholas. As with so many of the old valley families, the choice of sides was excruciating. It forced people to weigh loyalty against principle, kinfolk against friend, affection against duty. Newcomers to Tenonanatche, like Ebenezer Cox of Massachusetts, had little patience with equivocation; a man made up his mind according to his conscience and took his side. It was never that easy for Nicholas Herkimer.

Through the events of that spring, Cox seemed to ride at his side like an angry familiar, always badgering and pushing. Cox bridled at Herkimer, who had prosecuted him for unpaid debts a few years earlier, but most of all he doubted the resolution of the Palatine farmers and the willingness of their general to push them hard. "Cox and that Dutchman Schuyler be damned," the locals replied. "We won't serve under anyone but Honnikol." A brave statement, Honnikol might think, except that he too had every reason to doubt whether his German farmers would stand up to Mohawks in the forest or redcoats advancing with gleaming bayonets on an open field. Honnikol had experienced wilderness war and made the long, desperate marches, but that was twenty years earlier when he was a younger man. Now he would have to lead his boys with Schuyler's couriers tugging at one elbow and Cox and his Yankees tugging at the other. Brigadier General Herkimer was a lonely man. He was fighting for the independence of the United States of America, but he was no special friend of either Philip Schuyler or New England agitators.

First they made him send men to Ticonderoga; then, when that emergency had passed, to Fort George as freight-haulers, and now they wanted his battalions at a remote fort in the middle of a swamp. What they did not understand, and Herkimer kept trying to tell them, was that he had nowhere near enough men to both guard the settlements of the Mohawk frontier from Indian attack and maneuver to the advantage of regular forces. His men, farmers leavened with a few woodsmen, were in arms to defend their homes and neighborhoods from raiders, not to be dispatched to this post or that at Schuyler's whims. And yet this was exactly what had happened again. On the advice of Ahnyero and Kirkland, Herkimer was ordered to Unadilla to meet one last time with the war chief of the Mohawks, Thayendanegea, and offer concessions in exchange for Brant's pledge to refrain from attacking the Tryon townships. Herkimer was to make the march with 350 militiamen, and in the event that Brant refused to treat, he was to deal with him short of provoking an Indian war.

The long march from Fort Dayton at German Flats to Unadilla on the Susquehanna lasted almost a week in beautiful June weather. At Canajoharie, Herkimer and Cox met up with John Harper, whose scouts led them south by way of Lake Otsego. Ninety miles lay between home and the village of Unadilla, down forest trails through the heart of New York, and the expedition arrived at the junction of the rivers six days later, on June 20. Along the way Herkimer heard objections from Cox, Jacob Klock, and Peter Bellinger about his purpose in meeting with the renegade Mohawk. His battalion commanders were uneasy for good reasons. Brant despised Cox, who was George Klock's son-in-law; Jacob Klock had no use for his Uncle George, but resented Brant's threats against the family. Bellinger was just plain tired of being pushed around, and this long, hot, dusty journey into unknown dangers—only to hear what they had heard already—was enough to make him want to resign his commission. He was thinking about that when they arrived in a field near the town and began building a bower as a place of meeting.

"Yes, Captain Brant *will* meet with you; no, I do not know *when* Captain Brant will meet with you." Honnikol pointed his pipe at the Indian messenger and said, "Tell him an old neighbor is calling." "You are *all* old neighbors?" the messenger asked wryly. "Yes, tell him we are *all* old neighbors," Herkimer replied.[47] Brant would come, he knew, because the Mohawk's sense of his grand destiny required him to overawe his former friends. Nor would he offer violence, though he might threaten. The main question was what Herkimer would do if Brant refused his offer of truce. Cox was for welcoming him to council, shooting him, and ridding the region of a dangerous adversary. He argued that 350 men, amply supplied with powder and ball, could hold off Brant's braves. But cold-blooded assassination was not Herkimer's way. When Brant finally arrived from Oquaga, they agreed to meet in the bower, each bringing fifty unarmed supporters to witness the proceedings.

Many versions of the Unadilla meeting exist, but not a word from the two principal participants is found in the record. The meeting lasted two days, with the general's militia camped out in the field and Brant's corps sheltering under the eves of the forest. Once pleasantries and memories had been exchanged, the question arose as to why Brant had seized provisions from Unadilla, and by doing so, strayed from a strict policy of neutrality. Herkimer reminded him that this was unprovoked banditry. Brant begged to differ. Was it not also banditry to confiscate the property of loyalist Mohawks? Was it not banditry to hold the Anglican divine John Stuart and the wife of John Butler virtual prisoners on account of their political allegiances? How, Brant asked, were the king's faithful subjects to find justice under Philip Schuyler's unnatural regime?

Herkimer anticipated this response and, rather than trade further accusations, conceded that restitution would be made to Mohawk families injured by their patriot neighbors. Then, to the chagrin of many, especially Cox, he also allowed that the Reverend Stuart and Mrs. Butler would both be set free on his return to the valley. What the general asked in exchange from Brant was a simple statement reaffirming his neutrality in the contest between the Crown and its former subjects.

The Mohawk spoke eloquently to the point: "the Indians were in concert with the King, as their fathers and grandfathers had been. Herkimer and the rest had joined the Boston people against their king ... and Mr. Schuyler, or General, or what you please to call him, was very smart on the Indians at the treaty of German Flats, but was not at the same time able to afford the smallest article of clothing. Now the Indians were divided, but they were not frightened."[48]

Joseph spoke perfect English, notably more precise and fluent than Herkimer's, and while the general's manners and gestures were those of plain, ordinary folk, Brant's carriage was that of a British gentleman who had visited the court and been presented to the king. He was better educated than Herkimer and better traveled; he dressed in fine fabrics cut in the Mohawk fashion. The general wore as usual his stained blue waistcoat and leather breeches. He was described as a short man, thin and swarthy; his hair and eyes were dark, and he often looked as though he needed a shave. For all that his men revered and looked up to him, there was nothing avuncular about Herkimer. Like them, he had left a wife at home and often said he could not wait to get back to her. He would sit where he landed and smoke his pipe, but Brant's attitudes and superior demeanor would not put him off. Palatines rarely aspired to aristocracy, consigning that affectation to others as they strove to live contentedly in their ethnic solidarity. Brant claimed that he had 500 warriors at his call in the woods. Harper's scouts reckoned them at 200. With odds in their favor, Cox pressed for a fight, but Herkimer demurred; he wanted peace, and if Brant would not give him peace, he wanted to get his farmer soldiers home again where they belonged as quickly as possible. Someone suggested that they adjourn the inconclusive meeting until the next day and, to everyone's surprise, Brant accepted.

The devil was in the second day. An old militiaman, applying for a federal pension in the next century, remembered that as a young man he had accompanied Honnikol to Unadilla. Sometime during the proceedings, the veteran recalled, Colonel Cox exploded at Brant with a loud "Damn you!" and stood up. The Indians in attendance jumped up and ran for their guns, but Herkimer and his lieutenants pulled Cox down and tried to restore order. Honnikol took Brant by the arm and led him aside, telling him not to mind what Cox had said. "Herkimer talked very nice to him—Brandt was moderate too," the old soldier testified from memory.[49] But another old militiaman declared years later "that on the second day Herkimer gave him instructions to shoot Brant on the spot, but that Brant was always too wary for him to accomplish the job."[50] Whether the brawl in the bower threw off the appointed assassin's aim, or whether Herkimer thought better of the plan and moved the Mohawk out of the line of fire, or whether the story was true at all remains forever unknown. Writers have armed Cox with a pistol that misfired, cast aspersions on Herkimer's honor, found the account baseless and unlikely, or suggested that the concealed rifleman was only a precaution. To be sure, the stakes were very high. Thayendanegea was a formidable leader, with war experience and a large following of Native Americans and disaffected white loyalists. He ran a great risk in attending the Unadilla council, but if it was in Herkimer's better nature to greet him fairly, it was in Brant's nature to flaunt his power and independence in the face of Herkimer's yokels.

Brant's answer was a resounding "No!" He would remain a loyal subject of King George III; he would strive to unite Indians behind their rightful ruler, and he was leaving now for Oswego where he would meet John Butler, acting Indian Supervisor. There was nothing more to say, Herkimer realized, and as a storm came up from the northwest, as often it does in June in central New York, the two camps parted silently. The Indians on the edge of the wood began to fire their muskets in the air and whoop at the departing militia, but a great thunderclap and a sudden downpour put an end to their demonstration and, as the militia began the long trudge home in the chilling rain, the Indians dove for shelter into the nearby trees.

⚘ 9 ⚘

A RAVINE TOO FAR

Herkimer's militia was back in the Mohawk Valley only a fortnight when word arrived that New York's "Gibraltar of the North" had fallen. Two days after the first anniversary of the Declaration of Independence, the Northern Department evacuated Ticonderoga in the face of a superior enemy. The game was up as soon as Burgoyne's engineers cleared a road to the top of Mount Defiance and sighted artillery on the fort and Mount Independence across the narrows.[1] General St. Clair did what he was instructed to do in the event of the British securing the heights. He set his 3,000 men in retrograde motion, the bulk following him south along the Vermont border while the others, under Brigadier General Matthias Alexis Roche de Fermoy, moved by boat to Skenesboro with Ticonderoga's munitions and supplies.[2]

The most difficult maneuver in war, St. Clair knew, was the withdrawal of an inferior force in the face of a superior.[3] The British outnumbered him three to one, were better equipped, disciplined, and armed, and nearly surrounded his position. His plan for retreat was sound, but American forces at this point in the conflict lacked the coordination, discipline, and leadership to execute it.

Roche de Fermoy's soldiers, sensing their commander's desire to be away as fast as possible, panicked on the docks in the dark and flung themselves into any boat available; their general then succeeded in accidentally setting his headquarters afire and lighting up the chaos for the enemy to see, all at the same time one of his artillery detachments, securing the floating bridge between Ticonderoga and Mount Independence, was discovered dead drunk at its post.[4] As Mount Independence fell, the Americans fleeing south on Champlain aboard the surviving galleys of Arnold's fleet prayed that the huge iron chain stretching across the lake from Ticonderoga to Mount Independence would hold back pursuers.

In the event, the British Navy made quick work of the chain, and as the retreating Americans neared Skenesboro, they were under fire from enemy gunboats.[5] Within a few hours Arnold's surviving vessels were sunk or scuttled, the mills and warehouses at Skenesboro were burning, and survivors were floundering through a dismal wilderness labyrinth in hopes of reaching Fort Edward. Billows of smoke from captured Skenesboro could be seen for miles, and at this signal, native warriors screening Burgoyne's lightning advance converged on the forest trails leading south. Not all of Roche de Fermoy's frightened soldiers would reach Fort Edward; in years to come, road builders occasionally unearthed bones at the side of old trails where some had fallen in ambush.

General St. Clair's column, meanwhile, negotiated the treacherous forest road running along the eastern side of South Bay towards Hubbardton, Vermont. So narrow was this trail that his regiments often passed obstructions Indian file, leaving companies stretched out far behind. The weather was sultry, humid, with annoying cloudbursts, and many soldiers, short of sleep, hungry, and sick, fell out of line exhausted, driven nearly mad by mosquitoes and flies. St. Clair had placed his most reliable regiments at the end of the long column, closest to the onrushing enemy. In the middle of the column marched Seth Warner and his Green Mountain Boys, while at the rear colonels Hale and Francis, the best St. Clair had, rushed their tired men along just ahead of the enemy. These were New Hampshire and Massachusetts Continentals who did not fully appreciate how fast expert British light infantry could advance over difficult terrain. All the way south from Mount Independence, Brigadier General Simon Fraser was hot on their heels, closing to within three miles of the struggling rebels as night fell on July 6. Major Robert Grant, Fraser's spear point, was convinced that they would have the rebels in the morning, but what British regulars did not fully appreciate was how quickly the rebels could deploy and maneuver in deep woods.

If the rear of St. Clair's column had kept moving on July 6, closing up on the main body as ordered, the sharp and vicious fight at Hubbardton might never have happened and Schuyler could yet have skirted disaster with his infantry intact. Instead, Seth Warner and the Green Mountain Boys disobeyed orders; falling out of line to bivouac early in the evening, they effectively sent the New Hampshire regiments behind them into bivouac as well. Warner by this time was a savvy guerilla leader with extensive experience in woodland retreats. In his defense it might be said that his men were done in by an arduous march, many burdened with sick friends recovering from an epidemic of measles and unable to go farther without food and rest.[6] But the consequences of Warner's insubordination were realized the next morning when, at daybreak, while the New Hampshire men cooked breakfast beside Sucker Brook, Grant's infantry attacked with bayonets, scattering some, capturing others. The Americans fell back to a flat hilltop with few trees, formed line, and began to deliver a deadly return fire. Major Grant climbed a stump to see what was happening and fell dead at the feet of his men. One volley dropped twenty of his soldiers before they could even see their opponents or recognize that they had stumbled into a blocking force several hundred in strength. Over the next two hours the Americans had the better of the fight, as repeated attempts to turn their flanks were beaten back with heavy loss to the enemy.

This was nasty, murderous resistance, with Warner's men loading faster and firing more accurately than the redcoats. But as the day wore on and ammunition ran low, Warner knew that the decision would go to the side that reinforced first.

St. Clair heard the sound of battle to his rear and saw smoke rising above the treetops a dozen miles away. His aides were sent racing back to the formation closest to the fight with orders to turn about and reinforce the embattled rearguard, but the men of Colonel Bellow's regiment refused to follow their commander and plodded on towards the safety of the main body.[7] General Fraser, losing the fight and suffering severe casualties, was rescued by the appearance late in the day of Baron von Riedesel's Hessians, who lumbered into sight, massed on the flanks of the American line, and rolled them up. Hubbardton was an American defeat—at least 100 killed or wounded, over 300 captured. The gallant Colonel Francis fell in the fighting, and Hale was taken prisoner and sent to Ticonderoga. He later died in captivity. Seth Warner told men who escaped the encirclement to flee for the hills and make their way to Rutland as best they could. By now the fight had gone out of the Americans, and St. Clair was left to rush his tailless formation in the direction of the upper Hudson, keeping an anxious eye on the trail behind him.

But the British, too, had suffered heavily. Besides Major Grant, they had lost Captain Shrimpton of the 62nd Regiment and over 180 dead and wounded. Among the critically wounded were twelve officers. Fraser had little more than 600 men left, and these were in no condition to pursue St. Clair. Before they pulled out for Skenesboro, they tried to tidy up the wilderness battlefield, heaving some of the rebel dead into deserted houses at Hubbardton.[8] Their own wounded they tended in temporary hospitals on the outskirts of the plundered town. Sharp as the fight had been, Burgoyne had every reason to congratulate his officers. In eleven days of campaigning, they had swept through Ticonderoga, captured Mount Independence, driven the enemy south with heavy losses, and secured his main staging area on Lake Champlain. With justifiable pride he wrote to Lord Germain:

> I have the honor to inform your Lordship that the enemy dislodged from Ticonderoga and Mount Independent, on the 6th instant, and were driven, on the same day, beyond Skenesborough on the right, and to Humerton on the left, with the loss of 128 pieces of cannon, all their armed vessels and bateaux, the greatest part of their baggage and ammunition, provision, and military stores.[9]

The news would not reach London for six weeks and would be greeted with wild excitement by King George III as evidence of a most wonderful and decisive victory. And so it must have looked on maps of Colonial America. But in fact, as Schuyler might have told His Britannic Majesty, the victory did not mean much of anything. Burgoyne had buried himself in the heart of a trackless wilderness, and by the time

London came to celebrate his triumph, the general was already mired beyond escape in the swampy forests north of Albany.

Who came to know what, when, and how is the crux of the matter, and two and a quarter centuries after the fact, difficult to determine. News about the fall of Ticonderoga reached the Mohawk Valley—forty or fifty miles from Skenesboro—within the week, but news such as there was arrived garbled and incomplete. The Indian menace was on everyone's mind, and reports of Tory bands working behind the patriot lines set entire townships to double-bolting their doors.[10] Accurate details about the fight at Hubbardton probably never arrived in the Mohawk settlements. The battle occurred on the other side of the New England divide and therefore concerned people in New Hampshire, Massachusetts, and Maine more than patriots in German Flats. Back home in the New England provinces, the news about the fall of Ticonderoga had not yet sunk in by the end of July; when finally it did, the fury of the region's representatives knew no bounds. "Schuyler and St. Clair had been bought by silver balls fired over the walls at Ti," rumor ran. "They were scoundrels: the one a New York Dutchman, the other a onetime British officer, traitors both." Astute politicians read in the fall of Ticonderoga the setting of Philip Schuyler's star and the rise of Horatio Gates's, notwithstanding that Gates was the officer who failed to fortify Mount Defiance or alert St. Clair to the perils of his position.

The news arrived at Washington's headquarters at Morristown, New Jersey, by express rider on July 10. The dispatch delivered into the general's hands had been written three days before by Schuyler and announced that St. Clair had evacuated Ticonderoga. At first the commander in chief could not believe that the post was gone. Another dispatch delivered on July 11 convinced him, but also left open to speculation the whereabouts and condition of St. Clair's army. Washington, hard-pressed on all sides, called the loss "among the most unfortunate that could have befallen us," but he did not rush to judgment like many in Congress. John Adams, for example, confided to his wife, Abigail, "We shall never be able to defend a post until we shoot a general."[11] Whether he meant Schuyler or St. Clair is unclear, for these were the favorite targets of armchair strategists. Years would pass before the opinions of soldiers who had been on the spot were finally heard. Alexander Scammell called Ticonderoga "a perfect Mouse Trap, evacuated for want of men and the untenableness of the post."[12] Those who fell back, regrouped, and eventually saw their numbers and power swell beyond Burgoyne's knew how much they owed to the men who extricated them at the price of their own reputations.

Yet, in the moment all was confusion. Schuyler learned by July 7 that the post was gone, but he did not learn the location and condition of St. Clair's regiments until five days later. By then, survivors from Skenesboro were arriving with accounts of their escape from the British advance. What Schuyler discovered from them was that on July 8 Colonel Long, with several hundred men extricated from Skenesboro and reinforced by Colonel Van Rensselaer, had stopped the British dead in their tracks just short of Fort Anne. Burgoyne's pursuing regiments were stumbling through wastes and swamps without maps or guides. They could hear the voices of Americans in the dense woods, but could not see where they were until massed fire revealed their position. Despite the anger and recrimination breaking out behind the lines, and the spectacle of skulkers and deserters jamming the roads, Schuyler's hard core was not faring badly. He was making a fight of it and, on July 14, from Fort Edward, he wrote to Washington:

> Desertion prevails and disease gains ground ... for we have neither tents, houses, barns, boards, or any shelter except a little brush. Every rain that falls, and we have it in great abundance almost every day, wets the men to the skin. We are ... in great want of every kind of necessary, provision excepted. Camp kettles we have so few, that we cannot afford one to twenty men. ... our whole train of artillery consists of two iron field pieces.[13]

Artillery was not what the Northern Department required in mid-July. Schuyler, the old logician, seasoned in wilderness war, lamented the axes, tools, kettles and tents lost in the evacuation of Ticonderoga. He was getting ample food up to his troops from the Mohawk; what he needed to slow the invasion were shovels, picks, saws, and rope. He also made certain that no matter how many artillery pieces Burgoyne captured, the British found neither horses to drag them nor wagons to cart their provisions.[14] Washington for his part allowed his embattled officer to fight as he thought best. There would indeed be inquiries, Congressional investigations, and Schuyler and St. Clair were likely to be made scapegoats, yet the commander in chief, waging his own guerilla war, approved the methods of the unpopular New Yorker. Richard Ketchum summarizes the impression Schuyler often left:

> In his public utterances, in letters to George Washington and the Congress, it sometimes seemed that Schuyler had lost his nerve, which was certainly not the case. From the way he talked, you would have thought he saw a bottomless chasm opening beneath his feet, yet his actions were those of a man who knew exactly what to do and how to go about it in the most effective way. What he had accomplished was absolutely essential if the army was to be saved, but a retreat with no end in sight was not the kind of leadership to inspire confidence among the troops or the civilians who were running this war.[15]

What most frightened Schuyler were not several thousand British troops thrashing through the forests. These could be fended off until he found reinforcements to block them. The thrust through Stanwix into the breadbasket of Tenonanatche posed the greater peril. If anyone could overcome the logistics of distribution, the graft and corruption of procurement and transportation, the farms of the Mohawk and Schoharie were sufficiently productive to support armies larger than the American and British combined. For invaders, agricultural land made fast and easy marching, and just then an invading army was struggling up Wood Creek toward Fort Stanwix and the broad bottomland of the river system. This was the arm of attack Burgoyne should have reinforced, if he had understood the terrain.

Daniel Claus, restored as Indian Supervisor for Canada with Carleton's demotion, sent scouts out from Oswego in early July to reconnoiter Stanwix and the upper Mohawk. The party was led by a trusted Johnson retainer, John Deserontyon, who with his fellow Mohawks had helped Sir John escape to Canada in 1776. Scouting parties had been out before, but this one was expected to bring in prisoners from Gansevoort's garrison. This was the pretext for the mission, but to spread terror and insecurity was also on the agenda and, to that end, Claus dispatched the decidedly homicidal loyalist, John Hare, as a member of the patrol. They would come as close as they could to the fort, lay in wait, and snatch four or five captives.

While Gansevoort struggled to support his 700 men from 87 barrels of pork, 379 barrels of flour, and a single cask of rum, Willett struggled to keep his unruly work parties felling trees across Wood Creek, cutting sod for barrack roofs, and hunting fresh food. Everyone knew trouble was near, that the forests had grown perilous. But the true meaning of their situation far out on the western wing of the American line only became apparent after events of June 25.

On that afternoon a detachment of troopers from the 3rd New York under Captain James Gregg were detailed to fell trees and gather sod along Wood Creek. The tedious work, the warm breeze, and summer sun inspired Gregg and Corporal Madison to try their hand at pigeon hunting, passenger pigeons being good eating and much in evidence along the upper Mohawk. Intent on bagging their birds, Gregg and Madison went into the fields, losing touch with their work party. When the party heard two shots, they expected that Gregg and Madison had found their game. In fact, Deserontyon and Hare had found *them*. Both were hit but alive when Deserontyon buried a hatchet in Madison's skull and scalped him. Gregg took a glancing blow from the hatchet, was knocked cold, and scalped. The attack lasted all of two minutes. Popular accounts hold that Gregg's little dog later led soldiers to the scene of the attack, where they gathered up the severely injured man and his dead companion.[16]

On July 3, a few days before the fall of Ticonderoga, Stanwix received a second intimation of the danger lurking in the woods. A work detail under Ensign Spoor was up Wood Creek between old Fort Bull and the Carry when surprised by a war party. Spoor's men had no chance. Four were killed outright and scalped; five were bound and taken captive, including Spoor, and seven fled for their lives. One of the dead was then ritually mutilated as a further warning to the garrison of what they could expect. This attack, according to survivors, lasted all of three minutes. The prisoners were delivered a week later to Claus by Deserontyon and passed on to St. Leger for interrogation.

On July 27, while Schuyler harangued Herkimer for more militia to protect Stanwix, three farm girls berry-picking within sight of the fort were fired upon from the woods. Two of the children fell immediately and were dispatched and scalped on the spot. The lone survivor was hit twice in the shoulder by musket balls and critically wounded as she fled to the fort. These vicious murders, coming just as the wanton massacre of Jane McCrea inflamed settlers on the upper Hudson, drove home to families in the valley just what kind of enemy was approaching. The berry girls might have been from loyalist or patriot homes; Jane McCrea's folks were staunch Tories, and she herself was engaged to a Tory officer serving with Burgoyne. Once Britain's tribal allies were turned loose, however, killings of this sort would become unavoidable.[17]

Native Americans were paid $8 for prisoners or scalps, and for nearly two years had been encouraged by Guy Johnson and his family to stop at nothing in inflicting maximum punishment on white settlers. Above Albany, the fate of Jane McCrea was laid at Burgoyne's doorstep and would contribute to the swelling of militia companies gathering to stop him. On the Mohawk, the fate of the berry girls would be blamed on Joseph Brant, Daniel Claus, and Sir John Johnson. News of the outrage helped Nicholas Herkimer rally 800 militiamen over the next several days.

Gansevoort was sickened by the incident and immediately ordered the wounded and ill, with all women and children, downriver to the safety of Fort Dayton. He wrote to Colonel Van Schaick, commanding New York troops at Dayton:

> By the best discoveries we have made, there were four Indians who perpetrated these murders. I had four men with arms just passed that place, but these mercenaries of Britain came not to fight, but to lie in wait to murder; and it is equally the same to them, if they can get a scalp, whether it is from a soldier or an innocent babe.[18]

Incensed as he might be, Gansevoort read the lessons of the massacre. His soldiers had none of the requisite skills for uncovering enemies of the kind, nor the combat ability to encounter them. Warriors struck from ambush quickly and were gone in two or three minutes. His best protection was the fort, and to clear the fort of unwanted mouths before it could be invested was the reason for the orders of July 27. He needed musket balls that fit his ordnance or molds for fabricating bullets; he needed cannon-balls that fit his artillery, more powder, and implements for swabbing and cleaning guns. Most of all, he needed men to replace Herkimer's militia, withdrawn for duty elsewhere. This last struck Schuyler, caught up in a maelstrom of difficulties, the cruelest blow.

Herkimer had written to Gansevoort in mid-July:

> As the Time of my militia now stationed under your command at Fort Schuyler [Stanwix] will be expired this week I beg of you not to detain them longer. ... They will long for the Time in Regard to their Hay—and wheat harvest. I hope, therefore, that you'll grant them their Discharge next Thursday that they may reach home at the three weeks End, especially as one hundred and sixty Continental Troops are set off to day for Fort Schuyler to reinforce your Garrison.[19]

Schuyler, suspecting by now that Congress was acting to replace him with Gates, and still smarting from Herkimer's handling of the Brant affair at Unadilla, wrote furiously to the Brigadier:

> I am sorry, very sorry, that you should be calling upon me for assistance of Continental troops, when I have already spared you all I could ... For God's sake do not forget that you are an overmatch for any force the enemy can bring against you, if you will act with spirit.[20]

Herkimer's response by the end of the month was to pull out all stops and summon Tenonanatche to war in a rousing proclamation posted across the valley:

> Whereas, it appears certain that the enemy, of about 2,000 strong, Christians and savages, are arrived at Oswego with the intention to invade our frontiers, I think it proper and most necessary for the defense of our country, and it shall be ordered by me as soon as the enemy approaches, that every male person, being in health, from 16 to 60 years of age, in this our county, shall, as in duty bound, repair immediately, with arms and accoutrements, to the place to be appointed in my orders, and will then march to oppose the enemy with vigor, as true patriots, for the just defense of their country.[21]

As the grueling month of July drew to a close with thunderheads and dense, humid air hanging over the far-flung battlefield, General Burgoyne reached Fort Edward and occupied the post as his headquarters. Brigadier General St. Leger's artillery was just passing the great falls on the Oswego River, his Indian scouts far ahead at encampments along Wood Creek. Gansevoort and Willett had pulled in their pickets, waiting and watching for signs of the enemy, while in the valley to the east, Herkimer gathered his battalions. There was nothing for it now but to fight.

From his network of spies along the Mohawk, St. Leger learned that a convoy of bateaux delivering badly needed supplies was approaching Stanwix. His position on August 2 was nine miles from the fort on Wood Creek. Lieutenant Bird, with a mixed party of soldiers and warriors, had already reached the head of the creek near the Carry. St. Leger instructed him to intercept the convoy, and Bird, skirting the fort's defenses, struck out for the landing below the sally port. He arrived too late to prevent Wesson's Massachusetts Continentals with supplies of powder and ball from entering the fort. Bird's force overwhelmed the boatmen and then withdrew to the tree line to await St. Leger's main body. What they had seen was sobering.[22] As Claus warned, Stanwix looked crude and haphazard, yet was anything but a ruin. The walls were well-manned by Continentals and amply supplied with artillery.

Barry St. Leger, Lieutenant Colonel of the 34th Foot and acting Brigadier General in Burgoyne's expedition, had spent half of his forty years in the King's service, much of that time in North America. He had been at the sieges of Louisburg and Quebec, and could be expected to know his business. His advance from Oswego to Stanwix offered a model of wilderness conduct, with units well-separated and covering each other while they moved in ready file behind alert flankers. The lessons of the French and Indian War had not been lost on St. Leger and his officers. Rather, the force itself was too small for the mission. St. Leger brought with him 200 regular infantry from the 8th and 34th regiments accompanied by over 300 Tories of Sir John Johnson's "Royal Greens," a company of Tory Rangers under Colonel John Butler, and about 100 Hanau Jägers. He had 40 artillerymen equipped with two six-pounders, two three-pounders, and four small mortars called "cohorns." The white contingent numbered in all about 875 combatants, supported by several dozen Canadian militiamen. The Native American contingent under the leadership of Joseph Brant was placed at between 800 and 1,000 effectives. In truth, the right hook of Burgoyne's juggernaut was exactly the highly mobile, mixed and lightly armed force that Stanwix had originally been built to repel.

Not that this much consoled American troops when, on August 3, St. Leger's full might debouched from the forests and proceeded to encircle Stanwix with martial display. The reds, greens, and blues of the disciplined troops, drilling under their regimental banners, went far to intimidate the scruffy rebels watching on the parapets. But Brant's thousand warriors in full war paint, taunting the garrison with cries and gestures, left a more lasting impression on the defenders. This was what would befall them if they did not surrender, or possibly, even if they did. From these gruesome threats logically flowed the conclusion that there could be no capitulation. To the Americans, the simple fact that the howling savages seemed to outnumber the British soldiers dampened any psychological advantage St. Leger's demonstration might have achieved.

Gansevoort had paraded the garrison past a ritually slaughtered body recovered from Wood Creek; no one was under any illusions thereafter about what would happen if they fell into enemy hands. Men resolved to stick it out, many seizing on personal talismans. Willett wrote in his daily diary that the fort at this point was unassailable. Gansevoort clutched a letter from his brother Leonard that had just arrived on the last bateaux. It read: "I beg you and depend upon you and your Regiment not to be a disgrace to the New York arms. Your father flatters himself that you will conquer or die."[23] Other men required a public token. They demanded a flag. In the rush to ready Stanwix for battle, no one had thought to make a banner inclusive of all the people within the walls. Now, it is alleged, Willett stepped forward with the pattern for a national flag copied from an old newspaper. In this probably apocryphal story passed down for two hundred years in the Mohawk Valley, the flag would have stripes red and white—the white fashioned from old shirts and the red from the lining of Colonel Gansevoort's dress cape.[24] The blue background behind the stars was donated by Willett from the material of a British officer's cloak captured on its owner at Peekskill.[25] Sewed up in a rough and ready fashion, Stanwix's flag would fly through the siege, the first appearance in battle of an insignia approximating the Stars and Stripes.[26] Every morning, the flag was raised to drumbeats and an artillery salute. To insult an enemy, Gansevoort knew, was always worth the cost in powder.

St. Leger next sent a truce party under the well-known Tory, Captain Gilbert Tice, to demand surrender of the fort. The burden of his message was essentially Burgoyne's pompous pronouncement promising peace and protection to those who laid down their arms, with wilderness war to all others—except for, of course, women, babes, children, and the aged, who would be treated with clemency.[27] "Tell that to the berry girls," the garrison muttered behind piles of sod, and turned Tice out of the fort without a reply. On this signal Brant's warriors began their investment of the walls, sniping at the gun ports as St. Leger's diminutive artillery commenced bombardment. Yet, frightening as this barrage was to the fort's inmates, it inflicted almost no damage.

Behind St. Leger's theatrics lay a serious flaw. He did not have men enough to truly surround Stanwix, nor did he have firepower to breach the defenses quickly. Large detachments of his disciplined troops were assigned to clear fallen trees from Wood Creek, opening lines of communication to the rear. The shallow creek was especially cluttered and tortuous in the summer season, its banks crumbling, constricted, and smothered with poison ivy. Work details laboring in the foul waters to clear the way for bateaux quickly lost men to sickness and violent rashes.[28] From the moment of joining action, St. Leger's force suffered wastage at a higher level than Gansevoort's garrison.

Meanwhile, the siege settled into a snipers' war, with Brant's best marksmen taking up positions to harass the garrison. American sentries posted to the sentry box on the northwest bastion suffered especially galling casualties. On both August 4 and 5, at the break of dawn, a rifle ball fired from a distant oak mortally wounded the watchman on duty. On August 6 the garrison set up a scarecrow in the sentry box, wheeled a six-pounder into position loaded with canister, and waited for sunrise. As the expected ball blasted through the scarecrow's stuffing, the six-pounder fired its load into the oak. A Mohawk warrior identified as Ki, Brant's childhood friend from Canajoharie, toppled dead out of the tree with a Jäger's rifle in his hands.[29]

The same day, St. Leger set fire to the barracks foolishly built outside the fort and, as smoke from the conflagration drifted over Stanwix, he advanced closer to the walls. His skirmishers were met with sheets of musket fire as they came forward, and soon withdrew out of range. St. Leger could encircle Stanwix and try to seal it off from help, but he could not storm it without suffering exorbitant casualties.

Gansevoort, though, was boxed in, his lines of communication down the Mohawk closing rapidly. If he could drive back frontal attacks, he could not guarantee how long his ammunition and provisions would hold out. As a rule, in eighteenth-century warfare, a patient, well-supplied siege usually carried its objective. Critical, therefore, from Gansevoort's standpoint was the rapid deployment of a relief force to break the siege and roll up St. Leger's lines. That force—the only one available in the valley—would have to be the Tryon County militia. If Herkimer could join his 900 or so militiamen to Gansevoort's 750 Continentals, the Americans would approach parity on the battlefield. This was the message that Thomas Spencer, Ahnyero, carried to the Oneida village of Oriska, and thence to Herkimer at Fort Dayton.

Word of the attack on Stanwix reached Fort Dayton at German Flats on Sunday morning August 3. Herkimer immediately responded by ordering his brigade mustered and ready to march on Monday, August 4. To gather 900 men from scattered farms across Tenonanatche was no simple task, but so intense had alarms become in the previous days that most militiamen were ready and waiting for the signal to converge on Dayton. News of St. Leger's approach first reached the valley's Tories, carried by Mohawks recruiting for Brant's corps. Thus, by early August rumors of loyalists roaming neighborhoods and looking to molest patriots had been spreading from farmstead to farmstead. In the midst of this fear and confusion, Honnikol's call came almost as a relief: "drop what you are doing, snatch musket, ball, and bayonet, and report to Dayton. Be sure to remember your canteen." The masses of men moving down the dusty roads of the valley knew without being told that those who were able-bodied and did not report for duty would be counted. These were the Tories, who would be dealt with later.

Watching them straggle by Canajoharie in their dozens was a woman commonly referred to by British officers as Sir William's "relict," his common-law widow—Molly Brant. She had lived quietly in a well-furnished house above the King's Road on the outskirts of Kanatsiohareke, the Mohawk village, since her famous husband's death. What Molly certainly realized was that this gathering of martial power was aimed at and occasioned by her brother Joseph. She was well-informed, and as she observed her militia neighbors heading for muster, formulated an accurate assessment of their numbers, armament, and officers. In her report to St. Leger, dispatched by courier August 4, she described Herkimer's militia brigade in detail. She was almost forty miles from the British lines, but her message reached St. Leger by fast runners late on August 5.[30] Herkimer, like Philip Schuyler, never mistook Molly's loyalties, but also like his superior officer, Herkimer appreciated Molly's influence among her people and therefore declined to disturb her. She was doing nothing for her side that Thomas Spencer was not doing for his. But Honnikol's "softness," his forbearance with Indians, set in train bitter suspicions among some of his officers. This corrosive distrust proved more destructive to the patriots' cause in the end than any information Molly sent her brother. Her spying done, there was nothing for her but to sit and pray on the outcome of the battle. Both sides knew their enemy's strength and direction. Now what would matter most was who drew first blood.

Herkimer calculated that his column needed two days to reach Stanwix by the road running west from Fort Dayton. On the first day, they would proceed along the north bank of the Mohawk to the abandoned settlement of Deerfield, there to bivouac. On the morning of the second day, they would cross the river at the Great Ford and, arriving at the ruins of old Fort Schuyler (present-day Utica), turn onto the Albany road. From the tumbledown French and Indian War stockade, the army would move west along the road to a final bivouac in the vicinity of an Oneida village called Oriska, or "place of nettles."[31] The distance from Dayton to Deerfield was a long day's march of twelve miles. The distance from the Great Ford to Oriska was seven miles, and on the third day they proposed to cover the last six miles to Stanwix. Though the head of Herkimer's column reached the Oneida village on Oriskany Creek in late afternoon, August 5, the rear came no closer than modern Whitesboro, two miles east. With fourteen heavily laden oxcarts lumbering along between his 4th and 3rd battalions, Herkimer's column stretched more than two miles from head to tail. The accompanying wagons contained ammunition and provisions to sustain the brigade for two days. In the van, Colonel Ebenezer Cox's 1st battalion led the way, followed by Colonel Jacob Klock's 2nd and Colonel Peter Bellinger's 4th. The 3rd battalion, Colonel Frederick Visscher's, brought up the rear behind the wagons. This was the assigned order the brigade assumed after creating a depot at Deerfield, dropping off twenty-eight wagons, and detaching forty volunteers to guard supplies.[32]

Militia companies were trained to march in ranks of three. Even if they did not dawdle, they were still inclined to spread out over the countryside. Indeed, they paraded out of Dayton as snappily as their officers could wish, but this jauntiness did not last long on the dusty road under a hot summer sun. Foremost, these were farmers who could care less how a man carried his gun or whether he sauntered barefoot with his friends in the roadside grass. They knew where they were going and why, but few saw any point in aping professional soldiers or missing an opportunity to joke with family and neighbors. There were oxen to goad, loads to share, and favorite foods to pass around before encampment. For security, they trusted Honnikol, and when the fight drew near, relied on lifelong friends and family members. Whole settlements had answered Herkimer's call, turning out and marching together.

Tryon County had no available artillery, and while most officers were mounted, no detachments of cavalry. In wilderness warfare, these sister arms often proved more trouble than they were worth. The firepower of Tryon County came from .75-caliber Brown Bess muskets, along with a motley assortment of other firelocks. For close-in fighting, most men carried bayonets, hatchets, or knives. Each militiaman was issued twenty-five musket balls, two pounds of black powder, and a handful of flints. Men were expected to provide their own firelock picks, extractors, and firepan covers in event of rain. Few bothered to make up cartridges for fast loading; they carried their shot and wadding in multi-purpose shoulder bags, their powder in horns. Certainly these men could shoot—they had grown up on a wilderness frontier—but few had ever fired a shot at an enemy in anger. They had no uniforms, no flags, and no camp gear but kettles and frying pans. The majority wore felt slouch hats fashioned from discarded tri-corners, with identifying cockades in the hatbands.

As he moved out of Dayton, Herkimer's plan for the relief of Gansevoort was simple. He had had no direct communication with the colonel for some time and, under the circumstances, resolved to move to the fort as expeditiously as possible. This meant traveling the military road, built originally to supply Stanwix, even as it climbed through forested hills above the swampy southern margin of the river. With his remaining 760 troops and 14 carts, Herkimer had thought to push over the road and explode into the enemy's lines near the fort's landing. Yet, as he considered the terrain beyond Oriska, the idea seemed less appealing. Nineteen years before, as a captain in the provincial militia, he had helped build this road through the hills and swampy bottoms between Oriska and the Great Carry. The road was sixteen feet wide, corduroyed where it crossed marshy brooks, and it passed over densely wooded plateaus before descending to the fort. What made the road especially hazardous, Herkimer remembered, were the deep ravines traversing the plateaus—perfect places for surprise.[33] Historians suspect that another factor added to the peril—an extensive blowdown of trees had produced a tangled mass of roadside clutter. Microbursts, rare tornado-force storms, can devastate forests in mile-wide swathes, downing trees in interlocking patterns impossible to penetrate.[34] Sometime during the months preceding the Tryon militia's efforts to relieve the fort, such a storm occurred.[35] Eyewitness accounts agree on the confused jumble of deadfall that made the subsequent action especially localized and hellish. At Oriska, Herkimer welcomed into his command sixty Oneida warriors.[36] Behind Ahnyero, they would scout ahead over the road, alert for ambushes at which Joseph Brant was adept. The Oneidas did not like the feel of the road in this season, and Herkimer, from what he had seen, had to agree.

In his tent beside Oriskany Creek, Herkimer called for a squad of rangers to report. By stipulation of the Provincial Congress of the new State of New York, Captains John Harper and James Clyde of Schoharie had been authorized on July 17, 1777, to "recruit as fast as possible" a company of Tryon County rangers for special duty. These scouts were to be paid at Continental rates and awarded special allowances for food and equipment.[37] The three attached to Herkimer's brigade were Han Marks Demuth, Han Yost Folts, and Adam Helmer. All were expert woodsmen with intimate knowledge of local terrain. Helmer was the Mohawk Valley's champion runner; Demuth, known personally to Gansevoort, was a crack marksman and hunter.[38] Now Herkimer ordered them to slip through quickly to Stanwix. Once there, they were to inform the fort's commandant of the Tryon County strength and disposition. What Herkimer needed was a strong sally to pull Brant's warriors out of his way and into the open. With luck, the American forces could catch the British and their allies from both sides. Timing would be essential. Gansevoort was to fire three sequential cannon shots as soon as he was prepared to attack. The Tryon brigade would push the last six miles then at all-out speed to close the trap. As the rangers left on their mission, Herkimer judged that, with a sally from the fort, his militia could rush the road ahead with some assurance of success.

What he did not count on occurred early in the morning of August 6. At a meeting of his officers, he proposed delaying the last stage of the advance until the fort signaled its readiness or reinforcements arrived from Albany. He also announced that the Oneida war chief, Honyery Tewahangaraghkan, would accompany them with his wife, Senagena, who was known to wield a brace of pistols at her husband's side. The war chief's second captain was Henry Cornelius Haunnagwasuke who, with Ahnyero, his brother, and a warrior called Blatcop would help screen the advance into the forest. Also proudly present was the half-black Caughnawaga, Louis Atayataghronghta, who would later be famous as Colonel Louis, the highest-ranking native in the Continental service.[39] These were the best of the Oneida nation, and behind them followed threescore warriors imbued with faith in an American future and filled with Christian zeal owing in no small measure to Samuel Kirkland. They had to be conscious of what they were risking. By taking up arms against Brant's Mohawks, they were smashing their links to the ancient Iroquois League and laying themselves open to devastating retribution.

None of this mattered to Ebenezer Cox, who had no trust in Indians. He and the other officers present repudiated Herkimer's acceptance of Oneida aid. They did not need savages to help them deal with Brant and British invaders. What was more, after two days of marching down dusty roads and camping in the open, Cox spoke for the men when he refused to delay in pressing on to their objective. Now was the time; now was the hour. To hold back was cowardice. Herkimer looked to Klock and Visscher; they remained silent. Only his brother-in-law Peter Bellinger spoke up on his behalf, urging caution. The rebuke stung the brigadier deeply. Underlying Cox's vehemence was his dislike of the phlegmatic German, the slow, paternal, moderate leader who at Unadilla had let Joseph Brant slip through his grasp. Herkimer was used to ethnic slurs; he had been born a Palatine and grown up in the Mohawk Valley, where national group, clan, and church defined existence. But he could not stomach the charge of cowardice. This man, who in so many ways was the iconic American— generous, forbearing, courageous, pious—exploded now at the accusation that he, like his brother Hans Yost, serving with St. Leger, was a craven traitor to the patriot cause. "You want war?" he shouted in his heavily accented English. "I give you war! You'll see the enemy. ... And you'll be the first to run!"[40] And so, amidst rancor and doubt, the officers of the Tryon militia mounted up and moved out from Oriska onto the military road. The Oneida, who sensed the tension, chose to march between the 2nd and 4th battalions. The 4th came from the Kingsland and German Flats district and were known to them as friends.

The day before, in the British camp six miles away, a council of war had been called to consider developments. Molly's report of the departure of the Tryon County militia had alarmed everyone, for these battalions now threatened to shift the balance of power at Stanwix, handing momentum back to the Americans. Joseph Brant believed that Herkimer would forego a river landing under fire at the fort and make his approach over the old military road through the ravines. So much the better, he argued, for this was terrain he knew well. His Mohawks were on hand to smash Herkimer's hapless farmers and chase them back to Dayton. What he advised was an ambush in force, and he knew just where to spring it.

This proposal gave pause for thought. Sir John Johnson believed that a parley with the Tryon people could buy time to neutralize Stanwix, after which the militia would lose resolve and return to the settlements. John Butler tended to agree. Both men knew how pitiless a native ambush could be. Their present enemies were their erstwhile associates and tenants, and both hoped to return someday to their properties in the valley. Bushwhacking Tenonanatche's farmers did not seem the best way home to either man. Nor were the Seneca leaders comfortable with Brant's strategy. These leaders included such eminences as Cornplanter, Old Smoke, and the brilliant, young Red Jacket. They resented Thayendanegea's presumption of leadership, but most of all they were troubled by the Oneida presence among the Americans. Fractious nations were hardly unusual within the Iroquois League; the Senecas had themselves pressed the limits many times. Yet, Iroquois normally curbed their wrath and waited for recalcitrant brothers to fall back in line. The Senecas would not fight the Oneidas; moreover, they were mindful of promises of neutrality made to Schuyler and the Americans. They did offer, however, to follow Brant's corps as observers.[41]

It fell to St. Leger to make the decision. He was worried understandably about Herkimer's approach. With a regular force numerically inferior to the combined enemy, military expediency required that he divide and strike the Americans in detail or find himself overwhelmed in the open, where native forces were little help. St. Leger could not know how long his allies would willingly wait for victory or, for that matter, if he could even outlast Gansevoort. A soldier's soldier, St. Leger sensed the ferocity of Brant, the headlong willingness to hurt the enemy. If Brant believed he could destroy the militia and open the way into the Mohawk Valley, his daring deserved support. St. Leger appointed Sir John Johnson as overall commander, but appointed Joseph Brant to plan and coordinate the attack.

In the early morning of August 6, Brant positioned his forces. He chose as his ambush site a plateau formed by a deep ravine to the west and a steeper ravine to the east. The military road between these ravines ran through a densely forested stretch. Along the road, well concealed, Brant placed Mohawk marksmen. Where the road dipped down into the eastern ravine and crossed a creek over a corduroy bridge, he took up position with additional forces. Sir John with fifty of his Kings Royal New York Light Infantry (Johnson's Greens) was given the task of putting the cork in the bottle. As always in ambushes, the important first step was to stop the forward motion of the enemy. The Royal Yorkers, supported by Butler's rangers and a detachment of Hanau Jägers, were emplaced on the western lip of the western ravine in a position to decimate the head of a column descending into the declivity. Nearby, the pacifist Senecas took up their post of observation.

Brant's plan called for the head of the Tryon column to reach the western ravine just as the oxcarts, under observation by Mohawk scouts, were climbing out of the eastern ravine and the rearguard was crossing the eastern ravine's corduroyed bridge. At that moment the Royal Yorkers would halt the column with a volley; the Mohawks hidden on the plateau would rise up and fire into the flanks of the militia; and Brant and his warriors would fire and charge into the rearguard, cutting the militia off from retreat.

Between Brant's corps, Johnson's Royal Yorkers, and Butler's rangers, the Tory forces numbered approximately 800. Notably absent were British regulars, excepting a detachment of Hanau riflemen on Sir John's flank. The Battle of Oriskany would be between American Tories, patriots, and Native Americans of all political persuasions. Brant's brilliance lay in concealing his force from the approaching enemy. He knew how sharp were Oneida eyes and made certain in the early morning that his force left no broken branches, moccasin prints, or telltale signs pointing to their places of concealment.

Why did the Oneida not pick up on the ambush? Steeped in Iroquois tactics, did they not feel the strangeness of the forest? Why, for that matter, did Nicholas Herkimer allow his anger to override his deep misgivings? These are all reasonable questions.[42] The Oneidas, spurned by white men such as Cox, confused by the everlasting bickering of Tryon factions, marched beside those neighbors they trusted and followed them straight into the jaws of hell. When the smoke cleared, the Oneida were indeed moving fast, picking out targets, buying time for Bellinger's 4th battalion to regroup. Honnikol's anger—he had been steadily goaded and chivvied by ambitious know-it-alls—came as a response to class and ethnic rivalries long smoldering in the valley. By the time he had cooled down and regained his command composure, he could do nothing but lead on and listen prayerfully for three cannon to sound in the distance. By then, he was conspicuously mounted on his old white mare, riding up the eastern plateau between the 1st and 2nd battalions, directly into Thayendanegea's ambush.

Thomas and Henry Spencer were out ahead of the van, but could do nothing to restrain the 1st battalion's twenty forward flankers from plunging to the bottom of the western ravine and slaking their thirst in a bubbling brook of cool water. The only sounds in the forest were the jingle of bridles, the shuffle of feet, the incessant chatter of the militia. It was 10 AM, a hazy sun slanting through the trees, steam starting to rise from wet leaves. The day had dawned hot and humid, and after an hour's march, the drowsy militiamen loosened straps and opened shirts. Yet, something was not right, Ahnyero sensed, even as he watched Cox's scouts throw down their guns and flop beside the brook to drink. Brant's whistle had not sounded, but the sight of their enemy off guard had grown too much for the Royal Yorkers and rangers. From above the western lip of the ravine, their 200 muskets exploded into the prostrate men.

Bodies instantly splashed into the water. The Royal Yorkers and rangers held their place, reloading, but young Seneca warriors, thrilled with their first sight of kill, launched themselves into the ravine on top of the vanguard's survivors. Conrad Mowers, a private, observed the slaughter from the ravine's edge. The braves pierced bodies with spears, hacked off limbs with tomahawks, smashed skulls with war clubs, and scalped their victims with astonishing dexterity. John Casler from Canajoharie saw the muskets a moment before they fired and threw himself to the ground. In the confusion, he crawled into the trees and waited for the charging warriors to pass. Casler would survive the massacre—the only scout to do so.[43] Ahnyero probably fell in this action, along with his brother Henry and the Oneida chief Cohega.[44]

Joseph Brant, protégé of Tiyanoga, had learned well to set a trap. But as the ambush burst over Herkimer's column, Brant knew he was not in luck. The ambush had been triggered too soon; the oxcarts were just beginning to descend into the eastern ravine and the rearguard, Visscher's 3rd battalion, was still on the road to the east. Now, stunned by the smoke billowing up from the western ravine, the shouts and gunfire, the 3rd bolted back down the road out of the ambush. Brant could do nothing to hold back those Mohawks who now broke cover and started in pursuit of the rearguard. The best he could do was to pull his own loyal guard around him and plunge into the wagons at the rear of Bellinger's 4th.

At this moment Herkimer's column, expanding and contracting under volleys of fire, was probably half a mile long. In the front, Cox obeyed his general's orders and formed his companies to fire straight down the road into a swelling mass of attackers. Their first fusillade held back a score of shouting braves. Jacob Dieffendorf, a lieutenant in the 1st, ran a young Indian through with his sword, heard his name called, turned, and was shot in the face by another assailant. George Casler, seeing this, slammed the butt of his musket into the head of the man who had shot the lieutenant and finished him with his hatchet. As Cox's men reloaded, they were taken under fire by dozens of Mohawks and Tories who had worked into the deadfall to the north and south of the roadway. Muskets discharged practically in the faces of opponents. Militia who were not cowering in the bloody dirt now thrust out at the ambuscades with bayonets and climbed piles of brush to fall on the enemy with knives and fists. The 1st battalion had driven back one charge, but both flanks were now exposed as men fell in heaps to the hidden enemy. Cox, on horseback, rushed to rally his command, cursing troops in shock, even shooting a would-be deserter.[45] He was still trying to form lines when a ball struck him in the head and he slipped dead to the ground. His horse bolted back into the 2nd battalion's position, scattering men over the roadway.

Lieutenant Colonel William Seeber now took command of the 1st battalion, or what was left of it. The ranks, locked shoulder to shoulder on the road, elbows jostling as they tried to reload, had been thrust through, hacked, chopped, and even pulled out of line and captured by rushes of Mohawks and Senecas. The formal response to ambush had never worked for General Braddock or Colonel Williams, and there was no reason it would work now for the Tryon County militia. Herkimer had been wrong to hold his men on the road, and now, with their officers down, they crawled into the woods, scraped out firing pits behind trees and fell to fighting Brant's warriors in wilderness style. The problem for riflemen alone in the woods, however, was the half minute needed to reload between firing and missing. In that half minute, an intended target could close the distance to the shooter and brain him with a tomahawk.

Sir John Johnson saw the 1st battalion beginning to hunker down under the trees and judged the moment right to send an attack of Royal Yorkers straight down the road into their wavering line. He chose for the job Major Steven Watts and his young Highlanders—"six were Grants, five McDonells, four Rosses, three Murchisons, two Camerons, two McPhersons, and others with names like McLean, Chisholm, Ferguson, and Urquhart."[46] Before forming in the King's Royal New Yorkers, many of these men had followed Sir John out of the valley and over the Adirondacks to Montreal. They felt like—and indeed were—impoverished refugees, despised and exiled by German Protestant farmers whom they were now about to attack. Behind Major Watts, Lieutenant Singleton, and Lieutenant McKenzie, the Highlanders went in with claymores, bayonets, and a battle cry to shame the Iroquois. They proved the least of 1st battalion's woes.[47]

Major Samuel Clyde met them in the road and, shooting Sergeant O'Donnell through the heart, brought Lieutenant Singleton down with the same shot. Around him, men with knives and hatchets in hand dodged bayonet and sword thrust to close with the young Highlanders and end their threat. In the forest groves of Oriskany, edged weapons were the wise choice. There was little time to fuss with powder and ball.

When the 1st came under attack, Herkimer on his white mare was climbing the hill out of the eastern ravine. He spurred forward to find Cox holding his own. Returning to the top of the eastern ravine, where Klock's "Palatine Regiment," the 2nd battalion, was taking heavy fire from the trees, he learned that the brigade's staff surgeon, Moses Younglove, had been dragged into the underbrush by Indians and taken captive. Smoke was billowing out of the eastern ravine, where Brant had struck the supply carts, killing drivers and oxen. Brant was now embroiled with remnants of the rearguard and Bellinger's 4th battalion, stuck midway up the slope of the eastern ravine. In the first moments of the ambush, the 4th had lost Major Eisenlord, Major Clapsaddle, and 20 percent of its number.

At this juncture, Lieutenant Jacob Sammons brought word to Herkimer that Cox and Lieutenant Abel Hunt had been killed, and Lieutenant Colonel William Seeber was mortally wounded. William Seeber's son, Jacob, had taken command of the 1st; he had forced the battalion into a half circle facing the enemy on three sides, and was pouring fire directly into the charging Senecas. What Herkimer now knew, after all his worry and doubt, was that the Tryon County militia was in a desperate fight it could not win and dared not lose. He ordered Klock to move up and link to the 1st, then sent Bellinger down into the ravine among the plundered wagons to drag survivors back to high ground.

For Bellinger, who had watched the wagon drovers slaughtered below him, then witnessed Visscher's 3rd battalion flee from the brink of the eastern ravine, the order to rescue scattered militia, reform, and clear the high ground behind Klock came as a death warrant. The eastern ravine was full of dead livestock and mutilated bodies; the brook ran red with blood, and some Mohawks still rummaged in the carts searching for plunder or scalps. Enraged, Bellinger swung his heavy saber at one. To his complete astonishment, the man's head rolled away. The native warriors were glutted with plunder and grown careless with victory. Musket balls whined around them, but the 4th, aided by its Oneidas, somehow managed to sweep up the ravine and make contact with Captain Jacob Gardinier of the 3rd. Gardinier led fifty men who had declined to run. Until Bellinger found them, they had been fighting their own private war of survival on the slopes of the ravine. Now Gardinier brought Bellinger to Colonel Visscher and Lieutenant Colonel Veeder, who had fled in the first moments of the ambush, only to stiffen later and gather up their panicked soldiers. They blamed the brigade adjutant, Anthony Van Vechten, a long-time patriot leader from the Palatine district, for rushing through their command shouting "Run, boys, run or we'll all be killed."[48] Few of their men, fleeing for their lives down the road to Oriska with the Mohawks in hot pursuit, lived to tell their story. They were run down, killed, and stripped of their weapons. In years to come their skeletons would be found as far to the east as Oriskany Creek.[49]

Gathering whom he could from the abattoir of the east ravine, Bellinger led his augmented force back towards Klock's 2nd on the high ground between the ravines. Suddenly he spotted a young private, Adam Miller, from Visscher's routed battalion, darting away in terror. Out of the bush with several men popped Captain John Hare of Butler's rangers, the same who had ambushed work details in the vicinity of Stanwix. Hare seized the frightened boy, but before he could harm him, Bellinger fired. In that very instant the 4th's muskets found Hare and wrote finish to a notorious frontier menace.

Pushing back up the slope, the 4th with remnants of the 3rd chased away lurking snipers. Herkimer had instructed Bellinger to form on the high ground, deploy his squads in circular groups, and cover the rear. Klock's squads were in circles north and south of the road, while Seeber's 1st covered the road to the west. By now the militia battalions had lost their integrity; officers had been killed, and men struggled to survive beneath the trees in isolated pockets.

What alarmed Bellinger as he reached the top of the slope was the cluster of men milling around the general. Bellinger's brother-in-law was seated beneath a large beech tree. Dr. Petrie, the 4th's surgeon, was tightening the tourniquet on Herkimer's left leg where, six inches below the knee, a ball had shattered the bone. The same shot that passed through Herkimer had killed his mare. They pulled him out from under the horse, rushed him to the cover of the beech tree, and were trying to staunch the flow of blood. All the while, Honnikol sat calmly on his saddle giving orders. He had lit his ever-present pipe and, now smoking casually, explained what he wanted. Into the woods, two by two, he sent his remaining militia with jabs of the pipe stem. First man fires, and the second covers him if he misses. Try to make the first a rifle shot, the second a musket load of buck and ball for closer range. Don't run from the Indians. Keep touch with your left and right. Strip powder and ball from the dead, and remember to take their canteens. Leave the wounded where they lie; they're safer on the ground. Shot slammed into the beech tree around him, and his men wanted to move him to a safer spot. Herkimer would not have it. He struggled to free his hanger, jammed it into the ground, and told them, "No, I will face my enemy!" What many had not known, but Philip Schuyler had from tales of the old war, was that the little man from German Flats cared too much for his men to worry overly about his own safety; he was truly fearless under fire.

During the second hour of combat, the battered militia began to concentrate firepower, free up ammunition from the fallen, and respond to orders. These flowed down from Herkimer, wounded though he was. As the militia pushed into the trees, they came to close quarters with their enemy and the fighting grew hand-to-hand and merciless. No one will ever fully know what individuals experienced in those woods. There are the ghastly stories. Surgeon Truelove, being led away by captors, passed warriors slitting the necks of wounded militiamen, even drinking blood from torn throats. Truelove was in shock and would claim to see worse excesses later as a prisoner.

Of equal moment was the tragic ending of friendship. Lieutenant Abram Quackenbush of the 3rd battalion was edging up along the roadway when he heard a familiar voice. Adam had been a storekeeper in Glen, just south of Fultonville, and many Mohawks in the district had been his friends and customers. Now he glimpsed a familiar face under war paint. The brave who whispered to him was Bronkahorse, his childhood playmate, who urged him to surrender and stay safe. Quackenbush would not do it. The men were both fine marksmen and they now began circling each other through the trees. Bronkahorse fired first, and the ball barely missed Quackenbush's head; the storekeeper fired next, and killed his oldest and best friend.[50] At Oriskany, the bridge that Sir William and other early settlers had built between Europeans and Native Americans was being torn up plank by plank.

Captain Christopher Fox, resting on a log to nurse his injured arm, spied a wounded Mohawk crawling back toward the enemy lines. He was not letting this one get away. Running to the man, who seemed to plead for mercy, he drew his sword and stabbed him through the chest. His victim, by all accounts, was no one else than William of Canajoharie, Tagawirunta, Sir William's unruly son by Caroline, daughter of King Hendrick.[51]

Two veterans of the failed Canadian campaign were serving in Klock's battalion. "George Lonis took a shot and stepped back to reload and his mate, Henry Sits, replaced him. When Sits fired, his musket burst. Shaken but uninjured, Sits searched about for a replacement. Lonis was taking a bead when the ends of three of his fingers on his left hand vanished, shot off by an Indian who sent the ball through his hair above the ear."[52] Muskets were becoming fouled as the fighting continued. Guns burst or failed to fire, and hardened soldiers like Lonis and Sits took to clubbing opponents to death with their rifle butts. Even the forest was beginning to break down. Twenty feet up from the fire-swept road, one Seneca recalled, the trees were riddled with shot, the leaves torn, and branches down. No one had ever seen so much lead discharged in so small a space.

The worst for both sides were the comrades lost, often in confused moments that would leave the survivor wondering for the rest of his life if there had been something he could have done. Men would leave a wounded buddy, circle back returning, and find him tomahawked and scalped. Some would scrape out a shallow grave and at least say goodbye. Others searched for relatives among the bodies and failed to identify them. Scalping causes facial flesh to sag, making verification difficult. The wounds at Oriskany were especially horrific, and fathers, brothers, sons searching piles of dead for family members under fire often failed to find them.

Not so the Senecas, who soon learned how much their nation had to grieve. Catapulted into a battle that their elders had never resolved to join, the youngest Seneca chiefs raced down the open road from the western ravine to smash the bloodied 1st battalion. They were Hasquesahah (Axe Carrier), Dahwahdeho (Things on a Stump), Gahnahage (Black Feathertail), Dahgaiowned (Branch of a Tree), Dahohjoedoh (Fish Lapper), and Jeskaka (Little Billy). All had been confirmed as the rising might of the Seneca people in a council at Oswego in July. Now, with bloody weapons and new scalps tucked into their belts, they dashed 200 yards to reach the white enemy. "The bloodied men of the Canajoharie Regiment waited patiently for them," Allen Foote writes. "At about one hundred paces the order was given and a solid sheet of flame erupted in the direction of the Indians. The formation of braves was decimated. More than half of all of the Seneca chiefs and warriors to perish on this day were lost during these opening volleys, including the flower of the young leadership."[53]

The shocked Senecas limped back to the main body, where their elders berated them for the foolishness of their tactics. Never should they have frontally assaulted a line of guns like profligate white soldiers. The loss to their people in the deaths of seventeen young chiefs was incalculable. This was the future of the Seneca nation, left crumpled in the dust of the roadway. But the dying had only begun. Before the day was out, the formidable chief Gisugwatoh had been slain by the sword of Major Samuel Campbell of Cherry Valley, and the notable Cayuga leader Ghalto shot through the chest and taken prisoner.[54] In all, twenty-three Iroquois chiefs and nearly eighty warriors fell at Oriskany, the worst casualties among the Iroquois in living memory, and the numbers did not include Oneida losses. Little wonder then that Red Jacket, a great future leader and native diplomatist, took one look at the slaughter in the forest, gathered two Seneca companions together, and left immediately for Genesee. No one would ever blame him for saving his talents for tomorrow.[55]

By early afternoon the combatants on both sides were beginning to notice a peculiar phenomenon. Within the glades, the air was darkening. The suffocating clouds of humidity, polluted by a dense haze of gun smoke, had begun to circulate under the trees as a cool breeze brought sudden relief to the grimy survivors. Above the musket fire, thunder sounded, or perhaps at 1 PM these claps were the long-awaited signal cannon. A few drops of rain and then, as will happen in central New York, a veritable deluge fell from the heavens. The heavy rain brought most of the fighting to a standstill as men looked to keep flints and priming pans dry. For Tryon County the downpour came as a blessed relief, a time to regroup, to tighten lines and replenish ammunition. For the Native Americans, the storm seemed to confirm the evil omens of the day. In the Tory camp, Sir John used the interlude to rush up fresh reinforcements as the Royal Yorkers prepared to break through Herkimer's lines for once and for all.

But as Johnson's reinforcements left the siege lines around Stanwix for the battle in the woods, something else was stirring. Herkimer's rangers had reached the fort about noon, long after the ambush was sprung. Whether or not Gansevoort's men heard the din of firing a few miles away has never been established, but pursuant to Herkimer's request, the colonel prepared a detachment under Major Willett to sally from the fort and attack the enemy encampment. All morning they had been watching Indians leave their camp and move to the east. Something was up and certainly heading Herkimer's way. At one o'clock, Gansevoort fired three sequential cannon shots. As he unbarred the gates, the very storm that lashed the militia in the forest descended on the fort, delaying the sally. Then, at about two o'clock, Willett judged the rain had lightened and finally launched his attack of 250 Massachusetts and New York Continentals, which swept into the nearby Indian bivouac. There was no defense. The attack encountered only women and children.

Willett dismantled the camp quickly, stripping the Seneca hutments of all goods, blankets, implements, war booty, and munitions. From a distance, St. Leger could not discern what was happening; his regulars were on duty at Wood Creek and slow to respond. Sir John's reserves had left for the front. Lieutenant Bird's detachment was scattered. Willett had all the time in the world to break into Sir John's bivouac, strip the Royal Yorkers' tents of all effects, and rifle the rangers' huts. He captured six battle flags and a mountain of records. While his infantry formed to meet the anticipated British counterthrust, wagons rolled back and forth between the fort and the enemy camp loaded with plunder. The Americans filled wagons with supplies, personal goods, sundry treasures, and arms. They were especially careful to pilfer cooking implements, food, clothing, and blankets. From the gentlemen's tents they took wine and tobacco, writing materials, uniforms and accessories. Then, almost as quickly as they had appeared, they were gone, leaving their enemy languishing outside the walls impoverished, denuded, and embarrassed. Not a casualty was suffered on either side, but time would prove Willett's raid a catastrophic defeat for St. Leger.

The raiders came in with many scalps found in the camp, including those of the "berry girls," but they made certain that when the Senecas returned from battle, they would have neither food to cook nor pots to cook in, neither blankets to shelter under nor tenting to cover them in the night. The Mohawks, off with Brant, hardly fared better, and Sir John's entire correspondence now fell into patriot hands, an invaluable source for identifying loyalists in the valley. What infuriated the British regulars most, however, was the sight the next morning of six captured battle flags flying below the Stars and Stripes above the fort.

Yet this success did not immediately alter the course of the battle. Oriskany had become an infernal world unto itself, and the rains relenting, the killing began again. Pools of bloody water stood everywhere beneath the dripping trees. "Soon after the rain stopped, the Indians and Troops began to creep forward through the drenched undergrowth and rivulets of run-off," Blacksnake recalled. "I thought at that time the

Blood Shed a Stream Running down on the Descending ground during the afternoon, and yet some living crying for help. But [we] have no mercy ... for them."[56] Wounded opponents, found by both sides, were dispatched.

By 2 PM the battle had hardened into stalemate. Tories and their Indian allies controlled the woods, while the Tryon County militia clung to their defense of the high ground. The American lines were more pear-shaped than circular, with the current battle monument about where a pear is thickest and Herkimer's position southeast from the monument along the road outlining the left side of the pear.[57] The attack made by Sir John's Royal Yorkers in their final attempt to break the defenses and overrun the militia came down this road, passing the western ravine and cutting into the head of the enclosure where many of Colonel Visscher's remnants had taken position.

John Butler suggested a ruse to permit the Yorkers to close with the enemy before unleashing a bayonet charge.[58] They would be stumbling forward over a terrible tangle of bodies. What Butler proposed, and Sir John accepted, was that the "Greens" turn their uniforms inside out, with their white linings showing on the outside. Massachusetts Continentals often wore white hunting smocks in the field, and at a distance, the militia might very well mistake the Yorkers for timely aid arrived from Stanwix. By now everyone had heard firing from the direction of the fort; Native Americans were beginning to get word of the attack on their camp and slip away from the battle. If the Tories could break through in these closing moments, capture or kill Herkimer and scatter his militia, they would secure total victory. If they failed to penetrate the enemy lines, they would leave the grievously injured militia in control of the field, free to crawl back to the valley.

The Royal Yorkers came on in good order with arms at port, just as Continentals might have, and among the militia some stood up to cheer the sight of their approaching saviors. Then, men began to spot familiar faces in the ranks—faces of Tory neighbors from home. Still, no one fired. Captain Gardinier, of Visscher's 3rd, sprang forward shouting, "They're Tories, shoot, shoot," but the militia seemed frozen in hope. A militiaman ran toward his rescuers. They wrestled him to the ground and pinioned his arms.

Gardinier, a blacksmith by trade and a rough soldier, plunged into their midst with a spear—either a spontoon (a short pike) or a captured Indian weapon. Quickly he thrust through two Royal Yorkers before others were able to knock him down and pinion both his calves to the ground with bayonets. A third assailant jabbed his bayonet at Gardinier's chest, but the blacksmith caught it in his callused hand, pushed it aside, and pulled the man down on top of him. Somehow he tore himself loose of the bayonets in his calves, threw his human body shield into the air, and caught him on the point of the spear. The man killed was Lieutenant Angus MacDonald, one of the most despised enforcers among Sir William's loyal Highlanders. Gardinier raced back to the American lines and dove through just as the militia unleashed a blistering salvo into Johnson's Greens. Thirty of the Royal Yorkers fell in that blow, but the hundred or so Tories still standing charged for the militia lines and, in many places, broke through. These men who grappled with each other in the mud knew and hated each another. They never bothered to reload, but tore at their opponents' faces with knives, bayonets, and fingernails. Undoubtedly, the worst hand-to-hand fighting of the battle occurred in these seconds, but such ferocity could not sustain itself.[59]

About 3 PM, the fifth hour of the conflict, Johnson's Greens began to withdraw, dragging their wounded behind them. Many of Johnson's late reinforcements were novice soldiers who had had to face the fury of Oriskany survivors, men engaged for five hours in an unspeakable battle. Captain Jacob Gardinier was wounded thirteen times, had fought his way from the rearguard to the front of the column by the end of the day, and would not let an enemy off easily. The cry of "Oonah, oonah," the Iroquois signal for retreat, sounded through the forest as Joseph Brant recognized the folly of continuing attacks against this concentrated foe. Except for one last outburst, the fighting was all but over.

That outburst occurred as men attempted to roll Nicholas Herkimer off his bloody saddle onto a blanket litter stretched between two poles. A pair of Mohawks, lurking in the bush, took the chance to rush the general and kill him. The shots that felled them were probably the last to sound in the forest on August 6.[60]

What remained for the men of Tryon County was to extract their wounded as best they could, moving them out from under the blasted trees before the enemy returned. Return the natives would, to gather up their dead and scavenge the battlefield. The patriots were almost out of ammunition. Their unwounded numbered 150 powder-blackened survivors. What they observed now as they drew back down the mile of road to where they had entered the ambush would provide lifelong nightmares for many. Nearly 600 men from both sides had been mortally wounded in this dreadful place. Their bodies were strewn along the roadway and well into the woods as far as eye could see. Their wounds were traumatic and violent beyond description. As they pulled out, the last to leave spied a militiaman's body pinned high against a tree trunk by a bayonet. The socket jutted out of his chest. For many decades, long after the man's body had decayed and fallen to the ground, the rusting bayonet socket, jammed impossibly high in the bark of the oak tree, would serve to remind the people of Tenonanatche of the fury that once divided and destroyed them.[61]

From the foregoing accounts, one might conclude that Herkimer's command held its own against Tories and Indians. These accounts, however, are based on the testimony of militia who survived the battle and described their exploits for posterity. The truth of the day was more sobering. "August 9, To the Albany County Committee of Safety," Peter Dygert wrote, "The flower of our militia either killed or wounded, except 150, who stood the field and forced the enemy to retreat; the wounded were brought off by these brave men."[62] According to imperfect records, about 150 militiamen came through the ambush unscathed. Down from the plateau between the ravines during that late afternoon the able-bodied brought 200 or so wounded to the banks of Oriskany Creek. They were aided by late-arriving troops from the Deerfield depot, Fort Dayton, and Oneida villagers. Many of the severely wounded men would die over the next two weeks. The number of missing was placed at about 50, mostly captured. Half of these would die in captivity. The conclusion remains that Herkimer's force suffered nearly 400 dead on the field and an additional 100 lost as a consequence of the battle. The percentage of casualties to force is stunning. Over 80 percent of the Tryon militia were killed, wounded, or captured. The Tory infantry and Tory rangers lost about 100 dead; the Native Americans from 100 to 150—casualties that in themselves were extreme for Revolutionary War battles. Saratoga resulted in a combined patriot death toll of about 250 of all ranks, Monmouth about 450, the siege of Yorktown another 150. At the Battle of Long Island, it is doubtful that the dead on the field exceeded 250. Thus, historians assert that the Battle of Oriskany was the bloodiest of the American Revolution, which indeed it was. The new country would not experience a comparable intensity of violence until the fratricidal strife at Shiloh and Antietam.

But Oriskany, as we shall see in the next chapter, was much more than just a Revolutionary battle. The large number of Native Americans involved, the absence of British regulars, the familiarity and local origin of the combatants argues for a different interpretation. This was less a fight over nation building than over race, ethnicity, and cultural identification—the worst conflict possible in a plural society. Nor did the battle announce an end or a turning point to war; Oriskany, "the place of nettles," was just the beginning.

✣ 10 ✣

Sorrow on the Land

Behind their sod walls, Gansevoort's soldiers, alert to attack, watched the commotion in the Iroquois camp. As the Seneca men returned from battle, their women met them with accusations and blame. Gone were the goods, lost or stolen—silver and clothing, pots, tools, blankets, medicine bundles, even food, plundered from their bark huts. The Senecas' humiliation was complete, and the fort took comfort in their confusion. But this pleasure would not extend to the militia prisoners brought to the camps trussed and bound. Ten men were appointed to sate the rage and grief of the Native Americans. These, John Butler reported, "were conformable to the Indian custom afterwards killed."[1] What "conformable" meant was that after a night of taunts and jibes, they were tortured to death in sundry ways. Most prisoners of the Oriskany battle remained in the not-very-tender hands of the British and Tories. Sacrificial victims were marked by their prominent political position in Tryon County or alleged mistreatment of loyalists.

Captain Robert Crouse of the 1st battalion was resented less for his actions than for his intimidating size. A truly huge man, Crouse, a year and a half earlier, had led General Schuyler's New Jersey Continentals over the ice of the Mohawk to arrest Sir John at Johnson Hall. During the crossing he found the strength to wave a streaming regimental flag in each hand; this remarkable feat was now remembered. His tormentors in their anger and spite amputated his legs at the knees with hatchets, and having cut him down to "human size," forced him to walk on the bleeding stumps until he collapsed. Six others, forced to run a gauntlet of assembled Senecas, were clubbed to death in full view of the fort. According to surgeon Moses Younglove, many more were similarly maimed and murdered, and he himself came near to being killed by Lieutenant McGinnis, Sarah Kast McGinnis's son, an officer in Butler's rangers. In December 1777, Younglove testified before a Committee of Congress presided over by John Barclay:

> That [Major] Isaac Paris Esqr [1st battalion] was also taken and led by the
> Savages the same Road, without receiving from them any remarkable Insult

except stripping untill some Tories came up who kicked & abused him, after which the Savages thinking him a Notable Offender Murdered him Barbarously. That those of the Prisoners who were delivered up to the Provost Guard were kept without Victuals for many Days and had neither Clothes Blankets Shelter or Fire while the Guards were ordered not to use any Violence in protecting the Prisoners from the Savages who came every Day in large Companies with Knives and feeling the Prisoners to know who was fattest That they Dragged one of the Prisoners out with the most Lamentable Cries, Tortured him for a long time and the Deponent was informed by both Tories and Indians, that they eat [sic] him as appeared they did another on an Island in Lake Ontario.[2]

Younglove's full account contains many contradictions and probably is best understood as the deposition of a badly shaken man, but the death of Isaac Paris, a member of the Tryon County Committee of Safety, occurred much as he describes. Tories, not just Indians, took the opportunity to even old scores with their neighbors. Some prisoners of the Senecas, like John Spanable and Henry Walrath, experienced harsh treatment, but were eventually delivered unharmed to Albany and New York.[3] Wilderness captivity was chancy; the end could come abruptly, as it did for Crouse and Paris, or result in lengthy imprisonment, slavery, or a bartered exchange. Much depended on the personalities of captors and the disposition of their families in the aftermath of battle. Oriskany struck at the pride of the once invincibly united Iroquois and, as Johnson sensed, a quick success was required to restore their confidence. He urged St. Leger to bypass Stanwix and pursue Herkimer's demoralized militiamen into the valley. With 200 soldiers and Brant's Indians, they could easily sweep east through Tenonanatche into Schuyler's rear at Albany. Sir John warned that the Indians held the Americans responsible for their despoiled camp and dead chiefs at the moment, but should the British fail to deliver victory, the blame for the humiliations at Oriskany would fall on them. An understanding of the native mind eluded St. Leger. As a proper soldier in His Majesty's service, he categorically refused to disobey his orders by lifting the siege.

What he proposed, as trenches drew closer to the fort's walls, was a letter to Gansevoort. It was penned by his two highest-ranking prisoners—Frederick Bellinger, Lieutenant Colonel in the 4th and brother of Peter, and John Frey, Brigade Major on Herkimer's staff. Under threat of Indian torture, the men consented to assist the enemy by inscribing and signing the following:

It is with concern we are to acquaint you that this was the fatal day in which the succours, which were intended for your relief, have been attacked and defeated with great loss of numbers killed, wounded and taken prisoners. ... Our sincere advice to you is, if you will avoid inevitable ruin and destruction, to surrender the fort you pretend to defend. ... We are sorry to inform you that most of the principal officers are killed, to wit—Gen. Herkimer, Cols. Cox, Seeber, Isaac Paris, Captain Graves and many others. ... The British army from Canada being now perhaps before Albany, the possession of which place of course includes the conquest of the Mohawk River and this fort. [4]

This missive, accurate more than not, was delivered to Stanwix by Major Wesley Ancron and John Butler. Gansevoort declined to meet with either, or to reply in any way to the assertions represented. St. Leger scribbled on the back of the returned letter: "Gen. St. Leger, on the day of the date of this letter, made a verbal summons of the fort by his Adjutant General and Colonel Butler, and who then handed this letter; when Colonel Gansevoort refused any answer to a verbal summons, unless made by Gen. St. Leger himself, but at the mouth of his cannon."[5]

What Gansevoort realized by now was that the relief force had been defeated and that the besiegers creeping closer to his walls had ample time to work a breach. Yet, no one inside was of any mind to surrender, even after the enemy cut off water to the garrison. They dug a well, drank the muddy liquid, and thought this refreshment superior to falling into the hands of the Senecas. The British remounted their tiny cohorns as howitzers and attempted to shell the fort's enclosure. The Iroquois watched closely and quickly concluded that firing lead balls into sod bastions and dropping explosive peas over the walls was a monumental waste of powder. This was not their kind of war nor, after Oriskany, were they about to charge Gansevoort's gun ports. Their mutterings grew louder as small parties packed up and prepared to leave. In council after council, Brant, Johnson, Butler, Claus, and St. Leger tried to persuade them to be patient. But the terror provoked by the very presence of the Native Americans was part of the problem. If the fort could be brought to yield without a bloody assault, the native peoples would have to forego the accepted practice of slaughtering the defenders. With the Indian threat over their heads, the Americans were likely to fight to the finish, and that could consume several weeks. The restive chiefs were at least willing to consider the proposal—turning all prisoners over to the British—but only if they were allowed sole right to plunder the fort. Prospects of material gain had brought the Iroquois into the field in the first place, and their losses to date far outweighed gifts received. The chiefs' consent now allowed St. Leger to appeal to Gansevoort on humanitarian grounds. The tribes promised not to molest prisoners, burn homesteads, or otherwise terrorize inhabitants once they had passed through Stanwix into the valley. Supplied with this understanding, Ancron and Butler were able to return to the fort with a credible proposal for surrender.

They were admitted under a white flag, blindfolded, and led to the officers' quarters, where light refreshments were served. Colonel Gansevoort refused to meet with them—he would only treat with St. Leger—but he had delegated Lieutenant Colonel Willett to act on his behalf. Ancron presented St. Leger's argument, repeating assertions about Herkimer's defeat and Burgoyne's triumph at Albany. Under the circumstances, he urged the Americans to:

> Surrender now on favorable terms and be guaranteed protection for all members of the garrison. Or, if the fort had to be taken by force, he [St. Leger] could not restrain his savage allies from an indiscriminate massacre of its defenders. The Indians were so provoked by their recent losses of several favorite chiefs that they threatened to march down the valley and destroy all the settlements and their inhabitants, men, women, and children, and he [St. Leger] could not prevent it.[6]

Butler then gave his personal bond, as a man widely recognized and respected in the valley, that the terms offered would be faithfully kept—the Indians would not harm prisoners.

Lieutenant Colonel Willett's reply to this offer resounds famously down the years as a restatement of the principles for which the patriots fought:

> Do I understand you, Sir? I think you say, that you come from a British colonel, who is commander of the army that invests this fort; and by your uniform, you appear to be an officer in the British service. You have made a long speech on the occasion of your visit, which, stript of its superfluities, amounts to this, that you come from a British colonel, to the commandant of this garrison, to tell him, that if he does not deliver the garrison into the hands of your Colonel, he will send his Indians to murder our women and children. You will please to reflect, sir, that their blood will be on your head, not on ours. We are doing our duty: this garrison is committed to our charge, and we will take care of it. After you get out of it, you may turn around and look at its outside, but never expect to come in again, unless you come a prisoner. I consider the message you have brought, a degrading one for a British officer to send, and by no means reputable for a British officer to carry. For my part, I declare, before I would consent to deliver this garrison to such a murdering set as your army, by your own account, consists of, I would suffer my body to be filled with splinters and set on fire, as you know has at times been practiced, by such hordes of women and children killers, as belong to your army.[7]

Willett seizes the moral high ground, staking out the claim that Americans fight not for empire but civilization, that their enemy is the dark and secret savagery embraced by hypocritical Britons and unleashed upon the weakest victims. Ancron's representation makes no moral claim; it purports only to convey hard military facts. Herkimer's relief column has been defeated; Burgoyne has won in the east; the rebels at Stanwix are clearly without hope or resources. The statement about Burgoyne's progress was, of course, wishful, while given that the militia held the field at the end of the day, withdrew in good order, and inflicted severe casualties on the enemy drew into question the totality of Herkimer's defeat.[8] Willett could not know the truth of these matters, but he and Gansevoort would have been very foolish indeed to accept St. Leger's representations while Stanwix gave every indication of withstanding siege.

It is perhaps appropriate at this point to pose the awkward question: Who did actually win the bloody fight at Oriskany? In truth, what makes the question irrelevant is the difficulty of discerning any winners.[9] There were many losers—Herkimer and Cox, Brant, Johnson, Butler and St. Leger. They all left the field, if they left at all, with tarnished reputations or diminished options. But the greatest losers of all were the Native Americans who were drawn into the vortex against their better judgment, instincts, and interests. Mary Jemison, the white woman turned Seneca, always believed that at Oriskany her adopted people were "completely beaten."[10] She was not at Stanwix, but learned of the events at home in Genesee. Militarily, Brant, Johnson, and Butler triumphed over Herkimer, or so the butcher bill presented to Tryon County suggests. But in exchange, their success led to the demonizing of a people who until late had lived commiseratively with their neighbors on Tenonanatche. Native Americans and white Europeans usually chafed at each other, but Oriskany turned a low-grade conflict into a soaring conflagration. Brant, Butler, and Johnson had much more fight to give, but increasingly they would be striking at a foe motivated by racial hatred and a fierce desire for revenge. Willett knew his men despised the British for turning the Indians loose. They believed that in time they would free themselves from this foreign yoke, but they would never be free of the Indian threat until they had driven the Indians off their soil.

The worst that could happen, William Johnson and Conrad Weiser had warned, was an Indian war in the valleys of central New York and Pennsylvania, for the scattered hamlets and homesteads of the settlers were hopelessly vulnerable to Iroquois tactics, while the Iroquois themselves in their material needs were no longer self-sufficient or independent. Shickellamy and Skenando might have added that in their view the truly worst thing that could befall their people was for the Iroquois to war against European settlers while also warring among themselves. Yet this is exactly what happened in the wake of Oriskany. Like the white combatants on the Mohawk, "they, too, would become a divided people—nation against nation, clan against clan, lodge against lodge."[11] Innocent victims in time would far outnumber battlefield casualties as farms and villages struggled to survive without their men, and non-political Native Americans were squeezed between the fierce partisanship of their brothers and the racial stigmas of white society.

That August, the Oneidas and Tuscaroras received a bloody hatchet from Onondaga, signifying that their nations were now at war with the Iroquois Confederacy. The announcement was followed by a quick retributive strike against the

Oneida village at Oriska. Since these people had aided the enemies of their Mohawk and Seneca brothers in the late battle, Brant felt no compunction in burning their homes, scattering their livestock, and hunting down their warriors. Oriska ceased to exist as an inhabitable abode.

But the Oneida also knew where Thayendanegea's sister lived, high above the Mohawk in a finely appointed house. The Oneidas had learned from the Reverend Kirkland that Molly Brant had passed critical information about the Tryon militia to her brother, and now, with their own grief to assuage, they swept into the upper Mohawk castle at Canajoharie and drove out the inhabitants. Molly escaped from her house, fled to Onondaga, and eventually reached her relatives in Cayuga country, but the Oneidas entered her home and plundered her possessions. "From Mary Brant alone," Graymont writes, "Deygart and the Oneida warrior Honyery Doxtater obtained a rich haul which they divided between them. The treasure included 'Sixty half Johannesses, two Quarts full of silver, several Gold Rings, Eight pair silver Buckels; a large Quantity of Silver Broaches, Together with several silk Gowns.' Deygart's daughter amused herself by parading about in Miss Mary's purloined silks. Honyery moved himself and his family into Mary Brant's house."[12]

The Oneidas reached the Mohawk village of Kanatsiohareke on the north bank soon after and, chasing the dwellers into the hills, proceeded to remove wagonloads of corn and foodstuffs. They were on their way to Fort Hunter, where William Johnson had arrived in 1737, and to the lower castle of Tiononderoge, where the Anglican divine, the Reverend John Stuart, officiated at Queen Anne's chapel. By the time the Oneidas arrived, local militia from the lower valley had turned the venerable chapel into a tavern, serving rum from behind the ornate lectern. Little Abraham and his people struck out for hidden places in the hills, while 100 Mohawk warriors from the castle raced to Montreal to enlist in Burgoyne's campaign. No sooner were the Mohawks gone than John Stuart was arrested as a loyalist Anglican, friend to the Johnson party and associate of Joseph Brant. He would eventually be exchanged to Canada, where he would become chaplain to the 2nd battalion of Sir John's Royal Yorkers. But his chapel at Fort Hunter would by then have become a stable for army horses. Beneath the dirt floor, where his Mohawk parishioners had hidden it, rested the silver communion service presented to Fort Hunter by Queen Anne as a gift of faith. Eventually the Mohawk Anglicans would unearth their treasured heirloom and smuggle it to Kingston, Ontario.[13]

The Schoharie Creek empties into the Mohawk River at Fort Hunter, and up the Schoharie Valley in mid-August, Colonel John Harper won a notable victory over the Tories James McDonald and Adam Crysler at the head of a party of Mohawks. Crysler had secreted Indians on his sprawling farm in Vroomansland waiting for a moment to attack. When McDonald arrived from Niagara via the Susquehanna with twenty more Mohawks and a band of Tories, the two combined to raid farms in the middle valley.[14] Their plan was to meet up with St. Leger at Fort Hunter and set fire to Tenonanatche all the way to Albany. Harper raced to Albany, begged a detachment of Continental cavalry from the Committee of Safety, and returned in time to confront McDonald and Crysler. The Battle of the Flockey, as this engagement came to be called, was loud, head-on, and decisive.[15] The mixed band of McDonald and Crysler managed to fire one volley before they were driven into the forests. Behind them they left several casualties and most of their supplies. Suddenly, war had arrived in the Palatines' "land of Scorie," and while some militia marched for Fort Hunter to punish the Mohawks, others commenced an ambitious construction program to seal off the valley against the very people who once, in a bitter winter, welcomed their refugee forbearers. The forts built in 1777 to protect Schoharie would see desperate fighting over the next three years as the covenant between the Iroquois and the settlers continued to unravel.

Gansevoort needed to know the truth about the American situation in the valley. Someone therefore would have to break through the siege lines, reach Fort Dayton if possible, and return with solid intelligence. Willett volunteered to try, accompanied by Lieutenant Levi Stockwell, a seasoned woodsman acquainted with the river trails. For a second in command, ranked lieutenant colonel, to run the risk of a mission through enemy lines was highly unusual, but as Willett later explained, his good standing with the Tryon militia made his choice a logical one.[16] In the night following the interview with Major Ancron, Willett and Stockwell slipped out of the fort, through the British sentries and, armed only with spontoons, began a fifty-mile journey along the north bank of the Mohawk to Dayton.[17] Their wilderness trek was full of narrow escapes, and both men arrived two days later swollen by bites, starved, and half-drowned from fording flooded streams. But they learned to their joy that help for Stanwix was on the way. Gansevoort and his forlorn garrison had not been forgotten.

Schuyler heard of Herkimer's battle two days after the fact, and only the third day following was he aware that the "damned, clumsy Germans had been shot to pieces," as Dygert described. The general was on the verge of being replaced by Horatio Gates, the choice of Congress, but Gates was making his way to the North Country at a leisurely pace. He would not arrive until August 19, and in the meanwhile, Schuyler continued to command the Northern Department from his headquarters at Stillwater on the Hudson. Burgoyne was at Fort Edward, about twenty-four miles away, summoning reserves and supplies for a thrust towards Saratoga. At this point he outnumbered Schuyler two to one, but he had also dispatched a sizable Brunswick force under Lieutenant Colonel Baum—who spoke no English—to scour the countryside towards Bennington for provisions, horses for his dragoons, and any stray loyalist bands he might encounter. On the day Willett left Dayton for Stillwater, Baum set course for Manchester, Vermont, expecting to brush aside the remains of Seth Warner's Green

Mountain Boys. What he could not know, and Schuyler did, was that the irascible and commanding John Stark, favored son of New England, was raising the State of New Hampshire to block him. Stark had no use for Schuyler, and Schuyler no liking for Stark, but there would be a fight, and win, lose, or draw, it would buy time for Schuyler to rush help to his left flank.[18]

At a meeting of his staff on the morning of August 13, Schuyler announced that he would send a strong detachment from his army to the relief of Stanwix. He called for a volunteer from among his officers to lead the expedition. None responded. There were murmurs of disbelief that in the face of Burgoyne's threat, Schuyler would even think of diverting troops to the west. The general bit the stem of his clay pipe in two and threw away the fragments. He glowered at his staff. "I will take the responsibility upon myself, but Stanwix and the Mohawk Valley shall be saved. Where is the brigadier who will command the relief?"[19] Benedict Arnold, resentful of how Schuyler had been treated and aware that relieving Stanwix was vital to the American left flank, agreed to lead the column to Gansevoort's assistance. Arnold was Schuyler's old friend and subordinate. He and the Dutch patrician had traveled hard roads together. Sidelined now and no friend to Gates, Arnold itched for a chance to be in action.

The following day, Arnold departed Stillwater at the head of the 1st New York Regiment and 900 Massachusetts Continentals from Ebenezer Learned's brigade. Along the way he scooped up Willett and Stockwell, who briefed him on conditions at the fort. Arnold roused his troops with all the patriotic bombast he could command and paused frequently in river towns to inspire the local people with a spirit of resistance. He was stunned to find them sullen and uncooperative. Some resented being rescued by a Connecticut man leading a Massachusetts regiment; others had simply had enough of the war. Understandably, Arnold believed he had landed in a hotbed of loyalist sympathizers. Not until he entertained a delegation of Oneida chiefs, heading east to fight Burgoyne, was he told by eyewitnesses what had happened at Oriskany. The dimensions of the tragedy had begun to sink into the collective consciousness. The Snell family had sent six men to the fight, and not one returned. All four Seebers fell. Three Bellingers, three Wollebers, two Houses, and two Davises were killed. The valley patriots were bled dry, and yet notwithstanding, they would rise again to send a hundred militia to Arnold and another hundred to the New York regiments at Saratoga. What Arnold could not expect, however, were happy faces and cheering crowds.

At Little Falls he crossed the river with his surgeon to pay respects to the wounded Herkimer. The brigadier was at home in bed, his spacious house filled with children and attending relatives.[20] By now, ten days after the battle, his shattered leg had mortified and would require amputation. Arnold left his personal surgeon to attend to Herkimer, and with the story of the Tryon militia much on his mind, raced off to Fort Dayton to rejoin his command. Surgeon Johnson performed the operation, but since this was the first leg he had ever removed, he performed it badly. He was unable to suture the arteries closed or to staunch the slow hemorrhaging of his patient. Willett remained behind and witnessed the passing of Honnikol on August 16. The General seemed composed; he smoked his pipe incessantly and, wearing his spectacles, read from the family Bible brought to the New World by his Palatine ancestors in 1710. He opened to Psalm 38, beginning: *"Herr, strafe mich nicht in deinem Zorn und züchtige mich nicht in deinem Grimm./Denn deine Pfeile stecken in mir, und deine Hand drückt mich."* [O Lord, rebuke me not in thy wrath: nor chasten me in thy hot displeasure./For thine arrows stick fast in me, and thy hand presseth me sore.] Self-recriminations at his headstrong rebuke of Cox and the rush into ambush remained with him to the end.

Throughout the warm afternoon Herkimer faded. His amputated leg was given to two teenaged nephews to bury on the grounds of the house.[21] And thus he slipped away, one of Tenonanatche's heroes, to be almost immediately forgotten in the turmoil of revolution and Indian war descending on his beloved valley. Today, his body is thought to rest in the family graveyard close by his lovely brick Georgian house, but no one knows the exact location. In October the Continental Congress "directed that a monument be erected to the memory of Brig. Gen. Nicholas Herkimer, of the value of five hundred dollars." The amount was never received; the monument was never built.[22]

For all his energy and daring, Arnold at Fort Dayton had good reason to hesitate. He could count on perhaps 1,000 men to follow him to Stanwix, a number not greatly exceeding Herkimer's brigade, and he would need to travel the same military road that the poor Tryon County militia trod if his force was to reach Stanwix in time.[23] The Oneidas had warned him that Brant and his corps still invested the fort. They were as capable of ambushing Arnold as they had been Herkimer. Foremost in Arnold's thoughts was how to avoid Herkimer's fate. And now the answer to his quandary appeared in the extraordinary personage of German Flats's village simpleton, Han Yost Schuyler.

This famous Mohawk Valley story begins with Sarah Kast McGinnis's visit to the British camp at Stanwix. She and her two daughters, married to the Thompson brothers, had just been paroled from jail at Fort Dayton. They had been confined there on suspicion of treason. Frightened by the potential consequences of Oriskany, the local authorities decided to release them, and they lost no time in crossing the wilderness to the camp, where two of Sarah's sons served with Butler's rangers. The news they brought cheered St. Leger. Valley Tories, Sarah announced, were ready and willing to rise; they only awaited instructions from the approaching British forces to throw off their caution.

St. Leger, like his adversary Gansevoort, desperately needed help from the valley if he were to break the present stalemate. A Tory uprising in the rear of the Americans would serve his purposes well. Consequently, it was agreed that Walter N. Butler, John Butler's son, an ensign in the 8th regiment, would carry a flag of truce into the valley and confer with as many Tory leaders as could attend him. His group would make its way to the Shoemaker house on the outskirts of German Flats by forest roads and byways known to Private Han Yost Schuyler of Gray's Loyalists. Once there, Butler would rally the neighborhood for the king. The British persisted in believing, as the Johnson faction repeatedly told them, that many more loyalists inhabited the region than rebels. In that case, St. Leger reasoned, the mission might open communications with a sizeable number of supporters placed where they could cut the Americans' road to Stanwix.

What this wild scheme never entertained was the notion that the Shoemaker house stood only two miles from Fort Dayton, and that the garrison at Dayton would be delighted to find Tories flushed out of hiding. Young Walter Butler's boisterous parties drew many guests. Most were eager to hear news from sources reliable or otherwise. But along with the crowds came American officers, and they soon reported the goings-on at the Shoemakers' to Fort Dayton. The dream of a Tory uprising ended quickly when a hundred Continentals surrounded the house, overwhelmed Butler and his associates, and dragged them away in chains.

It happened that this event coincided with General Arnold's arrival, and as ranking officer, he was obliged to authorize the court martial of Butler and the others—not that such proceedings overly concerned him. Lieutenant Colonel Willett presided, and the court, to be expected, returned a verdict in all instances of guilty, sentencing the malefactors to death for treason. When Schuyler learned of Butler's capture, he ordered him remanded to Albany, where he would be interrogated and jailed. He was not about to allow one of the valley's patricians to be executed by order of a military court. As for Han Yost, he was Arnold's business, and Arnold, immersed in plans to relieve Stanwix, cared less whether he hanged or not. Who did care was Han Yost's mother, and she pleaded with the American officers to spare her son. Not only was Han Yost a distant relative of General Schuyler, his mother turned out to be Nicholas Herkimer's sister. Could they not see he was a fool? The Indians knew that he was touched and set apart by God. Han Yost had married an Oneida woman. He spoke fluent Oneida and Mohawk. He was a Tory, indeed, but could not explain what that term meant.

Arnold's officers took one look at his broad, grinning face and agreed that hanging him was probably beside the point. What they could do, on the other hand, was to set him free and send him back to his friends with a tale to tell. Suddenly, Arnold began to show interest. He saw a ploy that might work. Shoot the fool's coat full of holes and let him escape back to his Indians—so long as he warned them that Arnold was coming with thousands of men. Mrs. Schuyler had every reason to drill this lesson into her son, for on his successful recitation depended both their lives. Or so she was led to believe; Arnold could be a ruthless persuader.[24] Admittedly, this *ruse de guerre* was a long shot, but sending a frightened Han Yost off with an Oneida companion to spread alarm among the tribes played on the Indians' nerves. If the boy could spark one moment of panic among St. Leger's allies, there would be opportunity for Arnold to rush over the military road and meet the confused enemy in the open.

What resulted was more than a moment of panic. Han Yost entered the Iroquois camp with the most amazing story. Walter Butler was taken, yes, but more importantly Arnold was coming, and his army was like the leaves on a tree—3,000, 4,000, or more. Han Yost had been lucky to escape the hail of bullets tearing holes through his coat. The Native Americans did not need to be told that Benedict Arnold was Colonial America's best fighting general or that in battle he burned with a fury like the legendary warriors of old. Senecas, Mohawks, Cayuga, and Onondagas were conscious of the personalities of their opponents. St. Leger was no match for this man, whose temerity led him to cross the Maine wilderness in autumn and storm Quebec in a blizzard. If Arnold burst out of the woods with a few thousand riflemen, catching them in the open dawdling around the fort, he would destroy them root and stock. He was on his way, as Han Yost told them, and the time had come for choosing. Their choice, it turned out, was to make up for lost plunder by pillaging the camp of those who had let them down. They touched not the hair on the head of a British soldier or Tory, but they ran wild looting their possessions. No good alternatives remained for St. Leger. If he stayed and fought Arnold with only his white troops, he would be outnumbered. If he fought the Iroquois mutiny, he would just as likely be destroyed. He had supped with the devil and now, as the bill was presented, the acting brigadier could only lead his loyal troops back to the bateaux, abandon his camp and equipment, and push off down Wood Creek for the safety of Lake Oneida.

St. Leger explained his dilemma to Burgoyne in a letter dated August 27:

> I learned that 200 were already decamped. In about an hour they insisted that I should retreat or they would be obliged to abandon me. I had no other party to take, and a hard party it was to troops who could do nothing without them ... and therefore proposed to retire at night, sending on my sick, wounded and artillery down the Wood Creek, covering them by our line of march.[25]

This debacle played out over a single day, to the utter amazement of Gansevoort and his garrison. A threat so long anticipated in the Mohawk Valley, then resisted with terrible bloodshed, had in a summer's moment evaporated. Burgoyne's right-wing diversion had ended in abject failure, but at the moment the general was digesting far worse news.

On the 14th, as Baum's expedition crossed Rensselaer County towards the Vermont border, the Brunswick column began to encounter significant numbers of militiamen.[26] Suspecting that he faced more opposition than previously believed, Baum dispatched couriers to Burgoyne requesting reinforcements. His detachment, with recent augmentations, numbered about 800. Unknown to him, he confronted over 2,000 New England militia, with more on the way. The next day, rains fell heavily, and only on the 16th was Stark able to attack. In fierce fighting the Hessians were eventually surrounded and overrun. Baum died in the ensuing hand-to-hand combat, and by afternoon his column's only hope of survival lay with Colonel Breymann's approaching reinforcements. But Seth Warner was able to block Breymann. His Green Mountain Boys found revenge at last for their rough handling at Hubbardton. They clung to the flanks of the Hessians, demolishing their ranks. By nightfall, Breymann's 600 troops were in headlong retreat back to the Hudson.

The Battle of Bennington was fought entirely within New York State and was an extension of the struggle for the Mohawk / Hudson corridor.[27] Burgoyne's losses were severe: 207 of all ranks were left dead on the field; about 700, including 30 officers, were captured, and great quantities of arms and munitions seized. The Americans suffered 30 killed and 40 wounded. This was a subtraction the British could ill afford. Now, Burgoyne, with little hope of aid from Henry Clinton on the lower Hudson, had only his own grand army to command. His native allies had melted away; as he left Fort Edward, he had fewer than 50 scouts.[28] The Americans had several hundred Oneidas in the field by this time, and these would bring in over 150 scalps and 32 prisoners.[29] By the beginning of September, Burgoyne was outnumbered, short of supplies, and tactically blind. Shortly, he would meet old enemies in wait for him at Freeman's Farm and Bemis Heights—Daniel Morgan, Henry Dearborn, John Stark, Seth Warner, and Benedict Arnold.

This last adversary, above all others, would help shut down Burgoyne's invasion over the next forty-five days.[30] But on August 24, Arnold was still advancing with his fingers crossed through dense forests towards Stanwix. He reckoned that the Indians were not likely to ambush his column where Herkimer had fought. The reasons were soon apparent to everyone. "We had to march over the ground where Herkimer's battle was fought," Lieutenant William Scudder of the 1st New York recalled, "and as the dead had not been buried, and the weather warm, they were much swoln and of a purple color ... we must have marched over and very near, about four hundred dead bodies."[31] The Native Americans had removed their dead before the forest animals ravaged them. But no one from the valley dared enter the fatal woods until long after the battle and, in keeping with the harsh realities of wilderness warfare, the Tryon County dead were left to molder where they fell. Nature covered them gradually. In 1783 a young lieutenant of artillery, on the way to his post at Stanwix, saw "a vast number of human skulls and bones scattered through the woods."[32] Arnold's brigade passed over the military road with faces covered to mask the frightful smell. They made a small attempt to bury the dead, then rushed along, averting their eyes. Ahead, they would come down from the top of the ridge and see the bastions of Stanwix rising in green fields beyond the blue winding ribbon of the river. At that moment they would be able to form battle lines, as Herkimer had once hoped to do, and advance against the enemy, pressing him back onto the guns of the fort.

So might have happened, were there any enemies. But Han Yost had seen to that, along with the stubborn defenders who wore down the patience of the Native

Americans. The gates of Stanwix rolled open, and Gansevoort's tired and hungry men rushed out to join Arnold's column in jubilation. Not a trace of the Senecas or Mohawks remained, and so rapidly had St. Leger retreated down the creek that his own small force was beyond pursuit. By the time Continentals arrived on the shores of Lake Oneida, the British bateaux were vanishing over the horizon. Lieutenant Colonel Barry St. Leger, profoundly embarrassed, rejoined Burgoyne. He would be even more distraught when he learned in time of Arnold's trickery. In September he was posted to Ticonderoga to bolster its defenses against American raids. Once Burgoyne and his army surrendered, St. Leger conducted another evacuation, burning as much of Ticonderoga as possible and sailing north for Montreal in the first snows of November. Like Baron von Dieskau, twenty years before, St. Leger could argue that he was a good soldier dealt bad cards. His native allies had hindered him more than his American enemies. But he must also have realized that his steady habits of command, fixing him in place at Stanwix, were partly responsible for defeat. From the moment he marched out of Oswego at the head of a mixed force, he was engaged in Indian warfare, and the essence of such warfare was mobility. He had lacked the nerve to bypass Stanwix and slash into Tenonanatche with a killing stroke.

One might imagine that after victories at Stanwix, Bennington, Saratoga, and the forced abandonment of Ticonderoga, Tenonanatche would enjoy a measure of peace. The main stem of the American Revolution—Washington's fight for independence—had triumphed where the Mohawk met the Hudson. Now the army of Congress moved on and, following several defeats near Philadelphia, retreated in December 1777 to Valley Forge. The fight was not over, to be sure, but in the north the threat of invasion from Canada, the isolation of New England, and a powerful British presence astride the south-flowing rivers had been averted.

In fact, none of this brought peace to the valleys of central New York. Issues settled by the overthrow of Burgoyne tended to be more national in scope than local. A young country had demonstrated its potential. France and other overseas powers now resolved to support the Americans with materials of war. None of this mattered, however, to John and Guy Johnson, who were trying to fight their way home, or to Joseph Brant, who was trying to restore Native American unity under the king, or to the exposed settlers of Wyoming or Cherry Valley, who were simply trying to survive.

Nor had one bit of the old hatred abated as the patriot faction along the Mohawk and Schoharie began wholesale confiscation and sale of Tory properties. A deep winter sent both sides to ground; Joseph Brant's corps retired to Fort Niagara, while the patriot militia stacked arms and disbanded for the season. But the Tory command structure remained intact, biding its time in Canada. Philip Schuyler was gone from Albany, if not from the service, and the men and supplies he had stockpiled were now being sent to Washington's desperate army. In the north, spring would bring raids again, everyone agreed, yet how to hold off Brant and Butler's Indians and rangers no one could foresee.

An odd development marks these middle years of the conflict. At the outset, the Revolution was carried forward by localized insurrections using militia companies with little or no training. Where these partisans could strike quickly out of natural cover, they were a formidable threat to regular formations. General Washington and his staff were determined, however, to build a regular American army on eighteenth-century principles. Converting militia to Continentals with fixed terms of service and disciplined skills was progressing in central New York as 1778 began. The manpower available was increasingly going to a national purpose, while the British in Canada were discovering that localized guerilla actions, whether conducted by rangers or Indians, held the greatest promise for disrupting and demoralizing agricultural New York. The tables had turned, and soon regular American troops, cooped up within their palisades as the British had once been, would see spires of smoke rising from the defenseless countryside.

The ground began to thaw in mid-April, and scouts from the Schoharie Valley and Stanwix were able to detect a buildup of Tory and Indian forces along the upper Susquehanna, especially at Unadilla and Oquaga. Forty years after Sir William had pioneered travel down the Unadilla from the Mohawk Valley, trails from villages on the Susquehanna to Tenonanatche were well-trodden. One followed modern Route 8 to the vicinity of today's Mount Upton, then veered east along Route 51 across the Butternuts district to the west side of Lake Otsego. Just as now, this region was a rather remote corner of New York. The few settlers in the area did all they could to keep roofs on their cabins and their livestock safe. They would slam their doors shut rather than meet or interfere when herds of cattle driven south from the Mohawk passed their homesteads. From the head of Lake Otsego, German Flats was about twenty miles distant, Andrustown four miles. From the foot of the lake, Cobleskill lay twenty miles away and Cherry Valley twelve. If war irrupted from the south in 1778, the raids would come this way.

The people along the southern edge of Tenonanatche (roughly the line of today's Route 20) were not happy to see the winter pass. They expected the Tories and Indians to revenge last fall's setbacks by attacking their thriving towns, and they bombarded Albany and Congress with requests for military aid, of which there was little to provide. Reports of strong Tory parties flowing out of Niagara and into Indian country reached Samuel Kirkland at Stanwix from Oneida scouts. This threat could combine with threats from the Susquehanna, or move into the Adirondacks and attack anywhere along Tenonanatche's northern rim. It was not a question of would this happen, but only where and when.

In mid-spring, Philip Schuyler, serving in a quiet Hudson posting after his exoneration by court martial, wrote to Henry Laurens, president of Congress, on behalf of his endangered state. Schuyler believed that the Tory attacks would be worse than in 1777, and that the only course open to the Americans was a preemptive attack into Indian country. "This would not require," he argued, "a greater Body of troops to destroy Towns than would be necessary to protect the Frontier Inhabitants."[33] Schuyler was not indifferent to injustices done the Mohawks at Canajoharie and Fort Hunter, and he requested that the Tryon Committee do everything possible to find the perpetrators of the looting and restore stolen property. Yet, increasingly, and with great sadness, he viewed the Iroquois Confederacy as the main enemy.

The British had burned Schuyler's mansion and mills at Saratoga for military reasons, and he was only now beginning to suffer the financial consequences of their destruction.[34] In the charred ruins of the town of Saratoga, extreme patriots had turned to whipping suspected loyalists in the streets, tarring and even hanging them. This was just the kind of behavior Schuyler feared would follow the destruction of valley settlements, unraveling what little civility survived on the frontier borders. His understandable bitterness at being denied credit for a Saratoga victory he had done so much to assure was never publicly expressed, nor did it interfere with the continuation of his service to the Republic.[35] Congress welcomed his advice about the threat to New York, but in 1778 troops and supplies were not available for an invasion of Indian territory. That vast wilderness stretched from the Unadilla River westward, across the Finger Lakes region, to Lake Erie and Niagara. So long as the enemy could strike at settlements from this direction unimpeded, the frontiers of New York and Pennsylvania were hopelessly vulnerable.

Another adventurer arrived at Albany in May with a pressing request for troops. The Marquis de Lafayette held an appointment from the Board of War of Congress charging him to design and affect "an irruption into Canada." The old invasion plan, thought dead by most, had staggered to its feet again and found supporters willing to believe that French Canada would rise to a French general on a mission of liberation. Fortunately, this initiative was short-lived. What Lafayette found at Albany were a few hundred ragamuffin soldiers, poorly armed and trained and in no state of mind to fight. What the French general did next, on Washington's prompting, was to cancel the Board of War's project and, instead, survey the defenses of towns exposed to raids. Lafayette was appalled at the fortified houses in Cherry Valley; they might withstand a windstorm, but not a well-armed incursion. What the poor people needed, he reasoned, was a large, strong stockade to which they could retire with their livestock and valuables in an emergency. Lafayette, on Washington's authority, instructed the New York Committee at Albany to see to a stockade immediately. Washington could not provide troops, but he and his staff could help break the lockstep thinking of militia bureaucrats. Cherry Valley loved the idea of a stockade, and soon every other village in the threatened area was clamoring for similar attention. New York's authorities bitterly resented interference by His Excellency the General's staff in matters of local defense, but so imminent was attack that Albany swallowed hard and acted on Lafayette's recommendation. Cherry Valley got its fort.

Before he returned to Washington's headquarters, the marquis made the acquaintance of a young, educated, Tory gentleman confined under harsh conditions in Albany's dungeon. Supplicants on the young man's behalf came forward from several directions, and Lafayette was led to agree that Walter N. Butler, John Butler's son, warranted more civilized treatment. By training he was an attorney, and Walter pleaded his case well; Lafayette persuaded the local authorities to accept Butler's parole and remand him to a comfortable house outside the city, where he would remain under detention. Thus, all that the marquis managed to accomplish for Cherry Valley was inadvertently undone by his predilection for men of seeming reputation and refinement. The citizens of Tryon County could have warned that staunch Tories typically broke every code and violated every promise in the service of their king. Within a fortnight of leaving his dungeon, young Butler's friends helped him escape; native allies smuggled him up the valley into Indian country, and by June, Walter had rejoined his regiment at Niagara. The spoiled son of a formidable father, he seethed with resentment at his treatment under the patriots, vowing to redeem the family honor with fire and sword.[36] Cherry Valley and Tenonanatche would hear from Walter Butler again.

By May 30, people in the neighborhood of Cobleskill reported sightings of Indians in several directions. These parties were small—a few braves and Tories poking around the countryside—but at Schoharie Stone Fort, the lower of the three forts, Captain William Patrick, from Stoughton, Massachusetts, decided to take a closer look with forty Continentals from Colonel Ichabod Alden's Massachusetts line.

Patrick and his men had just arrived at Schoharie and were bound for Cherry Valley, where a new fort was under construction; they were regulars, trained but without experience in Indian war. As they marched west on the Cobleskill road, they encountered a local family fleeing east to Schoharie Stone Fort with household goods piled in a cart. These were the Warners. They too had seen small Indian parties crossing their fields at sunrise and were taking no chances. Patrick assured them that small groups were not likely to attack a strong farmhouse. Farmer Warner did not linger to explain to Patrick that small war parties could very quickly join together into very large war parties.

The captain continued down the road toward the Warners' abandoned house until he met two men crashing out of the brush; one clutched a wounded arm, the other carried muskets and a fishing rod. Bent and crouching as they ran, they threw fearful glances into the silent woods behind them. These were the Borst brothers, Jacob and Joseph. They had been fishing on Cobus Creek with John Freemire where a fallen tree formed a deep, shaded trout pool. Freemire was playing a large fish, the brothers cheering him, when a shot rang out and Freemire pitched headfirst into the creek. A second shot winged Jacob in the fleshy part of his upper arm, but he lurched for his musket and came up fast enough to shoot his charging assailant. Joseph, meanwhile, was wrestling on the ground with a tomahawk-wielding warrior when the warrior suddenly realized he was alone, broke from Joseph, and plunged into the brush. The brothers lost no time racing for the protection of the Warner home. A detachment of Cobleskill volunteer militia, led by Captain Christian Brown, was drawn to the scene by gunfire. They found Freemire dragged onto the bank and scalped, but no sign of the fallen brave.[37]

Captain Patrick welcomed the thirteen militiamen from Cobleskill and the Borst brothers into his command. He resolved to hold the stone farmhouse, located on an eminence above the road, as a forward post. No sooner was this decided than a small party of Indians and Tories fell out on the road and opened fire at the house. Patrick left a few regulars under Lieutenant Maynard to guard the improvised fort and set off in pursuit of the enemy with the balance of his force. This was never to be done when at war with Joseph Brant. The Patrick attack seemed to succeed at first; then, around a bend in the road, the detachment ran into the massed musketry of over 100 Indians and Tories—the small parties had indeed very quickly joined together. Patrick was shot through the groin and died in the roadway with half a dozen of his Continentals. The militia, tagging along at the rear, understood immediately what had happened and bolted for the rear. The regulars tried to retreat in order, but soon were running for the cover of the Warner place.

Lieutenant Maynard stopped the fleeing men in the road, positioned them at every window and behind every outhouse, and met the pursuing ambush with gusts of well-aimed fire. A few Indians were hit, and Lieutenant Maynard, firing coolly from a doorway, killed a Tory soldier named Christopher Service. While Maynard held the house with eight men, Captain Brown retreated with the main body towards Cobleskill. The fight at the Warner property was brief. Maynard was slain by a musket ball that tore open his throat. His body fell across the doorway. Private Jonathan Young tried to aid him, was hit in the side, and then, as he struggled to bar the door with a large knife in hand, was pierced by a lance. He was dragged clear of the house and stabbed to death. His assailant opened his body, cut out his heart and threw it to the side, then, dragging out his intestines, wrapped them around the limb of a large tree and into Young's dead left hand.[38] This was the kind of taunt the raiders liked to leave their pursuers. The effect on late-arriving rescuers was usually horror and nausea, but slowly the realization would dawn that this could happen to them too on a walk in the woods.

Captain Ian McDonald, in charge of the Tories, succeeded in setting the Warner house on fire. The six surviving troopers were killed as they attempted to escape, or burned to death in the conflagration. Of Patrick's command, one sergeant and four regulars would eventually return to Schoharie Stone Fort; thirty-six were killed or captured. The militia under Brown arrived at Cobleskill only slightly in advance of the raiders. They were able to roust out the civilians with nothing more than the clothes on their backs and send them running for Schoharie. Then they, too, were overwhelmed by attacks from every side. Brant's combined force of Tories and Native Americans numbered over 350. They had negotiated the trails from Unadilla undetected, and breaking into small scouts as they approached their objective, came together only after they had swept the immediate neighborhood of organized resistance. They had plenty of time to finish off the militia, rustle the stock, and plunder the houses before setting Cobleskill ablaze. The village contained twenty structures; many were two-story clapboards, for Cobleskill was then less a frontier bastion than a thriving farm community on the verge of becoming what nineteenth-century America would call "small town." By nightfall the village was totally destroyed. Seven days later, Abraham Wempel, in charge of militia stores, wrote to General Ten Broeck, commander of the militia at Albany:

> I have buried the dead at Cobus Kill, which was 14 in number; found five more burnt in the ruins of the House of one Yurry Wainer, where the Engagement has been; they were Butchered in the most Inhuman manner; burnt ten houses and Barns, Horses, Cows, Sheep & c. lay dead all over the fields. ... [Ps.] I forgot to mention in mine of this date that the people of Cobus Kill, whose houses and Effects are burnt, only came off with what they had upon their Backs, have apply'd to me for provisions. I shall be glad to know wether they can draw out of public stores or no.[39]

Legend holds that thirty or so braves were killed in the Cobleskill attack and their bodies buried in a marsh near the Warner house. No evidence supports this conclusion, and in all likelihood Brant's losses were a half dozen braves and one Tory private. Brant was the first of Niagara's guerilla leaders into the field that spring. He arrived at Oquaga in mid-April and began recruiting intensively for his new campaign. Hard-core supporters probably numbered about 100 Mohawks, 50 valley Tories under Ian McDonald, and a band of white volunteers. This last group is of great interest.

As the raiding war continued, Brant's corps, almost entirely Mohawk or Six Nations at Oriskany, increasingly welcomed white recruits. The local people who joined Captain Brant at Oquaga in 1778 were content to soldier for British pay and plunder under a leader they trusted. They were quick to adopt native dress and tactics, but beneath this veneer they were tough, ruthless mountain folk with long-smoldering resentments. They came largely from the hill country of the upper Delaware branches, the lower Catskills, south of the fertile valleys of central New York. Isabel Kelsay describes them:

These Loyalists were not wealthy men intent on protecting their privileges. Actually they were very poor men, mostly tenant farmers, and they had a hard struggle trying to eke out a living from stony ground which they had leased for two or three lives, or longer, from the owners of the great semi-feudal estates in the Catskills or the Helderbergs. ... These people—for who knew what dangerous plots such Tories might hatch?—were feared and resented by the rebels from the very beginning of the war.[40]

It went without saying that the hill people above Cokeose (Deposit) and east to the Susquehanna tended to despise Dutch landlords and Palatine farmers, and being largely Scots-Irish, found more in common with Sir William's people than with the farmers of the prosperous valleys. What made Joseph Brant's force attractive to them had everything to do with their grinding poverty compared to native peoples. This was more common than might be imagined given the general fruitfulness of the land. Colonel Peter Gansevoort observed: "It is remarkable that the Indians live much better than most of the Mohawk River farmers, their Houses very well furnished with all [the] necessary Household utensils, great plenty of Grain, several Horses, cows and wagons."[41] Gansevoort was describing Tenonanatche settlers, not hardscrabble farmers from the West Branch of the Delaware River. Brant's appeal to such people was as revolutionary as any idea whirling through New York. He offered revenge, but also new beginnings under the king's patent in old bought-up lands.

The reason for the raid north was simple. Brant needed livestock to feed his growing army, and the best place to find hogs, sheep, and cattle was in the fat agricultural belt of Schoharie. Of course, any fear he might instill into farm communities was also to be desired; the predictable outcome of terror was fewer fields cultivated, more homesteads abandoned. But what steered the May 30 raid to Cobleskill was an incident along the way from Otsego. The raiding party shot down a dispatch rider from Cherry Valley. Until Brant read his dispatches, he was aiming at that very town. Now he discovered that a fort was under construction there and that a regiment of Continentals was deployed to protect the builders.[42] This was the kind of high-risk attack that never appealed to Brant after Oriskany. He might indeed win a great victory over the rebel soldiers, but even a great victory could spell long-term defeat for the many fewer Native Americans in his command. The whites could always replace losses; the Iroquois could not. His raiders turned to the east and, spreading out, began their carefully rehearsed approach to Cobleskill.

Andrustown, twenty or so miles northeast of Cobleskill, had been a long time found-ing. The first settlers, seven families in all, had cleared the ground for the village by 1723.[43] Between then and the end of the French and Indian War, Andrustown managed to attract only a few additional homesteaders. One, John Powers, was an outspoken Tory, and in 1777 the town expelled him from his home with threats of tar and feath-ering. Powers struck out for Oquaga, and along the way shared his indignation with Joseph Brant, who now learned that the farms of Andrustown were exceptionally rich in livestock and winter wheat. The wealthy Tunnicliff family owned an estate called the "Oaks" on Canadarago Lake near Andrustown, but while John Tunnicliff Jr. was a patriot serving with the Albany County militia, his ever-resourceful father leaned to the Tories. Brant would bypass the Oaks when he attacked Andrustown July 18, 1778.[44]

The raid came in right off the head of Lake Otsego, swept through the tiny ham-let of Springfield on a heading for present Jordanville, and caught the population of Andrustown (north of today's Warren) gathered around the town's single bake oven. It was a sunny Saturday morning when the village turned out to bake bread; several farmers were harvesting winter wheat in the fields, and a newlywed couple held court in a circle of friends on the town green. The attack arrived without warning. The out-lying plowmen were struck first, and their young helpers, racing for home and guns, were cut off by the sweep of the assault. In the village center, townspeople who sensed the threat and bolted for cover were shot; those who cowered in shock around the oven were taken prisoner. The new bride died, and her husband clutched his wife's body to his breast weeping. At Brant's direction, he was passed over and left to his grief.[45] Some women were unavoidably slain, but males of military age, eleven to sixty, often received no quarter. Their scalps were worth $15 apiece at Niagara.[46]

According to witnesses, Brant did everything possible at Springfield to spare women and children, and did so again at Andrustown, but raiders tended to lash out in fury at the defenseless people in their power.[47] Outrages occurred, and only after prisoners were trussed, scalps counted, houses pillaged of portable goods and set afire, would discipline be restored. As the smoke from burning Andrustown joined with that rising from Springfield, the raiders vanished down Oak Creek, heading for Otsego and the trail to Unadilla. Ahead of them, they drove a herd of livestock; behind them came wagons loaded with stolen goods and sacks of flour; at the rear of the wag-ons marched fourteen prisoners. At least as many more had been killed between the two villages. Some of the captives would surface eventually in Niagara or at Montreal; some would never be heard from again. Yet the most critical loss of all to the patriot cause was the community of Andrustown. The settlement, so arduously established, would never be rebuilt. Wheat was left to rot in the fields, and in seasons to come, superstitious people would avoid the patch of blackened earth where the village had once stood.[48]

News of Andrustown quickly reached the length of Tenonanatche, conflated with other stories of frontier massacres and murders of isolated families. The most persistent rumor, however, and one all too soon confirmed, was of a terrible raid on the Pennsylvania frontier, where more than 1,000 were believed to have perished at the hands of Brant, Butler, and their Indians. Accounts of destruction in the Wyoming Valley emanated from Stroudsburg, across the Delaware River from New Jersey, where many hundreds of refugees arrived in the weeks before the Andrustown raid. They told of seven forts arranged on both sides of the Susquehanna, north and south of Forty-Fort and the Wilkes-Barre stockade, all surprised and undone by Tory treachery or John Butler's devilish stratagems. In fact, two of the forts were abandoned, one belonged to a notorious Tory family, and two others were surrendered for lack of garrison to hold the walls. How the Wyoming Valley, a patriotic hotbed with hundreds of militia, could fall into such dire straights was not at first clear.

As the crow flew, Wilkes-Barre lay 130 miles south-southwest of German Flats, but the Mohawk settlements, joined by kinship and history to Pennsylvania's Lebanon Valley, had no special ties to Wyoming. The beautiful valley had been claimed by Connecticut, and several infusions of Connecticut pioneers over the mid-eighteenth century had built its farms and hamlets. What connected New York to the Wyoming Valley in July 1778 was a shared enemy. Rumors to the contrary, Joseph Brant and his Mohawks were not that enemy. They were nowhere near Wyoming on July 3.[49] Colonel John Butler, Brant's rival for leadership among the Iroquois nations, came out of Niagara in the late spring with the fighting might of the Senecas behind him. He and war chief Sayenquerraghta led upwards of 800 Senecas, Cayugas, Onondagas, and Tuscaroras down the Forbidden Path through Indian country to the junction of the Chemung and Susquehanna rivers at Tioga.[50] Butler commanded an additional 400 rangers and Royal Yorkers, swelling the raid aimed at Wyoming to 1,200 experienced campaigners. Encamped at Tioga, they built the canoes and rafts that would float them to within reach of the valley's homes.

Colonel Nathan Denison and Colonel Zebulon Butler, commanding the valley's militia, knew the raid was coming and had raised 450 troops to meet it. What they did not know was how large the enemy force was, and John Butler did everything to keep them from learning. The militia gathered at the Forty-Fort stockade spotted only small detachments of enemy, who fled when confronted. As the valley's homes began to go up in flames, John Butler cunningly set fire to the small stockade he had been using as a headquarters.[51] Immediately, the militia assumed that the raiders, inferior in numbers, were withdrawing from Wyoming. Cooped up in the fort, they clamored to be set free to pursue.

In a repetition of the Oriskany tragedy, commanders Nathan Denison and Zebulon Butler advised waiting until more was known, but the militia rioted, calling both worthy men cowards and traitors. Militia organizations had the authority to elect new officers, and the Wyoming volunteers soon found leaders of a stripe to gratify their desires. Behind their intimidated colonels, they formed and advanced towards the enemy's burning headquarters. At first, rangers and Indians scattered, inflicting only a galling fire. Then, as so often happened in frontier war, the trap slammed shut. The 450 entered a bare, coverless meadow, easily enfiladed from two sides. Far from outnumbering their adversaries, the Wyoming militia now was outnumbered three to one. As the raiders' muskets fired from the fence and tree line, whole ranks of militia went down at once. This was the signal for the Senecas to close in behind and cut off retreat. The fight lasted only minutes, leaving three-quarters of the patriots dead on the field or floating face down in the river where they had fled to escape. John Butler surveyed the ruin of his king's enemies and rested satisfied with the carnage. He was able to protect a few prisoners, but many were hauled away, tied to trees, and tortured to death.

With the muskets needed to protect the walls lost, the forts of Wyoming surrendered one after the other. Butler was able to prevent his native allies from molesting women and children as he turned the panic-stricken inhabitants loose to find shelter and safety outside the valley. Those at the Pittston and Jenkins forts began a forty-mile trek across the wilderness to Stroudsburg without food, clothing, or shelter. Unavoidably, many lost their bearings, wandered into switchback ravines, and ultimately died of exposure. Some evacuating Wilkes-Barre farther south stumbled into a deep, dismal swamp—still called the Shades of Death—to perish from starvation and drowning. Civilian casualties of the Wyoming raid have been placed as high as 2,000, and though this number is probably excessive, mortality among the young and infirm was doubtless severe.[52] Since he had saved their scalps, their sorrows troubled Butler's conscience not at all. He wanted civilians out of the way as expeditiously as possible to free his work forces. The raiders needed all of two days to complete the destruction of the valley, burning every home, barn, and structure, firing the fields, slaughtering livestock down to cats and dogs, and dismantling the remaining forts.

The Wyoming massacre of myth and legend—the core account that spread like wildfire through the Northeast—had less to do with the fate of the militia, the plight of the refugees, or the massive demolition of the settlement than with a grisly incident in the aftermath of the battle. Queen Esther (Esther Montour) the great-grandchild of a French grandee and the Seneca chieftainess Kithinay, emerged from the raid as an apparition of destruction, a fearsome figure who would haunt the frontier imagination for decades. Before the Wyoming events, Esther ruled a large, thriving Seneca town at the mouth of the Chemung, inherited from her mother, French Margaret. She was married to the warrior chief Eghobund, by whom she had one son, Gencho. The chief died of natural causes at Queen Esther's Town in 1773.

Tall, full-figured, and straight as a tree, the stately widow often addressed the Onondaga Council with impressive effect. She was conversant in English and French, literate, and nominally Christian. Over the years she had argued eloquently for peace with the settlers, and had only recently set free white prisoners taken by the Senecas. This was before Gencho, a novice warrior with Butler's raiders, happened to be killed by a militia patrol, scalped, and mutilated. Something snapped in mother Esther at this point or, as the terrified Senecas believed, something mad and demonic now entered into her nature. She became an uncontrollable thing, painting her naked body in black and white circles and crying out for vengeance. On the evening following the Wyoming battle, she ordered nineteen prisoners formed in a circle around a prominent boulder. One after the other, captive heads were forced down on this rock and Esther, gleaming in the dancing firelight, crushed her victim's skull with a war club, crying out at each blow, "Gencho." Two of the nineteen prisoners escaped from the circle around the brain-splattered stone. Their account became the story of the "massacre," while the Senecas who pursued them into the brush quickly lost interest in the fugitives and returned to watch the last of the sacrifices with morbid fascination.

This tale reached the Mohawk at the end of August 1778. It was told in taverns up and down the Hudson Valley, in inns along the Schoharie, and everywhere the chilling narrative reminded white Christians that the dark forests still held sinister forces worshipped by the red man. How much truth adheres to the legend of Queen Esther is very questionable. Prisoners were indeed executed, but not necessarily by Esther Montour.[53] Compared with the enormity of damages inflicted on Wyoming's settlers by John Butler, James Caldwell, and other white Tory gentlemen, her alleged crimes added only a grim coda to the catastrophic event. The Wyoming raid stands as one of the worst frontier disasters in United States history.

A few days before the Wyoming debacle, Washington's army, away in New Jersey, fought Henry Clinton's retreating regiments to a standstill. The British had been running from Philadelphia to New York when a force of 13,000 Continentals, well-trained, uniformed, and heavily armed with artillery, intercepted them. The Battle of Monmouth was fought on European principles in North American heat and humidity; its outcome proved to all but the most obdurate that the Americans had not only survived Valley Forge, but had emerged with an army very nearly equal to the king's. This good news might have cheered patriots on the smoldering frontiers, had they not lacked the men and cannons to protect their own women and children. The Wyoming Valley sent 1,000 recruits to Washington's army, but when Wyoming begged Washington's headquarters for a company of Continentals to meet the anticipated raid, these soldiers were withheld until after Monmouth. By then it was too late, as it was already too late for German Flats. The cost of winning the American Revolution was not paid for only on battlefields with the British Army, but all across the backcountry and along the contested borders where a pioneer people struggled to endure.

Ilion gorge is a deep fissure carved by Steele Creek in the southern wall of Tenonanatche. Where the creek now drops precipitously along Route 51, smoking in the early morning sunlight, an old colonial road connected German Flats and the Mohawk bottomlands (the towns of Herkimer, Ilion, Frankfurt, Little Falls, Danube) with communities on the southern plateau. Steele Creek rises in the high swamps that also feed the Unadilla, but flowing north from that watershed over the rim of the valley, it had long ago carved out a direct path to the Mohawk towns from Lake Otsego and points south.[54] The Ilion gorge required to be patrolled in the fall of 1778 if German Flats was to sleep securely. Rumors of an attack being readied by Brant spread widely in August, and a plan was developed for sheltering inhabitants in forts Dayton, Klock, and Herkimer when the alarm sounded. But an alarm would have to sound, and the only way Brant was likely to break into German Flats unannounced was from Ilion gorge.

A year after Oriskany, Tryon County had too few militiamen to protect the population. Without a detachment of Continentals, they could never hope to fight off raids of the size that burned Andrustown and Cobleskill. But Fort Herkimer could send out small parties of scouts to scour the southern approaches. On September 11 one of these parties had worked its way up the gorge and towards the headwaters of the Unadilla. Four men, ordered out by Peter Bellinger, braved the ambushes and perils of capture to watch the trails converging on Steele Creek. In the late afternoon of the 11th, they collided with 300 Tories heading for German Flats. Behind Captain William Caldwell's command came Joseph Brant with 150 Mohawks eager to punish the patriots of the valley for harm done their people. The Herkimer patrol galloped for the gorge, and one scout out of the four, John Helmer, survived the dash to reach the flatlands and warn the inhabitants.[55]

People reached their sanctuaries safely, as Brant no doubt expected they might. He had no interest in flailing the townsfolk, only in destroying their wealth. Bypassing the forts, his 450 raiders attacked the town with fire, and despite a ferocious thunderstorm, quickly succeeded in burning down over 120 structures—virtually the entire settlement. Raiders had attacked German Flats during the French and Indian War, but nothing like this devastation had occurred before. When they emerged from their forts, the citizens found neither shelter for the winter nor livestock for meat and milk. Their clothing and household utensils were gone, their harvests trampled and ruined. On the brink of inclement weather, more than 1,000 were utterly and irremediably destitute. They could throw themselves onto the charity of friends and family in the valley, but none of these could tell after the German Flats raid whether a similar devastation would not be visited on them as well.

The Northern Department of the Army of Congress was under the temporary command of General Stark of Bennington fame, and Stark's attention was focused principally on the Hudson Valley. The general, however, was no stranger to marauding; he had been a lieutenant in Rogers' Rangers at the time of the St. Francis raid and understood that the way to stop incursions was by long-range counter-incursions against an enemy's bases. Stark could not allow the New York frontier to go up in flames. Hit Unadilla and Oquaga, he therefore advised, and hit them hard. If the vipers are caught off guard, destroy them; if they escape, at least destroy their nest. Governor George Clinton of New York and General Ten Broeck approved this operation, and by the end of September instructed Colonel William Butler (no relation to Zebulon or John and Walter) to move with troops from the 4th Pennsylvania line to the destruction of the Indian towns. Butler had just arrived at Schoharie Stone Fort with his Pennsylvania regiment and a company of Daniel Morgan's riflemen. He picked his best woodsmen for this deep strike and, ordering them to travel light, departed Schoharie on October 1 with 260 men.

Most of the way south, the weather was wet and windy; the riflemen, lightly clad and without tents, suffered severely. Finally, on the morning of October 4, creeping through heavy mist, they broke into Unadilla and captured a Tory named Glasford. He was the only prisoner taken, for the town was deserted. The Indians had pulled back, or possibly were setting a trap beyond the town. Using Glasford as a guide, Butler cautiously probed towards Oquaga (today's Windsor) where, in the chilly evening, his troops waded the Susquehanna up to their armpits in the swirling current and stormed into the town with bayonets fixed. The assault was unnecessary, for Oquaga too was deserted. Not that the troops failed to sense eyes watching them from the forests. They banked up more campfires than needed to give an impression of strength, and lay on their guns in the night, carefully watching until dawn. In the morning they began the destruction of a town Colonel Butler called, "the finest Indian town I ever saw; on both sides of the River there were about 40 good houses, Square logs, Shingles & stone Chimneys, good Floors, glass windows &c."[56]

For half a century Oquaga had existed as a meeting place for European settlers and Native Americans; the village was a highly successful cooperative venture where dialogue could settle disputes and promote understanding. That was until war made Oquaga a base for Tory raiders and renegades. Oquaga was Joseph Brant's favorite town after Canajoharie and the longtime home of his wife's family. While Butler burned Oquaga, Brant was raiding in the Neversink Valley of the Catskills, too distant and too depleted in munitions to interfere. Yet, the Americans went about their demolitions soberly. These homes had to remind them of their homes far away in Pennsylvania and Virginia. This was not a dirty Indian village with scalps curing on lodge poles. This was a place where the otherness of the enemy seemed far less.

Butler left one house standing at Oquaga, the house of Good Peter, the saintly Oneida who many years before had advised Samuel Kirkland about his mission to the Senecas. Then, moving as fast as he could to avoid ambush, he raced back to Unadilla, burned the entire town except for Glasford's house, and set out for Schoharie with only enough livestock and provisions to get his men home. The expedition that was intended to write "finished" to the raiding season of 1778 cost the Americans one casualty—a drover who wandered far off the road at Oquaga and took a bullet in the head.[57]

Unknown to New York authorities, while William Butler was paying back the destruction of German Flats, Colonel Thomas Hartley, commanding on the northern frontier in Pennsylvania, was pushing up the Susquehanna with 200 men to attack Indian settlements. He destroyed Sheshecunnunk (Queen Esther's Town) and Tioga in revenge for Wyoming, and then, learning that Walter Butler was on the Chemung with 300 Tories, retreated toward Wyalusing. Seneca warriors attacked Hartley there and were beaten off, suffering severe casualties. At this point, about October 1, Hartley sent a message to the Senecas. He accused them of murdering women and children, of burning prisoners, and desolating settlements. If this continued, Hartley warned, American forces would force their way into Indian country and destroy the land and people of the Senecas with fire and sword.[58]

The Iroquois received the message and were incensed. Yes, they replied, there had been families murdered along the West Branch of the Susquehanna by irresponsible warriors, but at Wyoming, women and children had been spared. The militia was destroyed in revenge for Oriskany and Stanwix. Moreover, the report of burnings was exaggerated. Queen Esther had not been at Wyoming; the story was concocted by Americans to cover their own inexcusable military blunders. The Senecas especially resented Hartley's inclusion of Colonel Nathan Denison in his command, for Denison had been captured and paroled at Wyoming and had taken up arms in violation of his oath. Henceforth, they would give no quarter to Americans, since they could not conceive of fighting the same enemy twice. Two hundred years later, it is impossible to disentangle the charges and counter-charges behind this conversation. Hartley retreated with threats to soon come again with an army that could destroy the Senecas, and the Senecas, for their part, always hot-tempered and vengeful, responded that they would make the rivers flow red with blood of the *Bostonnais*.

In their own councils, the Senecas had doubts. Chief Great Tree and a delegation of warriors had visited Washington in New Jersey; they testified to the growing power of the Americans and the presence of French officers in the American camp. Great Tree, however, would not hear of an attack on Indian country; it would have to be resisted if it came. The Seneca nation had always preferred the French to the British; many had distrusted Sir William Johnson, and many now strongly disliked the arrogant Tories. In their slow and deliberate way, the Seneca war leaders—Cornplanter, Red Jacket, Sayengueraghta, and Blacksnake—considered whether the American cause was winnable. Many inclined to believe it was, but they were pledged to the British, and not least because their sole source of trade goods was at Fort Niagara. How much they were willing to suffer for this relationship would now be tested.

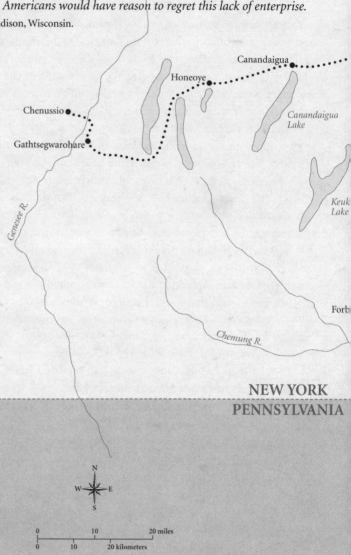

THE SULLIVAN-CLINTON EXPEDITION, 1779

Sullivan did not push on beyond Chenussio to Niagara, the main British base.
Over the next two years, Americans would have reason to regret this lack of enterprise.
Mapping Specialists, Ltd., Madison, Wisconsin.

Lake Ontario

— Ft. Niagara 75 miles

Chenussio

Gathtsegwarohare

Honeoye

Canandaigua

Canandaigua Lake

Keuk Lake

Genesee R.

Chemung R.

Forb

NEW YORK

PENNSYLVANIA

N
W E
S

0 — 10 — 20 miles
0 — 10 — 20 kilometers

•••• Expedition Route
✼ Battle Site

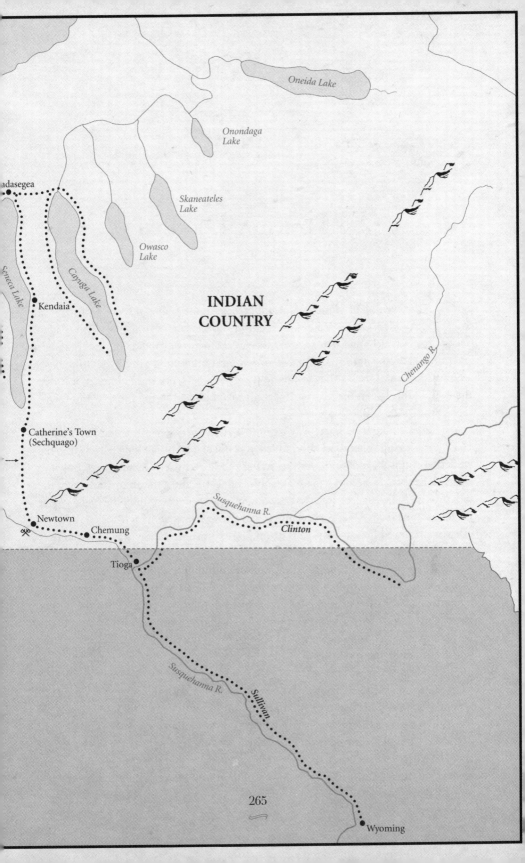

Oneida Lake

Onondaga Lake

Skaneateles Lake

Owasco Lake

adasegea

Seneca Lake

Cayuga Lake

Kendaia

Catherine's Town
(Sechquago)

INDIAN
COUNTRY

Chenango R.

Newtown

Susquehanna R.

Chemung

Clinton

Tioga

Susquehanna R.

Sullivan

265

Wyoming

❖ 11 ❖

To Make a Desert

On the evening of Monday, November 9, Sergeant Adam Hunter's patrol out of Fort Alden, Cherry Valley, was spending its third night along the south road to the Susquehanna. The weather was exceedingly cold and damp, and Hunter's men, after camping in the dark for two nights, were requesting a fire. Miles from base, southeast of Lake Otsego, they found no trace of raiders, nor did Hunter expect that they would this late in the season. He let his men build a roaring fire to warm themselves against the chill.

Hunter thought he knew why he pulled every dirty assignment at Fort Alden. His luxury-loving colonel, Ichabod Alden, was not about to lead long patrols into the wilderness himself, and junior officers in the 7th Massachusetts remembered only too clearly what befell Captain Patrick at Cobleskill. Let Hunter tramp up and down the hills around the village; he was the one who fell asleep on guard duty the night Walter Butler escaped from Albany. He claimed that a mysterious woman drugged him, but everyone believed he was just plain drunk. His punishment now was to watch over Cherry Valley in all kinds of weather.[1]

Early in November Colonel Alden received another warning from Fort Stanwix about a large Tory and Indian party heading in his direction. He discounted the likelihood of an attack this late in the fall and assured the alarmed citizens that the 7th was more than adequate to protect them. Some had begun to move their valuables into the half-completed stockade. Alden reminded them that the installation was not a warehouse and made them remove their property. Added to doubts about the colonel's military competence was the discovery that Alden, a Massachusetts man descended from Mayflower pilgrims, was an insufferable snob, contemptuous of New Yorkers in general. Yet he and his regiment, innocent of any knowledge of frontier war, were all the good people of Cherry Valley had between them and an enemy who had already destroyed Cobleskill, Springfield, Andrustown, Wyoming, and German Flats.

The Cherry Valley fort, named by Alden after Alden, had been built by townspeople from materials dumped at their doorsteps. Following local practice, they enclosed the area surrounding their village church and graveyard with a stout log stockade.[2] At Albany, Peter Gansevoort requested command of Cherry Valley's defenses; he and the 3rd New York had proven themselves at Stanwix. But Gansevoort's application was dismissed in favor of a New England commander and regiment. Political strife between New York and New England continued unabated in Congress, and even growing evidence that agricultural production was declining along the Mohawk did nothing to stem sectional rivalries. Congress desired to help the embattled farmers of New York, but Congress, suffering a crippling shortage of qualified officers, was not above driving square pegs into round holes.

The village of Cherry Valley, thirteen miles south of the Mohawk, was one of the most prosperous in central New York, a tribute to the intelligence and industry of its inhabitants. Settled by devout Presbyterians from Scotland and Northern Ireland, the town remained predominantly patriot, though several prominent loyalist families resided peacefully within the village. Cherry Valley sent many citizens to Oriskany, not the least of whom were Thomas Spencer (Ahnyero), Samuel Clyde, and Samuel Campbell. The community nestled in a well-watered vale at the foot of mountains covered in May by wild cherry blossoms. Roads through the village connected Albany, fifty miles away, with the headwaters of the Susquehanna, and German Flats, fifteen miles away, with settlements of the lower Schoharie. Symbolically, no less than materially, Cherry Valley was too vital to be left at risk.

Yet Colonel Alden did nothing to improve the town's security. Fort Alden had two artillery pieces, but no platform to open fields of fire over the walls. The stockade lacked loopholes and banquettes on which troops could stand and fire.[3] Although Alden had 250 trained Continentals, he cancelled this advantage by failing to construct barracks within the fort. He quartered his soldiers on the town, refusing to hear warnings that in an Indian attack his men would have no time to reach the stockade. He himself was quartered at the comfortable mansion of Robert Wells, where he enjoyed the society of Wells's large, lively family.

Sergeant Hunter was quartered the morning of November 10 on the damp ground, next to the warm embers of a large fire. The fire, a bad idea, had attracted unwanted company. He awoke to find a familiar face close to his and a knife across his throat. Captain Walter Butler had a few questions for his onetime jailer, and the penalty for declining to answer was obvious. Three hundred Tory rangers surrounded the small scouting party, while from sounds in the dripping forest many more were moving up. They had found a disused trail running parallel to the south road, and slipped passed Hunter's watch. Now, a few poked through the encampment searching for food and rum. Rangers and Senecas had not had a fire in weeks, and marching 200 miles on a few handfuls of parched corn had left them hungry and irritable.[4]

By the time Hunter was done talking, Walter Butler knew that the Cherry Valley garrison was spread through the village. This meant that the soldiers would try to get back to the stockade when attacked, and outside the stockade they would find Butler and his rangers waiting for them. Hunter and his two corporals were taken prisoner by the rangers; the other six were dragged away by the Senecas and not seen again.[5] They were likely the first casualties of the Cherry Valley raid, and probably took the brunt of the Iroquois rage over the destruction of Oquaga and Tioga. Butler, in command of his first raid, should have sensed the mood of his allies and taken precautions in deploying them. His plan was to use the Senecas to flush the settlers and soldiers out of the houses—this on the condition that Little Beard, Little Billy, and Mary Jemison's husband Hiakatoo promised not to harm women and children. They seemed grudgingly to agree to these provisions, but Butler should have made certain.[6]

Joseph Brant, who had joined Butler's raid at Chemung after visiting the ashes of Oquaga, was free to lead his band wherever he pleased. He and Walter were not getting along particularly well. The young captain, meticulous about military etiquette and proud of the appearance of his father's ranger companies, objected to the fact that Brant's ragged volunteers wore pieces of yellow lace on their hat brims.[7] He also announced that they should all be enlisted in Butler's rangers for the duration, upon which ninety of Brant's men deserted. Thayendanegea would go into the Cherry Valley massacre with only sixty or so loyal Mohawks behind him. They would do what they could to prevent the worst, but their efforts were not sufficient to curb the rioting Senecas.[8] The delicate social network of Tenonanatche extended to Cherry Valley, where both Joseph and Molly Brant had friends.[9] But the Senecas, from the interior Finger Lakes country, cared little about nuanced relationships with white villagers. Walter Butler, himself a child of Tenonanatche, would feel the shame of this raid all of his life and would never again campaign with a main force comprised of Seneca braves. He brought 300 rangers to Cherry Valley, but over 400 Iroquois, not counting Brant's contingent.

Throughout a rainy November 10 the raiders sheltered in the pine forests a few miles from their objective. Their original plan was to attack at night, but a torrential downpour upset the schedule and the assault was advanced to the next morning. At first light, sleet and snow were falling over the area. Masked by swirling mists, the Senecas under Little Beard closed on the house of Robert Wells, a few hundred yards southwest of the fort. The large house was built on a knoll, and as Little Beard and his warriors approached, Joseph Brant raced through a plowed field attempting to cut them off. Wells, Cherry Valley's most respected citizen, had often opened his spacious home to Brant and other notables as they traveled south to the Susquehanna. He was of loyalist sympathies, inclined to present himself as a neutralist. No matter his politics, all agreed that Wells was a pious citizen of unfailing kindness and decency. The more the pity then that Brant lost his race to intercept Little Beard's warriors.

The Senecas swept the porch of awakening soldiers. The eleven men, who should never have been billeted at the house in the first place, reacted too slowly to the emerging threat; they managed to squeeze off a few wild shots before a massed volley cut them down. In a moment they were overrun, tomahawked, and scalped.

Little Beard, with Walter Butler at his side, crashed through the door. Butler grabbed Lieutenant Colonel Stacey and his aides as prisoners, while Little Beard with his warriors charged upstairs, knocked down the door to a bedroom and found the Wells family kneeling in prayer. They slaughtered Wells, his wife Mary, his three sons, and his brother John. As they scalped these victims, Seneca women broke into the lower story of the mansion and began plundering table settings and silver. In the kitchen, loyalists dressed as Indians and wielding tomahawks murdered and scalped the family's three African servants. Wells's daughter Jane dashed out of the house for safety. Little Beard pursued and seized her. A Tory who knew the young woman interceded and grabbed Little Beard's arm. The warrior flung him to the ground and buried his hatchet in the girl's skull. Jane's aunt Eleanor escaped into an orchard beside the barn. Rolf Hare, a ranger known for his cruelty, tracked her to where she hid beneath the leaves. He dragged her out and hacked her to death. Hare flung her dismembered arm into a tree where it seemed to be reaching, when found, for a wizened apple.[10]

Colonel Alden heard the terrified screams and slipped out the back door of the Wells house. He began running for the fort. Joseph Brant, who by now could do nothing for the Wells family, pursued him, dodged a ball from the colonel's pistol, and tomahawked him within sight of the fort's entry.[11] Troops who had made it to the fort could only fire through the half-opened gate; they slammed the portal shut when Butler and his rangers peppered them with small arms fire, leaving their colonel's body lying scalped at the side of the road. Outside the stockade, with nothing to fear from the soldiers within, several hundred raiders ran amok through Cherry Valley.

The Mitchel and Dunlop families were all but wiped out amid scenes of horrifying brutality. The Seeber family, resisting staunchly, were burned to death in their cabin. Fifteen soldiers washing their clothes in the creek near the fort were surprised and slaughtered. But most difficult to comprehend then and now was how children and young people were cut down even as their parents were taken prisoner. Women and children had not been harmed at Oquaga, Tioga, or Unadilla. Nothing explains the scale of savagery visited on Cherry Valley, beyond the inexplicable failure of Walter Butler to anticipate and control the contagious fury of his raiders. As Butler conducted fruitless feints against Fort Alden, his rampaging warriors butchered women and children for no military purpose other than sadistic pleasure. In the absence of leadership, they lost all sense of discipline. Arlen was not the only incompetent in the field that terrible morning.

Even in an age when a single bomb destroys hundreds of lives indiscriminately in a crowded marketplace, when total war is commonplace, there remains something especially hideous about the fate of Cherry Valley. The killing was intentional, deeply personal, and cruel as it could be. Infants were shot at their mothers' breasts, dismembered, flung into the snow. An old man, shielding himself with his family's Bible, was found with the book pinned to his chest by a lance. Bodies were mutilated, and according to one account even gnawed.[12] Atrocities committed by Seneca warriors in their lust for blood and revenge were equaled by many of Butler's rangers, and if Brant and his Mohawks saved some women and children by turning a blind eye to their escape to the woods, the destruction and desecration of life carried out by their side was nonetheless despicable. And they knew it. Lieutenant William Hare, a ranger, had helped save old Reverend Dunlop from being scalped. He wrote in an after report:

> The Evening before the attack the Chiefs promised to observe the same humanity they had with Colo Butler [at Wyoming] instead of which they exerted the most horrid barbaritys, the bloody seen is almost past discription. I think it hath determin'd Captains Butler and McDonald from ever having more to do in such a service where Savages make the principle part of the army.[13]

It is easy to blame Hiakatoo, Mary Jemison's husband, for his bestial behavior at the Dunlops', or to blame Little Beard for the murder of the Wells family, but Seneca warriors were raised from childhood to endure pain, whether their own or others', to strike ruthlessly at an enemy, and to make no distinction between man, woman, or child. On their ability to create terror and inflict maximum punishment depended the integrity of the Iroquois empire in the century preceding the Revolution. But the world had changed, as the Mohawks and Oneidas understood, and the old ways no longer guaranteed the safety of the People of the Long House. Young Seneca warriors tended to be the rustic cousins of the league. They were the last to realize that, while killing soldiers was warfare, killing women and children was atrocity, and atrocity could bring retributions in kind from their American opponents. Mohawks at Cherry Valley would not lift a hand against Iroquois brothers, but Brant and Kananaron did everything possible to restore a measure of proportionality to Seneca actions.

At the height of the massacre, over 180 people cringed in their hiding places in the woods, huddling together as the snow fell, praying that the Tryon County militia would come to their rescue. Indeed, the militia was coming under Colonel Klock, but it was coming very slowly, fearing every step of the way to collide with a raid larger than it could handle. By the next morning, when 400 militiamen approached the town, the raiders were gone. Everything that had been Cherry Valley, except Fort Alden, had been burned to the ground. The remains of the dead lay scattered in the roadway. Wolves had wandered off the mountains in the night, and many of the corpses were mangled beyond identification. Some would not be found until the spring thaw of 1779.

All that remained was to lead the civilians out of the valley and down to the frightened Mohawk settlements where they could find shelter. At Fort Alden, Major Daniel Whiting, now the senior surviving officer of the 7th Massachusetts, organized his remaining troops into burial parties. They found thirty-three women, children, and infants scalped and sprawled in the charred wreckage along with nearly one hundred additional dead, including soldiers. Dozens of people were missing—taken prisoner—and while many of these would be set free on the south road, some would stumble shocked into the forests and succumb to the cold miles from a cherished home that no longer existed.[14]

The massacre at Cherry Valley confirmed settlers' darkest premonitions, and as the ferocity of the raid became known, many families along the ridges of Tenonanatche made plans to move to the shelter of the Hudson Valley come spring. Some did not wait that long; they abandoned their cabins and fled eastward by sleigh in the depths of the winter. Two things were apparent—the seasonality of wilderness war in New York was giving way to warfare around the year, while militia organizations, designed to protect inhabitants, were increasingly unable to cope with large consecutive raids at all times from all directions. For every village or hamlet attacked, there were dozens of isolated farms and cabins set to the torch. In the hardest-hit areas, agriculture was at a standstill. Foodstuffs previously sent down the south-flowing rivers to Washington's army ceased to arrive. And, in 1779, Washington himself would take a hand in trying to find an answer to New York's Indian crisis.

The first retributive raid proposed by his Excellency to George Clinton, New York State's first governor, was against a richly symbolic target—the village of Onondaga. Here, until 1776, the great Iroquois council fire had burned for a quarter of a millennium in the famous Long House. The Onondaga nation generally supported the British; a number of Onondaga warriors had been present at Cherry Valley and Washington instructed Clinton to destroy the village completely and to take as many Onondaga hostages as possible.

On April 19, under cover of darkness, Colonel Goose Van Schaick[15] and 558 soldiers of the 1st and 2nd New York line marched from Fort Stanwix to Lake Oneida. There, in a chilling drizzle, they launched bateaux at present-day Verona Beach for a voyage across the lake into position north of the Indian town. They were to surprise and burn the sprawling town of Onondaga (site of Syracuse) in revenge for Cherry Valley. The previous summer, Colonel Gansevoort, still in command of the 3rd New York at Stanwix, had sent a party to burn Oswego in revenge for German Flats. Increasingly, the war in New York State had become a tit-for-tat contest, with the heavy raid against Onondaga at the start of the planting season intended to send a strong message to the British, Tories, and their native allies that American forces too could play the guerilla game. Van Schaick, whose father was mayor of Albany, was an unusual figure among Dutch families of the upper Hudson. He was a skilled professional soldier, who as a young officer in 1758 took a French musket butt to his face at the Battle of Ticonderoga. The resulting wound never healed.

Van Schaick and his regiments had been active in patriot service since the invasion of Canada, and while they were always short of men and supplies, they could be counted on to carry out a long-range amphibious mission. Notwithstanding, General James Clinton,[16] the governor's brother, warned Goose against allowing his men to mistreat Onondaga women. The purpose of the raid was not just to kill braves, but also to take hostages who might be exchanged for white settlers captured on the frontier. Thus Clinton to Van Schaick:

> Bad as the savages are, they never violate the chastity of any women, their prisoners. Although I have very little apprehension that any of the soldiers will so far forget their character as to attempt such a crime on the Indian women who may fall into their hands, yet it will be well to take measures to prevent such a stain upon our army.[17]

Both sides at this point in the struggle were highly sensitive to negative publicity. The news of Cherry Valley and other massacres reaching the British public brought storms of recrimination against the government. Washington and Clinton wanted no soil attaching to American actions in the eyes of the world. Yet, in the event, Van Schaick's soldiers, according to Onondaga testimony, treated several women prisoners loosely. Regrettably, the people fighting wars often have different aims from those conducting them. New York's 1st and 2nd regiments wanted revenge for victims like the Wells family. After all, the Wells daughter may have been left a virgin, but she was tomahawked and scalped nonetheless. The Onondaga prisoners were at least taken away alive. Much more than this, Van Schaick's lieutenants seemed unable to deliver.

After sleeping on their weapons in a swamp north of the town, they and their Oneida scouts broke into Onondaga out of the morning mist, killed twelve braves, and captured thirty-four men, women, and children.[18] They then plundered and demolished the town, including the ceremonial Long House. In a few furious moments, one of the most sacred sites of Iroquoian culture was desecrated and ruined. Van Schaick's soldiers retreated toward Fort Brewerton with their captives, boarded twenty-four bateaux left behind at the lakeside, and escaped to Fort Stanwix without loss. The strike was deemed a brilliant success. On the other side, fifty houses were torched, and the survivors, destitute and homeless, were left little choice but to gather up their remaining possessions and depart for the shelter of Fort Niagara and the generosity of the British.

How many of these Native Americans ever understood the connection between the Cherry Valley massacre and the abrupt demise of their own town is a good question. The misery descending on them and other Iroquois in this time of division and fragmentation must have seemed to most incomprehensible. They noticed the

Oneida moving among the Americans, and would never forgive them. As for the soldiers, they were as the British had described them, and they were from this day forward the enemy.

Joseph Brant revenged Onondaga a few months later in a sharp defeat of patriot militia at Minisink Ford on the Delaware River. In late July, probing reports that the Americans were preparing an army for invasion of Indian country, Brant led eighty-five warriors down the Delaware by canoe to the village of Minisink (present-day Port Jervis). They attacked and burned the town, but found that most of the cattle—the primary reason for the raid—had been driven into the woods. Inhabitants were also sparse, most having sought shelter in the town's stockade. Brant's report to Colonel Bolton at Niagara offers a glimpse into the raider's tactics:

> I arrived here last night from Minisink [Ford], and was a good deal disappointed that I cou'd not get into that place at the time I wished to do, a little before day; instead of which I did not arrive 'till noon, when all the Cattle was in the Woods so we cou'd get but a few of them. We have burnt all the Settlement called Minisink, one Fort excepted, round which we lay before, about an hour, & had one man Killed & one wounded. We destroyed several small stockaded Forts, and took four Scalps & three Prisoners; but did not in the least injure Women and Children. The Reason that we cou'd not take more of them, was owing to the many Forts about the Place, into which they were always ready to run like Ground Hogs.[19]

Brant's assurances to Bolton that women and children had not been injured reflected his own views on conducting war, as well as increased pressure from British leadership to prevent further Cherry Valleys. In any case, Thayendanegea had arrived too late in the day to surprise many civilians. Even a hundred miles south of the Mohawk Valley, settlers previously undisturbed were now alert to the war's threats. Brant could burn their towns, but his opportunity to wreak havoc on their families was diminishing. Not until two days later, at Minisink Ford, would militia throw caution to the wind and offer him a chance to bloody the hatchet.

Lieutenant Colonel Dr. Benjamin Tusten's detachment from Goshen, New York, responded rapidly to the raid. One hundred and twenty strong, they pursued Brant, slowed by his plunder and cattle, to the place where the Lackawaxen River enters the Delaware. Tusten, a physician by profession, deduced that his opponent was likely the infamous Joseph Brant, with a force almost as large as his own. He counseled a guarded approach even as his executive officer, Major Samuel Meeker, jumped into his saddle, flourished his sword, and with the impetuosity that repeatedly led militia to disaster, cried: "Let all the brave men follow me. The cowards may stay behind!"[20] As in the past, most followed.

Before long they found forty of Brant's men wading the river. Forming ranks, the militia fired on them. Colonel John Hathorn arrived on the scene at this point and, outranking Tusten, assumed command. But Hathorn failed to notice that half of Brant's force was still on his side of the river and had begun to slide in behind his position. Surprised in the rear, many of the militia fled. Hathorn retreated with others in good order, but Tusten was driven away from the river with fifty men over several steep ledges and through deep forest.[21] This spot on the Delaware was then one of the craggiest and most impenetrable places in New York State. It was a "howling" wilderness, so-called because at night the hills came alive with the cry of wolves. From the moment Tusten's militia fought its way up the wooded hillside in retreat from Brant's warriors, the Battle of Minisink passed from history into the fog of legend. No one today knows with certainty what next befell the Goshen volunteers. The men formed a square in the woods atop the hill and appear to have fought to their last cartridge. The fight lasted five hours until Brant found an undefended point in the line and led his warriors through the defenses. Doctor Tusten was tending wounded under an overhanging rock. In forest warfare, where each combatant fought for himself, no one heeded officers. The doctor turned to helping as best he knew how. The worse for him. When Brant's warriors broke through to the hilltop and charged into his makeshift hospital, they slaughtered the physician and his patients.[22]

Over forty militiamen died in the Battle of Minisink—Brant claimed his warriors took forty-odd scalps—but many more militiamen were wounded, some mortally. Colonel Hathorn put a good face on the action in his report to Governor Clinton, yet in the aftermath many locals referred to the battle as a massacre.[23] So remote and terrible was the site that more than forty years went by before a party from Port Jervis climbed the hill above the ford and gathered up the bones of the fallen.[24] By then it was impossible to tell what had transpired. Some militiamen who were too severely wounded to be brought down from the top or taken prisoner were dispatched by the Mohawks out of mercy.[25] The militia had fled and night was coming; the wolves waited. Hard rules these, but an accepted part of woodland fighting. Brant lost three dead and suffered ten wounded in the fight for the hilltop. One of the casualties was his dear friend, John, a severely wounded Tuscarora.

What Brant took away from Minisink besides victory and meat for his table was certain knowledge that a major American force was readying to invade Indian country. He wrote to Bolton: "I find the enemy certainly intends an expedition into the Indian Country, & having built strong Forts—by last accounts they were at Wyoming, perhaps by this time they may be at Shimong [Chemung], where I have sent my Party to remain 'till I join them; I am now seting off with 8 men to the Mohawk River, in order to discover the Enemy's motions."

He discovered on reentering Tenonanatche that Brigadier General James Clinton had gathered an army of 2,000 men at the bottom of Lake Otsego for a descent of the Susquehanna. The Susquehanna flows out of the lake as a shallow creek, and since the summer had been unusually dry, the creek was impossible for boats to navigate. Clinton ordered a dam constructed across the outlet, and while he scoured central New York for supplies to feed his four regiments of New York line and militia detachments, the waters of Otsego rose steadily. On August 11, with his troops and supplies stowed in bateaux, Clinton ordered the dam opened. The waters of the lake were three feet higher than normal, and their sudden escape carried the invasion fleet over the rocks with banners flying, drums and fifes playing. The New York division of Washington's long-awaited attack on Iroquoia had been launched. Eleven days later, after descending the Susquehanna in fine weather, Clinton's division met the main army under General John Sullivan at Tioga. Sullivan had brought 2,400 men, mountains of supplies, and a pack train of artillery upriver from Wyoming. Joined now, they were ready to forge a way into Seneca country, engage the Iroquois if they resisted, find and destroy their villages, and take as many hostages as possible.

Brant at Minisink had sensed the readiness of Sullivan at Wyoming, but had missed the imminence and size of Clinton's attack. After razing a small hamlet on the Mohawk, Brant fled for old Oquaga, only to arrive just ahead of Clinton's flotilla. The Yorkers had paused on the way to burn Indian villages and search for renegades. At one settlement they discovered two of Butler's rangers home on leave. Since both were known to have been at Cherry Valley, Clinton, despite the lamentations of their families, had them strung up on the spot. Natives spotted by Clinton's scouts were usually fired upon. Brant narrowly escaped these far-ranging parties, but as he moved southwest from Clinton's line of advance, he was forced to evade aggressive probes sent out by Sullivan as he ascended the river towards Tioga. Sullivan's practice differed little from Clinton's—where his troops found villages, they were burned; where they met Indians, they were captured for interrogation or shot. The main army had spent weeks at Wyoming amid devastated homes; they called the place "the valley of bones" and shuddered at the stories told by surviving inhabitants. At the onset of the campaign, they were fired with a determination to expunge the perpetrators of all such barbarities.

Samuel Kirkland, one of the few participants in the expedition knowledgeable about Indian country and acquainted with Seneca ways, had been appointed chaplain of the army.[26] Viewing the devastation along the Susquehanna, he placed the blame on George III: "Are these the fruits & effects of thy Clemency O George, thou tyrant of Britain & scourge to mankind! May *He*, to whom Vengeance belongs, pour forth his righteous indignation in due time."[27] Kirkland was careful to mute his condemnation of the Seneca people, but since Seneca homes, not His Britannic Majesty's, lay in the path of the invasion, they foremost would feel the wrath of the American crusaders. Indeed, Washington intended them to bear the brunt. In his orders to Sullivan, he wrote that the goal was: "the total destruction and devastation of their settlements and the capture of as many prisoners of every age and sex as possible to be held as hostages—the only kind of security to be depended on for the behavior of the Six Nations. ... The country is not to be merely *overrun* but *destroyed*."[28]

In January, Washington had begun plans to capture Niagara by sending an army across New York and Pennsylvania. To this purpose he consulted Philip Schuyler, who dissuaded him from pressing too far into a wilderness little known. Displaced Iroquois were usually thrown back upon His Majesty's resources for material support, and the British at Niagara were finding Indian demands increasingly onerous. Thus, to make the New York and Pennsylvania frontiers safe again, Schuyler reasoned, the army's aim should be to increase Niagara's burden by destroying the homes and crops of the offending Senecas. Let the campaign penetrate as far as Chenussio on the Genesee River, sweeping the shores of Lake Seneca bare of habitation. On withdrawal the army could then destroy the towns and orchards lining the banks of Lake Cayuga. After initial skirmishes, no one expected the Iroquois to contest the passage of a disciplined army 4,000 strong. Of course, in this plan the enemy who stood to suffer most, especially during the coming winter, would be women, children, and the elderly. Between famine, disease, and exposure to the elements, the vulnerable people of the Long House would pay the highest price for outrages committed by British-led warriors. According to twenty-first-century standards, an attack of this nature against a civilian population, with the intent of causing massive loss of innocent life, is defined as genocide. The offensive being waged on the frontiers by British, Tory, and Indian forces was no less so, and while some Americans with tender consciences objected to Washington's methods, they could not argue with the goals of the undertaking.[29]

That Washington could even conceive of such a campaign was the result of having fought the enemy to a stalemate in the Northeast. The British held New York City, but were rapidly shifting their strategy southwards. In the weeks before the launch of Sullivan's campaign, Americans would win battles at Stony Point and Paulus Hook, penning Henry Clinton tighter into the city and lower Hudson. This was the right time for the Continental Army to deal with the Indians, and to this end Washington sent Sullivan three New Jersey regiments under William Maxwell, three New Hampshire regiments and one New York under Enoch Poor, three Pennsylvania regiments and one Maryland under Edward Hand, and three New York regiments under James Clinton. This was the seasoned core of the Continental service, led by the best brigadiers in the army. Washington and staff planned the expedition meticulously. The divisions would not trail three-pounder cannon and grasshoppers (small antipersonnel cannon) into the attack, but the same artillery park that had shelled Clinton at Monmouth—nine- and twelve-pound cannon with howitzers—and they would be supplied with French goods, food and arms captured by American privateers from

British ships, and the best provisions Congress could purchase from New York, Pennsylvania, New Jersey, and Connecticut. Sullivan would be the first American general since the invasion of Canada four years earlier to lead an aggressive expedition into an unknown and alien country.

He was not Washington's first choice for the command. Philip Schuyler and Horatio Gates had turned the commander in chief down in light of the campaign's arduous field requirements.[30] Sullivan was a rigorous thirty-nine, but with a mixed record. He had fought in Canada during the retreat, been captured at Long Island during the great rout and, after exchange, fought bravely at Trenton, Princeton, and Brandywine. But Sullivan was of a cautious disposition, where Washington sought a leader who would move quickly and decisively. Four years of helter-skelter survival had taught Sullivan much, and he had no intention, despite Washington's urgings, of moving without ample supplies, moving without scouting his front, or striking without overwhelming force. This would be the advance of a tough national army with a determination to find and kill—not a militia dash for glory.

By the time Brant reached Chemung, he found it burned to the ground. Before the American crusade lurched forward, light infantry had moved out ahead, clearing the ground. The main army followed behind over terrible roads at sometimes a modest three miles a day. Brant had time to locate John and Walter Butler encamped at Chucknut, a small village near the larger settlement of Newtown (present-day Elmira). The Butlers mustered 180 rangers, including a small detachment from the King's 8th regiment. They had been in the field for months and were weary and ill. Senecas and Cayugas, who should have been in the vanguard of the defense, were responding sluggishly; only a few hundred had yet arrived. Delawares, whose villages also lay nearby, promised two hundred warriors but sent thirty. With Brant's corps forming again around its leader, the force available to block the Forbidden Path was not much more than Walter Butler had led to Cherry Valley. Even after Sullivan detached several battalions to protect his supply lines, the invading army outnumbered the defenders four to one. The British governor of Canada, Lieutenant Colonel Haldimand, had assured the tribes that their lands were under no threat from the Americans. He rushed now to send troops south to their aid, but even the wilderness-wise Sir John Johnson could not reach the Chemung before Sullivan had come and gone.

There was no help for it but to contest this invasion or face massive defections of Iroquois from the British cause. Brant and the Butlers counseled retreating into the interior, harassing the Americans as they came forward and waiting for the tribes to shrug off their torpor. Right now they were in no mood to fight; many argued that fighting white men in a white man's war was best left to British forces. Even news that the "Great Sun," Colonel Daniel Brodhead,[31] was leading 600 soldiers from Fort Pitt over the Alleghenies into western New York did nothing to rouse the ardor of the Senecas. They sent a small party to stop him; Brodhead ambushed the party and continued forward to burn villages and destroy crops per Washington's orders.[32] Given their normal aggressiveness, the Senecas' passivity seemed strange, but this attitude probably reflected how tired they had grown of the long, divisive war.

Relations between the allies were often difficult. Tories did not always see eye-to-eye with Indians, "colored people," especially when fighting ceased and all hands turned to digging. Some Seneca leaders resented Brant, whose very prominence among whites inclined them to stubbornly disregard his advice. John Butler could negotiate with war chiefs, but he and his rangers too were often shunned, and in late August 1779, with disaster staring all in the face, the Seneca leaders rejected Butler's recommendations. They had made up their mind to ambush the Americans at Newtown no matter how large the opposing force. Their ambush would be sprung from a half-mile-long ridge that squeezed the road between its densely wooded slopes and the Chemung River. This was the road Sullivan's army would have to take.

But Sullivan was not advancing headlong as Nicholas Herkimer had into the ambush at Oriskany. Edward Hand's Pennsylvanians led the way, and James Parr's three companies of Morgan's riflemen led the Pennsylvanians. The woodsmen slipped forward silently in advance of the cumbersome infantry, searching for signs of ambush with a practiced eye. Brant, in fact, had designed the chiefs' ambuscade in the fishhook pattern sprung at both Oriskany and the Bloody Morning Scout. Rangers and Indians dug in on the slopes of the ridge under trees, and Brant expertly camouflaged their position with piles of deadfall and still-green branches. The plan was to volley into the right flank of the marching Americans; Walter Butler would then punch into the head of the confused enemy while Brant's Mohawks cut off retreat, forcing the milling troops backward into the river. Which might well have worked if Sergeant Samuel Poleman of the 4th Pennsylvania had not climbed a tree with a spyglass and studied the wooded slope of the ridge. He quickly discerned glistening colors that should not have been there—painted bodies stripped to the waist for work in the hot sun.

Sullivan needed less than thirty minutes to devise a battle plan answering the circumstances. He had ordered the column stopped in place and Colonel Proctor's artillery unlimbered 300 yards from the ambush site. This was the reason that the army had dragged and floated the artillery all the way from Wyoming, for nothing broke up an ambush like a screaming barrage of hot metal. At 3 PM, Hand would move out to a position on the enemy's left flank, threatening to assault the ridge. Poor and Clinton with 1,700 infantry between them would traverse rough country and swing around the ridge to take up position in the enemy's rear. Meanwhile, Ogden and the 1st New Jersey would use the defilade provided by the riverbank to take position on the extreme right flank, cutting off the line of retreat. At 4 PM sharp, Proctor was instructed to open fire with everything he had, strafing the hidden entrenchments from end to end. This would be the signal for Hand to begin his demonstration and for Poor and Clinton to mount their assault for the summit. Sullivan's plan was complex, comprehensive, brilliant—the sort of professional maneuver militia could never hope to emulate. Of course, Sullivan also outnumbered and outgunned his opponents substantially.

By the time Brant realized that his ambush was discovered and that solid lines of infantry were moving to surround him, shells were crashing into his breastworks, exploding behind them, and pinning down his riflemen in a hail of grapeshot. Proctor threw solid shot, exploding shells, bar, grape, harrow teeth, and bushels of spikes at the rangers and Indians, and although the barrage killed relatively few, it terrified most. Any chance of ambush was hopelessly disrupted now as trees crashed down over the trenches and volleys of musket fire from Hand's regiment raked the line. But the real threat, Brant soon realized, was Poor's and Clinton's assault intended to cut off escape and drive his force into Ogden's arms. What saved the Tories and Indians from annihilation at Newtown was the delay between the barrage and the main attack, for Poor had to advance over difficult ground and Clinton had to swing even farther right along Poor's flank. As the New Hampshire regiments climbed the ridge, the rangers and Indians who had survived the bombardment fought furiously. At one point they all but surrounded Colonel George Reid's 2nd New Hampshire until Lieutenant Colonel Henry Dearborn wheeled his 3rd New Hampshire around and broke the attack against Reid.

The American assault was at bayonet point and in places overran the Indian position, inflicting many casualties. Brant and his Mohawks were seen everywhere, attempting to hold back the converging forces of Hand, Ogden, Poor, and Clinton. Survivors streamed through a gap between the latter and succeeded in bringing off many wounded. The Americans pursued them until dark, wounding more and killing an indeterminate number in the woods to the north. Atop the ridge, the ground steamed from the barrage Proctor had poured on the entrenchments; blankets, personal effects, camp gear lay strewn across the bloody gorse, and near where Poor's troops had broken the defense, the bodies of twelve male Indians and one female were found stripped and scalped. Later, John Butler admitted to losing five rangers in the defeat, but their bodies were dragged back, along with a number of Indian dead, from the scene of the fighting. In the morning, when triumphant American troops burned Newtown and set about destroying the village's extensive planting fields, they found many traces of the injured, including a blood-spattered canoe adrift in the Chemung. American losses at Newtown amounted to three dead and thirty-nine wounded, five of whom died of their wounds the next day. Sullivan had broken down the door to Indian country, but to everyone's amazement he appeared to have also broken the spirit of the redoubtable Iroquois.

For all the thunder and fury of the massive American advance, the casualties suffered by the Senecas at Newtown should never have proven decisive. In a different state of mind, the Senecas might have retreated, regrouped, and contested one of the gorges or swampy places through which Sullivan had to pass. Their homes and fields were at stake, and sooner or later British reinforcements would have reached them. Instead, they ran, emptying their villages and leaving behind well-built and highly developed settlements to the torch of the enemy. Thayendanegea and John Butler begged them to turn and fight; their pleas fell on deaf ears as, all across the Iroquois heartland, a thriving Indian population pulled up roots and evacuated. Some fled to the hills or remote valleys, while others moved closer to Niagara to avail themselves of British support.

Just what made the setback at Newtown so intimidating to the Senecas is difficult to discern. Clearly, even with many uncounted dead, they did not suffer warrior losses approaching, let alone surpassing, Oriskany. The Americans, jubilant at their flight, offer no particular reasons for their sudden and total demoralization. The identity of the dead found on the battlefield could perhaps explain this loss of confidence, but the names of the thirteen dead have never been established. William J. Stone, Joseph Brant's first biographer, writes of the event fifty years later, claiming:

> It was believed that the King of Kanadasagea [Kayingwaurto] had been killed at Newtown. He had been seen on his way thither, and had not returned. From the description given of his dress and person, moreover, it was believed by General Sullivan that he had seen his body among the slain.[33]

The King of the Senecas was much revered. His loss, with the subsequent desecration of his body, could have gone far toward discouraging his people, but only if they also concluded that the sacred spirits guarding the Forbidden Path had abandoned their cause. These mysterious powers warding the back door to Iroquois country were palpable enough to frighten most of the Oneida scouts accompanying Sullivan into deserting.[34]

Many of the leaders of the Seneca nation were at Newtown before or during the battle. Red Jacket, characteristically, left the encampment before the fighting began. Cornplanter was engaged on the West Branch of the Susquehanna during this time, but Little Billy, Blacksnake, Little Beard, and Ganiodaio were present and survived the defeat. Allan Eckert alleges that "Gu-cinge, Rozinoghyata of the Onondagas, Kayingwaurto of the Senecas, Captain John of the Mohawks, and the middle-aged Seneca woman Queen Esther" were killed in the last stand against Poor and Clinton.[35] If so, their earthly remains did not find an easy grave. Lieutenant Barton of the 1st New Jersey wrote in his journal:

> At the request of Major Piatt, sent out a small party to look for some of the dead Indians—returned without finding them. Toward noon they found them and skinned two of them from their hips down for boot legs: one pair for the Major and the other for myself.[36]

Tracing the whereabouts of individual Iroquois leaders during this period is close to impossible, yet most of the eminences Eckert mentions seem to pass away at the time of the battle and are not heard from again. Certainly they had the prestige to take charge from Brant and Butler but, being older and slower, might also have been trapped in the entrenchments by the folly of their tactics. The shock of the Seneca nation at the outcome of Newtown suggests losses not immediately apparent in the record. What is beyond dispute, however, is that, following the battle, the road to Sechquago, Kendaia, Kanadasegea, Canandaigua, Honeoye, Kanagha, and Geneseo was uncontested.

The American march into Indian country brought little sight of the Native Americans, who fled the columns as they approached, but along the route the advancing Americans made startling discoveries. On everyone's lips during the first lovely days of September were praises for the agriculture and solidly built villages found. Sullivan's was a literate army replete with diarists, letter writers, journal keepers; they wrote for themselves and for families at home with the fervor and frequency of Union soldiers eighty years later. What they had to say often reflected well on the enemy. At Newtown they came upon vast fields of corn, some stalks an amazing eighteen feet high, gigantic pumpkins and squash, great tracts of varied beans enough to fill every man's mess cup to overflowing. Lieutenant Beatty took part in destroying "150 acres of the best corn that Ever I saw (some of the stalks grew 16 feet high) besides great quantities of Beans, Potatoes, Pumpkins, Cucumbers, Squashes & Watermelons." At Newtown he saw "Good buildings of English construction burned there."[37]

Christopher Ward captures the record of destruction in a medley of soldiers' accounts:

> On the 31st Catherine's Town, thirty houses, another village of eight, and a third of twenty, with their cornfields and orchards, were destroyed. Appletown was burned on the 4th of September, and Kindaia's thirty neatly built and finished houses made a fine bonfire on the 5th, while the army was employed in destroying corn & fruit trees, of which there was a great abundance. Many of the trees appeared to be of great age. Two days later, one detachment burned the chief town of the Senecas, Kanadaseagea, eighty houses, and destroyed a great number of fruit trees; another put an end to Schoyere. Canadaigua, a very pretty town, very compact & neatly built with thirty houses much better built than any I have seen before went up in flames. Honeoye and Kanagha followed.[38]

For three weeks Sullivan's march of destruction blazed a way across that country that someday would comprise the Finger Lakes wine district, the peach and apricot orchards of Cayuga, the fertile granary of the Genesee Valley. He describes in letters to Washington and Congress the extent of the damages: "The number of Towns destroyed amounts to 40, besides scattering houses. The quantity of Corn destroyed ... must amount to 160,000 bushels, with a vast quantity of vegetables of every kind. Except for one Town ... about 80 miles from Genesee, there is not a single Town left in the Country of the five nations."[39] By the time the army turned back for Wyoming, the troops had become vegans, subsisting almost entirely on vegetables. Sullivan knew that an army marched and fought on salt pork, beef, and bread, but these commodities were in short supply. The Senecas surrendered their towns and crops, but they saved their people and livestock. If one of Sullivan's goals was to take hostages, the great expedition by that measure failed resoundingly. After Newtown, few contacts were made with the inhabitants of Iroquoia.

The lack of engagement, the absence of prisoners or hostages, combined with interminable marching over difficult terrain and mindless destruction of homes and orchards nagged at the troops. Many were farmers and builders; it went against them to fell ancient fruit trees and burn habitations. They dug their hands into the soil and saw that it was good; when the war was over, some promised they would return to this place of fish-filled lakes, rolling fields, and dark, fertile ground. Both General Hand and Lieutenant Colonel Dearborn, responding to the grumbling in the ranks, protested the intensity of the demolition, but Sullivan had his orders and was following them to the letter. By adhering to Washington's instructions, the Americans, according to one nineteenth-century historian, engaged in "the ruthless destruction of the greatest advance in civilization that the red men in this country have ever attained."[40]

The sermons of the Reverends Wheelock and Kirkland adjuring the natives to put down the bow and take up the plow had been fulfilled beyond all expectations in Seneca country. Seneca women grew the miraculous corn the soldiers harvested, but in Seneca practice, men cleared, broke, and plowed the fields.[41] The creative effort of these energetic people was everywhere in evidence, and perceptive Americans, to their great surprise, saw for the first time that Indian settlements often surpassed their own in productivity and permanence.

The destruction of their heartland terrified the Iroquois. Years later, when he visited President Washington, Cornplanter recalled the lasting impression left by the invasion: "When your army entered the country of the Six Nations, we called you Town Destroyer: and to this day when that name is heard our women look behind them and turn pale, and our children cling close to the necks of their mothers."[42]

Women look behind them, in Cornplanter's testimony, and grow pale at the destruction of their homes, but where were the Seneca men? Many Americans realized that they had missed the target. Major Jeremiah Fogg concluded in his diary, "The nests are destroyed, but the birds are still on the wing."[43]

The dire consequences of Sullivan's failure to locate and subdue the Seneca warriors was about to be felt by Lieutenant Thomas Boyd and his Oneida scout Hanyost Thaosagwat. Near Conesus Lake on September 13, the intrepid Boyd, a pathfinder with Morgan's rifles, blundered into an ambush laid in preparation for Sullivan. John and Walter Butler with rangers and 400 braves were waiting for an opportunity to avenge Newtown. Boyd ruined the ambush, but he was quickly surrounded and subdued. He, Sergeant Parker, and Hanyost were taken prisoner, while the rest of the patrol were scattered or killed. The Senecas wasted no time chopping the Oneida to pieces in their anger, but they saved Boyd and Parker for special attention once the two had been interrogated. "Parker and Boyd were tortured in the most excruciating manner," Graymont writes, "being whipped, stabbed, having their nails, tongues, and eyes plucked out, and their ears cut off, and finally being decapitated."[44] According to Mary Jemison, who witnessed the scene at Chenussio (Geneseo), Boyd's belly was opened and his intestines drawn out. What remained of the lieutenant was on display for Sullivan to see as he rode into town. The flayed skull was placed on a log at the entrance, staring through empty sockets in the direction of the intruders.[45] The tortured and mutilated remains of the two men were nearby, a sight not to be forgotten by those who discovered them.

By committing savageries on the bodies of Boyd and Parker, the Senecas were not just venting a childish rage. They left an unmistakable sign for the Americans that they were not beaten and never would be. Through their victims, they made a gift to the god of war, hoping that in the torment of the dying men, the spirits of those slain by Sullivan's army would find release and rest. As for the living, they had no choice now but to follow the British father across the sea; he, at least, would feed his children in their time of need. Barbara Graymont explains: "The war became very personal to the Iroquois. If they did not have a cause before, they had one now. They would not lay down the hatchet until the British did, and then, only reluctantly."[46]

After one of the worst winters of the century, the ice lingered long on the Mohawk River. Five feet of snow blanketed the ground, and wild animals everywhere perished from the cold. In what remained of the Indian towns, suffering was intense during this winter of winters, as many died from poor nutrition and exposure to the winds. The frigid conditions did not impede Joseph Brant and others from gathering to punish the Americans. But neither did it inhibit emissaries for peace from trying one last time to reverse the slide into disaster.

At the end of February, Brant was leading a war party of 200 warriors east towards Tenonanatche when he spotted four figures, black against the white expanse, struggling towards him on snowshoes over the drifts. He soon realized that they were Iroquois, bound for the west, bearing signs of parley. The leading figure was Skenando, seventy-three years old, war chief of the Oneidas and Brant's former father-in-law. Accompanying him was Tigoransera (Little Abraham), peace chief of the Mohawks, Agorondajats (Good Peter), the Oneida holy man, and Unaquandahoojie (White

Hans), a Mohawk sachem from Fort Hunter. The delegation had left Stanwix days before with a message from Philip Schuyler to the then-resident Indian superintendent at Niagara, Guy Johnson. Since these ambassadors, Brant surmised, were arriving with another stale peace offer, he had no intention of interrupting his mission to help them through the snow. He sent them on their way with cold greetings. Brant was leading the first raid of the year against Oneida settlements to the east.

Of all the embassies sent out in New York over the war years, this was perhaps the most perilous. Schuyler was still Indian Supervisor for the Northern Department, and when he asked for volunteers to make this wintertime journey to Niagara, he found only these four willing to go. Skenando and Good Peter were firm patriot supporters, but Little Abraham and White Hans remained, as they had always been, strong neutralists. What the Senecas might do to this party in the wake of last summer's devastations, or how the irascible Guy Johnson would respond to their arrival, was problematic. The ostensible reason for the diplomacy was an exchange of prisoners, which both sides desired. The deeper purpose was to show the Iroquois an alternative to their British policy, offering them a return to their lands in exchange for peace. Schuyler was the first American leader to appreciate the failure of the Sullivan campaign and to fear reprisals against the New York frontier. If that frontier could be driven back by raids and spoliation to Albany and the Hudson Highlands, any peace settlement between the exhausted British and the equally exhausted Americans might end by awarding abandoned sections of upstate New York to British Canada.

Schuyler's concerns reflected those of the large landholders; Skenando's reflected his fear that the British in defeat might desert the Six Nations entirely and leave Indian country wide open to rapacious white settlers. The four elders knew that there was much to discuss, even with their implacable foes.

Guy was having none of it. He refused to allow the chiefs to circulate freely among the Indians at Niagara, interrogated each individually and, meeting the four collectively, flung back their peace belts with contempt. The Johnson party's main objective was the preservation of grants certain to be lost if the Americans retained the Mohawk. For them, loyalty to King George was nonnegotiable, and Guy believed that he spoke for Sir John, Joseph Brant, Molly Brant, Daniel Claus, New York's loyalists, and a majority of the Six Nations.

Sayenqueraghta (Old Smoke), Six Nations Joint War Chief, and Kananaron (Aaron Hill), Mohawk war chief, confirmed this position, berating the Oneidas and neutralists for countenancing the destruction of the league. Old Smoke conveniently forgot that he had signed a treaty in 1775 at Albany pledging the neutrality of the league in the looming confrontation. Now he confessed to being at a loss about what to do with these peace emissaries, and while the matter was under advisement, and with the complicity of Guy, he consigned the four old men to the darkest and dankest dungeon of Fort Niagara. The embassy was at an end. In the black hole of the fort, without blankets, fire, or adequate food, Little Abraham sickened and died. The three remaining ambassadors survived, but not without lasting damage to their health from a winter's sojourn below water level on the icy shores of Lake Ontario.

By the end of February, Brant had burned several Oneida villages, raided German Flats once more, and ambushed a supply train bound for Stanwix. The fort, stuck out on the western edge of settlement, was again in desperate condition, but Stanwix increasingly mattered little as raids from the west slipped past it into the valley. During the first four months of 1780, almost 500 Iroquois warriors and Tories went out from Niagara on raids against the New York frontier. After July, bands of 400 or more were constantly ranging across the Mohawk and Schoharie valleys, the upper Susquehanna, and lower Adirondacks.[47] These parties, varying in size from a dozen to a hundred, were led by Little Beard of the Senecas, Fish Carrier of the Cayugas, Cakadorie of the Onondagas, and Rowland Mountour. They scourged settlements that were rebuilding from previous depredations and struggling to survive in the wake of a disastrous harvest season and severe frosts. Governor George Clinton, surveying the damage inflicted on Tenonanatche's farms by the inclement weather, lamented: "Bending under a load of Debt, and groaning under an accumulation of Distress We entered the year 1780 with universal Dismay, as the Hand of God had been upon us in blasting our crops the preceeding Harvest."[48]

The tale of these early raids is repetitive—a home burned here, a hamlet attacked and massacred there, six scalps taken, an old man captured with two of his grandchildren, the old man unable to keep up, slain and scalped, the scalp waved in the face of the two children to make them move faster, more prisoners dragged to Niagara, more families torn asunder or left in mourning over their dead. Joseph Brant might act with humanity towards his victims on occasion, but the majority of raiders did not, and Brant himself could little control the behavior of his marauders. The British were waging a "war of posts" against New York State, and this meant relentlessly striking towns and defenses protecting the approaches to Albany and the upper Hudson. Here was the reason that Brant destroyed Harpersfield at the head of the Schoharie Valley in early April, struck at Cherry Valley for a second time, and once more damaged Cobleskill. Add German Flats, Little Falls, Neversink, and Minisink to the list of targets destroyed, and a straight line from north to south appears across the map of central New York State. The raids of 1780 were not opportunistic, but carefully envisioned and coordinated.

In Sir William's time, the frontier between settled lands and Indian country had more or less followed the Unadilla River. That frontier now lay thirty miles to the east, and with attacks against the Schoharie Valley, would be shoved another thirty miles eastward towards Albany and the Hudson. Nor did the forts of central New York offer much deterrence. If blockhouses and stockades were small and undermanned, they were destroyed; if they were heavily garrisoned, they were bypassed. The objective was to drive communities away from the land through terror, while methodically devastating homes, crops, and livestock. Everything that Washington had unleashed on Indian country in 1779 was coming back to the patriot settlements with interest in 1780. The great, expensive expedition, glorious in its progress against the opponents of liberty, had in fact succeeded in leaving the people of New York more vulnerable, more isolated, and less protected than before Sullivan's army had marched.

By the end of April 1780, the national cause stood to lose Charleston and much of South Carolina, a colony only slightly smaller in population than New York. North Carolina, a colony larger than New York in population, was also in danger of being overrun.[49] The focus of the war was shifting rapidly to the south, where great wealth, and possibly the survival of American independence, hung in the balance. Washington clearly did not have the resources to protect central New York, contain enemy forces in New York City, and turn back British encroachments in the Carolinas; in truth, given the state of the army, Washington wondered if he had the resources to do any of the above.[50] And so again, as the Continental service faced fresh emergencies, the citizens of New York were left with only their own militia to shield them.[51]

A fortuitous raid down the Champlain corridor almost a year earlier had demonstrated to Governor Haldimand that incursions by regular troops against the Americans were still possible using the old warpath from St. Johns to Fort Edward. An intrepid British major, Christopher Carleton of the 29th Foot, had succeeded in penetrating to the headwaters of the Connecticut River by this route and also sending a strong detachment into Johnstown on the Mohawk.[52] He reported the American defenses down everywhere, with only small squads of militia guarding Crown Point, Ticonderoga, Fort George, Fort Edward, and the Sacandaga blockhouse. While the Indian raids of early 1780 struck at towns between the Susquehanna and Mohawk rivers, the back door to Albany was left wide open.

The Royal Navy controlled Champlain from St. Johns to South Bay, even while American militia detachments continued to hold the key land points. Moreover, some Vermont settlers, disaffected with Congress and following Ethan Allen's example of defiance, had entered into negotiations with Haldimand toward the creation of an independent Republic of Vermont. These were not inclined during the spring of 1780 to interfere with British movements on Champlain aimed at the New York shore.[53] Nothing stood in the way of Sir John Johnson leading his Kings Royal Regiment, reinforced with troops from the 53rd, 29th, 34th, and Hanau Jägers, south against the eastern flank of Tenonanatche in a movement recalling Burgoyne's advance. Ample whaleboats and bateaux were on hand, and Johnson had only to wait for better weather in May to embark.

The situation of the Americans in New York was described by Colonel Goose Van Schaick in a letter to Governor Clinton dated May 17:

I should not be surprised if all the settlements to the Northward of the Mohawk and the Westward of Hudson's River were shortly either destroyed or abandoned. ... I am incapacitated to draw forth the militia for want of provisions. ... Drafts from the militia have been made. ... but being unfurnished with provisions were obligated to disband. [Two days later he wrote again:] ... the Militia of Tryon County have as good as refused to turn out ... the frontier settlements are breaking up fast & if some remedy is not soon applied, Schonectady will be our frontier Settlement. ... Your Excellency's feelings must daily increase on the account of the distressed situation of our Affairs relative to supplies for the Army & the naked situation of our Western & Northern frontiers for the want of men & provisions.[54]

By May 1780 the authorities of Tryon County had resorted to drafting able-bodied men from sixteen years of age to sixty for service in the militia. Any declining to serve were liable to incarceration and their properties held open to confiscation. Loyalists and neutralists remarked bitterly on the vaunted freedom promised by the American cause in the face of impressments and seizure of private goods. Not only was the frontier "breaking up fast," but the civil guarantees for which patriots fought were being eroded before their eyes. Along the edges of Tenonanatche, militia formations refused their orders, preferring to remain close to threatened families in defiance of a government that could neither provide for its military nor protect its civilians.

The consequence was that Sir John landed at Crown Point with over 500 soldiers and Native Americans, cut overland to the southwest, skirting Schroon Lake, and entered Johnstown through the Scotch Settlement on May 21. Now, the order of business was reversed. Notorious patriots, those who had imprisoned Tories and stolen their property, were hunted down and executed. The 3rd Battalion of the Tryon County militia was too weak to resist the invaders; a dozen were killed and scalped, and their commander, Lieutenant Colonel Volkert Veeder, taken prisoner. The raid destroyed over 120 barns, mills, and houses, and a large depot of military stores.[55] Then, as quickly as he had appeared, Sir John vanished back into the forests, burdened now with prisoners and loyalist civilians who hoped to find freedom from persecution in Canada. Johnson's well-disciplined regulars moved quickly over the mountainous terrain, aware that Brigadier General ten Broeck and 1,700 Albany County troops were close behind. The British won the race, and by the time the Albany levies reached Crown Point, all that could be seen were a few last bateaux disappearing down the lake.

The first Johnstown raid not only allowed Sir John to rescue his silver plate and other valuables buried at Johnson Hall, but the successful conclusion confirmed him in his conviction that a large-scale incursion with regular troops into the heartland of New York was feasible. In his short stay at Johnson Hall, he ordered an attack on Caughnawaga (Fonda) a few miles upriver from Johnstown. The village, like many more on the river's north bank, was undefended and burned easily. Caughnawaga happened to be the site of the first liberty pole in Tryon County. Johnson remembered, and he remembered the insolence of the rebels. During the next three months, while Joseph Brant destroyed Little Falls, Fort Plain, Canajoharie, Norman's Kill and Vroomansland on the Schoharie, Haldimand and Sir John designed a plan to level the valleys in the greatest raid of the war.

Since this was to be the payback for Sullivan's invasion, Haldimand had no difficulty enlisting Iroquois participation. He could count on Brant's corps, Butler's rangers, the King's Royal New Yorkers, companies of British regulars and Hesse-Hanau jägers, along with several loyalist detachments—in all, about 2,000 effectives. And with luck, these disciplined and seasoned campaigners would cut through Clinton's demoralized militia easily, encircling the Mohawk and Schoharie valleys in a simultaneous pincer attack.

Haldimand planned the attack for October, when harvest was over and grain and foodstuffs vital to Washington's famished army lay in barns awaiting transport. The destruction of the 1780 crop was to be British Canada's contribution to the war efforts of Henry Clinton and Lord Cornwallis. But Haldimand was anxious as well about possible attacks on Canada from a French fleet in the St. Lawrence and American troops above Albany. To obviate these threats his pincer would sweep through the forts on Champlain and Lake George to strike Ballston, south of Saratoga, a short march from Schenectady. This bold thrust would have the virtue of drawing the enemy's response northward and away from the main attack on the valleys, while also demolishing bases within range of Montreal. Command of the Champlain arm was wisely given to Major Carleton, already familiar with the terrain and experienced at working with native auxiliaries, and to Captain Munro of the King's Royal New Yorkers, whose assignment was to destroy Ballston and link up with the valley force. The arm sweeping towards the Schoharie from Oswego would be under the command of Lieutenant Colonel Sir John Johnson, accompanied by Captain Brant and his volunteers. Their task would be to enter the Schoharie in the south and march north to the Mohawk, burning everything in their way. Joining Munro near Schenectady, they would proceed together up the Mohawk Valley leveling towns, villages, crops, and farms. This raid would exit by way of the Onondaga River to Oswego.

Only a highly trained and superbly equipped force could think of undertaking a mission of such length and complexity on the edge of winter. Brant's Native Americans, inured to long travel by hidden paths through all seasons of the year, would be vital for screening and sustaining the long approach. For fighting power, Sir John would deploy companies of the 8th, 34th, and 53rd British line, a small artillery detachment, Lieutenant Colonel John Butler's rangers, and several contingents of loyalist troops. Old Smoke, Cornplanter (Seneca), Hung Face (Cayuga), Sagwarithra (Tuscarora), and Seth's Henry (Mohawk) were the native war chiefs whose warriors would fan out from the main column to fire settlements as Sir John passed. They were under instructions to spare women and children, but to kill any man found in arms.

The Oswego expedition was late in assembling and departing, and Sir John realized immediately that any junction with Munro or Carleton was unlikely. Since he knew where he was going and how to get there, this failure of coordination troubled him not at all. He would need luck to tear through the heart of New York with 1,000 men and get out again, and Sir John was feeling lucky. His boats carried him up the Onondaga River (today's Oswego River) into Onondaga Lake. Near the town, burned by the Americans the previous year, the raiders disembarked, sank their bateaux for safekeeping, and struck out bearing south and east.

Sir John's plan was to reach the headwaters of the Unadilla, about forty miles distant, descend the river to a point above the Susquehanna, follow Schenevus or Charlotte Creek northeast to Panther Creek (Kennanagara), and follow Panther Creek into the Schoharie just above the Upper Fort at Fultonham. The first stages of this route lay across Oneida lands made desolate by raids. Kanowarohare was a charred ruin, the surrounding fields abandoned and overgrown. Nearby villages were gone, burned to the ground, and travelers passing through this landscape for a day did so without meeting signs of life. Oneida who had survived the rage of the Senecas and Mohawks were clustered now outside the walls of Fort Stanwix for protection, or had relocated to filthy, impoverished camps in the direction of Albany. A few hundred had simply capitulated, turning up with hands out at Niagara, where Guy Johnson fed them on the condition that they renounce their alliance with the Americans. No prying eyes, therefore, saw the silent men climbing Chittenango gorge and marching eastward on the south road in the bright October sunlight.[56]

The march to the Schoharie covered nearly 160 miles of central New York—through forests, swamps, and mountainous terrain—taking only eight days to arrive at Sir John's first target. Along the way a network of Tory sympathizers supplied food, shelter, and directions. They also pointed the raiders to patriot homesteads. By the time the column reached the lower Unadilla and Butternuts district, there was no longer any need for stealth. Smoke from burning farms could be seen for miles around, and in Albany, Colonel William Malcolm of the New York levies was aware and alarmed at the size of the raid. Not that there was much he could do about it. Carleton had ambushed and annihilated a militia company at Bloody Pond and captured Fort George; he was demolishing villages on the upper Hudson that were only just recovering from Burgoyne's invasion. Munro had sacked Ballston and was retreating north to Canada with Albany militia hot on his heels. Malcolm had nothing to spare.

The farmers of the Schoharie Valley knew that a raid was coming, and they knew what a raid could do to their farms. In August, Brant's and Seth's Henry's Mohawks harrowed Vroomansland at the foot of Vroman's Nose, the Corn Mountain or *Onistagrawa* of the Iroquois. They caught people hoeing in the fields, women doing wash or cooking in their kitchens, and they slaughtered them with their children. About twenty houses were burned and twelve people murdered. Inhabitants would never forget August 9 as the date of the Vroomansland massacre. In the aftermath they gathered up the bodies found along the valley flats and buried them at the Upper Fort. Most were unidentifiable, and their gravestones read simply "Vroman."[57]

As a consequence of this experience, no one in October waited at home to learn what Sir John intended. As soon as word reached the valley of raiders coming in from Panther Creek, everyone fled to the Upper Fort at Fultonham. When the Tory column was spotted, the cannon in the blockhouse of the fort fired the alarm, and this sound, reverberating through the valley, warned settlers four miles away to flee into the Middle Fort outside Middleburgh, or old Weisersdorf.[58] From there, word spread like chain lightning north down the valley to the Lower Stone Fort outside Schoharie village, where a large body of militia gathered.

The Schoharie stockades were built in frontier style with logs at least a foot in diameter. They enclosed buildings at their center, often of stone, and were protected by blockhouses at two of their four corners. Their construction was proof against light artillery. At the Upper and Middle Forts, 200 militia were supposed to report on the alert to man loopholes and blockhouses. Each fort had a three-pounder cannon mounted in a blockhouse, and each was well supplied with powder and provisions. Sir John wasted no time attempting to subdue the Upper Fort, but aimed at the Middle, from where his forces might spread out north and south along Schoharie Creek. A day of skirmishing between patrols from the fort and companies of British regulars followed. Johnson ordered up his three-pound cannon and observed with disappointment how little effect mortars or artillery had on the fort's structure. On the second day he sent forward a party of truce led by Captain Andrew Thompson of Butler's rangers, hoping to bluff the garrison out of their works.

Inside the Middle Fort, Major Melanchton Woolsey of the New York levies was all for entertaining a parley; he commanded a few score state troops leavened with a detachment of Continentals and militia. They were opposing over 700 Tories and Indians. At this critical point Timothy Murphy of Morgan's rifles, a private, took it upon himself to advise Woolsey, his commanding officer, not to treat with the enemy. Woolsey was about to slap Murphy into irons when he realized that the fort's defenders were behind the rangy frontiersman and that Murphy's famous rifle was aimed at his chest. This was the rifle that sniped Brigadier Simon Fraser at Saratoga, helped Murphy escape from the ambush of Boyd's patrol at Geneseo, and shot down over two dozen Indians. Woolsey, of course, thought twice, and Murphy, climbing the wall, sent a ball winging at the truce party. Three times the brave Captain Thompson tried to deliver Sir John's message to the commandant of Middle Fort, and three times Murphy drove the flag-bearers back with murderous intent. He knew well what had happened to Boyd and Parker, and had no interest in surrendering to a vengeful enemy with memories of his exploits. Thus the insubordinate private saved Middle Fort.[59] Sir John dallied outside the walls only long enough to burn every house and barn in the neighborhood.

On the following day when Sir John appeared at the Lower Stone Fort four miles to the north, the valley behind him was shrouded in smoke from burning farms and fields. The weather was cold but dry; a strong west wind blew, and conflagrations set by the marauding Indians raced over fields of stubble and up the mountain draws. The smoke rising above the Schoharie was visible from the outskirts of Albany, where the smell of charred wood filled the afternoon air. Sir John fired his small cannon at the Stone Fort three times, leaving a ball embedded in the eaves of the roof, but this attack was meant only to pin the local militia inside the structure while parties of incendiaries fired the substantial village.[60] Once the houses and barns were nicely ablaze, the raid moved on, northward over an old Indian trail to Fort Hunter in the Mohawk Valley.

The great raid, reaching the Mohawk, seemed to pick up fresh energy from loyalists brought out of hiding with repressed resentments. Fort Hunter was soon destroyed with their help, and settlements all the way to Schenectady were set ablaze. Johnson now resolved to move westward along the north bank, cut two miles into the interior, and destroy the granary of Stone Arabia. This old Palatine community was celebrated for its waving fields of wheat, a beautiful church, and a way of life offensive to none. On October 19 the war came to Stone Arabia with a vengeance as Brant's vanguard crashed into a patrol of Massachusetts levies from the nearby Fort (Isaac) Paris.[61] The patrol fell back onto the support of Colonel John Brown who, with 380 Tryon County volunteers, Oneidas, and Massachusetts levies, was forming a line to stop the raiders.

Brown was a veteran officer; he had served extensively in the first stages of the invasion of Canada, and in 1777 had helped to cut Burgoyne's communications, capturing Mount Hope and the outer works of Ticonderoga. He was a distant relative by marriage of Benedict Arnold, whom he heartily detested. In late 1780, Brown was proud of having perceived Arnold's true colors before other men realized his perfidy.[62] None of this mattered much now as Sir John attacked him behind a wall at the bottom of a hollow—a miserable position to defend while outnumbered two to one. Brown was shot off his horse and killed as Brant and Butler's rangers flanked the American position and rolled up the defenders. If Brown thought he was buying time for Colonel Van Rensselaer's Albany militia to reach him, he did not buy enough. His defending farmers and militia lost 100 combatants in dead, wounded, and captured. They abandoned their colonel's body and fled without removing vital papers from his pockets. Sir John would shortly know the disposition of Colonel Van Rensselaer's levies and militia now closing on him from the east. Brown died at age thirty-six on the exact day and hour of his birth.[63]

The first field engagement of the raid was over and won, but the second, more dangerous to Sir John by far, was about to begin as Van Rensselaer's forces negotiated the narrow road at Anthony's Nose and groped west to find the raiders before they could cross to the south side of the river.[64] It was late in the afternoon by the time the militia, weary with marching and hungry, came within range of the enemy. Along the north bank they absorbed the Oneidas of Lt Colonel Louis (Atayataghronghta) and troops of the Canajoharie militia, and moved into houses and hedgerows between Fort Nellis and the post road two miles west of Fort Klock. Sir John could not attempt to cross the river without dislodging this force on his left, and ordered a general assault by the Royal Yorkers and British infantry against the forming Americans. Their attack was driven back handily, and as the Tories and Indians dug in to meet Van Rensselaer's counterattack, Colonel Dubois, commanding the American right, flanked Sir John's position and routed his native auxiliaries. The Iroquois fled the field and opened the way for Van Rensselaer to sweep the enemy into the river. The British suffered heavy casualties, but Sir John's luck held. The autumn day was nearly done, and the American commander, concerned with the general confusion in his ranks and the growing darkness, withdrew his troops at the moment of victory. He bivouacked three miles to the rear, waiting for morning, while of course Sir John seized the respite to rush his several hundred men over the river and set them on their way to Onondaga and the waiting boats. The Battle of Klock's Field ended with no positive results to show except the capture of the raiders' three-pounder cannon and a score of wounded infantry and Indians.[65] A more decisive commander than Van Rensselaer might have finished Sir John on the spot, and in doing so saved New York another year of agony.

In all of its parts, the great raid of October 1780 covered close to 900 miles in an astonishingly short period. Sir John claimed to have destroyed several hundred thousand bushels of wheat, several thousand head of livestock, and many more structures: houses, barns, mills, warehouses, and factories than Sullivan's campaign had. What was more, he and Carleton returned to Canada with hundreds of scalps and numerous prisoners. Over the span of fourteen months, from the commencement of Sullivan's invasion of Indian country to the conclusion of Johnson's sweep of the Mohawk and Schoharie valleys, the new State of New York suffered devastating casualties and destruction. From Geneseo to Esopus, from Skenesboro to the Allegheny foothills, settlements and communities of all kinds—Native American, African American, European American—were ravaged and torched. The cost of the damage was incalculable, the lives lost and disrupted immeasurable. From the edge of the frontier to a few miles outside Albany, huge swaths of burned-over land were visible before the winter snows covered them, and across the Mohawk and Schoharie valleys little enough food was found to feed survivors, let alone ship provisions to Washington's starving Continentals. No wonder that the first months of 1781 would bring mutiny and discontent in the cantonments at Morristown and Pompton, New Jersey.

The news was nowhere good for patriots as 1780 passed into 1781. In August, Gates succeeded in losing the army of the Southern Department, Charleston was lost, and galling defeats were inflicted on American forces at Lenud's Ferry and Waxhaws. In December, General Nathaniel Greene arrived in North Carolina to take command of a demoralized army that was ill-clothed, ill-nourished, and ill-armed. No one was certain what Greene could do to reverse the tide of defeat. And in New York, Governor George Clinton wrote to Congress:

> We are now arrived at the year 1781, deprived of a great Portion of our most valuable and well inhabited Territory, numbers of our Citizens have been barbarously butchered by ruthless Hand of the Savages, many are carried away into Captivity, vast numbers entirely ruined, and these with their Families become a heavy Burthen to the distressed Remainder; the frequent Calls on the Militia has capitally diminished our Agriculture in every Part of the State. ... We are not in a Condition to raise Troops for the Defence of our Frontier, and if we were, our Exertions for the common cause have so effectually drained and exhausted us, that we should not have it in our Power to pay and subsist them. In short, Sir, without correspondent Exertions in other States and without Aid from those for whom we have not hesitated to sacrifice all, we shall soon approach to the Verge of Ruin.[66]

There was no exaggeration in Clinton's complaint. New York State was bankrupt, its capacity to export food sharply diminished. New York could no longer defend itself, or if so, just barely. Yet the dark night of the national cause was nearing an end. One year from the date on which Sir John broke into the Schoharie Valley (October 19), Cornwallis's troops marched out of Yorktown to surrender. Along Tenonanatche, this last year of the war would see untold suffering among the valley's survivors before a glimmer of hope appeared.

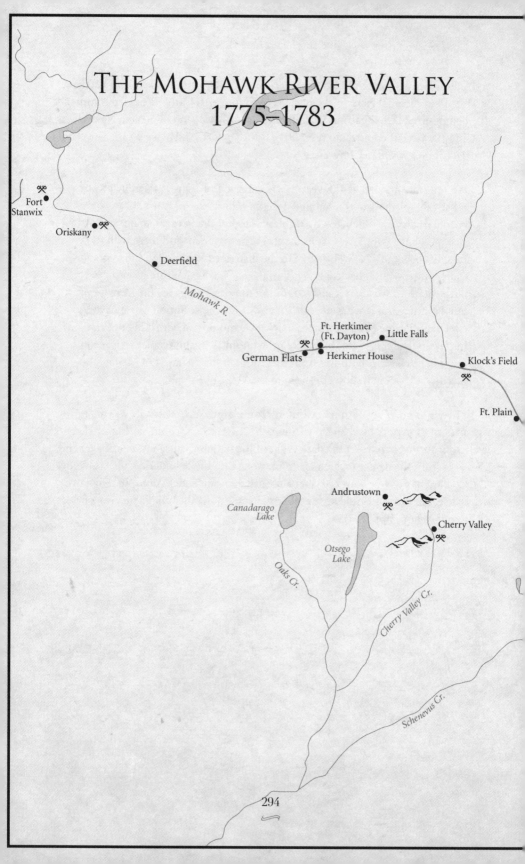

THE MOHAWK RIVER VALLEY
1775–1783

Fort
Stanwix

Oriskany

Deerfield

Mohawk R.

Ft. Herkimer
(Ft. Dayton)

Little Falls

German Flats

Herkimer House

Klock's Field

Ft. Plain

Andrustown

*Canadarago
Lake*

*Otsego
Lake*

Cherry Valley

Oaks Cr.

Cherry Valley Cr.

Schenevus Cr.

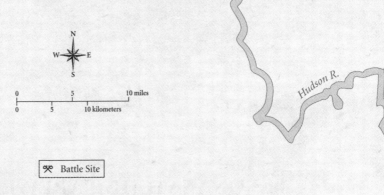

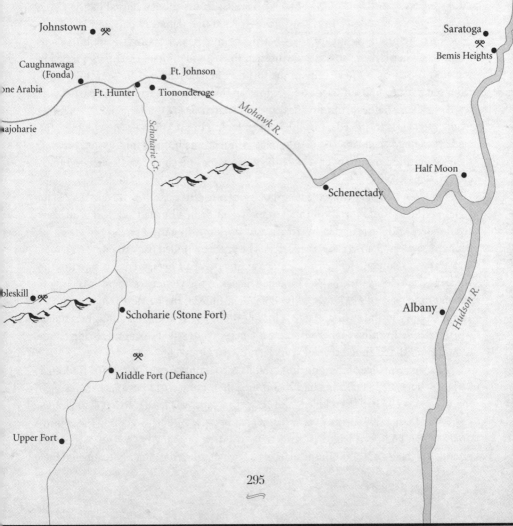

During the eighteenth century the valley communities stretched from Albany to Fort Stanwix, from Lake Otsego in the south to Johnstown in the north. The great raids of 1780 and 1781 entered the valley beyond Stanwix, swept up the Schoharie to Johnstown, and exited to the west.

Mapping Specialists, Ltd., Madison, Wisconsin.

Johnstown

Caughnawaga
(Fonda)

one Arabia

Ft. Hunter   Tiononderoge   Ft. Johnson

najoharie

Schoharie Cr.

Mohawk R.

Saratoga

Bemis Heights

Half Moon

Schenectady

bleskill

Schoharie (Stone Fort)

Middle Fort (Defiance)

Albany

Hudson R.

Upper Fort

⁂ 12 ⁂

TENONANATCHE FAREWELL

After a winter of heavy snowfalls, the Mohawk flooded in the spring, sweeping away portions of Fort Stanwix's walls. To the misery caused by the rising waters was added a fire of suspicious origin that damaged barracks and parapets. Even before these misfortunes befell, the inmates of Stanwix were bitter and mutinous. They lacked provisions, winter uniforms, and military essentials. Firewood was now so scarce in the vicinity of the fort that fatigue parties were sent miles away from the walls to find sufficient timber to keep the garrison warm. These parties suffered steady casualties from hostiles, and on March 2, 1781, a large detachment of woodcutters was surprised and wiped out by Joseph Brant.[1] In their wretchedness the soldiers blamed their officers, themselves, the turncoats in their midst, but above all their do-nothing commander—he of the great name and small results, General Robert Van Rensselaer.

That Van Rensselaer faced a board of inquiry for his handling of New York State levies at Klock's Field meant nothing to men penned in a burned-out fort eroded by river waters and surrounded by Tories and Iroquois. In early May, to the alarm of Mohawk settlers, Stanwix was evacuated. The garrison pulled back to Fort Herkimer, and Stanwix's gates, defended since 1777 at great cost of lives, were left open to the wilderness. No longer were there Oneida villages in the vicinity or many settlements left standing west of Herkimer to be defended. Indeed, the hardest thing to find in Tryon County in the spring of 1781, Joseph Brant could attest, was an intact house worth razing.[2] In ruins, Stanwix became a sanctuary for wild beasts and roving bands of raiders until reclaimed several years later by the United States.[3]

As a consequence of raids during 1780, Tryon County reported that 700 buildings had been burned, 354 families had abandoned their homes, 613 persons had deserted to the enemy, 197 had been killed, and 121 taken captive. These were civilian casualties. More than 1,200 farms were uncultivated because of enemy action. Three hundred women had been widowed, and 1,200 children orphaned.[4] "A land nature had intended to be lovely and bountiful," Larry Lowenthal writes, "had been turned into a bloodstained, fearful place. Instead of solid homesteads surrounded by rich fields, a succession of 24 ominous forts marked the 80-mile route up the Mohawk."[5]

Forts Nellis, Frey, Klock, and Keyser, all still standing, were examples of domestic buildings converted into blockhouses to shelter the local population. Forts Plain, Planck, Paris, and Rensselaer were militia installations garrisoned and protected by stockades. Planting fields at any distance from these fortified points were often left fallow in 1781 as too risky to cultivate. Even in the vicinity of the forts one man stood guard while another plowed, both ready to flee for safety at the first sign of marauders. Life in the cramped, dirty forts, filled with squalling children, communal cooking and living, was harsh in the extreme, and those who could escape the conditions seized at the opportunity. They moved east to the safer Hudson Valley or to western Massachusetts. The frontier, as Van Schaick had feared, was falling to pieces.

Tenonanatche was not just a place of white settlement; it was a world of Iroquois families as well, and in 1781 these were equally desperate and destitute. The Mohawk upper and lower castles had been fought over and torched several times, and by 1781 were largely uninhabitable.[6] After raids, the few Native Americans remaining in proximity to the white towns were often caught up and molested in revenge for harms done by their tribe. Little wonder then that many had decamped for the west or for British protection at Fort Niagara. The case of the Oneidas was especially pitiful. Because many, though not all, had supported the Americans, their villages west and south of Stanwix had been destroyed by British forces and their allies in retaliation. They were thrown back onto the slender charity of their friends for shelter and sustenance. For a time the Oneidas found safety beneath the walls of Stanwix, but by late 1780 they were relocating to camps for displaced people east of Schenectady. François-Jean de Beauvoir, Marquis de Chastellux, a major general with the French Forces, inspected New York in December and wrote of a visit to one of these camps:

> The Indian village Mr. Glen conducted me to is nothing but an assemblage of miserable huts in the woods, along the road to Albany. He took me into the hut of a savage from the Sault Saint Louis, who had long lived at Montreal and spoke good French. These huts are like our barracks in time of war, or like those built in vineyards or orchards, when the fruit is ripe and has to be watched at night. The framework consists only of two uprights and one crosspole; this covered with a matted roof, but is well lined within by a quantity of bark. ... In addition to the savage who spoke French, there was in this hut a squah, who had taken him as her second husband, and was bringing up a child by her first husband; two old men composed the remainder of this family, which had a melancholy and poor appearance. ... All that I could learn from the Colonel [Glen], or from the Indians, was that the state gives them rations of meat and sometimes of flour; that they also possess

some lands, where they sow Indian corn, and go hunting for skins, which they exchange for rum. They are sometimes employed in war, and are commended for their bravery and fidelity.[7]

In fact, "there were fifty-four women, ninety-three men, and two hundred fifty-nine children in this camp destitute of both food and clothing and reduced to the indignity of receiving whatever charitable handouts the general poverty of the countryside permitted." As Barbara Graymont observes, not all of them would survive the winter: "Lieutenant John Sagoharase of the Oneida Wolf Clan was one who perished as a result of the miserable living conditions."[8] Sagoharase had been awarded a battlefield commission by General Schuyler. The Oneida at the start of 1781 were declining in numbers. Casualties among the warriors had been especially heavy, and cold and famine took a steady toll of women and children. Congress and the United States, Schuyler argued, were honor-bound to remember the services of loyal Indians and, as Indian Agent for the Northern Department, he petitioned Congress tirelessly to appropriate funds for blankets and clothing, food and other necessaries. In the meantime, he met the need of such Oneidas as the Marquis encountered out of his own pockets, which indeed were not as deep as they had once been.

Schuyler thus lived to inherit the burden that Sir William Johnson put down only in death. His government ignored and rebuffed him until, on February 24, he turned to the New York State Legislature with a last offer. He would advance 1,000 Spanish dollars to the state on his personal credit toward the purchase of clothing for the Indians, if only the state would appropriate the balance required to meet the obligation. In the event, the state came through with half of what Schuyler asked, and Congress with a recommendation that $6,464 in Continental money be drawn on the Treasury of New York to purchase clothing for these "unfortunates." By December, the date of the Marquis's visit to Schenectady, neither food nor clothing had arrived from Congress. Merchants who had agreed to provide for the Indians now declined to do so as the state treasury defaulted payment and the Continental currency fell to near worthless.[9] That winter many Oneida families were housed in barracks at Schenectady that they shared with state troops. Women and young girls would be raped in these barracks, and wounded Oneida war veterans beaten for being "filthy" Indians. In this bitter season, it seemed to many that America's loyal friends fared far worse than America's enemies.

The Marquis was fortunate to avoid becoming a war prisoner himself. Even in a wintry December, raids continued in the neighborhood of Albany, as he reports:

As we were preparing to set out, one of these savages entered his [Colonel Glens'] house: he was a messenger dispatched by their hunters, and came to announce that a party of one hundred and fifty Senecas and several Tories had been seen a few miles from Saratoga, and that they had even carried off one of their young men. This messenger spoke very good French and very bad English; born of a Canadian, or perhaps European, father, he had mixed with the savages, amongst whom he had lived twenty years, from preference for this unrestricted life (*libertinage*) rather than from any other motive. The news he brought was not very encouraging.[10]

What strikes this foreign visitor, removed from routine dangers, is the conditional nature of border warfare. Along the frontier, mortal outcomes often depended on the plural relationships of adversaries. Native Americans might speak perfect French and remember the Quebec of New France, or be English to the core and communicants of Queen Anne's chapel, or American and followers of Samuel Kirkland, or Dutch- and German-leaning in their modes of worship and allegiance. Of course, they could also follow the old ways, fighting to preserve their spirit world against European influences. Some were allied to settlers by blood and kinship, by economic necessity and partnership, or estranged from their neighbors by perceived wrongs and misunderstandings. Whoever they were, however, in 1781 they inhabited a country disintegrating before their eyes.

The Tuscarora and Stockbridge people, closely associated with the Oneidas, withdrew to the upper Chenango Valley, beyond harm, where they could build villages and find ample game. Outside of Fort Niagara, Senecas, Mohawks, Cayugas, and Onondagas, still grieving for towns destroyed in 1779, moved to Buffalo Creek and attempted to restore their shattered communities. In the autumn of 1780, they succeeded in harvesting their first crops. But very few would ever return to Tenonanatche or make the long journey to Onondaga again. With British and Tory help, the Iroquois had driven the frontier back, erasing farms and white settlements. Yet they benefited not at all from this bloody triumph. During the process, the unity of the Six Nations was lost, and where once the Haudenosaunee, People of the Long House, ruled unchallenged, they now passed furtively in the dark as feared and hated interlopers. Too many irreplaceable warriors had been lost. Nor did the Iroquois leadership fail to see that Britain no longer mustered sufficient military might in Canada to conquer and reclaim Tenonanatche. The indefatigable settlers would endure and prevail. The Marquis de Chastellux anticipates the consequences:

> As an advanced guard, they [the Iroquois] are formidable, as an army they are nothing. But their cruelty seems to augment in proportion to their decrease in numbers; it is such as to render it impossible for the Americans to consent to have them longer for neighbors; and a necessary consequence of peace, if favorable to Congress, will be their total destruction, or at least their exclusion from all the country this side of the lakes.[11]

From the perspective of white settlers, the spring of 1781 was all about enduring. Six years of strife had brought nothing but chaos and devastation to the rich river valleys of New York. Even General Schuyler, in his mansion on the outskirts of Albany, was not safe from intruders in the night. On a summer evening, Schuyler and his family were gathered in the drawing room when the guards warned him of attack. The family bolted the doors and windows and retreated to the upstairs rooms while Schuyler found his pistols and took up position at a window. The war party was smashing at the door when Schuyler's wife Catherine remembered a baby left in its rocker on the ground floor. An older daughter, Margaret, ran downstairs and snatched up her younger sister just as the raiders crashed through. She fled up the stairs and was narrowly missed by a tomahawk that buried itself in the banister. Schuyler's gunfire from an upper window attracted attention, and before the war party could find and make away with him, they were rousted out of the house by the reinforced guards. It had been a close call with potentially great consequences, but what the Schuyler family experienced was also being inflicted on families everywhere across central New York in 1781.[12]

A civil war brings out the worst in a community, and the strife raging across Tenonanatche turned up its share of thugs, assassins, incendiaries, and sociopaths. Like the Missouri-Kansas border clashes of eighty years later, formal military campaigns seemed to give way to guerilla actions, which eventually devolved into mindless banditry and pillage. The fighting among the fortified houses on the Mohawk was often of this kind, and wherever a farm was surprised and a family massacred, Joseph Brant received the blame. In fact, Brant during much of 1781 was engaged against George Rogers Clark in the Ohio country. In late August he ambushed an American force led by Colonel Archibald Lochry on the trail from Fort Pitt to Sandusky and killed or captured the entire detachment. But Brant had many imitators who would meet little resistance riding through the tormented valleys at the head of a dozen brazen renegades. Often as not, these bands were composed of whites, some few defiant Tories, but many best described as border ruffians and outlaws. They left no witnesses to their depredations, and they scalped and mutilated victims to place the blame on Indians.

Clashes of irregular and regular forces were constant along the frontier. Private Henry Grim, in an affidavit filed for a service pension fifty years later, tells of such a moment in July on Steele Creek:

> About two months after my arrival my Captain and about eighteen or twenty others, including myself, went out on a scouting party towards Fort Schuyler to a place called Steele's Creek about three miles from Fort Herkimer. There we were discovered by a party of Tories. A skirmish ensued in which Capt. Ellsworth, Sergeant Montgomery and one John Sauts, a private, were killed. There had formerly been a settlement at Steele's Creek but previous to the time that I, Henry Grim, and my associates reached there, it had been laid in

ashes. I, Henry Grim, was wounded in this skirmish by a rifle ball in my side. That the party returned to Fort Dayton but next day a party was sent out to bring in the bodies of the deceased which were interred in the old burial ground of the Old Stone Church near Fort Herkimer.[13]

On July 2 a state ranger detachment under the command of Captain Solomon Woodworth left Fort Dayton for a patrol up West Canada Creek. Woodworth led forty-nine men accompanied by six Oneida scouts. The West Canada, more river than creek, offered a difficult but viable route out of the Adirondacks into the heart of German Flats; acquainted with reports of enemy activity along the river, Woodworth set out to sweep the upper reaches. According to the reports of survivors, the scouts warned that the tracks being followed showed a party twice the size of Woodworth's and advised that the rangers call for reinforcements. Woodward insisted on pressing forward fearlessly in the tradition of Oriskany. "The chicken-hearted can stay behind," he told his troops and promptly marched into an ambush across Kast's Bridge in the vicinity of Fairfield. These were not renegades Woodworth encountered, but a substantial war party of Onondagas and Cayugas led by a British officer, Lieutenant Jonathan Clement, of Guy Johnson's Indian Department. The first volley from the raiders killed or wounded half of Woodworth's men, and in the brief fight ensuing, the captain and ten more of his command fell. The Oneidas extricated themselves and reached Fort Dayton safely, but only ten of the rangers returned. In the 1850s bones were found in a farmer's field near where the ambush had been sprung and were reburied beneath an old beech tree outside Fairfield. To the end of the war, the woodland trails north and south of the Mohawk remained perilous.[14]

A few days after the Steele Creek ambush on the south bank of the river and the slaughter of the Woodworth patrol on the north bank, a major raid swept into the small village of Currytown, two miles south of Canajoharie. Currytown had been brushed by raiders before, but the inhabitants had fled to a stone house fortified by Henry Lewis and escaped serious harm. This time they were caught in the fields at noontime by a party of over 400 raiders led by a local Tory, John Doxtader. The attackers were after scalps and plunder, and as they broke out of the forests, they were shooting. More than three dozen people were killed or captured before they could reach the safety of their improvised fort. Their homes were looted and then burned. The attackers loaded the stolen goods into farm wagons and moved upland, heading south towards Cobleskill. This unsavory crew was unusually large and dangerous. Near Sharon Springs, surrounded on several sides by marshlands, they camped for the night of July 9.

Moving toward them, climbing the escarpment that encloses the Mohawk Valley, were 170 soldiers led by Colonel Marinus Willett, the hero of Fort Stanwix. That spring, at Governor Clinton's urging, Willett relinquished his commission in the Continentals to accept command of the Mohawk Valley's militia. What he discovered on stepping down to this responsibility was that of the 2,500 militiamen on the rolls of Tryon County at the beginning of the war, only 800 remained vaguely available. Of the original 2,500, Willett wrote: "I don't think I shall give a very wild account if I say, that one third have been killed, or carried away captive by the enemy; one third removed to the interior places of the country; and one third deserted to the enemy."[15] That Clinton could provide this famously energetic officer with no more than 170 regular troops spoke to the exhaustion and bankruptcy of the American cause in New York. Willett got what the governor had left to give.

Albany County, as hard-pressed as Tryon County, had sent its only companies north to General Gansevoort at Fort George. There, British raids were expected daily, and the prospect of open war between Vermont and New York loomed still. Many Yorkers in the Champlain corridor were fed up with Washington's war. They were ready to defect to Montreal along with like-thinking Vermont discontents. The only force available to block a potential march on Albany was at Fort George, and Peter Gansevoort could spare nothing to help his old comrade in arms.

In the early morning of July 10, having missed an opportunity to attack Doxtader at night, Willett learned from his Oneida scouts the location of the enemy encampment. A single path led onto the solid ground surrounded by the cedar marshes, and that entrance was heavily guarded. The New York levies were outnumbered better than two to one; to assault the enemy frontally seemed suicidal. Willett, determined to attack, opted for a reverse ambush. He sent ten men straight into the enemy's bivouac with orders to fire on the sentries, then turn and run. As expected, Doxtader's mob left their breakfast fires to chase down these intruders, and as they emerged from the marsh, ran head first into the massed muskets of Willett's troops. Many fell in the first volley, and survivors, retreating out of the crescent of fire, were surprised to be overtaken by troops advancing at bayonet point behind an exuberant leader. Willett's magic had begun to transform his New Yorkers. Where they had never thought of going, he would lead them, and suddenly they were rediscovering the drill, the precision, the discipline they had lost in the face of repeated defeats. Rapidly loading and firing, they swept through the Tory encampment like an avenging wind, taking prisoners, recapturing loot plundered at Currytown, and pushing aside the shocked Iroquois. Doxtader's Native Americans lost more than twenty warriors in the counter-ambush, and more as the encampment was overrun, while the white renegades taken alive paid for their brutalities at Currytown with summary execution. This did not prevent Doxtader and a considerable number of raiders from slipping away, but they fled the swamps of Sharon without their belongings or provisions for the long journey home.[16] The message they would deliver to Governor Haldimand was that the Mohawk Valley was aroused and fighting back.

Admittedly, the Battle of Sharon Springs was a small skirmish in the larger scheme of the war, but coming when it did, Willett's victory lifted morale across central New York, reminding patriots that if their government was helpless, they themselves were not. Christian Schell, a veteran of Oriskany, was attacked in his fortified cabin by Donald McDonald, a Tory leader of refugee Scots. McDonald arrived at the cabin door with more than sixty Tories and Indians, but Schell refused to surrender. While Christian and his three sons fired, his wife and daughters loaded. When the smoke cleared, McDonald had withdrawn with his wounded, leaving eleven dead behind. The Schells set an example for other families scattered in isolated homesteads across Tenonanatche.[17]

Farther up the valley, in September, a company of militia ambushed the infamous Captain Caldwell of Butler's rangers leading 100 Tories and Indians from Niagara. The raiders suffered sharp losses, and with their surprise visit spoiled, they fled to the west without inflicting further damage.[18] Suddenly the moribund militia was waking up under the prodding of Willett. After Sharon Springs, those disgusted with the ineptitude of their appointed leaders resolved to fight for a man in whom they could believe. Willett was a radical Whig, a fervent revolutionary who in 1775 had come out to fight the British in the streets of Manhattan with his bare fists. For six hard years he had slogged on for "the rights of man," making soldiers from the men he was given and sharing their hardships in innumerable cold and hungry camps. They knew him to be more than just courageous; he was lucky in battle. The question now was whether he could recruit and train them fast enough to shield the valley against another devastating raid from Canada. The hour was late for both sides, and Haldimand stood ready to throw his regular regiments into one last attempt to smash Schenectady and capture Albany.

Later, Willett would describe the great raid of October 1781 as "a fine Detachment of Troops [sent] upon such a Paltry Business," but he would also admit that his scouting system, based on Oneida eyes, failed totally. Almost 700 raiders under the overall command of Major John Ross of the King's Royal New Yorkers and Walter Butler of Butler's rangers landed at Oswego and followed the Oswego River into Oneida Lake. Nothing prevented them from landing at the mouth of Chittenango Creek and pressing inland beyond the scenic falls to a high plateau with a clear trail to the defiles of the Mohawk Valley. These approaches had once been warded by Fort Stanwix, but Stanwix now was abandoned. The Oneidas who might have spotted this formidable force moving up were far to the east. Willett had no idea that the enemy was upon him until Ross and Butler swept through Currytown, burning what Doxtader had left intact. They next ravaged Warrensbush, where Sir William Johnson first resided in the valley, and made their way along the south bank of the Mohawk towards the Johnstown crossings.

The rising columns of smoke told everyone in the valley that a major raid was coming in, but this attack owed little to Native American stealth. Only 100 Indians participated, and Ross later said of them, "the promised succor of the Indians is a

mere illusion; they are the refuse of different tribes with no leader."[19] Without prominent native leadership or tribal support, the enterprise depended almost entirely on
veteran companies of Johnson's Royal Yorkers, the 8th, 34th, and 84th British regiments,
and four companies of Butler's rangers. These soldiers navigated the valley's wood-
lands with all the speed and ease of Iroquois warriors, and while they brought no cannon—having learned from Sir John's mishaps the previous year—they far surpassed
Willett's force in fighting quality.

Yet, for all their advantages, they succeeded only in burning out the last remaining tract of intact farmland in the valley and storming into Johnstown. What happened to the plan to reach Schenectady or Albany? It appears that Ross feared being
"Burgoyned"—balked and surrounded by an enemy swelling in numbers. The chase
was up behind him, and troops moving down from the Champlain corridor could
trap him in the flat, piney country west of Schenectady. He opted to cross the river
into Johnstown instead, destroy patriot homes and depots, and set up headquarters at
Johnson Hall. This was where the Tryon County militia found him.

Willett first learned of the raid on October 24 at his headquarters in Canajoharie. Over the next twenty-four hours he raced to intercept Ross, calling in troops from
where he could. Governor Clinton had begged Massachusetts to send troops to the
New York frontier, and fortunately for Willett, Major Aaron Rowley had arrived a few
days before with a small detachment of Massachusetts State levies. Between the long-
suffering Tryon militia, Rowley's 60 troops, and contingents of Continentals and New
York levies, Willett was able to rush to Johnstown with 400 men—200 or so fewer than
Ross and Butler had gathered at Johnson Hall. There were no preliminaries, no negotiations. Willett threw his troops straight into the British lines forming outside the
village and then, defying conventional wisdom, divided his inferior force in the face
of the enemy. He sent Rowley's command, augmented with New Yorkers, to sweep left
around the flank while he and the Tryon militia advanced with artillery support from
the right. Their artillery support was provided by a single six-pound piece that would
be captured and recaptured several times during the afternoon.

Private Henry Grim, with the Tryon militia, remembered the fight a half century
later as violent and confusing. He was never aware of fleeing, but he admitted to "being
overpowered and driven out of the bush by Tories and Indians."[20] The Battle of Johnstown was a set-piece fight in relatively open terrain, where militia could not be counted
on to hold their ground. Daniel Morgan at Cowpens and Nathaniel Greene at Guil-
ford Courthouse bargained with their militia for two well-delivered volleys, after which
the volunteers were free to flee. Willett got many more volleys out of his militia before
they broke and ran. But they would break, he knew, as they had on every major battlefield of the war once the noise and confusion of battle overwhelmed their senses. He
and his officers did not try to stop them. They dashed back to the village instead and
met the winded men as they straggled in shamefacedly. Calming them and restoring
their ranks, Willett led Tryon County back into the struggle just in time to save Rowley.

As Willett's militia broke in front of the advancing British, Rowley slammed into the right flank of the enemy with his 100 men, loosing volleys of musketry through the hedges and bushes. This staggered Ross and forced him to wheel right to face the new threat. His forces were pummeling Rowley when, in the gloomy gray light of the late-October day, Willett's reorganized militia returned to the field, recaptured their artillery piece, and fired repeatedly into the confused and crumbling left flank of the British. Redcoats were falling in heaps, and Tories, charging the militia in desperation, now found that Willett's revitalized forces outnumbered them. As daylight faded, Ross and Butler withdrew towards the north, leaving many British soldiers dead or wounded on the field. Tory casualties were somewhat less, but still severe, and this at a cost to the Americans of about 100 dead or wounded. Both sides were badly mauled at Johnstown. But Ross and Butler were far from home, gravely weakened, and low on ammunition. They had marched 125 miles, destroyed three towns, and fought one pitched battle. Now the trick would be to escape Willett before he could rest, reorganize, and mount a full pursuit.

Willett calculated that the raiders would cross to the south bank of the river and attempt to leave by the route they had arrived. He sent a ranger party to find their boats on Oneida Lake and destroy them. As it happened, this mission failed. But Butler had no intention of retracing his approach through angry and aroused communities; he proposed escaping along the north bank of the river into the Adirondacks. This move took Willett by surprise. On October 26, Willett crossed to the south bank of the Mohawk with about 200 troops and rushed to Fort Herkimer, where he could find additional reinforcements to interdict the enemy. At German Flats he learned that Ross and Butler had eluded him and were making for West Canada Creek. They could either press on from there to Raquette Lake in hopes of finding the lake chain free of ice or sidle northwest towards the Black River and reach Oswego from the east. Willett realized that if he could not make contact with the fleeing raiders, his hard-fought victory at Johnstown would count no more than Van Rensselaer's dilatory efforts at Klock's Field the year before. But the countryside was turning out, beginning to savor his triumph over British soldiers. At Fort Dayton, from where Nicholas Herkimer had marched, frontiersmen hungry for revenge had begun to arrive and enlist. When Willett's column moved out on October 28, his force numbered over 500 muskets and was accompanied by 60 Oneida scouts.[21] The Oneidas were like hounds to the chase, and where they could cut in on the raid's stragglers there were likely to be few survivors.

At first, Willett's route followed poor Captain Woodworth's path, but Ross and Butler stayed out ahead with the bulk of their companies. Intermittent snow had begun to fall, the temperature was dropping, and the forest was endless and dismal. The Americans followed the enemy's path by discarded packs and personal effects. The enemy ran, according to a letter from Willett to Clinton, "in an Indian file upon a constant trot, and one man's being Knocked in the head or falling off into the woods never stoped the Progress of his Neighbour."[22] Yet, moving through the accumulating snow as fast they could, Willett's force never quite reached Ross. Some distance above today's Hinckley Reservoir, at a place on the West Canada called the Jersey Fields, the British column struggled across the turbulent stream. Gunshots were heard as the forward elements of the pursuit sniped at the escaping soldiers. Willett did not arrive until this action was long over and the column far ahead. What he saw on the far bank of the stream was a mutilated body already partially shrouded by snow. The man, according to Willett, had been shot in the head, tomahawked in the face, and scalped. The pockets of the corpse yielded a strange document, again according to Willett. The paper he read on the banks of the West Canada, October 30, 1781, in a rising blizzard, informed him that Walter N. Butler was commissioned an Ensign in the King's 8th Regiment of Foot effective June 1777.

What now seems certain is that Captain Walter Butler, alleged monster of the Mohawk, was killed by an Oneida Indian at age twenty-nine on West Canada Creek with a shot to the head. Everything else about his life and death is open to interpretation. Willett did not record his experiences until forty years later, in his late eighties, and by then had grown vague and forgetful. Why his adversary was carrying an old commission, and what happened to the document, has never been settled. Another variant of the story tells that the paper announced Butler's death sentence, passed by military tribunal at Fort Dayton during the summer of 1777; Willett had presided over that court martial. This neat piece of irony is complemented by another legend. The Oneida who shoots Butler charges across the creek to find him still alive. Butler begs for quarter. The Oneida raises his hatchet and says, "I give you Sherry Valley quarter," and strikes him dead. Butler, of course, was identified with the massacre at Cherry Valley. His body lay where it fell on the banks of the West Canada beneath a blanket of snow. Willett's frontiersmen passed it in pursuit of Ross, dishonoring it each in his own manner. When they were gone, loyalist friends smuggled the corpse back down to the Mohawk and transported it to Schenectady, where in the dead of night the body was interred in the nave of St. George's Anglican Church. According to tradition, the body rests today in an unmarked grave beneath the second pew off the right aisle of St. George's.[23] In the divided house of Tenonanatche, one person's heinous war criminal became another's courageous partisan worthy of a respectful burial.

The connection of Walter Butler with an Anglican church built by Sir William Johnson in the heyday of the Mohawk barony resonates with border loyalties. The first rector, the Reverend Doty, fled to Canada to become the chaplain of a loyalist regiment. The congregation, comprised largely of merchants and mill owners, included a number of crypto-loyalists, some few of whom were willing to bury the Tory in secret. The Butlers were hardly pious Christians, but they were men of property, deeply devoted Crown subjects, and loyal members of the Church of England. After Walter's death, American troops stripped St. George's of ecclesiastical furnishings and turned the building into a military barracks—without finding the elusive corpse. As a punishment for this perceived intransigence, the parish would struggle for many years after the war to reestablish itself.

As for Ross and the retreating British raiders, they suffered steady casualties in their flight until Willett called off the pursuit. By then the weather was worsening, the Americans were strung out and disorganized, and the enemy had doomed himself to punishment by nature. As Willett observed, "to the Compassion of a starving Wilderness, we left them in a fair way of Receiving a Punishment better suited to their Merit than a musket ball, a Tomahawk or Captivity."[24] No one is certain how many of Ross's troops reached Canada or died in the retreat up West Canada Creek. Several hundred regulars arrived at forts Oswego and Oswegatchie over the following weeks desperate from exhaustion and exposure. They arrived to news that even before they engaged Willett at Johnstown, Lord Cornwallis had surrendered his army at Yorktown. The catastrophe was complete. The world had turned upside down, and nothing would ever be the same again for British, Tories, or Native Americans in New York. The last full-dress battle of the Revolution had been fought at Johnstown, and the King's men had lost.

Along the Mohawk, where violence continued to break out sporadically until 1783,[25] the fear of raids, Indian war, and invasion lifted slowly, while at Niagara, where many could not accept the fact that the war was over, preparations for a campaign in 1782 continued. Brant led a large raiding party out from Oswego in the spring of 1782, but he had no sooner reached Oneida Lake than a messenger from Governor Haldimand called him back. Delicate treaty talks were underway and had reached a critical stage. This treaty, once negotiated and the terms published, would make Haldimand gasp and Joseph Brant break down and cry.

Refugees returning to the Mohawk Valley in the period between 1783 and 1784 found hardly a barn or house standing from Fonda to German Flats. Johnstown was severely damaged, Canajoharie had been burned to the ground, and dozens of hamlets were only discernible amidst the sprouting weeds by their charred timbers and toppled stones. Graves lined the dusty roads, and in the deep forest glades, skulls glinted in the moonlight. Few crops had been planted after 1782, and livestock had vanished long ago. The bones of cattle and sheep dotted the green meadows, and burned-out farm wagons clogged the country lanes. Game was scarce in the years following the war, and settlers even scarcer. One could walk—for there were no horses to ride—from the ruins of Andrustown to the ruins of Oneida Castle thirty miles away and meet never a soul. As Peter Sailly observed of German Flats in the springtime of 1784: "The most beautiful country in the world now presents only the poor cabins of an impoverished population who are nearly without food and upon the verge of starvation."[26]

The human toll of six years of war is difficult to measure. Perhaps a third of Tenonanatche's prewar population had been killed, dragged into captivity, or listed as missing—a total in excess of 10,000 people. Another third fled the valleys for the safety of one side of the lines or the other. The remainder stayed and suffered and, as the war ended, attempted to restore their lives. Peter Sailly, a French immigrant, visited the widow of a fellow countryman, Isaac Paris, murdered at Oriskany. She lived in the neighborhood of Stone Arabia, a district he found surpassingly beautiful but subsisting still under the pall of war and massacre:

> This brave man [Isaac Paris] was Colonel of Militia, originally from L'Orient, France, I believe. He has a brother in Philadelphia with whom I am acquainted; and had also many friends in Nantes. His widow has a mill in good condition, but it lacks water. She manufactures potash. Near her residence we passed through a section of country called "Stone Arabia." It is one of the finest sections I have seen in America. ... The soil is fertile and the inhabitants will be prosperous if they do not again undergo the evils of war, from which they have suffered by the loss of their houses and cattle, stolen and burned by the Indians. They have since then built a small fort into which they can retreat in case of any new incursion, if peace does not render the tardy precaution unnecessary.[27]

The people of the valleys could not be certain that the fighting and dying had ended. Native Americans were not aware of having been beaten, nor were they inclined to sue for peace. Even as the British Empire moved to cut loose its American colonies, surrendering the present borders of New York State with all forts, what remained of Iroquoia's hostile nations planned new and more devastating raids. The underlying reality, perceived by British authorities, rendered these aggressive intentions delusional. In 1784 the Iroquois numbered about 6,000, controlling fully half of New York State while compressing New York's population of 240,000 colonists into the other portion. The Oneida, for example, numbered no more than 600 men, women, and children, and claimed possession of several million acres in the center of the state. Canada counted no more than 100,000 British subjects poised north of 2,500,000 victorious Americans.[28] The main British army in North America had gone into captivity in Virginia, while General Carleton's garrison in New York City, several thousand strong, was ordered to assume a purely defensive posture. With a large French contingent now among Washington's Continentals, the British government had more pressing concerns than the discontents of its allies. The Crown risked losing Canada as well as the thirteen colonies if the war could not be brought to a rapid conclusion.

A new era was dawning on the Mohawk, Peter Sailly realized, and he predicted a surge in resettlement, of which he wished to be a part:

There is but little commerce upon the Mohawk. The inhabitants are poor since the war. It is nevertheless a desirable location as this part of America will soon be thickly peopled. The rich lands will attract settlers. ... I returned to Fort Henry, twenty-four miles from Johnstown, upon the Mohawk, to purchase some excellent lands, but I could not agree with the proprietors as to the terms.[29]

On September 3, 1783, even as inhabitants were returning slowly to the devastated communities of New York, the Treaty of Paris and Versailles was signed, concluding the American Revolution. The final document differed little from the 1782 draft. In no version of the treaty establishing American independence and America's rights to territory south of the 45th parallel from the Atlantic Ocean to the Mississippi River was Native America mentioned once. The forts of Niagara, Oswego, and Detroit were to be surrendered to the government of Congress as soon as practicable, with no reference to Native America. Legal debts were to be honored by both countries, citizens would be indemnified for actions committed during the late war, and American loyalists would be entitled to compensation from Britain for damages and losses suffered, without mention of Native America. The Americans were not going to bring up the subject, and the British dared not. They were seen to have fueled Indian war across the frontier from the Northwest Territory to the mountains of North Carolina. In Paris, where the silken representatives of Europe's crowned princes met to settle the fate of North America's peoples, no one spoke for the Iroquois or any other Indians. There was no notice of the Six Nations because there were no longer six nations, only affiliated tribes.

The Iroquois League was now left entirely inside the territory conceded to the new American republic and outside the boundaries of British Canada, the native people's main refuge and succor during the final days of the war. Alan Taylor summarizes: "For the United States, a nation verging on financial collapse and unable to defend its long frontier against Indian raids, the peace treaty was a stunning diplomatic victory."[30] To those on the ground closest to the consequences, the settlement was a colossal betrayal. Haldimand remarked to a friend: "My soul is completely bowed down with grief at seeing that we (with no absolute necessity) have humbled ourselves so much as to accept such humiliating boundaries. I am heartily ashamed and wish I was in the interior of Tartary."[31]

For the Johnson party in Canada, the outcome was rife with hypocrisy and cowardice. The independence of the Iroquois people as a self-governing and regulating entity within the white world had been cast aside without their consent or approval. All that Iroquoia had been assured and promised by Sir William Johnson was now as nothing before the advance of Yankee land speculators and homesteaders. Little surprise therefore that British officers stationed at frontier outposts withheld the terms of the Treaty of Paris from the Indians as long as possible. The rage exploding among Mohawks,

Senecas, and Cayugas as word spread from American officials and Oneida couriers and threatened to disrupt the Northwest fur trade and enflame the Canadian frontier.

John Deserontyon, the Mohawk war chief, exclaimed, "Our minds are in pain. ... The disgrace is almost killing us." Joseph Brant charged, "England has sold the Indians to Congress." At Fort Niagara in May 1783, Brigadier General MacLean, fearing the outbreak of Indian war, reported: "They told me they never could believe that our King could pretend to cede America what was not his own to give ... that the Indians were a free People subject to no Power upon Earth, that they were faithful allies of the King of England, but not his Subjects—that he had no right Whatever to grant away to the States of America, their Rights or Properties."[32]

Lord Shelburne, a party to the treaty negotiations, did not agree that Britain callously disregarded the welfare of her Indian allies. In a long speech before Parliament he observed disingenuously: "in the present treaty with America, the Indian nations were not abandoned to their enemies; they were remitted to the care of neighbours, whose interest it was as much as ours to cultivate friendship with them, and who were certainly the best qualified for softening and humanizing their hearts."[33] The idea of leaving Iroquois hearts to be softened by loving neighbors in New York State was so wide of the mark as to be ludicrous, but beneath the notion lay a cynical calculation. Parliament too had been outraged at the savage enormities practiced on the frontier settlements and, in a mood now to mollify American cousins, was willing to throw the Indians overboard. The American secretary of war, Benjamin Lincoln, had no difficulty picking up the matter where Shelburne had left it. He announced, "that all the Tribes and Nations of Indians who live to the Southward and Westward of the line agreed on [at the peace treaty], must no longer look to the King beyond the water, but they must now look to the Great Council, the Congress of the United States at Philadelphia."[34] This was a Congress bankrupt and wrestling with intractable problems, and into the vacuum left by the struggling central government stepped New York State under Governor George Clinton.

Haldimand feared an Indian uprising in the wake of the treaty, much like Pontiac's Rebellion of 1763. Beyond Niagara, Joseph Brant was actively seeking the support of western tribes that once had banded together to besiege Detroit and destroy British outposts. Indeed, Sir William had suffered several grievous episodes attempting to restore stability to this region on which Canada's fur trade depended. Now that the United States was due to take over Niagara, Detroit, and Michilimackinac (Mackinac Island, Michigan), Haldimand envisioned a return to border violence and commercial disruption. On these grounds he delayed the promised surrender of forts under his control.[35] But Native Americans, Iroquois and others, did not rise up and strike at

British or American outposts. There was much anger, but no bloodshed. Haldimand succeeded only in fixing Congress's attention on the westernmost boundaries of Iroquoia and on the vexing question about Indian citizenship within the United States. Who were these people and where, if anywhere, did they belong?

Aaron Hill (Kananaron), Brant's lieutenant and an influential Mohawk leader, believed that, because the Treaty of Paris made no mention of the People of the Long House, they were an independent nation and bound by no agreements between the Americans and British. Technically, they were still at war with the United States. But the People were still party to the Fort Stanwix Treaty of 1768 negotiated between Sir William Johnson and tribal leaders. That treaty line, running from Stanwix to the Unadilla to the Susquehanna and on to the Ohio, was the legal western boundary of such territory as had subsequently become New York State after the creation of the United States. The Mohawks recognized that their lands along the eponymous river were lost, but the lands claimed by the Oneida, Tuscarora, Onondaga, Cayuga, and Seneca peoples remained mostly to the west of the Fort Stanwix line and were therefore in Indian country, a territory distinct from Canada or the United States.

Hill's conception was a shrewd attempt to stymie American advances into Iroquois territory while also shielding for a time the Lake Ontario, Lake Erie, and Niagara peripheries awarded to the United States by treaty. Congress was having none of it. James Monroe of Virginia understood the issue in terms of jurisdiction:

Whether these Indians are to be considered as members of the State of New York, or whether the living simply within the bounds of a State, in the exclusion only of a European power, while they acknowledge no obedience to its laws but hold a country over which they do not expect, nor enjoy the protections, nor any of the rights of citizenship within it, is a situation which will even in the most qualified sense, admit their being held as members of a State?

The answer to which, Monroe concluded, was "that the Iroquois were autonomous Indians whose management is committed by the confederation [Acts of Confederation] to the U. S. in Congress assembled."[36] The western borders of Iroquoia, settled by the Treaty of Paris on the Niagara River and shores of Lake Erie, established that the Iroquois people, an autonomous political entity, were the responsibility of the Congress of the United States. On October 3, 1784, at the ruins of Fort Stanwix, federal treaty commissioners opened a council with the Iroquois that was meant to address Hill's claims and settle the issue of Indian rights within the new federation. "I now for the first time hear men, savage in almost every respect, harangue on important subjects with eloquence, force, and coherence, "wrote Griffith Evans from Pennsylvania, who with other delegates to Stanwix in 1784 discovered the cogency and integrity of Iroquois thought.[37] But undercutting the celebrations and oratory of the occasion were efforts by New York State to undo any agreement achieved by federal representatives.

New York State agents made certain that large quantities of rum were available and serious deliberations interrupted frequently by raucous lacrosse games. Governor George Clinton wanted the right to negotiate for Iroquois lands without the interference of Congress. New York's position was that the Covenant Chain agreement of decades earlier constituted consent by the Iroquois to their inclusion in the province, later state, of New York and thereby corroborated their status as citizens of the state outside federal jurisdiction. When Hill returned to the original claim that the Six Nations constituted an independent political entity, the commissioner from Virginia, Arthur Lee, told him bluntly: "Again you are mistaken in supposing that, having been excluded from the treaty between the United States and the King of England, you are become a free and independent nation and may make what terms you please. It is not so. You are a subdued people." Lee subsequently observed, "They are Animals that must be subdued and kept in awe or they will be mischievous, and fear alone will effect this submission."[38]

Lee's words echo Washington's in his instructions to General Sullivan on the eve of the 1779 campaign. Aaron Hill had made the mistake in Virginian eyes of assuming equality between Americans and Iroquois. He had come to this point of view in the world of Tenonanatche, but Tenonanatche was no more.

George Clinton would never utter the racial epithet "animals" that Arthur Lee so glibly spoke. Clinton was given to saying very little in fact, but he had fought the British Indians, served through the nightmare years of the raids, and as New York's first governor was determined to see that the fruits of patriot sacrifice were not lost by Congressional shilly-shallying. Clinton despised Tories, and resented Massachusetts with all therein, but he never denied New York's responsibility for the welfare of Native Americans. The problem arose, Alan Taylor observes, in that "Clinton could never accept them as prospering landlords with economic power over the state's white citizens. ... The governor and his commissioners meant for the Indians, instead, to remain tributary to the state, paying in periodic installments of land for occasional relief of their hunger and poverty."[39]

Clinton was born in Orange County near Middletown, the son of an Irish immigrant. In his youth he enlisted in a provincial regiment, serving in several campaigns against the French and Indians. Large, laconic, reserved, he nonetheless projected a political astuteness and empathy that reminded many old settlers of William Johnson. Clinton, like his friend and fellow French and Indian War veteran, Marinus Willett, was proud of his working-class origins, but his beginnings did not keep him from reading law, becoming clerk of the court of common pleas, or being elected to the New York Assembly. He would become the longest-serving governor of any state and eventually vice president of the United States under Thomas Jefferson and James Madison.

As a member of the Continental Congress, Clinton voted enthusiastically for the Declaration of Independence before leaving Philadelphia to serve as a brigadier general of militia. As governor, years later, he would refuse to support ratification of the

U.S. Constitution until the Bill of Rights was appended.[40] Beneath his silent exterior contemporaries found a radical Whig never forgetful of the hard knocks common people took in dealing with their betters. Which meant that he was a born adversary of Philip Schuyler and federalism, and indeed defeated Schuyler for the governorship of the state in 1777. Now, the two men were locked in controversy over the future of the Indians and the land they claimed to possess.

Schuyler recognized the pressure building for settlement of western New York, the vast territory penetrated by Sullivan, but any attempt to dispossess the Iroquois, he believed, would only drive them further into the arms of the British in upper Canada, thereby constituting a grave threat to the United States on the Great Lakes. Schuyler argued that the nations should be entitled to retain their lands in the center of the state. Living beside and among white settlers, he reasoned, the Iroquois would be integrated into the economy of the region and slowly adapt to new ways. Forgiving damages done during the late war was the first step towards resurrecting the multicultural model of prewar Tenonanatche. By the mid-1780s, settlers on the Chemung and Susquehanna had reconciled many of their differences with the Senecas and Delawares and appeared to live among native people without fear.[41] These hopeful developments occurred outside the sphere of British influence. But the population pressure of the 1780s would increase greatly during the 1790s, and as game grew scarce along the old frontier, tribes were tempted to sell out to the highest bidder and move westward to preserve their way of life. Clinton was determined that New York State would be that "highest bidder" and that profits from land sales to land companies be used to fill the state's empty coffers.

From Clinton's perspective, Schuyler's recommendation did not address the essential problem of burgeoning settlement. The Whigs of New York had fought for six long years to break down the barriers to expansion erected by the British Crown on behalf of Native American clients. Sir William's world had been overthrown. Pioneer New York could no longer be restrained within the 1768 treaty lines of Stanwix. But standing between visions of a new prosperity, of the Finger Lakes and Genesee Valley regions under cultivation, were fewer than 600 Oneida Indians clinging to tribal hunting lands stretching from Oneida Lake to the Susquehanna.[42] To reach the rich soils of the Senecas and Cayugas, the tide of settlement would have to breach and inundate a broad belt of Oneida land comprising the Unadilla and Chenango valleys. In 1784 at Fort Stanwix, the Oneidas were assured by Congress that: "It does not become the United States to forget those nations who preserved their faith to, and adhered to their cause, those therefore must be secured in the full and free enjoyment of their possessions."[43] Similar promises had been made by the State of New York, but the critical point remained, in Clinton's mind, whether the Oneidas could be brought to sell, thereby opening the western lands of the state to development.

Congress, mindful of land profits, was no less determined to assert its primacy in all territorial transactions involving Native Americans. Fortunately for Clinton, Congress had no money, and under the Articles of Confederation seemed unlikely to find any.[44] The Commonwealth of Massachusetts, with a royal patent predating New York's own, was in excellent legal position to purchase and resell Iroquois lands in the interest of restoring its own treasury. Fortunately for Clinton again, Massachusetts had few friends among the rich and influential magnates of the Hudson Valley. Massachusetts seemed always to arrive at the auction after the barn doors had closed. What was at stake beyond federalism and Native American sensibilities was the territorial integrity of New York State. Clinton somehow found the means to buy out the Oneidas, sell land to Congress, earn huge profits from land companies, and deliver the proceeds to his bankrupt state government. In the process he also found several parcels of attractive property for himself, but Sir William had done no less, and Clinton paid for his purchases.[45] Most of the money earned from Indian lands ended up, sooner or later, in the pockets of New York State or wealthy developers.

But what could Iroquois people do with money? They had traded land in hard bargaining with white men for more than a century, but while they might trade for luxury goods or peace, they seldom exchanged land for pecuniary gain. To hand over hunting grounds for specie was tantamount to selling their tribal birth right and plunging their people into slavery. No institution of the colonial world more appalled Native Americans than the practice of bondage. With hunting grounds gone and no alternative livelihood open to them except agricultural work, they would become day laborers on lands they once claimed as their own. Good Peter (Agorondajats) said as much in 1785 to New York State's commissioners gathered at Fort Herkimer: "Since last Winter We had determined not to sell any of our Lands, and that the Boundaries fixed should remain. The United States have informed Us that the Soil of our Lands was our own, and we wish your Assistance to prevent your People from coming among Us for that purpose."[46]

Good Peter added, "These lands are very dear to Us; as from thence We derive the Rags which cover our Bodies." He went on in his opening remarks to contrast what had happened to the Stockbridge Indians who, because they had been reduced to poverty as a result of losing their land, had come to live with the Oneidas. "This would be our Case should we sell our Lands as they have done. While the Indians had all their Lands, they were important ... but since they have parted with their Lands, the case is altered."[47]

Yet, the condition of the Oneidas in the wake of the war was desperate. Their villages on the upper Mohawk remained in ruins, while traditional subsistence, a mixture of light agriculture and hunting, continued to fail. Oneida Lake was rich in fish, and nearby families benefited from this bounty, but across Tenonanatche the nation at large lived in degrading poverty. Joseph Brant, passing through the village of Kanowarohare in the summer of 1784, described the Oneidas—hardly his favorite people—as "continually drunk with stinking rum." The Oneidas had dreamed of replacing the Mohawks as Tenonanatche's leaders, and with the expulsion of the Mohawks from the valley, they appeared to succeed.[48] But little happiness this brought them now, as they became the easternmost Iroquois nation and closest to the intruding whites. Their demoralization was apparent in deteriorating family life and destructive habits; even Samuel Kirkland, who had led them to war on the side of the Americans, admitted in a letter to his wife in 1785 that they had become "filthy, dirty, nasty creatures—a few families excepted."[49]

Good Peter tried to hold out at Fort Herkimer by offering New York tracts of relatively worthless land, but Clinton weighed in against his proposals, reminding the Oneidas that they were few in numbers and their holdings vast in area: "We fear You have lost your good opinion of Us, by making a proposal which, if accepted, would make the Government of the State tributary to You."[50] Good Peter struggled on, but under pressure from Clinton eventually conceded that "We suppose however it [the land] will be sold by the next Generation, and We wish that we may be suffered to breathe a little upon it." By the end of the negotiations, June 27, 1785, factionalism and greed among the Oneidas had tilted the conclusion in Clinton's favor. They agreed to part with a tract beginning ten miles up the Unadilla and comprising over a half million acres. The dam had broken, and in quick succession New York was able to conclude several more purchases totaling millions of acres between the Unadilla and the Chenango. Flush with money and in a generous mood, the Oneidas decided to award Kirkland and James Dean generous properties for their long services.[51] Indeed, federal law would eventually challenge the legality of these sales and gifts, but by then many of the People of the Standing Stone, the dwindling Oneida nation, would be gone from the lands of their fathers and the companionship of other Iroquois people. By the 1830s only a remnant remained in New York State; the majority, impoverished and landless, had moved to the Wisconsin Territory to begin life anew.

The story of treaties made and broken, of swindles and shady bargains struck with people who often could not read agreements set before them, is shameful in the extreme and not the least so because the native people defrauded had fought loyally at the side of Americans in desperate hours. Schuyler could not protect them any longer, nor could Kirkland. The Oneida were set in the path of a juggernaut that would not cease rolling until nearly all of New York State was under private ownership and poised to become the industrial and agricultural heartland of the new republic. Good Peter saw greed and racism at work in the state's policies; later, he recalled: "The voice of the birds from every quarter cried out 'You have lost your country—You have lost your country—You've lost your country! You have acted unwisely and done wrong.' And what increased the alarm was that the birds who made this cry were white birds." When well-meaning citizens complained about the treatment of the Oneidas, the low prices paid for their acreage, the deviousness characterizing the cessions of territory, they were told that the Oneidas themselves were to blame for acting unwisely.

Clinton left Fort Herkimer for New York City having achieved an astonishing coup. The state bought 460,000 acres for the paltry amount of $11,500. It would subsequently resell 350,000 of these acres to land companies for $126,000. Clinton had invented a money machine. Thus was the pattern established by which New York, in the period of one decade, would succeed in securing Iroquois lands to the full extent of its envisioned boundaries. Native people rejoiced in their newfound wealth, until the morning when they awoke to find themselves without property or influence. Clinton was no Sir William who would keep an eye out for their welfare. Alan Taylor concludes:

> New York triumphed by ignoring the United States, by coercing the Oneidas, and by compelling Massachusetts to compromise. But New York's surging prosperity and power alarmed its neighbors in the smaller adjoining states. No longer perceived as weak and vulnerable, New York now seemed too powerful for the confederation to control.[52]

What Clinton accomplished in turning New York from a colonial backwater into potentially the most powerful of the new states could be measured in miles of prime, virgin land acquired for settlement. At the end of the war, New York's frontier had been driven back to the Schoharie Valley, and while the state could claim jurisdiction to the gates of Fort Stanwix on the upper Mohawk, it scarcely controlled what it claimed to own. By 1795, a decade after the agreement at Fort Herkimer, New York's writ extended effectively to Niagara and the shores of Lake Erie.

The federal government closed New York's window of opportunity in a series of treaties culminating with the Treaty of Canandaigua signed between the Oneida nation, members of the Haudenosaunee confederacy, and the United States in 1794. Thereafter, only the president of the United States, with the approval of the Senate, would have power to negotiate and sign treaties with Native American people. War chief John Skenando signed for the Oneidas at Canandaigua and President George Washington for the United States of America. The Iroquois received assurances that henceforth they and their property, including reservations granted by state government, were under the jurisdiction of only the United States, and that they as an autonomous people were in no way beholding to New York. In effect, only the U.S. could negotiate the sale of Indian lands with the consent of tribal authorities.[53] During the same year the federal government made $5,000 available to pay veterans' benefits to Oneida, Stockbridge, Brotherton, and Caughnawaga warriors who had aided the American cause.

It was too little and too late but, in light of the political history, perhaps unavoidable that the Oneida would find their lands gone, their lives changed, and their tribal identity challenged as the flood of settlement swept west beyond the old barriers. This immense energy, released by unscrupulous New York land companies, had been building from the moment American troops followed Sullivan over the Forbidden Path into Indian country, encountering the stunning resources and fertility of Iroquoia. The last two decades of the eighteenth century would see thousands of pioneers rush into the new state from New England and Pennsylvania. They would brush aside the Oneida as they did the prewar structures of Tenonanatche.

Under the leadership of Joseph Brant and John Deserontyon, many Mohawks displaced from Canajoharie and Fort Hunter found new homes at Grand River, Ontario, and along the Canadian shore of the lake. Years would pass before London's intent regarding them was made known, and during this interim, Indian wars raged in the Kentucky and Ohio country, Senecas flush with land sale money aided Mohawk brothers starving in Canada, and Tory exiles found land grants in the neighborhood of their onetime allies. The history of the resettlement is vast and complicated, but it is not the story of Tenonanatche.[54]

Nor are the subsequent lives of John Johnson, Guy Johnson, John Butler, Daniel Claus, or Molly Brant pertinent to the later years of the Mohawk Valley. They had lost their homes there forever, but would become in exile founding citizens of British Canada. Over the years, Tory veterans sought out their old leaders, and John Johnson distinguished himself not only as Canada's Indian Supervisor, but also as a generous patron of loyalists seeking new starts in an alternative land. Whether Johnson openly revisited his lost domains on the Mohawk during his remaining lifetime is unclear.[55]

The mark he and others left on upstate New York is seen in a multitude of places designated "forts," "battlefields," or "massacre sites" dotting the counties that once comprised Tryon. Nor, after all these years, are the old stories forgotten. They are deeply woven into the mythic memory of people still residing on the land, and the common theme of their narration is loss. Descendants are justly proud of forebearers who defeated a foreign enemy at Stanwix or Saratoga but, for the most part, British troops did not destroy the Mohawk Valley—the residents did, as well as each other in the cruelest manner possible. Loss—not just loss of life, but loss of the common stuff that holds humanity together—scarred the survivors and shaded the recollections they left to posterity. Loss is what gives the wind in the valley its special remorsefulness, the fog and lake-effect snow its isolating loneliness. Something happened here that was more intense, more shattering, than the ordinarily sorrowful consequences of war.

In the beginning, everyone brought to the wilderness what they already understood. Sir William built a manorial system because he knew that system at home, and if he labored all of his life to advance an empire, he did so because the empire advanced him and his. The Dutch transplanted their mercantile culture to a hostile land filled with hunters and gatherers. They stayed in their towns and cities and tried not to venture far into the forests. The Palatines knew little else than farming and persecution. They had been driven out of the Rhineland and across the sea. In time, their valley farms leveled the primeval forests and their thick-walled homes became permanent features along new rivers. New England had only beliefs to offer, and these its missionaries spread widely through the valleys along with radical political visions. Joseph Brant to the end of his life never referred to patriotic Americans except as

"Bostonians." The marvel was how these disparate cultures coexisted so long beside each other and beside the indigenous people of the forests, the Iroquois.

The unwritten compact of Tenonanatche, river between the mountains, was compromise in the interest of a common good—not that the "common good" ever seemed equitable to everyone. William Johnson and James Logan, Peter and Philip Schuyler, Conrad Weiser and Nicholas Herkimer were translators and negotiators between the clashing desires of widely divergent people. They found their essential counterparts in Tiyanoga, Shickellamy, Skenando, Thayendanegea, and Ahnyero. The success of the early Mohawk settlement, its survival through the French Wars and Pontiac's Rebellion, demanded that the residents of the valley recognize the striving of their neighbors and the common, flawed, humanity all shared. This was the living covenant chain, the Haudenosaunee symbol of a linking interchange between all beings. What broke the chain forever were acts that flung aside caution, counsel, and compromise in a foolish termination of dialogue.

When Guy Johnson left Jacob Sammons lying beaten in the dust of the highway at Fonda, the chain had begun to break. When Guy decamped from the valley surreptitiously, abandoning his broader responsibilities and sending the evil birds of war to the ears of the Iroquois, he was not only disregarding the welfare of Native Americans long attached to his family, but calling down murder and mayhem on his Whig neighbors. Caught up in a dream of privilege and empire, this man of slight learning and small understanding had forgotten where he lived. Tenonanatche was never shire land, and the simple farmers and tradesmen of the valley never willing peasants.

But were Philip Schuyler and the Dutch magnates who chose the American cause any less swollen with pride and ambition? Schuyler was inflated by his appointment as major general in charge of the Northern Department, and in one of the most ill-advised campaigns in colonial history led an enthusiastic but inexperienced army into Canada. He should have known that this aggression would break the chain, alarming loyalists along the Mohawk and Hudson and precipitating armed conflict throughout Tryon County. Schuyler would come to his senses and eventually take charge of a long, grinding retreat that contributed to the winning of the war. But his policy of backing Kirkland and separating the Oneida nation from the Iroquois League inadvertently led to the collapse of the league and the breakup of the last effective forum for addressing the Indian crisis in New York.

Yet Joseph Brant, perhaps more than anyone else conversant with the terms of the conflict, failed to seek peace at the last possible moment when peace, or at least armed neutrality, might have prevailed. Imbued with the autocratic principles of the Johnson party, the fiery partisanship of his sister Molly, and fresh from his reception at the Court of St. James, he spurned the olive branch offered by Nicholas Herkimer on the banks of the Unadilla. This was a month before Oriskany. After Oriskany, the Mohawk Valley would be laid open for five long years to terrible depredation. Brant himself destroyed twenty-five towns and hamlets with most of their population. He boasted of sparing women and children, but often these innocents escaped the tomahawk to be dragged off for ransom in Canada. *C'est la guerre*, Brant offered in defense, but this was little excuse coming from the most brilliant prewar citizen of Tenonanatche, a leader respected and envied on all sides for his remarkable abilities.

In the end, they all grew tired of each other—these people white and native who lived between the lines of the cultures. Sir William was heartily sick of Indians on many occasions, and Shickellamy in his response to the know-it-all Weiser expressed a similar impatience. Kirkland testifies to how difficult life among the Senecas was for him, and Brant rails over George Klock and the doddering pace of white justice. In the last days of the war, Schuyler was too sick to meet with the Oneidas. Abandoned, Good Peter wore himself out arguing against the relentless land-hungry Governor Clinton, only to watch the heartless legal process wear down his people's inheritance. These are the documented examples of frustration and chagrin; the undocumented instances experienced by ordinary Native Americans and white settlers can only be imagined. To find a way between the reality of white expansion and the necessity of native survival was to find the true river between the mountains. The search exhausted the best minds of both sides to no avail. For when the War of Independence came, as Sir William feared, there was too little goodwill remaining to curb the knives of the angry and disappointed, those who now threw all caution to the wind and for their own party, ideology, or gain assaulted their neighbors.

Sir William had believed that education was the best answer, but he had been unable to establish serviceable schools on the Mohawk. Instead, he sent Joseph Brant and others to Wheelock's Academy in Connecticut, where Brant met Kirkland. Johnson swallowed his Anglican distaste for Puritans and dissenters in his search for a solution to the Indian dilemma. Now, twenty years after his death and on the far side of a destructive war, 600 citizens from Schenectady and surrounding communities realized their dream of establishing a college free of all sectarian interests and ethnic biases. Concerned subscribers met first in 1779, two years after Burgoyne's defeat and during high hopes for Sullivan's campaign. Their interest was premature; raids over the next two years reached to the outskirts of Schenectady. Yet the lower Mohawk towns would escape the scourge and by 1794 raise sufficient funds to found Union College. Union was the first institution of higher learning chartered under the Regents of the State of New York, and the very name of the college trumpeted the birth of the nation.

Significantly, the curriculum leading to the bachelor degree was to be predominantly scientific and secular, with French instruction held equal to Latin and Greek. Over the next century this college, raised out of the ashes of the valley, would produce one U. S. president (Chester Arthur), seven cabinet secretaries, fifteen U. S. senators, ninety-one members of the House of Representatives, thirteen governors, numerous diplomats, judges, missionaries and generals, and ninety college presidents, including the first presidents of the University of Illinois, the University of Iowa, the University of Michigan, Vassar College, Smith College, and Elmira College. Franklin Delano Roosevelt's father and Winston Churchill's grandfather would go to Union,[56] but very few Indians were invited to attend.

Seventy-five miles upriver, on a hill overlooking a town that would some day be named for George Clinton, Samuel Kirkland responded to the belief that the education of whites and Native Americans together was in the interest of the developing United States. While he appealed to his denomination, Harvard College, and the Massachusetts Indian Society for monetary support, he petitioned the State Regents to charter his Hamilton-Oneida Academy, arguing "the mutual Benefit of the young and flourishing settlements of Emigrants to said County and the various Tribes of Confederate Indians."[57] Alexander Hamilton would lend his name to the academy and serve on its board of trustees—his only contributions to the institution. Kirkland was by then a substantial landowner in the valley, thanks to the Oneidas, and donated the land on which Hamilton College would eventually be built. The evolution from academy to college was torturous in the absence of reliable funding. New England settlers, pouring into the hills above what would some day be Utica, clamored for decent education, but they had no interest in Kirkland's plans to educate Iroquois. Unfortunately, the Oneidas themselves put forward very few candidates, and following state charter in 1812, Hamilton, like Union, went on to produce statesmen, politicians, jurists, and academics in the service of the new nation, but few Indian graduates.

Twenty-five miles due south of Fort Stanwix, the immense Oneida forests stretched from Tenonanatche to the banks of the Susquehanna. The wilderness extended on both sides of the Chenango River and was penetrated only by a few Indian trails. In overview, this country was hilly and covered with hardwood trees of great height. The soil was rich with limestone just under the surface, handy for building. By the late 1780s, New York State and the U.S. Congress had begun to dispose of packets of the Chenango Valley to state and Continental veterans in fulfillment of enlistment promises. The most prominent of the new landholders was a battlefield hero, Colonel William S. Smith, sometime aide to generals Sullivan, Washington, and the Marquis de Lafayette, husband of Abigail Adams, John Adams's daughter, and in time an American ambassador to Spain.[58] Smith carved six townships out of the Chenango Valley and, towards the end of his long career in public life, lived there himself. He left the early pioneering to others. By 1790 he had sold land to Samuel Payne and fellow immigrants from Lebanon, Connecticut—evangelical Baptists by persuasion—who leveled the forests and built the roads connecting their town of Hamilton with the Mohawk Valley.

On a bright autumn day in 1794, Payne climbed through the virgin forests to the side of a high hill outside Hamilton. He owned the land and intended to clear it. As the first tree fell, he knelt to pray, dedicating to the service of God his wilderness acres—or so the story goes. For this act marked the beginning of Colgate University, a college with a seminary, that began as the Baptist Education Society in 1817 and grew over the subsequent decades to cover Payne's hill. Colgate in its early years would send many missionaries to Asia and Africa, educated men who could fashion dictionaries and translate scripture into exotic languages, but Colgate would send very few missionaries to Native America. The Great Awakening that had so fired Kirkland, Dean, and Occom at Wheelock's Academy had passed. Now, as America rushed westward in the new century to the Mississippi, it seemed to push aside native peoples without a thought. The country looked outward for new greatness and often forgot those who had lived nearby in its humble beginnings.[59]

Institutions like colleges and academies have a way of cropping up in the wake of cultural dislocation; they are harbingers of new social resolves, and never far behind them come revolutions in industry, transportation and communication. Indeed, within four decades of Samuel Payne's pious assault on the Oneida wilderness, the Chenango canal passed through the bustling village of Hamilton, connecting the new city of Utica on the Mohawk with the new city of Binghamton seventy-five miles away on the Susquehanna. The ashes of the great trees burned in the clearing of the land went to make soap on a commercial scale never seen before, and in time the produce was barged down the Erie Canal to New York City for shipment to the world.[60] The pace of change along the Mohawk River was dizzying, and in the exuberant making of a new nation, the painful past was often romanticized, mythologized, or simply forgotten.

And why should selective memory not prevail? Modern Iroquois nations are at least as interested today in reservation rights, gambling franchises, and tobacco sales as they are in lamenting the dismal treatment of their people in the eighteenth century. We are all one people now; we move on; we get it done. But who we are we learn from comparing ourselves to the past, if only we are able to see that past through judicious eyes. Bringing yesterday into focus is not the purpose of a book or a school of thought, but the function of a healthy society. Would we be different people if Schuyler had not delayed Carleton at the end of 1776, if Willett had lost at Johnstown, if Good Peter had held off Clinton's demands? Indeed, many viewpoints are possible on the subject of Tenonanatche, and this book represents only one. To engage views, as many as life and circumstance allow, is to participate in a long dialogue, negotiating differences, accepting exceptions in just the way the peoples of the Mohawk Valley failed to do on the edge of a devastating upheaval. We try to learn from their mistakes.

Notes

Introduction

1. Te-non-an-at-che translates as "river flowing through the mountains," which indeed the Mohawk does from west to east. The Iroquois nations living along the banks of the river had many names for it. "Mohawk" was not one. Tenonanatche denotes the river's most essential feature. See Codman Hislop, *The Mohawk* (New York: Rinehart, 1948), p. 31.

2. General Philip Schuyler, hero of the Revolutionary War, invested heavily in an engineering project to canalize the Mohawk in 1792. A few years later the effort ended in financial collapse. Capital requirements to accomplish this vast undertaking demanded the resources of nation and state. See Peter L. Bernstein, *Wedding of the Waters* (New York: W. W. Norton, 2005), pp. 24, 48–49.

3. Bernstein, p. 48.

4. The beauty of the Mohawk Valley, especially in spring or autumn, can be appreciated by driving west on Route 5 between Fonda and Little Falls. Sweeping panoramas of the river can be enjoyed from the northern ridge of the valley in the vicinity of Ephrata and Stone Arabia. The industrial towns of the region are now struggling to recapture an earlier charm and prosperity.

5. Remington Rand was founded at Ilion on the south bank of the river, across from Herkimer, while General Electric made its earliest home at Schenectady. These are only two of many famous brands associated with the valley.

6. Numerous colonial wars in the seventeenth century fixed the lines between France and Britain and Britain and Holland for domination of North America. In so doing the wars profoundly affected Native America. But the conclusion of Queen Anne's War (1713) and the relative peace initiated for two decades led to notable changes in settlement. Peace allowed heavy immigration into the Mohawk, Schoharie, and Hudson valleys. The arrival of thousands of Palatine refugees in central New York between 1710 and 1713 marked a decisive turn in the crown colony's development.

7. Alan Taylor, *The Divided Ground: Indians, Settlers, and the Northern Borderland of the American Revolution* (New York: Alfred A. Knopf, 2006), pp. 16–18.

8. Charles C. Mann, *1491: New Revelations of the Americas Before Columbus* (New York: Vintage, 2005), p. 370. Mann notes: "The evidence is unclear, but the ancestors of the Five Nations [the Haudenosaunee: Mohawk, Seneca, Cayuga, Oneida, Onondaga], neighboring bands of gatherers and hunters, may have lived in their homeland since the glaciers retreated from the Finger Lakes—the eleven deep, narrow lakes that lie like cat scratches across central New York State."

9. "League" or "Confederation" often appears interchangeably in older sources referring to the Iroquois. In fact, "League" referred to the ancient peace compact between the nations of the Haudenosaunee, while "Confederation" signified a complementary body concerned with politics and foreign policy. See James H. Merrell, *The Lancaster Treaty of 1744 with Related Documents* (New York and Boston: Bedford/St. Martin's, 2007), p. 12.

10. These would become the Six Nations with the addition of the Tuscaroras about 1713. The Tuscaroras, an Iroquoian people, were driven out of North Carolina by massacre and enslavement and took shelter under the Five Nations. The following is from the Tuscaroras' home site: "The chiefs of the Five Nations, in conference with Gov. Hunter at Albany, Sept. 25, 1714, acquainted him with the fact that

the Tuscarora Indians are come to shelter themselves among the Five Nations; they were of us and went from us long ago, and now are returned and promise to live peaceably among us. And since there is peace now everywhere, we have received them." For an account of the tribe's sufferings, see Alan Taylor, *American Colonies: The Settling of North America* (New York: Viking Penguin, 2002), pp. 234–235.

11. Dean R. Snow, Charles T. Gehring, and William A. Starna, eds., *In Mohawk Country: Early Narratives about a Native People* (Syracuse, N.Y.: Syracuse University, 1996), p. xxiii.

12. This interpretation of the Haudenosaunee relationship to Mohawk country is open to charges of romanticism such as Hugh Henry Brackenridge, supreme propagandist of the American Revolution, leveled against Eastern Indian-lovers: "the original right of these aborigines to the soil is like the claim of children; it is mine, for I saw it first." See Joseph J. Ellis, *After the Revolution: Profiles of Early American Culture* (New York: W. W. Norton, 2002), p. 90.

13. Alan Taylor, *American Colonies*, p. 293. Britain acquired Acadia, Newfoundland, Hudson Bay, and the West Indian island of St. Kitts.

14. All of Johnson's biographers stress his Irish origins, but Fintan O'Toole, *White Savage: William Johnson and the Invention of America* (New York: Farrar, Straus and Giroux, 2005) explains the Celtic mind of Sir William and the cultural and psychological heritage of his followers most fully. See pp. 58–69.

15. Estimates of civilian casualties versus displacement are, of course, only approximate. Besides the exile of Tories and Iroquois loyal to the Crown, war deaths among the population possibly approached 25 percent. An example of the ferocity of the fighting is described by John Ferling: "The fight was savage and primordial, as civil wars tend to be, for in this desperate engagement [Oriskany] Loyalists fought rebels who once had been their neighbors, and Indians fought Indians with whom they had once joined hands in the Six Nations Confederation. Every man knew that the vanquished would never leave this forest. No quarter was given. None was asked." *Almost a Miracle: The American Victory in the War of Independence* (New York: Oxford University, 2007), p. 231; also pp. 558–559 for estimated casualties.

16. Under a Thruway overpass are traces today of an ancient mining road that once linked the Hudson Valley to eastern Pennsylvania. Over this road a community, indentured and impoverished, once migrated from upstate New York to the Lebanon Valley. Their march made them a new people, afterward to be called *Pennsylvania* Dutch as opposed to *New York* German. The route ran from Albany down the Hudson to Esopus (Kingston) where, meeting the Rondout-Neversink Road, it led on to Minisink and the Delaware River. For the importance of the mining road, see Paul A. Wallace, *Conrad Weiser: Friend of Colonist & Mohawk* (Philadelphia: University of Pennsylvania, 1945), p. 35.

17. This statement is true of the Sullivan campaign in 1779. The intent was genocidal but, fortunately for the Iroquois, the result was not. Yet, over the years of warfare, the Six Nations were bled dry by casualties, famine, epidemic, and displacement. See Barbara Graymont's epilogue in *The Iroquois in the American Revolution* (Syracuse, N.Y.: Syracuse University, 1972), pp. 292–296, for a concluding appraisal.

18. The battles of King William's War, Queen Anne's War, King George's War, the French and Indian War (or Seven Years War), and War of Independence were fought disproportionately in the province of New York—many on or within a day's march of the Mohawk. The strategic location of the state and the state's water highways accounted for this up to and through the War of 1812.

19. John Ferling, *The First of Men: A Life of George Washington* (Knoxville: University of Tennessee, 1988), pp. 314–315. This is attested by a letter from Washington to New York's Governor George Clinton, August 12, 1783.

20. Patricia Nelson Limerick, "Haunted America," from *Sweet Medicine: Sites of Indian Massacres, Battlefields, and Treaties* (Albuquerque: University of New Mexico, 1995), p. 121.

21. More historic signposts are found in the Mohawk Valley than elsewhere. The State Historic Marker Program, which was managed by the Education Department's State History office as an active field program from 1926 to 1966, has now become an advisory and database management program. The archives of that program, as well as the records of over 2,800 historic markers across the state, are maintained by the Museum of the State of New York. For further information on the old gold and blue markers and many nationally designated sites, view: http://www.nysm.nysed.gov/services/srvmarkers.html.

22. Gordon S. Wood, *The Radicalism of the American Revolution* (New York: Vintage, 1993), p. 6.

23. See O'Toole, pp. 339–341, for an appreciation of Cooper's debt to the world of Sir William Johnson.

Part I

Chapter 1: On an Indian River

1. For a list of contentions between the colonies in the early eighteenth century, see William R. Polk, *The Birth of America* (New York: Harper Perennial, 2006), pp. 300–301. The contest for land was no greater than the commercial competition carried on among the colonies for natural resources and manufacture.

2. When Washington was twenty-two, his failure to control a war party lost in the Pennsylvania forests resulted in the unintended murder of thirty-five-year-old Joseph Coulon de Villiers de Jumonville, a captured French ensign, by an Indian scout in Washington's employ, Tanaghrisson. This episode, with other misadventures in the Ohio territory during peacetime, precipitated the opening events of the French and Indian War, which in turn avalanched into the Seven Years War of worldwide proportions. For an account of these developments, see Fred Anderson, *Crucible of War: The Seven Years War and the Fate of Empire In British North America, 1754–1766* (New York: Alfred A. Knopf, 2000), pp. 5–7.

3. Polk, pp. 197–202.

4. Carl Bridenbaugh, *Cities in Revolt: Urban Life in America, 1743–1776* (New York: Capricorn, 1964), pp. 5, 216. New York City in 1743 was still a village, containing 11,000 inhabitants; by 1775 it would number 25,000. Boston had a declining population in 1743 of about 16,000, and Philadelphia a rapidly growing population of 11,000 that would reach 40,000 in 1775. The interior numbers for this period are difficult to ascertain, but Albany is thought to have numbered several hundred families.

5. Anderson, p. 26.

6. The story of Céloron's celebrated mission is graphically retold by Allan W. Eckert, *Wilderness Empire* (Boston: Little Brown, 1969), pp. 112–121. For the account of the role of the Marquis de la Galissonière in this act and French policy in general, see Francis Parkman, *Montcalm and Wolfe: The French & Indian War* (New York: Da Capo, 1995), pp. 21–30.

7. Polk, p. 157: "In the 1780s Pennsylvania had 78 cleared roads; Massachusetts had 143, and New York only 57 miles of post road capable of supporting carriages and wagons. Mail between New York and Boston moved once a week in summer and once every two weeks in winter. Delivery took four or five days."

8. Parkman, p. 18.

9. It is difficult to estimate how many slaves were held in bondage in upstate as opposed to downstate New York. Certainly there were fewer upstate than on Long Island, but Sir William Johnson brought slaves with him from Boston and sent occasionally to New York City for additional servants, as did many wealthy families in the Mohawk Valley. A better indication of the extent of slavery in upstate was the significant number of black partisans serving with Tory bands during the Revolution in hope of their eventual freedom. See Simon Schama, *Rough Crossings: The Slaves, the British, and the American Revolution* (New York: Harper Perennial, 2006), pp. 113–114.

10. For New York City's famous tolerance, see Russell Shorto's account of New Amsterdam's Dutch roots and folkways in *The Island at the Center of the World: The Epic Story of Dutch Manhattan & the Forgotten Colony That Shaped America* (New York: Doubleday, 2004).

11. Anderson, p. 38.

12. Milton Hamilton, the Johnson biographer most to be trusted, holds that the journey to the Mohawk departed Boston by land and crossed the Hudson at Albany: *Sir William Johnson—Colonial American, 1715:1763* (Port Washington, N.Y.: Kennikat, 1976), p. 8. It seems far more likely that Johnson would have sailed to New York, outfitted, and been availed of the efficient Albany packets.

13. Michael Tyrrell obtained a lieutenancy in Colonel William Gooch's regiment of Virginians in 1740. He wrote to his cousin, May 28, 1741, about participating in an attack on Cartagena: "I delight in war though I have seen great slaughter and several changes since I seen you. … If the French disturb you in America, our Regiment will be sent to New York where I hope to have the pleasure of seeing you in good health. Please to remember to all friends and best respects to Dr. Barclay, Mr. and Mrs. Dillon, to Catty and all that inquire for me." Sir William Johnson, *The Papers of Sir William Johnson*, ed. James Sullivan (Albany, N.Y.: The University of the State of New York, 1921), I, pp. 10–14. The letter is notable for casting light on the people Johnson first came in contact with on the Mohawk.

14. James Thomas Flexner, *Mohawk Baronet: A Biography of Sir William Johnson* (Syracuse, N.Y.: Syracuse University, 1979), pp. 10–14.

15. The "new" fort erected in Schenectady, the Mohawks' *Schonowe* or "Gateway," was completed in 1706 and named Queen's Fort. The fortifications are long gone, but the plan of their construction is remembered on a monument in the square of the present-day Stockade District. For a detailed account, see W. Max Reid, *The Mohawk Valley: Its Legends and Its History* (New York: G. P. Putnam, 1907), pp. 69–70.

16. Flexner, p. 17.

17. The impression is derived from correspondence between the two men and later between Johnson and Warren's widow.

18. Woods Creek was a twisting, tree-shaded water connecting the Great Carry on the Mohawk with Lake Oneida to the west. Negotiating its swampy length was notably hazardous in war and exhausting at any time. Yet goods could not be sent west or east from Lake Ontario without traversing Woods Creek. Cooper, who had himself been an ocean sailor, captures the consternation old salts felt on sailing inland seas in his character of Cap in *The Pathfinder.*

19. The growing independence of the colonies during the early eighteenth century is described by Polk in "Mother England Loses Touch," pp. 126–143.

20. For a lively account of the pirate and the governor, see Richard Zack, *The Pirate Hunter: The True Story of Captain Kidd* (New York: Hyperion, 2003).

21. Theodore Roosevelt, *New York: A Sketch of the City's Social, Political, and Commercial Progress from the First Dutch Settlement to Recent Times* (New York: Charles Scribner, 1906), vii.

22. There are few more romantic or enigmatic stories in New York annals than the accounts of Catherine Weisenberg. For twenty years she would be William Johnson's housekeeper, mistress and mother of his three legitimized children. Flexner, pp. 25–27, accepts that she was from Madagascar, because no Weisenbergs appear to have lived on the Mohawk at this time. He accepts that she was purchased from the Phillipses, as valley tradition holds, and that she was not married initially to Johnson. Reid, an older source, asserts that the couple was eventually wed by the Reverend Dr. Henry Barclay, p. 113.

23. St. John's church in Johnstown, built by Sir William and also his burial place, was destroyed by fire in 1836. Under the chancel was found his tomb, and when the church was rebuilt on a slightly altered plot, the tomb was left outside the new building. When the sarcophagus was relocated and opened in 1862, the skeletal remains wore a gold ring, dated June 1739–16. Embedded in the hip was the musket ball that Johnson received at the Battle of Lake George: Reid, p. 205.

24. Flexner, p. 25.

25. Hamilton, p. 33.

26. Ibid.

27. A good way to be introduced to the sweep of New York City's history is through Ric Burns, *New York: A Documentary Film* (Steeplechase Films, 1999), I–VII. PBS began broadcast and distribution of this documentary in 2001.

28. Reid, pp. 84–91.

29. Reid, pp. 94–97.

30. Two Barclays are found in the historical record. The Reverend Thomas Barclay, chaplain of Fort Orange (Albany) was called to the service of Queen Anne's chapel between 1708 and 1712. The Reverend Henry Barclay succeeded William Andrews, and served from 1735 to 1745, when he was appointed rector of Trinity Church, Wall Street, New York City. He rewarded himself amply with Mohawk lands, but in all other respects was an energetic and devoted minister of the gospel.

31. "In 1614 Dutch traders established a year-round presence on the upper Hudson by founding Fort Nassau, later relocated and renamed Fort Orange, with an associated village called Beverwyck ('ëBeaver Town'). During the late 1620s, Fort Orange had only about fifty Dutch inhabitants, about half fur traders and half soldiers, all employees of the monopolistic Dutch West India Company": Alan Taylor, *American Colonies: The Settling of North America* (New York: Viking Penguin, 2001), pp. 251–252. Note that the foundation of Albany precedes Plymouth Rock by six years and is older than New Amsterdam, i.e., Manhattan. For the story of the Van Rensselaer's hold on the surrounding region, see Russell Shorto, *The Island at the Center of the World: The Epic Story of Dutch Manhattan and & the Forgotten Colony That Shaped America* (New York: Doubleday, 2004), pp. 131–134. By the time Johnson came to Albany, the

fortifications of Fort Orange were more thought on than actual.

32. Flexner, p. 15. In the vicinity of Warrensburgh, *Chuctenuda* as it was known, other settlers struggled to make a go of it. On the border of Johnson's property, a community of free blacks tilled the soil and worked to clear farms. See Hamilton, pp. 11–13.

33. Johnson, I, pp. 4–7.

34. Johnson, I, pp. 7–8.

35. The trail ran close to present Route 8 in the Unadilla Valley and was reached by skirting Lake Otsego through the hills to the southwest. Cooper's Natty Bumppo, the original "leatherstocking" hunter, was probably modeled on one David Shipman, familiar to the novelist in his youth. Susan Fenimore Cooper remembered that "during the 1790s the old hunter by the name of Shipman had frequently come down from his home in the Otsego hills to offer his game at Judge Cooper's door —... His rude equipment, dogs, and rifle had much attraction for the lads of the house." Alan Taylor, *William Cooper's Town* (New York: Vintage, 1996), p. 53. Leather leggings were a fashion acquired from the Iroquois, and Shipman's hunting grounds, stretching southwest to the Susquehanna, still define the heartland of the Leatherstocking region in New York.

36. The introduction to *The Last of the Mohicans* (1826) studiously avoids crediting Johnson with the naming of Fort Edward, Fort William Henry, and Lake George. Cooper says only, "The loyal servants of the British crown had given to one of these forest-fastnesses the name of William Henry, and to the other that of Fort Edward, calling each after a favorite prince of the reigning family." Cooper found the name "George" applied to the romantic lake almost too commonplace for words, and substituted "Horican" for Lake George in his fiction. Recollections of the Revolution, and of blame attaching to the Johnsons in New York for its long and bloody course, lurks just beneath the surface of *The Last of the Mohicans*, where a shift in taste from Imperial British fashions to Republican American values colors all the landscape and characterization.

37. Fintan O'Toole, *White Savage: William Johnson and the Invention of America* (New York: Farrar, Straus and Giroux, 2005), pp. 174–175. Also Flexner, p. 137.

Chapter 2: Muster at Albany

1. Daniel K. Richter and James H. Merrell, eds., *Beyond the Covenant Chain: The Iroquois and Their Neighbors in Indian North America* (University Park, Pa.: Penn State University, 2004), p. 16.

2. Richter, p. 31.

3. Alan Taylor, *American Colonies: The Settling of North America* (New York: Viking Penguin, 2002), pp. 268–269.

4. Milton Hamilton, *Sir William Johnson—Colonial American, 1715:1763* (Port Washington, N.Y.: Kennikat, 1976), p. 210. At a meeting of the nations at Oswego in 1756, Johnson ceremonially removed the petticoats from the Delaware in token of their restored status.

5. Fintan O'Toole, *White Savage: William Johnson and the Invention of America* (New York: Farrar, Straus and Giroux, 2005), p. 42.

6. William R. Polk, *The Birth of America* (New York: Harper Perennial, 2006), p. 201.

7. Many accounts exist of the foundation and history of the Iroquois Confederacy. For one, see Bill Yenne, *The Encyclopedia of North American Indian Tribes* (New York: Random House, 1986), pp. 120–121.

8. Beside the old rectory, the only surviving building of Queen's Chapel at Fort Hunter, a gold and blue sign marks the spot where Joseph Brant worked with the Reverend John Stuart to translate the Book of Common Prayer, the Anglican missal, into the Mohawk language. For details see Isabel Thompson Kelsay, *Joseph Brant, 1743–1807: Man of Two Worlds* (Syracuse, N.Y.: Syracuse University, 1986), pp. 132–134.

9. Allan W. Eckert, *The Conquerors* (Boston: Little Brown, 1970), pp. 685–689.

10. There is a kind of doomed glamour shared between the conquered Irish and hard-pressed Iroquois that accounts for their fierce attachment to a natural life and their mutual comprehension of the tragic hero, according to Fintan O'Toole in his very Irish biography of William Johnson, *White Savage*, pp. 32–35.

11. W. Max Reid, *The Mohawk Valley: Its Legends and Its History* (New York: G. P. Putnam, 1907), pp. 98–112.

12. James Thomas Flexner, *Mohawk Baronet: A Biography of Sir William Johnson* (Syracuse, N.Y.:

Syracuse University, 1989), p. 40. For Johnson's growing prominence during King George's War, see pp. 59–79.

13. Flexner, p. 58.

14. For elucidation of this complicated decision, and the government parties behind it, see Fred Anderson, *Crucible of War: The Seven Years War and the Fate of Empire in British North America, 1754–1766* (New York: Alfred A. Knopf, 2000), pp. 66–73.

15. Anderson writes: "In fact, events had reached a stage at the beginning of 1755 that made war between Britain and France all but inevitable. The origins of that war lay in a skein of developments so tangled that neither Newcastle nor any other diplomatist in Europe could fully have unraveled, let alone controlled, them": p. 72.

16. For the details of Johnson's appointment, see Hamilton, pp. 114–118.

17. Anderson, p. 99.

18. Robert Leckie, *A Few Acres of Snow: The Saga of the French and Indian Wars* (New York: John Wiley, 1999), pp. 282–283.

19. Leckie, p. 285.

20. Walter R. Borneman alludes to the captured documents in his recent account of the battle and its aftermath in *The French and Indian War: Deciding the Fate of North America* (New York: Harper Perennial, 2006), pp. 56–57.

21. For the standard account of Braddock's defeat, see Lee McCardell, *Ill-Starred General: Braddock of the Coldstream Guards* (Pittsburgh: University of Pittsburgh, 1958). For a reappraisal, consult Anderson, pp. 94–106. Thomas Gage, Horatio Gates, Washington, and even Daniel Boone and Daniel Morgan were present at the Monongahela; not one of them ever criticized Braddock for his generalship. Washington always held that the poor discipline of the British troops caused the debacle. This did not avert the vilification of Braddock as a proud and obstinate fool in legend and popular story thereafter. Also attributed to the general at his last: "We shall better know how to deal with them another time": Leckie, p. 286. Indeed, the British army would need many more years before it learned the lesson of wilderness ambush.

22. Eckert, p. 301.

23. Flexner, pp. 135–136. "Lyman wrote Johnson that, if the women were not instantly banished [from camp], the Northern saints will either mob or privately destroy them.'" Certainly there is no evidence that the young militia were ever so inclined.

24. Francis Parkman, *Montcalm and Wolfe: The French & Indian War* (New York: Da Capo, 1995), p. 171. Parkman tends to laud the Massachusetts effort. "Forty-five hundred of her men, or one in eight of her adult males, volunteered to fight the French." Flexner tends to depict New England as a cross Johnson was compelled to bear. Regional controversies over the battle obviously did not cease with the creation of the United States.

25. Sir William Johnson, *The Papers of Sir William Johnson*, James Sullivan, ed. (Albany: The University of the State of New York, 1921) v. I, pp. 456–459.

26. Johnson, v. I, pp. 512–516.

27. Johnson, v. I, pp. 663–665.

28. Flexner, p. 136.

29. Parkman, p. 172.

30. Romanticized views of Brant's exploits can be found in many places, such as Howard Thomas's *Joseph Brant: Thayendanegea* (Utica, N.Y.: North Country, 1984), pp. 31 ff. The standard nineteenth-century biography is William L. Stone, *The Life of Joseph Brant—Thayendanegea* (Buffalo, N.Y: Phinney, 1851), 2 vols. The definitive account of Brant's life is Isabel Thompson Kelsay's *Joseph Brant 1743–1807: Man of Two Worlds* (Syracuse, N.Y.: Syracuse University, 1984).

31. Kelsay, p. 387. Daniel Claus, Johnson's son-in-law, was instrumental in advancing this project by which Brant met the Bishop of London and the Archbishop of Canterbury. The rectory at Fort Hunter where Brant was said to have begun his translation is still standing and designated by a gold and blue historical marker.

32. A statue of Father Jogues, crucifix aimed toward the water, presently stands two hundred yards or so from the site purported to be Johnson's headquarters at the Battle of Lake George.

33. *View of the Lines at Lake George* by Captain Thomas Davies (c. 1737–1812) is in the collection of

the Fort Ticonderoga Museum. This oil painting provides cover art for John R. Cuneo's *Robert Rogers of the Rangers* (Ticonderoga, N.Y.: Fort Ticonderoga Museum, 1988). Lieutenant Davies was with Amherst in 1759 during the Lake Champlain expedition.

34. Johnson, II, p. 9.

35. Anderson, pp. 120–121. See also maps of Johnson's deployment in Johnson, II, pp. 2, 4, 7.

36. Johnson, II, pp. 6–9.

Chapter 3: The Battle of Lake George

1. Fred Anderson, *Crucible of War: The Seven Years War and the Fate of Empire In British North America, 1754–1766* (New York: Alfred A. Knopf, 2000), pp. 124–125. Because Boscawen succeeded in capturing only a few ships, France received, according to Anderson, not only justification for hostilities, but also the means to threaten the frontier of every American colony. On July 18, Charles de Levis, duc de Mirepoix, French ambassador to the Court of St. James, left London in a fury. He did not know yet of Braddock's fate on July 9. Dieskau disembarked at Quebec on June 23 with his troops.

2. Because of Braddock's defeat, the frontier in Pennsylvania was pushed back to within 100 miles of Philadelphia. Seven hundred people died on the frontier in the weeks immediately following the defeat. The only positive development achieved by Braddock and Shirley was the strengthening at home of William Pitt, who in the aftermath of 1755 observed: "I believe that I can save this nation and that no one else can." See Alan Taylor, *American Colonies: The Settling of North America* (New York: Viking, 2001) p. 430.

3. The ruins of the old French Fort St. Frédéric still stand at Crown Point, near the massive remains of later British fortifications. The point, where the lake narrows drastically, was fortified from the end of the seventeenth century as New France's southern bastion. Notwithstanding, Dieskau found the 1737 renovation dilapidated and inadequate. St. Frédéric had a sinister reputation in New England. From this place raiders fanned out into the English settlements. Captives and scalps taken passed back through St. Frédéric on the way to Montreal. For the 1735 plans, see John R. Cuneo, *Robert Rogers of the Rangers* (Ticonderoga: Fort Ticonderoga Museum, 1988), pp. 84–85.

4. Francis Parkman, *Montcalm and Wolfe: The French & Indian War* (New York: Da Capo, 1995), p. 174, after Parkman's translation from the *Archives de la Marine* and the correspondence of Dieskau and his adjutant Montreuil.

5. Allan W. Eckert, *Wilderness Empire* (Boston: Little Brown, 1969), p. 326; Parkman, p. 174.

6. Louis Antoine de Bougainville, *Adventure in the Wilderness: The American Journals, 1756–1760*, Edward P. Hamilton, trans. (Norman, Okla.: University of Oklahoma, 1990), pp. 174–175.

7. Fort Carillon, to become Fort Ticonderoga, had the distinction of being built of stone in the style of a Vauban fortress. It was a remarkable undertaking given the circumstances, but as the Americans would learn to their discomfort twenty-seven years later, Ticonderoga was poorly sited to defend the Champlain channel. Worse, it was easily commanded by nearby heights, whereon Burgoyne placed his artillery. See Richard M. Ketchum, *Saratoga: Turning Point of America's Revolutionary War* (New York: Henry Holt, 1997), pp. 28–29 ff.

8. James Thomas Flexner, *Mohawk Baronet: A Biography of Sir William Johnson* (Syracuse, N.Y.: Syracuse University, 1979), pp. 138–139.

9. Sir William Johnson, *The Papers of Sir William Johnson*, James Sullivan, ed. (Albany: The University of the State of New York, 1922), II, pp. 14–15.

10. Eckert, p. 327.

11. The occasion is recorded in Johnson, II, pp. 16–17.

12. Flexner, p. 144.

13. About three miles outside of Lake George village, south on Route 9, the ravine is visible in the vicinity of the Williams monument. This monument is marked by a gold and blue sign difficult to see from the highway. The military road to Fort Edward ran through this wooded ravine. Hikers today can climb through the ravine just as Tiyanoga did, with Williams at his rear. On top of the ridge, where the ravine ends, stands a motel called the King Hendrick. At the bottom of the ridge, also on Route 9, is the Colonel Williams Resort Motel. Lake George village may be a battlefield site, but the beautiful lake remains a popular vacation destination.

14. Milton Hamilton, *Sir William Johnson: Colonial American 1715:1763* (Port Washington, N.Y.:

Notes

Kennikat, 1976), p. 162. Hamilton quotes Daniel Claus on Hendrick being a "heavy old gray headed" man. Claus was fond of the old sachem he called "Henery my Father."

15. This scene is borrowed from Allan Eckert, *Wilderness Empire* (Boston: Little Brown, 1969), p. 337.

16. Parkman, p. 177.

17. Flexner, pp. 145–146, derives these details from Daniel Claus, *Narrative of his relations with Sir William Johnson*; *Documents relative to the colonial history of the State of New York*; *Documentary History of the State of New York* (New York: 1904), p. 14; and N.Y. *Mercury*, 9/15/1755. Eckert follows this version, while Anderson adheres to Parkman's sources.

18. Fintan O'Toole persists in referring to the men of the Bloody Morning Scout as "British." Braddock's regiments were "British," his wagon men, Daniel Boone and Daniel Morgan, "American." Williams's soldiers were "American," or so our sectionalism urges us to insist. Otherwise, O'Toole has the fight vividly and accurately depicted in *White Savage* (New York: Farrar, Straus and Giroux, 2005), pp. 139–140.

19. The facts of the situation are from Hamilton, p. 163; the dramatic words from Eckert, pp. 340–341.

20. Quotations are from Parkman, p. 179, drawn from the journals and correspondence of Seth Pomeroy and Surgeon Williams. The hospital that Williams and Pynchon established is thought to have been at a point now marked by a gold and blue sign 200 feet northeast from Johnson's headquarters tent on the Lake George Battlefield Campgrounds.

21. Flexner, p. 150. The story is told in *Dialogue entre le Maréchal de Saxe et le Baron de Dieskau aux Champs Élysées*, most likely written by Dieskau himself.

22. Johnson, II, p. 74. The house to which Dieskau was evacuated belonged to Philip Schuyler, then a serving quartermaster. Schuyler would be named major general by act of Congress twenty years later. He met Dieskau on the occasion of his captivity in Albany. Fintan O'Toole construes a lengthy acquaintanceship between Johnson and the French general while both are in recovery. Dieskau had fought at Fontenoy, where the Irish Brigade of the French Army helped turn the tide of battle. Johnson owned a book on this famous campaign. O'Toole, pp. 30–31.

23. Hamilton, p. 172.

24. Anderson, p. 762, n. 24. Markers for Bloody Pond are found beside Route 9 where the military road, entering the ravine, turned uphill. Here Lt. Coles checked Dieskau's advance, allowing Williams's survivors to escape. The pond itself, such as it is now, is found deeper in the woods than the pond directly off the highway.

25. Flexner, p. 146, and Eckert, p. 349, find this account convincing. Hamilton, p. 162, sticks closely to Claus's contemporary account in holding the women responsible.

26. Parkman, p. 182.

27. Denis Diderot, *Mémoires de Diderot* (1830), I, p. 402.

28. 1759, "the wonderful year," as it came to be called in Britain and the colonies, saw Wolfe capture Quebec, Amherst capture Ticonderoga and Crown Point, and Johnson capture Oswego and Niagara. This after disappointing, even catastrophic, campaigns in 1755, 1756, 1757, and 1758. By the summer of 1760, Amherst had captured Montreal, and the power of France in North America was broken for all time. French forces had been outnumbered, outgunned, outspent, and strangled by blockade. They had also been undone from within by graft and corruption. Britain would enjoy this expensive victory only a short time before bills came due and the American colonies declined to pay.

29. Flexner, pp. 301–302.

30. Flexner, p. 111.

31. "Montcalm was horrified by the style of warfare he encountered in America and did everything in his power to make his operations conform to civilized standards as he understood them. He may have lived long enough to regret it": Anderson, p. 136. Notwithstanding, the destruction of Fort William Henry amidst scenes of notable barbarity and the hard handling of the Black Watch on the lines of Ticonderoga went far toward making Montcalm an object of fear and blame.

32. De Bougainville, p. 235.

33. Edward P. Hamilton, *The French and Indian Wars: The Story of Battles and Forts in the Wilderness* (New York: Doubleday, 1962) p. 201. Hamilton follows Parkman in doubting what Webb could have done

even if he had elected to march out. He would have needed to leave some of his 1,600 behind to guard Fort Edward and the road to Albany. Monro had 2,200 regulars and provincials in Fort William Henry or encamped nearby. Montcalm commanded upward of 8,000, including Indians. The poor quality of artillery at Fort William Henry was also to blame; many of the guns burst. Webb could well have been ambushed on the road to Lake George, much as Colonel Williams had been on the Bloody Morning Scout. Except for the garrison at Fort Edward, there were no British forces north of the headwaters of the Hudson, only green militia. Capitulation might have seemed the least of the evils confronting Webb. On balance, allegations of cowardice are probably exaggerated.

34. De Bougainville, p. 333.

35. For plans of the fort, see Cuneo, pp. 84–85. Rogers and his brother Richard conducted raids against Ticonderoga (Fort Carillon) from Fort William Henry. The rangers were active at the site up through the siege. See also Stephen Brumwell, *White Devil: A True Story of War, Savagery, and Vengeance in Colonial America* (New York.: Da Capo, 2004), pp. 87–96.

36. Parkman, pp. 277–287. Parkman dwells at great length on the savage practices of Montcalm's Indian allies and de Bougainville's great trepidations about their probable behavior.

37. Since the Fort William Henry garrison was afflicted with smallpox, many of the corpses disinterred were infected. Warriors carried the disease home, causing great mortality among the western tribes on their return. Richard Rogers succumbed at William Henry to smallpox. His was one of the bodies desecrated: Cuneo, p. 54.

38. Walter R. Borneman, *The French and Indian War: Deciding the Fate of North America* (New York: Harper Collins, 2006), p. 94. Parkman follows an account by Lévis estimating that fifty or so prisoners were murdered out of the column, in addition to those killed in the infirmary. As many as 700 were dragged off, however, "stripped and otherwise maltreated": Parkman, p. 297. The French were able to buy back or secure several hundred of these Indian captives.

39. Throughout the colonies, the massacre at Fort William Henry was followed by a great public outcry damning the perpetrators and promising severe revenge against the Indians. The *New York Mercury* thundered: "Surely if any nation under the heavens was ever provoked to the most rigid severities in the conduct of a war, it is ours! Will it not be strictly just and absolutely necessary, from henceforth … that we make some severe examples of our inhuman enemies, when they fall into our hand": Borneman, p. 95.

Chapter 4: A Rumored Gift

1. Sanford H. Cobb, *The Story of the Palatines: An Episode in Colonial History* (New York: G. P. Putnam, 1897), pp. 77–79.

2. While Queen Anne certainly wished to extend her charity to these oppressed coreligionists, the evidence points rather to land speculators among the American proprietaries as instigators of the immigration. See Cobb, pp. 50–58, for the terms of the dispute. During the period in question (1680 to 1780), approximately 500,000 southwestern Germans left the Rhineland for new homes. Only about 20 percent voyaged to America; the majority moved eastward into Hungary or Russia and lands recently vacated by the receding Ottoman Empire. Alan Taylor views the migration to America by way of Britain as an example of the push/pull principle in immigration. "Why, then, did so many Rhinelanders undertake such a daunting journey across an ocean to a strange land? There were push factors. No united realm, Germany was subdivided into many small principalities, frequently embroiled in the great wars of the continent. … Authoritarian princes heavily taxed their subjects. … Most princes also demanded religious conformity from their subjects. … In addition, a swelling population pressed against the limits of the rural economy." If this was the push, all that was needed on the other side was a pull, and this took the form of rumor, or conflated rumors, advertising the Crown's intentions and promoting the promises of North America. See Alan Taylor, *American Colonies: The Settling of North America* (New York: Viking Penguin, 2002), pp. 318–319.

3. Cobb, pp. 126–127.

4. Edwin G. Guillet, *The Great Migration* (New York: Thomas Nelson, 1937), p. 131.

5. Taylor, p. 294. "Scots gentlemen became conspicuous as colonial officials, including the royal governors Robert Hunter of New York, Alexander Spotswood of Virginia, and Gabriel Johnson of North Carolina." Thwarted in their own drive for empire, Scots made the most of the English Empire and, after

1707, according to Taylor, Scots outnumbered the English as New World settlers.

6. John Romeyn Brodhead, *Documents Relative to the Colonial History of the State of New-York*, ed. E. B. O'Callaghan (Albany, N.Y.: Weed, Parsons, 1855), 5, 113.

7. Gottlieb Mittelberger, *Gottlieb Mittelberger's Journey to Pennsylvania in the Year 1750 and Return to Germany in the Year 1754* (Philadelphia, 1898), pp. 25–28. The indentured servant that Mittelberger describes was known as a "redemptionist." In exchange for the price of passage, the immigrant agreed to labor three to four years. Redemptionists were a vital part of Pennsylvania's economy. Taylor believes that Mittelberger exaggerates. Safe transport of redemptionists was in everyone's best interest. See Taylor, p. 320.

8. James Alexander and William Smith Sr. defended John Peter Zenger in 1735. Both were subsequently disbarred by Chief Justice James DeLancey, and Andrew Hamilton of Philadelphia successfully took up the case. For the importance of Alexander and Smith in early Revolutionary politics, see Barnet Schecter, *The Battle for New York* (New York: Walker, 2002), pp. 17–24.

9. Cobb writes: "There can be no doubt that, had Hunter pursued a just course towards the Palatines, they would not have denied him the certificate demanded, and he himself would have come nearer to just treatment by the Treasury": p. 245. Hunter was owed reimbursement—no one denies—and except for resentment directed at him by his late charges, resentment more properly aimed at Livingston, he would have received it.

10. Codman Hislop, *The Mohawk* (New York: Rinehart, 1948) pp. 94–99.

11. Cobb, pp. 124–125.

12. Paul A. W. Wallace, *Conrad Weiser 1696–1760: Friend of Colonist & Mohawk* (Philadelphia: University of Pennsylvania, 1945), pp. 7–8.

13. Cobb, p. 80.

14. Cobb, pp. 117–120.

15. Cobb, p. 105.

16. Joseph Addison, *The Spectator*, No. 50, Friday, April 27, 1711 (New York: Dutton, Everyman's Library, 1964), I, pp. 150–151.

17. Fintan O'Toole in *White Savage: William Johnson and the Invention of America (New York: Farrar, Straus and Giroux, 2005)*, pp. 11–15, describes Tiyanoga's visit and Addison's subsequent fabrication of the Hendrick letters. The visit of the four so-called chiefs was indeed a publicity stunt funded by Peter Schuyler, Philip Schuyler's grandfather and mayor of Albany, in interest of drawing attention to French encroachments along the New York frontier.

18. Cobb, p. 107.

19. Cobb, pp. 114–115.

20. The march from the vicinity of Saugerties to the headwaters of the Schoharie likely followed the Devil's Path route towards modern Tannersville, between Plattekill Mountain and High Peak, an exceptionally rugged pass.

21. Wallace, p. 120.

22. Vincent J. Schaefer, *Vroomans Nose: A Study* (Fleischmanns, N.Y.: Purple Mountain, 1992), p. 36. The site of the old Indian village is marked by a gold and blue sign about a half mile east of the eastern base of the Nose.

23. The great poverty of the Palatines at this time is attested to by both Native Americans and Dutch settlers. Wallace, pp. 16–23.

24. C. Z. Weiser, *Conrad Weiser* (Reading, Pa., 1876) contains the English version of the autobiographical diaries entitled *Conrad Weiser's Tagebuch*, later translated by Dr. Hiester Muhlenberg of Reading. Essential passages are reproduced in Wallace. The quality of Weiser's prose vies with any produced in early eighteenth-century America for narrative power and psychological insight. His account of Native Americans and of life on the frontier opens a window into the otherwise obscure history of settlement in early colonial New York and Pennsylvania.

25. Wallace, p. 29.

26. Hislop, pp. 111–113.

27. Cobb, pp. 251–257.

28. Wallace, p. 31.

29. Wallace, pp. 36–36.

30. Logan was an early patron of Benjamin Franklin. For an appreciation of the power of patronage in pre-Revolutionary America, see Gordon S. Wood, *The Radicalism of the American Revolution* (New York: Vintage, 1992), pp. 74–76.

31. Wallace, pp. 39–49.

32. Wallace, p. 552.

33. Flexner, p. 59.

34. Wallace, p. 133.

35. Hiester H. Muhlenberg, M.D., was born at Reading, Jan. 15, 1812, son of the distinguished Rev. Henry Augustus Muhlenberg, pastor of the Trinity Lutheran Church of Reading, afterward member of Congress and ambassador to Austria, and at the time of his death the candidate of the Democratic Party for governor of Pennsylvania.

36. Wallace, p. 81 ff.

37. Wallace, p. 81 ff.

38. Wallace, p. 82.

39. Wallace, pp. 82 ff.

40. Wallace, pp. 83–85.

41. Wallace, p. 88.

42. Wallace, p. 88.

43. See James H. Merrell, *The Lancaster Treaty of 1744 with Related Documents* (New York and Boston: Bedford/St. Martin's, 2007), Part One.

44. Wallace, pp. 175–183.

45. Isabel Thompson Kelsay, *Joseph Brant 1743–1807: Man of Two Worlds* (Syracuse N.Y.: Syracuse University, 1986), pp. 67–68.

Chapter 5: The Missionary

1. The first Recollect fathers entered New France in 1615, the first Jesuits in 1625. Among Protestants, Johannes Megapolensis (Johann van Grootstede) was the first to preach to Native Americans of the Mohawk Valley, in 1643. See Dean R. Snow, Charles T. Gehring, and William A. Starna, eds., *In Mohawk Country* (Syracuse, N.Y.: Syracuse University, 1996).

2. Sir William Johnson, *The Papers of Sir William Johnson*, ed. James Sullivan (Albany, N.Y.: The University of the State of New York, 1921), V, p. 59.

3. Fred Anderson, *Crucible of War: The Seven Years War and the Fate of Empire in British North America, 1754–1766* (New York: Alfred A. Knopf, 2000), p. 637.

4. Kevin Phillips, *The Cousins' Wars: Religion, Politics, & the Triumph of Anglo-America* (New York: Basic, 1999), pp. 116–119. At Fort Stanwix in 1768, Johnson succeeded in negotiating a grant of land from the Six Nations in exchange for guaranteeing their homelands in western New York. The Nations agreed to open lands south of the Susquehanna and Ohio rivers to white settlement. In New York, the Fort Stanwix line veered southeast from present Rome to the Unadilla River, then ran from the junction of the Susquehanna and Unadilla to the West Branch of the Delaware at Deposit. The line then swept westward to Owego, beyond Binghamton, and from Owego on the Susquehanna, sharp west to the headwaters of the mighty Ohio. Lands lying west of the Unadilla, to the north of the Susquehanna and Ohio, were denominated Indian lands. All else—a vast grant of territory stretching over the Appalachians—was open to white settlement. The Six Nations had surrendered lands not even occupied by the Six Nations, but home to the Delaware, Mingo and Shawnee nations whom the Six Nations held in subordination. Yet the Fort Stanwix treaty line, for all its injustice, came as close as any previous agreement to satisfying all sides. Nonetheless, the Reverend Eleazar Wheelock, a firebrand for Native American conversion, sent a mad visionary, Reverend Jacob Johnson, to protest the treaty and denounce the wilderness Antichrist (Sir William) and his popish minions. See James Thomas Flexner, *Mohawk Baronet: A Biography of Sir William Johnson* (Syracuse, N.Y.: Syracuse University, 1989), pp. 324–328, for an account of the conference and its participants.

5. The Iroquois of the mid-eighteenth century were totally dependent on European goods for their lifestyle. O'Toole records a note from a Tuscarora sachem sent to Sir William: "Sarah the wife of Isaac Gives

her kind love to your honour. And Desires the favour of a little Chocolate if you please." Fintan O'Toole, *White Savage: William Johnson and the Invention of America* (New York: Farrar, Straus and Giroux, 2005). p. 50.

6. Samuel K. Lothrop, "Life of Samuel Kirkland," *The Library of American Biography*, Second Series, Jared Sparks, ed. (Boston: Little Brown, 1855), Vol. XV, p. 133.

7. For a description of Wheelock's educational program and effect on students, see Isabel Thompson Kelsay, *Joseph Brant 1743–1807: Man of Two Worlds* (Syracuse, N.Y.: Syracuse University, 1984), pp. 83–85.

8. Flexner, p. 291.

9. Johnson, V, p. 60.

10. Lothrop, pp. 133–134.

11. Walter Pilkington, ed., *The Journal of Samuel Kirkland* (Clinton, N.Y.: Hamilton College, 1980), p. 88.

12. Pilkington, p. 3.

13. Pilkington, p. 3.

14. James Thomas Flexner, *Mohawk Baronet: A Biography of Sir William Johnson* (Syracuse, N.Y.: Syracuse University, 1989), p. 288.

15. Pilkington, p. 4.

16. Lois M. Huey and Bonnie Pulis, *Molly Brant: A Legacy of Her Own* (Youngstown, N.Y.: Old Fort Niagara Association, 1997), pp. 25–26.

17. Pilkington, p. 6.

18. Lothrop, p. 143.

19. James E. Seaver, *A Narrative of the Life of Mrs. Mary Jemison* (Norman, Okla.: University of Oklahoma, reprint of 1823 account), chapter 3.

20. Pilkington, p. 11.

21. Pilkington, pp. 23–25.

22. Pilkington, pp. 13–14.

23. Lothrop, p. 140

24. Pilkington, p. 43.

25. Allan W. Eckert, *The Conquerors* (New York: Bantam, 1981), p. 729.

26. Eckert, p. 730.

27. Anderson, p. 545.

28. Eckert, p. 730.

29. Eckert, p. 730.

30. Eckert, p. 634.

31. Pilkington, p. 29.

32. Pilkington, p. 35. Kirkland's account of arriving at Johnson Hall includes surviving a storm on Lake Oneida in a flimsy canoe and seeking help for his adopted brother's sister-in-law among the Oneidas.

33. Flexner, p. 290.

Chapter 6: A Revolutionary Idea

1. See www.courts.state.ny.us/history/elecbook/fulton/pg1.htm. Johnstown courthouse is the only colonial courthouse in the State of New York still in daily operation, and one of only five in the nation. Sir William wrote: "I am now carrying on a handsome building for a Court House, towards which I shall contribute £500." The bricks were brought from Holland. The triangle for summoning sessions was made from a piece of bent iron still in the belfry today and still in use to announce assembly. The courthouse was only partially finished when, on September 8, 1772, the first Court of General Sessions to be held west of Albany was convened. Present as judges were: Guy Johnson, who was to succeed Sir William as Superintendent of Indian Affairs for the Northern Zone; John Butler, who was with General Braddock at Fort Duquesne and later commanded Butler's rangers during the Revolution; and Peter Conyne, who served with distinction with the Tryon militia during the Revolution.

2. Gordon S. Wood, *The Radicalism of the American Revolution* (New York: Vintage, 1992), p. 88.

3. Wood, p. 128.

4. Wood, p. 88.

5. James Thomas Flexner, *Mohawk Baronet: A Biography of Sir William Johnson* (Syracuse, N.Y.: Syracuse University, 1989), p. 335.

6. The core of Tryon County was comprised of six districts stretching along the north and south banks of the Mohawk. In the east, the Mohawk District encompassed the lower Mohawk castle and Schoharie Valley; in the center, the Palatine District stood north of the river; while the Canajoharie District, including the upper Mohawk castle and Cherry Valley, lay south; in the west, the Kingsland District was north of Fort Stanwix and the German Flats District south of the river to the headwaters of the Susquehanna. Sir William's land holdings were concentrated within these districts, as were the holdings of most of the Johnson party.

7. George Croghan was of great assistance to Sir William in translating tribal demands and mapping the interior of the wilderness. He spoke more dialects than Johnson and had penetrated deeply into the trans-Mississippi. As a reward Croghan received a large parcel of land in Cherry Valley from Sir William. See Reuben Gold Thwaites, *Early Western Journals: 1748–1765* (Lewisburg, Pa.: Wennawoods, 1998), p. 51.

8. Despite cyclical downturns in the economy, the fundamentals for prosperity had been firmly established in the colonies by 1776. See Thomas Fleming, *1776: Year of Illusions* (New York: W. W. Norton, 1975), p. 23. "British taxes cost the 2,250,000 Americans of 1776 at most 3 percent of their over-all national income—between $3 million and $7 million a year." Americans paid on average $1.20 a year per capita in taxes. Their exports to England very nearly equaled England's exports to the colonies.

9. Even aging and ill, Sir William enjoyed abundant creature comforts, scandalizing the valley on many occasions with the extent of his sexual appetite. He had a fourteen-mile road laid through the forest to the shores of Lake Sacandaga, and there built Fish House, his own private pleasure resort. Two shots fired in the air usually brought Susannah Wormwood, a beautiful young girl, running to his side. She bore Sir William a son in his silver years, his last child: Flexner, pp. 337–338.

10. Isabel Thompson Kelsay, *Joseph Brant, 1743–1807: Man of Two Worlds* (Syracuse N.Y.: Syracuse University, 1986), p. 121.

11. The Boston Massacre of 1770 had found a counterpart in New York City during the same year. Bloody fights broke out in lower Manhattan with quartered British troops. "Wages in both cities," Kevin Phillips writes, "already depressed because of an economic slump, were reduced in 1770 by the willingness of moonlighting British troops to accept cut-rate employment. In prewar Philadelphia, by contrast, the greater working-class radicalization and emergence of class warfare are partly explained by the absence of British troops to play the unifying role of an external enemy": *The Cousins' Wars: Religion, Politics, & the Triumph of Anglo-America* (New York: Basic, 1999), pp. 89–90. New York City's reaction to British troops found no echo along the Mohawk in 1772; in fact, what frightened central New Yorkers was the total absence of British forces along the frontier.

12. Guy Park Manor, a stunningly beautiful Georgian villa, stands along Route 5 on the western outskirts of Amsterdam, N.Y. The interior is significantly altered, but the façade looks much as it did in Guy Johnson's day.

13. Allan W. Eckert, *That Dark and Bloody River: Chronicles of the Ohio River Valley* (New York: Bantam, 1996), pp. 13–16.

14. Flexner, p. 314.

15. Mineral springs are found at Sharon, Richfield, New Lebanon and, of course, Saratoga. All were within close reach, and Sir William tried them in order to find relief from his wound and circulatory problems. Eckert asserts that his main malady was syphilis; Flexner that he was generally run-down from rich living, excessive drink, and food; all agree that he suffered excruciating pain throughout his life from the lead ball embedded in his hip. He apparently bled profusely from the smallest cuts, was also arthritic, cirrhotic, and probably the victim of arteriosclerosis.

16. Flexner, p. 314.

17. Lois M. Huey and Bonnie Pulis, *Molly Brant: A Legacy of Her Own* (Youngstown N.Y.: Old Fort Niagara Association, 1997), p. 49.

18. Kelsay, pp. 133–134.

19. Flexner, p. 320.

20. Allan D. Foote, *Liberty March: The Battle of Oriskany* (Utica, N.Y.: North Country, 1999), p. 81.

21. For the role of Scottish Highlanders in the American Revolution, see Phillips, pp. 202–207.

22. Anderson, pp. 634–635.

23. Anderson, p. 636.

24. Sir William Johnson, *The Papers of Sir William Johnson* (Albany, N.Y.: The University of the State of New York, 1921), V, p. 6.

25. Johnson, IV, p. 843–844.

26. Johnson, V, p. 7.

27. George Washington expressed himself as clearly opposed to the Proclamation of 1763: "I can never look upon that proclamation in any other light (but I say this between ourselves) than as a temporary expedient to quiet the minds of the Indians." Benjamin Franklin came closer still to the reason for disregarding the Proclamation in an address to the British House of Commons in 1766: "The trade with the Indians, though carried on in America, is not an American interest. The people of America are chiefly farmers and planters; scarce anything that they raise or produce is an article of commerce with the Indians. The Indian trade is a British interest: it is carried on with British manufacturers, for the profit of British merchants and manufacturers": Eckert, p. 653.

28. Gordon S. Wood, *The Radicalism of the American Revolution* (New York: Vintage, 1993), p. 126.

29. Kelsay, p. 145.

30. Eckert, p. 65.

31. Flexner, p. 346.

32. See Don R. Gerlach, *Philip Schuyler and the American Revolution in New York, 1733–1777* (Lincoln, Neb.: University of Nebraska, 1964), pp. 248–250, for detailed accounts of the New York Assembly's transactions at this time; Barnet Schecter, *The Battle for New York: The City at the Heart of the American Revolution* (New York: Walker, 2002), pp. 53–54 for a contemporary view of the Canadian threat; and Richard M. Ketchum, *Saratoga: Turning Point of America's Revolutionary War* (New York: Henry Holt, 1997), pp. 13–14, for Congress's wishful thinking.

33. John Jay was hardly an ardent revolutionary. As late as January 1776, he, James Duane of New York, Andrew Allen of Pennsylvania, and William Livingston of New Jersey were closeted with Thomas Lord Drummond over a plan to reconcile the Crown to the colonies. These middle-state representatives told Drummond, "they were not prepared to plunge themselves into a civil war merely to humor a set of people [the New England delegates] who were obnoxious to them." Jay was less concerned with Canada's threat to New England than with New England radicals drawing New York into a pointless and bloody conflict. See Thomas Fleming, *1776 Year of Illusions* (New York: W. W. Norton, 1975), pp. 142–143.

34. Gerlach, pp. 285–286.

35. The main contingents attending the Second Congress for New York represented New York City, Long Island, and Albany County almost exclusively.

36. John Ferling, *Almost a Miracle: The American Victory in the War of Independence* (New York: Oxford University, 2007), p. 71.

37. Schuyler was outraged at the treatment of Skene, no matter his political persuasion. By seizing his farm, boatworks, and forge, the patriots violated private property. "A set of people," he remarked, "calling themselves a Committee of War embezzled everything." Schuyler eventually gave orders that Skene's possessions be restored "in order that no disgrace may be brought on our cause by such lawless proceedings": Gerlach, p. 285. From the outset, there were deep and abiding disagreements about the meaning of "liberty."

38. Christopher Ward, *The War of the Revolution* (New York: Macmillan, 1952), I, pp. 68–69. Of the many histories of the war, Ward's remains among the most comprehensive, readable, and finely detailed.

39. Ward, p. 69

40. Fleming, pp. 48–50.

41. *World Almanac of the American Revolution*, L. Edward Purcell and David Burg, eds. (New York: World Almanac, 1992) p. 44.

42. Ketchum, p. 15.

43. James L. Nelson, *Benedict Arnold's Navy* (New York: McGraw-Hill, 2006), p. 342. Nelson explains, "Ticonderoga, situated by the French to resist a move from the south, was not ideally placed to defend against an attack from the north."

44. Ward, I, p. 64.

45. Ferling, p. 47.

46. Ward, I, pp. 139–140.

47. W. J. Wood, *Battles of the Revolutionary War* (New York: Da Capo, 1990), p. 35.

48. Ward, I, pp. 145–146.

49. Kelsay, p. 157.

50. Kelsay, p. 162.

51. Ward, I, p. 151.

52. Ward, I, p. 153.

53. Ward, I, p. 158.

54. Arnold's march from Augusta, Maine, up the Kennebec, the Dead and Chaudière rivers to Levis, and across the St. Lawrence to Quebec, remains one of the great wilderness adventures. The story is resoundingly told by Kenneth Roberts in the novel *Arundel*. This was a New England effort, and the New York effort, creeping northward from St. Johns, paled by comparison. For a brief synopsis of the ordeal, see W. J. Wood, pp. 41–44.

55. Montgomery's body was eventually returned to his home, New York City, and interred beneath the porch of St. Paul's Chapel on lower Broadway. The monument can be viewed beside the entrance to the church, the oldest surviving public building in the city and the rest station for thousands of rescue workers in the aftermath of the September 11 tragedy.

56. Schuyler House is maintained by New York State as an historic site. Located at 32 Catherine Street in downtown Albany, the core building of the original estate suggests the good taste and refinement of the family that built it in 1760. The Schuylers inhabited an earlier house in Albany, and to this older residence Johnson sent the wounded Baron Dieskau to recuperate in 1754. Philip Schuyler and Dieskau became fast friends. To the house on Catherine Street also went General Burgoyne following his surrender and the Baroness von Riedesel with her children. Although the servants disliked serving a British general, Burgoyne was treated as an honored guest by Schuyler's wife, the beautiful Catarina van Rensselaer. Few who visited Schuyler House ever departed feeling neglected.

57. Ketchum, p. 38. Schuyler was especially solicitous of Franklin's health, sending him back to New York with his own carriage and servants.

58. Ward, I, pp. 196–197.

59. Phillips, p. 141.

60. Gerlach, p. 9, for Schuyler's early education; see also, pp. 11ff. for his respectful relationship with Native Americans.

61. Gerlach, p. 283.

62. Ketchum, p. 336.

63. Ketchum, p. 36.

64. Ketchum, p. 36.

Chapter 7: Estranged Neighbors

1. The scene described is found in Isabel Thompson Kelsay, *Joseph Brant, 1743–1807: Man of Two Worlds* (Syracuse, N.Y.: Syracuse University, 1986), pp. 149–150.

2. See Kevin Phillips, *The Cousins' War: Religion, Politics & the Triumph of Anglo-America* (New York: Basic, 1999), for an analysis of ethnic and religious determinants of side, pp. 219–221. William L. Stone, *The Orderly Book of Sir John Johnson* (Albany: Joel Munsell, 1882), believed the Tories to have been more numerous than the patriots, but less active in meeting the uprising, pp. 16–17. W. J. Wood, *Battles of the Revolutionary War*, rehearsing the reasons for St. Leger's diversion, emphasizes the political purposes of the expedition. St. Leger hoped to capitalize on the fact that "The Mohawk was a hotbed of Toryism centered on a Tory stronghold": p. 116.

3. Codman Hislop, *The Mohawk* (New York: Rinehart & Company, 1948), pp. 155–157.

4. Hislop, p. 162.

5. Barbara Graymont, *The Iroquois in the American Revolution* (Syracuse, N.Y.: Syracuse University, 1972), p. 63.

6. Allan W. Eckert, *The Wilderness War* (New York: Bantam Books, 1982), pp. 52–53.

7. Kelsay, pp. 146–147.

8. Kelsay, p. 147.

9. Kelsay, p. 673, *Gage papers.*

10. Eckert, pp. 60–61.

11. Kelsay, p. 673, *American Archives,* Fourth Series, 2:911.

12. Eckert, p. 64.

13. Kelsay, p. 121.

14. The first trading post and fort built on the Oswego site dated from the 1720s and was located on the left bank of the Oswego River as it enters Lake Ontario. This was Fort Oswego, as distinct from Fort Ontario located on the right bank. Shirley rebuilt the tottering edifice in 1755, and Montcalm burned it in 1756. By the time Guy arrived at Fort Ontario, the trading post was still active, but the fortifications, repaired by Sir William Johnson in 1759, had been allowed to decay.

15. Kelsay, p. 152.

16. Graymont, p. 68, *Claus papers: Public Archives of Canada.*

17. Kelsay, p. 153, quoted from *Minute Book of Tryon County Committee of Safety.*

18. Gavin K. Watt, *Rebellion in the Mohawk Valley* (Toronto: Dundurn, 2002), pp. 37–38.

19. Graymont, pp. 65–66.

20. Eckert, p. 84, New York Colonial Documents.

21. Eckert p. 85.

22. Eckert p. 86.

23. Graymont, p. 81.

24. Graymont, p. 86.

25. On the north side, the Adirondack forests are drained principally by the Oswagatchie, Raquette, Grass, and St. Regis rivers flowing into the St. Lawrence; on the east side, by the Ausable and Saranac rivers flowing into Champlain; on the south side, by the Sacandaga flowing into the Hudson and the East and West Canada creeks flowing into the Mohawk. Flowing westward into Lake Ontario are the Black and Beaver rivers. These rivers, with their feeder lakes, form a dense webwork of navigable channels connected to the Northeast's major waterways. See Paul Scheider, *The Adirondacks: A History of America's First Wilderness* (New York: Henry Holt, 1997) for a detailed account.

26. Milton W. Hamilton, *Sir William Johnson—Colonial American, 1715:1763* (Port Washington, N.Y.: Kennikat, 1976), p. 35.

27. H. C. Burleigh, "A Tale of Loyalist Heroism," *Ontario History,* Vol. 13, No. 2 (1950), pp. 92.

28. Hamilton, p. 162. William Johnson was especially aggrieved at the loss of McGinnis and Ferrall; they had come into the country with him and were loyal friends and servants.

29. Ida Kast House and Mildred Kast Conrad, *Mohawk Valley Kasts and Allied Families* (Herkimer, N.Y.: Herkimer County Historical Society, 1985), pp. ix–xiii.

30. Gavin K. Watt, *The Burning of the Valleys: Daring Raids from Canada Against the New York Frontier in the Fall of 1780* (Toronto: Dundurn, 1997), p. 237, and also *Rebellion in the Mohawk Valley* (Toronto: Dundurn, 2002), p. 173–174.

31. Kelsay 177–179.

32. For American support of the rebellion on the Mohawk, see Eckert, p. 88.

33. Graymont, pp. 82–84.

34. Eckert, p. 87.

35. See Fintan O'Toole, *White Savage: William Johnson and the Invention of America* (New York: Farrar, Straus and Giroux, 2005), p. 11–12, for the role of Peter Schuyler, mayor of Albany, in the visitation of the chiefs.

36. Graymont, p. 84.

37. This flight would entail several notable defeats. At Trois Rivières, General Thomas's 2,000 collided with Burgoyne's 8,000. The Americans lost over 400 troops; the British, under a dozen. Thirty miles from Montreal an American force surrendered without a fight at the Cedars, and as a consequence Montreal, Sorel, and Chambly fell.

38. John J. Gallagher, *The Battle of Brooklyn* (New York: Sarpedon, 1995), p. 67.

39. Graymont, p. 90.

40. Walter Pilkington, ed., *The Journal of Samuel Kirkland* (Clinton, N.Y.: Hamilton College, 1980), p. 117.

41. Graymont, p. 92.

42. Snow, et al., p. 275.

43. Snow, et al., p. 275.

44. Snow, et al., p. 277.

45. Snow, et al., p. 278.

46. Snow, et al., p. 280.

47. Watt, p. 30.

48. Graymont, p. 94.

49. Eckert, pp. 91–92.

50. Barbara McMartin, Lee M. Brenning, and Peter O'Shea, *The Northwestern Adirondacks: Four-Season Adventures through the Boreal Forest and the Park's Frontier Region* (Woodstock, Vt.: Backcountry, 1990), p. 129.

51. Watt, p. 31.

52. Watt, p. 32.

53. Snow, et al., p. 280.

54. Ward, I, p. 389.

55. Ward, I, p. 385.

56. Watt, p. 47.

Chapter 8: At the Barricades

1. Kevin Phillips, *The Cousins' War: Religion, Politics & the Triumph of Anglo-America* (New York: Basic, 1999), pp. 276–277.

2. Phillips, p. 276.

3. Richard M. Ketchum, *Saratoga: Turning Point of America's Revolutionary War* (New York: Henry Holt, 1997), p. 43.

4. http://www.famousAmericans.net/NicholasHerkimer/.

5. Christopher Ward, *The War of Revolution* (New York: Macmillan, 1952), I, p. 389.

6. In mid-April 1776, Schuyler ordered Hermanus Schuyler to Skenesboro to begin turning the town into a shipyard. Schuyler had been building bateaux at Fort George on Lake George to support the Canadian campaign. He now wrote to John Hancock, president of the Congress, that he was "under the necessity of building a number of Batteaus far Exceeding what Congress ordered." In fact, Schuyler had ordered Hermanus to begin building gondolas. The idea of contesting the lake originated with him. James L. Nelson, *Benedict Arnold's Navy* (New York: McGraw-Hill, 2006), pp. 227–228.

7. Ward, I, p. 387.

8. For a detailed account of the building of Arnold's fleet, see Nelson, pp. 227–241.

9. John Paul Jones also found that the privateers, lucrative and free-wheeling, drew off able seamen from naval service. Until sailors were better paid, Jones warned, the American Navy would never become formidable. Evan Thomas, *John Paul Jones: Sailor, Hero, Father of the American Navy* (New York: Simon & Schuster, 2003), pp. 68–69.

10. Thomas Fleming, *1776: Year of Illusions* (New York: W. W. Norton, 1975), p. 390.

11. Ward I, p. 386.

12. Richard Varick, Schuyler's secretary, was tireless in his service to the Northern Department. He was a master logician and quartermaster responsible for bringing together the resources required by generals Schuyler and Arnold. He rose to become inspector-general at West Point after 1780, and was the first aide-de-camp to General Arnold, whom he greatly admired as a soldier. It is said that when Arnold's defection was made known, Colonel Varick was almost insane for several days. Towards the end of the war, he joined Washington's military family, and following the war, served as New York City's mayor from 1791 to 1801. See http://www.famousAmericans.net/RichardVarick/.

13. Ward, I, p. 386.

14. Kenneth Roberts, *Rabble in Arms* (New York: Doubleday, 1933), p. 241.

15. Ward, I, pp. 388–389.

16. Fleming, p. 390, discusses the consequences of Carleton's decision.

17. Ward, I, p. 392.

18. Ward, I, p. 392.

19. Ward, I, p. 392. Arnold received nothing that he requested.

20. Fleming, p. 392.

21. Ward, I, p. 393.

22. Ward, I, p. 394.

23. Nelson, p. 301.

24. Nelson, p. 320.

25. All of Arnold's attacks on Quebec were mounted at night, one in a blinding snowstorm.

26. Fleming, pp. 397–398.

27. http://www.historiclakes.org/vbrp/vbr12b.htm.

28. Fort Stanwix was renamed Fort Schuyler in 1776. An older Fort Schuyler, on the present-day site of Utica, was recognized as derelict. The fort in Herkimer village (German Flats) was named Dayton; other forts in the district were named Franklin, Montgomery, and Paris, after Isaac Paris.

29. Walter Pilkington, ed., *The Journal of Samuel Kirkland* (Clinton, N.Y.: Hamilton College, 1980), p. 118.

30. Isabel Thompson Kelsay, *Joseph Brant 1743–1807: Man of Two Worlds* (Syracuse, N.Y.: Syracuse University, 1986), pp. 185–186. Good Peter and other Oneidas at Oquaga were happy to welcome Thayendanegea home, but the sentiment in the village remained in favor of neutrality. "Most of them were not eager to join in the war," Kelsay observes. "Like the entire Six Nations, there were a few at Oquaga who favored Britain, a few who favored the rebels, and a much larger number who felt as Fort Hunter's Little Abraham did: they just wanted to live in peace with both sides."

31. Pilkington, p. 113.

32. Barbara Graymont, *The Iroquois in the American Revolution* (Syracuse, N.Y.: Syracuse University, 1972), p. 239.

33. Pilkington, p. 120.

34. Graymont, p. 113.

35. Carleton's restraint in employing native warriors was one part pragmatism and one part idealism. Edmund Burke would eventually (1779) deliver a three-hour oration in Parliament on the immorality of using "offspring of the devil against civilized people." William Pitt also blamed the government for attempting to subjugate a brave people by hiring foreign mercenaries and untamed red men. Graymont, p. 161. Carleton knew more than either Burke or Pitt about Indian war and its consequences.

36. Kelsay, p. 189.

37. Kelsay, p. 189.

38. The Forbidden Path into Seneca country began by the fork of the Susquehanna at Tioga and continued on to the Finger Lakes. For most of the eighteenth century, the path was closed to white travelers unless accompanied by Seneca braves. The Forbidden Path was not only the back door into Indian country, but the most direct route from Oquaga to Niagara.

39. Allan W. Eckert, *The Wilderness War* (Boston: Little Brown, 1978), p. 116.

40. Ketchum, p. 113.

41. Ketchum, p. 118.

42. Gavin K. Watt, *Rebellion in the Mohawk Valley* (Toronto: Dundurn, 2002), pp. 60–61.

43. Larry Lowenthal, *Marinus Willett: Defender of the Northern Frontier* (Fleischmanns, N.Y.: Purple Mountain, 2000), pp. 14–15.

44. Schuyler ordered Colonel Goose van Schaick with a detachment of 150 Massachusetts Continentals into Tryon County. The men were scratched together from Brigadier Ebenezer Learned's brigade and led by the state's senior major, Ezra Badlam: Watt, p. 76.

45. Baron Roche de Fermoy could be considered, along with numerous other foreign appointees commissioned by Congress, a soldier of fortune. His inadequacies would cost the patriots dearly at Ticonderoga, but his presence also reflected the severe officer shortage prevailing in the American army. A similar lacking accounts for La Marquisie's forwarding to Stanwix as chief engineering officer.

46. Watt, p. 143.

47. Walter D. Edmonds, *Drums along the Mohawk* (Syracuse, N.Y.: Syracuse University, 1997, original edition 1936), p. 161.

48. Claus to Knox, Oct. 16, 1777, and Watt, p. 83.

49. John Dusler, Feb 12, 1833, declaration, Brant MSS., 3F40–41, quoted from Kelsay, p. 195.

50. William L. Stone, *Life of Joseph Brant—Thayendanegea* (Buffalo, N.Y.: Phinney, 1851), 1: 184–185.

Chapter 9: A Ravine Too Far

1. W. J. Wood, *Battles of the Revolutionary War 1775–1781* (New York: Da Capo, 1995), pp. 138.

2. W. J. Wood, p. 139.

3. Christopher Ward, *The War of Revolution* (New York: Macmillan, 1952), I, pp. 410–411.

4. Ward, I, p. 412.

5. Colonel Pierce Long commanded the armada sailing from Mount Independence and Ticonderoga to Skenesboro, and failed to push on quickly or to sight guns overlooking the lake's narrows. Ward, I, p. 414, also Richard M. Ketchum, *Saratoga: Turning Point of America's Revolutionary War* (New York: Henry Holt, 1997), pp. 222–223.

6. Ketchum, p. 190.

7. Michael Stephenson, *Patriot Battles: How the War of Independence Was Fought* (New York: Harper Collins, 2007), p. 295.

8. Ketchum p. 209.

9. Ketchum, p. 230.

10. Ketchum, p. 188.

11. Ketchum, p. 219.

12. Ketchum, p. 220.

13. Ketchum, p. 248.

14. Not without justification, Stephenson compares Schuyler to Marshal Kutuzov, p. 297.

15. Ketchum, p. 252.

16. Alan Taylor, *The Divided Ground* (New York: Knopf, 2005), p. 136, offers an account of Colonel Frederick Visscher, who was scalped and left for dead much like Gregg. The victim stood a chance of survival once infection had passed, but was required to wear a hat or skull cap for the rest of his life.

17. Jane McCrea's story is told in many places. For the classic nineteenth-century view, see George Scheer and Hugh Rankin, *Rebels & Redcoats* (New York: Da Capo, 1987), pp. 269–270; for a more current appreciation, Gavin K. Watt, *Rebellion in the Mohawk Valley* (Toronto: Dundurn, 2002), pp. 138–139, 303.

18. Watt, p. 114.

19. Watt, p. 115.

20. Watt, p. 92.

21. Watt, p. 100.

22. Allan W. Eckert, *The Wilderness War* (Boston: Little Brown, 1978), p. 140.

23. Watt, p. 120.

24. Max Reid, *The Mohawk Valley: Its Legends and Its History* (New York: G. P. Putnam, 1907), p. 416.

25. Larry Lowenthal, *Marinus Willett: Defender of the Northern Frontier* (Fleischmanns, N.Y.: Purple Mountain, 2000), pp. 26–27.

26. The first appearance of the striped flag of union was on January 1, 1776, at Cambridge: L. Edward Purcell and David Burg, *World Almanac of the American Revolution* (New York: World Almanac, 1992), p. 68.

27. Burgoyne's pronouncement to his Indian allies ran roughly as follows: "We go from here into battle with those Rebels, but before we do there are certain laws and customs of war to which you must agree to conform. I positively forbid bloodshed when you are not opposed in arms. Women, children, and old men, as well as those of our enemies who become our prisoners, must be held sacred from the knife or hatchet, even during the time of actual conflict": Eckert, p. 119.

On the Bouquet River, June 20, Burgoyne issued a manifesto to all Americans: "Let not people consider their distance from my camp provides them safety. I have but to give stretch to the Indian forces under my directions—and they amount to thousands—to overtake the hardened enemies of Great Britain. If the frenzy of hostility should remain, I trust I shall stand acquitted in the eyes of God and man, in executing the vengeance of the British government against the willful outcasts." Ketchum, p. 141.

28. Watt, p. 132.

29. Watt, p. 197; Eckert, p. 145.

30. Lois M. Huey and Bonnie Pulis, *Molly Brant: A Legacy of Her Own* (Youngstown, N.Y.: Old Fort Niagara Association, 1997), p. 45; Isabel Thompson Kelsay, *Joseph Brant, 1743–1807: Man of Two Worlds* (Syracuse, N.Y.: Syracuse University, 1986), p. 203.

31. Old Fort Schuyler, not to be confused with Fort Stanwix, which also was called at that time Fort Schuyler, moldered quietly on the south bank of the Mohawk across from Deerfield. The word "oriska" in the Oneida dialect signifies "nettles," and "oriskany" meant "place of nettles." The creek to this day is densely enclosed by growth. It rises twenty miles to the south of the Mohawk in Eaton, New York. The Albany road of the eighteenth century lies beneath modern routes 69 and 5S.

32. Herkimer's wagons, forty or so in number, carried ammunition and provisions for two days. These were meant to provide rations additional to the rations carried by individual militiamen. Presumably, the staple foodstuffs were salt pork and flour.

33. Watt, p. 157.

34. An example of recent microburst devastation can be found along the upper reaches of the Oswegatchie River on the borders of St. Lawrence and Herkimer counties, New York.

35. Allan D. Foote, *Liberty March: The Battle of Oriskany* (Utica, N.Y.: North Country, 1999), p. 145; Gavin K. Watt, *Rebellion in the Mohawk Valley* (Toronto: Dundurn, 1997), p.159, n. 415, p. 374.

36. Watt, p. 152.

37. Foote, p. 200.

38. Walter D. Edmonds, *Drums along the Mohawk* (Syracuse, N.Y.: Syracuse University, 1997, original edition 1936), pp. 373–383.

39. Watt, p. 152.

40. W. J. Wood, p. 122.

41. Old Smoke (Sayenqueraghta) was the war chief of the Seneca's Turtle Clan, while Cornplanter (Gayentwahga) was chief of the Wolf Clan. Both were fearsome opponents who would figure significantly in later raids on the Mohawk. Blacksnake (Dahgayadoh) survived the wars of the Revolution and 1812 to be interviewed subsequently by Lyman Draper. The "Blacksnake Conversations" are a source of much information on Oriskany and the Wyoming massacre from the Seneca viewpoint. See Barbara Graymont, *The Iroquois in the American Revolution* (Syracuse, N.Y.: Syracuse University, 1972), p. 340.

42. W. J. Wood, p. 124; Ward, II, p. 485.

43. Foote, p. 150.

44. Eckert, p. 154.

45. William L. Stone, *Life of Joseph Brant—Thayendanegea* (New York: 1838), I, App. IV.

46. Watt, p. 170.

47. Watt, p. 171.

48. Foote, p. 153.

49. Few militiamen, encumbered by their standard kit, could outrun Iroquois warriors over a flat forest track. The accuracy with which the pursuer could throw a tomahawk generally ended the race. Herkimer told his men never to run; that was what the enemy, dressed in all his frightfulness, expected, and usually the outcome would prove fatal.

50. Foote, p. 156.

51. Debate continues over the death of William of Canajoharie at Fox's hands. Kelsay, p. 206, credits the account of his death at Oriskany despite reports of later sightings in the Mohawk Valley.

52. Watt, p. 172.

53. Foote, p. 152.

54. The scarcity of prisoners at Oriskany is testament to the ferocity of the fighting and the reluctance on both sides to encumber their actions with captives. Without settled lines in the smoky forest, and without officers, individual soldiers and warriors fought savagely for survival.

55. Red Jacket appears on the fringes of several engagements—Oriskany, Wyoming Valley, Newtown, Kanadasegea—yet never as a full combatant. Brant called him "the cow killer" because he buried his hatchet in a cow and boasted later that its blood was an American's. The Seneca enjoyed tales of Red Jacket's cowardice. These did not prevent him from becoming the leading orator of his nation, an advisor to sages, and a positive influence on the direction of his people in the bitter years following the Revolution.

56. Watt, p. 177.

57. For a diagram of the disposition of the lines, see Watt, p. 183.

58. John Butler wrote to Carleton: "the Indians shewed the greatest zeal for His Majesty's Cause, and had they not been a little too precipitate, scarcely a Rebel of the party had escaped." He added that their behavior "exceeded anything I could have expected from them": Kelsey, p. 206. The senior Butler's cold, dispassionate comments reveal the perceptions of a master tactician, a brilliance that would bear bitter fruit for the patriots at Wyoming.

59. W. J. Wood, p. 128.

60. W. J. Wood, p. 129.

61. Foote, p. 164.

62. Foote, p. 180.

Chapter 10: Sorrow on the Land

1. Barbara Graymont, *The Iroquois in the American Revolution* (Syracuse, N.Y.: Syracuse University, 1972), p. 136.

2. Papers of the Continental Congress, "Moses Younglove Declaration," December 1777, transcribed by William Markland, National Archives & Records Administration, M 247-70, 157, pp. 85–87.

3. Allan D. Foote, *Liberty March: The Battle of Oriskany* (Utica, N.Y.: North Country, 1999), p. 175.

4. Allan W. Eckert, *The Wilderness War* (Boston: Little Brown, 1978), p. 164–165.

5. Eckert, p. 165.

6. Christopher Ward, *The War of Revolution* (New York: Macmillan, 1952), II, p. 489.

7. Larry Lowenthal, *Marinus Willett: Defender of the Northern Frontier* (Fleischmanns, N.Y.: Purple Mountain, 2000), p. 31; also, William Marinus Willett, ed., *A Narrative of the Military Actions of Colonel Marinus Willett, Taken Chiefly from His Own Manuscript* (New York: G. & C. & H. Carvill, 1831), pp. 57–58.

8. Foote, p. 182.

9. See Graymont for a judicious evaluation of the claims, pp. 136–142.

10. Graymont, p. 141.

11. Graymont, p. 143.

12. Graymont, p. 147.

13. W. Max Reid, *The Mohawk Valley: Its Legends and Its History* (New York: G. P. Putnam, 1907), p. 94.

14. Edward A. Hagan, *War in Schohary* (Schoharie, N.Y.: Schoharie Stone Fort Museum, 1980), pp. 3–5.

15. *Die Fläche*, High German for "plain," was anglicized as "Flockey."

16. Lowenthal, p. 32.

17. Willett Bridge over the Mohawk at Rome, New York, is said to be built on the spot where Willett and Stockwell slipped through the British sentries.

18. Richard M. Ketchum, *Saratoga: Turning Point of America's Revolutionary War* (New York: Henry Holt, 1997). Ketchum characterizes Stark as "proud, touchy, difficult, cantankerous, contrary, ornery, determined, and as independent as a hog on ice," p. 286. New Hampshire troops would follow no one else. He was a brilliant tactician, but lacked Schuyler's grasp of broader issues. Stark was a veteran of Rogers' Rangers; he had fought with distinction at Bunker Hill, on the retreat from Canada, and at Trenton and Princeton. But by refusing to join his New Hampshire forces with the Continental Army on the Hudson, he became in Schuyler's view a loose cannon.

19. Ward, II, p. 489, from Isaac N. Arnold, *The Life of Benedict Arnold* (Chicago: 1880), pp. 153–154.

20. Herkimer had no children of his own.

21. Herkimer's home on the south bank of the Mohawk by Little Falls, New York, is a well-preserved historic site. The interior has been restored to reflect the furnishings and décor of August 1777. The family burial plot adjoins the house and gardens.

22. Foote, p. 186.

23. Arnold's choices—the trails Willett and Stockwell followed (too slow); attack by bateaux (not enough available); the military road through Oriska. Note that the trench line had approached to within 150 feet of the wall at this point.

24. Eckert, p. 175.

25. Foote, p. 185.

26. Baum originally intended to reach Manchester, but when Burgoyne learned of the militia's depot at Bennington, Baum's objective was changed. He departed Fort Miller and camped the first night on the Batten Kill, four miles away. The German column moved slowly. The next day they followed the Hoosic River to the town of Cambridge where, on Owl Creek, they made first contact with militia detachments sent out by Stark to impede Baum's marauding Indians. The battlefield, reached on the 15th, lay about seven miles to the southeast of Cambridge: Ward, I, p. 425.

27. The Hampshire Grants, long claimed by New York State, became Vermont only after 1777. The boundaries between the future states of Vermont and New York were then, like many state boundaries, questionable. Although the Bennington monument stands today in Bennington, Vermont, the battle site on the Walloomsac River is found several miles away in New York State.

28. Ketchum, p. 382.

29. Graymont, p. 150.

30. See Michael Stephenson, *Patriot Battles: How the War of Independence Was Fought* (New York: Harper Collins, 2007), pp. 303–309, for a concise and colorful account of Arnold, Dearborn, and Morgan at the battles of Freeman's Farm and Bemis Heights.

31. Gavin K. Watt, *Rebellion in the Mohawk Valley* (Toronto; Dundurn, 1997), p. 259.

32. Foote, p. 186, "Testimony of Lt. Alexander Thompson, 2nd Artillery, Continental Army." The remains, such as could be found, were gathered up by farmers in the early nineteenth century and buried in unmarked locations. This was as the forest itself had begun to give way to planted fields.

33. Graymont, p. 164.

34. Ron Chernow, *Alexander Hamilton* (New York: Penguin, 2004), pp. 135–136.

35. Chernow, pp. 101–102, for Hamilton's and others' reactions to Gates.

36. The Mohawk Butlers claimed origin from Thomas Butler, Black Tom, Earl of Ormond and faithful lieutenant to Elizabeth I in her Irish wars. Reid, pp. 220–221.

37. Eckert, pp. 202–203, for most colorful account; also, Isabel Thompson Kelsay, *Joseph Brant, 1743–1807: Man of Two Worlds* (Syracuse, N.Y.: Syracuse University, 1986), p. 216; and Hagan, pp. 10–11.

38. Eckert, p. 204.

39. Hagan, p. 11.

40. Kelsay, 189–190.

41. Alan Taylor, *The Divided Ground: Indians, Settlers, and the Northern Borderland of the American Revolution* (New York: Alfred A. Knopf, 2006), p. 98.

42. The dispatch that Brant read was bogus, planted in the rider's saddlebags to deceive captors. The real message was probably lost with the rider. Cherry Valley on May 30 was totally vulnerable. The new stockade was hardly begun, and the town's main military presence was a handful of militia: Eckert, p. 201.

43. The name of the seven families, as commemorated on a monument to the Andrustown patriots found near Warren, New York, were Bell, Crim, Frank, Hower, Lepper, Osterhout, and Stauring.

44. The Tunnicliff mansion had been burned during the French and Indian War. At that time John senior was in London. He and his family returned to their Mohawk property in 1772. The stream flowing out of lovely Canadarago is still called Oaks Creek.

45. These details are borrowed from Eckert, p. 265.

46. For comparative values see Eckert, pp. 522–523. British authorities denied paying for scalps, but Native American testimony left no doubt that they understood scalps to be worth goods.

47. Kelsay, p. 224.

48. Today, it is difficult to locate the precise location of old Andrustown. The village stood northwest of Warren and southeast of Jordanville in what are now empty fields.

49. Kelsay, p. 221.

50. The Forbidden Path, the back door to Seneca country, roughly followed the Chemung River west-northwest to the village of Canisteo at the heart of Indian country. Its use was forbidden to all except Iroquois.

51. This was Fort Wintermoot, inhabited by Tory sympathizers.

52. Eckert, pp. 534–535.

53. The execution stone, a piece of quartz streaked with red, still lies not far from Forty-Fort on what was then the shore of the Susquehanna. The scene of the wild woman Esther dancing against the firelight with her club raised found numerous graphic representations in the nineteenth century.

54. East Winfield is now the town on Route 20 closest to the Steele Creek spring.

55. Graymont, p. 178.

56. Graymont, p. 181.

57. Graymont, p. 182.

58. Graymont, p. 180.

Chapter 11: To Make a Desert

1. The account of Adam Hunter appears in several sources. I use the version described in Susan Murray-Miller, *Five Days in November: The Cherry Valley Massacre* (Cobleskill: Times-Journal Press, 2003), pp. 1–3. Some attribute Hunter's willingness to talk to his loyalist sympathies.

2. Barbara Graymont, *The Iroquois in the American Revolution* (Syracuse, N.Y.: Syracuse University, 1972), p. 185. This design had been used at Fort Herkimer and Schoharie Stone Fort. Since churches were often the strongest buildings in a community, they made excellent defensive positions while also providing instant barracks for displaced people.

3. Allan W. Eckert, *The Wilderness War* (Boston: Little Brown, 1978), p. 291.

4. Christopher Ward, *The War of the Revolution* (New York: Macmillan, 1952), II, pp. 634–635.

5. Isabel Thompson Kelsay, *Joseph Brant, 1743–1807: Man of Two Worlds* (Syracuse, N.Y.: Syracuse University, 1986), p. 230.

6. Kelsay, p. 231.

7. Murray-Miller, p. xvii.

8. John Sawyer, *History of Cherry Valley from 1740 to 1898* (Cherry Valley, N.Y.: Cherry Valley Historical Association, 1997), p. 32. This 1898 account contains recollections of survivors interviewed in the nineteenth century. Brant's efforts to save women and children are widely attested to and have become a part of the historic record.

9. Murray-Miller, p. 40.

10. There are no significant disagreements between accounts of the survivors and after-action reports submitted at Niagara. Some of the more ghastly details, seemingly exaggerated, are confirmed by several eyewitness sources. See Murray-Miller for a summary of losses house by house during that morning.

11. Brant's part in Alden's death is a received story often repeated in more or less graphic detail. Graymont, Ward, and Kelsay pass it over, noting only that Alden died in the first few minutes of the attack. Eckert elaborates on Brant's role and is followed by Murray-Miller.

12. Eckert, pp. 309–310.

13. Kelsay, p. 233.

14. An old woman, Mrs. Cannon, the mother of Jane Campbell, was unable to keep up with her captors. Despite her daughter's pleading, she was tomahawked and left dead in the middle of the roadway: Murray-Miller, p. 55.

15. The name "Goose" derived from Van Schaick's grandfather's patronymic, "Gossen."

16. James Clinton was the father of DeWitt Clinton, whose energy and genius would bring the Erie Canal to fruition in the next century.

17. Graymont, p. 196.

18. The Americans took thirty-four prisoners—two chiefs, six warriors, twelve women, thirteen children and one white man—and killed twelve others. Mike McAndrew, "Troops Kill Onondagas," Syracuse *Post-Standard*, Monday, August 7, 2000.

19. Brant correspondence, http://www.sullivancountyhistory.prg/places.htm.

20. Ward, II, p. 636.

21. Hathorn correspondence, http://www.albertwisnerlibrary.org/~wisner/Factsand History/Minisink. htm.

22. The Minisink battlefield site is well marked and accessible today, with a self-guided tour stopping at the overhanging rock where Tusten and his wounded were slain. The Mohawks not only dispatched one of the few physicians available on the Delaware frontier, but also took the scalp in Minisink village of one

of the few schoolmasters, Jeremiah Van Auken, who in death saved his fleeing students: Graymont, pp. 199–200.

23. Kelsay, p. 252.

24. http://www.minisink.org/minisinkbattle.html.

25. Kelsay, p. 252; Graymont, p. 201. One exception to the execution of the wounded and captive Americans was John Wood, who flashed Brant the Freemason's sign of distress. Brant, like most of the Johnsons, was an enthusiastic Mason and spared Wood's life. Wood later admitted to not being a Mason at all, but by then the killing fury had passed. He was taken prisoner to Niagara. Whatever supposed humanitarianism lay behind killing wounded soldiers, the sorry fact was that, in 1779, wherever fighting occurred, British troops and Tory raiders increasingly offered no quarter to surrendered Continentals and militiamen.

26. Kirkland had been a young missionary in 1765 traveling to Kanadasegea with Sir William Johnson's blessings.

27. July 5, 1779, to Mrs. Jerusha Kirkland, Kirkland MSS.

28. Ward, II, p. 639.

29. Eckert, pp. 399–400.

30. Washington explained that he had wanted Schuyler for the command, but Schuyler no longer wished a field command under Congress; Lee and Putnam were unacceptable; and thus Gates was offered the command with the provision that, if he rejected the proposal, he would send the letter of appointment on to Sullivan. Gates's reply to Washington was peevish: "Last night I had the honor of your Excellency's letter. The man who undertakes the Indian service, should enjoy youth and strength; requisites I do not possess. It therefore grieves me that your Excellency should offer me the only command to which I am entirely unequal. In obedience to your command, I have forwarded your letter to General Sullivan": William J. Stone, *Life of Joseph Brant—Thayendanegea* (Buffalo, N.Y.: Phinney, 1851), II, chapter 1.

31. Colonel Daniel Brodhead and the 8th Pennsylvania played a decisive role in the Ohio country during the last years of the Revolution, defeating the Delawares at Coshocton. His agnomen, "Great Sun," was a term of respect given Brodhead by Seneca adversaries: Kelsay, p. 254.

32. Graymont, pp. 214–215.

33. Stone, II, Chapter 2.

34. Kelsay, p. 261.

35. Eckert, p. 442.

36. Graymont, p. 213.

37. John Sullivan, *Journals of the Military Expedition of Maj. Gen. John Sullivan against the Six Nations of Indians* (Albany: State of New York, 1887), p. 186.

38. Ward, II, p. 643.

39. Ward, II, p. 644.

40. Sidney G. Fisher, *The Struggle for American Independence* (Philadelphia: 1908), II, p. 245.

41. Graymont, p. 216.

42. Graymont, p. 192.

43. Sullivan, p. 101.

44. Graymont, p. 217.

45. Eckert, p. 493. For contemporary accounts of the finding of Boyd and Parker, see http://members.aol.com/liv18thc/newtown.html. That John Butler did nothing to save Boyd, whom he found an intelligent officer, has been held against Butler father and son down the years. Lieutenant Rudolphus Van Hovenburgh, 4th New York, records in his diary for September 14th: "A women who was prisoner among them came to us who informed us that the Squaws did not like to leave their place and persuaded the warriors to make peace with us but Butler would not hear to that and order'd them to goe to Niagra and also Says that the Indians Brought the Prisoners to Col. Butler, but he gave them over to the Indians for Satisfaction for the damages we had done to them. ..." The woman who was a prisoner might have been Mary Jemison. She lived at Chenussio and lost her home and possessions in the destruction of that town.

46. Graymont, p. 220.

47. Graymont, p. 228–229.

48. Graymont, p. 224.

49. L. Edward Purcell and David F. Burg, *The Almanac of the American Revolution* (New York: St. Martin's, 1992), p. 232. Of the nine largest colonies, New York remained sixth in population, following Pennsylvania, Massachusetts, Virginia, North Carolina, and Maryland. Moreover, most of New York's population was concentrated in and around New York City.

50. For Washington's opinions about militia and the Continental soldier, see his letter to George Clinton, reproduced in Gavin K. Watt, *The Burning of the Valley: Daring Raids from Canada Against the New York Frontier in the Fall of 1780* (Toronto: Dundurn Press, 1997), pp. 256–259.

51. By mid-1780 many states were increasingly relying on a category of troops called levies to fill the gap between regular army and militia. Unlike militia, who served locally in an emergency, New York or Massachusetts levies enlisted for nine months, could be dispatched across state borders, and were generally uniformed. Their state of training and effectiveness, however, was no improvement on the militias'.

52. For an account of this raid, see Watt, p. 72.

53. New York lost its northeastern counties during the war to the independent Republic of Vermont, a creation of disaffected small farmers determined to escape New York's land claims. New York obstructed Vermont's admission to the Union, but Congress, fearful of New York's growing power in the wake of the war, blocked all attempts by Governor Clinton to regain the Vermont region. See Allen Taylor, *The Divided Ground*, p. 154.

54. Watt, p. 76.

55. Watt, p. 79.

56. No certain knowledge is found of Johnson's route to the Schoharie after arriving at Onondaga. It is reasonably certain that he followed the Unadilla. The creeks mentioned by modern name flow eastward toward the Schoharie and may well have been his path.

57. Vincent J. Schaefer, *Vroomans Nose: A Study* (Fleischmanns, N.Y.: Purple Mountain, 1992), p. 46; and also Kelsay, p. 294.

58. This was the center of the Palatine settlement in the Schoharie dating back to the 1720s, as indeed Vroomansland was once the property of Adam Vrooman of Schenectady. Middleburgh, the "middle fort," was previously known as Weisersdorf, named for Johann Weiser, the father of Conrad Weiser, who grew up in the neighborhood and met Shickellamy on Onistagrawa.

59. Edward A. Hagan, *War in Schohary* (Schoharie, N.Y.: Schoharie Stone Fort Museum, 1980), pp. 38–39. After Yorktown, a battle in which he served, Murphy returned to the Schoharie Valley for the remainder of his life. He is buried beneath an appropriate monument in Middleburgh cemetery.

60. The Stone Fort remains as a museum located on the north side of the town of Schoharie. The hole in the eaves is still visible and the three-pound ball is on exhibit in the museum's collection.

61. Isaac Paris had been captured at Oriskany and murdered. He was one of the earliest members of the Tryon County Committee of Safety.

62. Arnold deserted to the British on September 25, 1780, after plotting to surrender West Point and its garrison of 3,000 to the enemy. The shock to his many admirers in upper New York State was shattering.

63. Brown is buried in the graveyard behind the Stone Church in Stone Arabia under a modest marker. Many of the men who fell in the battle are also buried there. The church is located on Route 10, three miles north of Palatine Bridge, New York.

64. Anthony's Nose, a round knob rising on the north bank of the Mohawk, constricted the King's Highway into a narrow defile. Across the river, the even higher Noses provided an unparalleled view of the upper valley. In the face of a lurking enemy, this was a dangerous place to rush through, and the American militia had to clear the position before they could move west safely. The Noses are slightly below Keater's Rift near the present-day site of Kanatsiohareke.

65. The most complete account of Klock's Field appears in Watt, *The Burning of the Valleys*, pp. 223–239. Casualties are not clear, but the likelihood is that Sir John got the worst of it. He commanded 600–700, while Van Rensselaer's force amounted to about 900. The following day, Governor George Clinton arrived with reinforcements to bring the pursuing force to 1,500. This hardly mattered in the end, since the Americans had pushed off in the wrong direction. The great raid circumvented Fort Herkimer and Fort Stanwix and most likely returned to Onondaga by way of Chittenango Creek.

66. Graymont, p. 240.

Chapter 12: Tenonanatche Farewell

1. John C. Devendorf, *Battles and Raids in the Province and State of New York, 1609–1814*, http://www.fortklock.com/Battles.htm.

2. Isabel Thompson Kelsay, *Joseph Brant, 1743–1807: Man of Two Worlds* (Syracuse, N.Y.: Syracuse University, 1986), p. 315. Although Brant was reported everywhere in Tenonanatche during 1781, he was in fact in the Ohio country and environs of Detroit through most of the year.

3. In July 1784 a French immigrant, Peter Sailly, described the fort as "no more than a rampart of earth, now overgrown with thorns and bushes." Sailly's description of the Oneidas and others in the wake of the war suggests a measure of recovery. Dean R. Snow, Charles T. Gehring, and William A. Starna, eds., *In Mohawk Country: Early Narratives about a Native People* (Syracuse: Syracuse University Press, 1996), p. 295–299.

4. Daniel E. Wager, "Col. Marinus Willett: The Hero of the Mohawk Valley," an Address Before the Oneida Historical Society, Utica, New York, 1891.

5. Larry Lowenthal, *Marinus Willett: Defender of the Northern Frontier* (Fleischmanns, N.Y.: Purple Mountain, 2000), p. 53

6. The upper castle was located at Canajoharie; the lower, Tiononderoge, at Fort Hunter. Except for Fort Rensselaer, Brant had burned the white settlement and castle at Canajoharie. The lower castle at Fort Hunter was a hotbed of Tory activity and had been destroyed by militia in the aftermath of the Schoharie raid.

7. Snow et al., p. 294.

8. Barbara Graymont, *The Iroquois in the American Revolution* (Syracuse, N.Y.: Syracuse University, 1972), p. 242.

9. Graymont, p. 243.

10. Snow, et al., p. 293.

11. Snow, et al., p. 294.

12. Graymont, p. 246.

13. Revolutionary War Pension Application for Henry Grim, submitted October 18, 1832, at Herkimer County Courthouse. Herkimer County archives at http://herkimer.nygenweb.net/henrycrim.html.

14. Jeptha R. Simms, *The Frontiersmen of New York* (Albany: George C. Riggs Publisher, 1883), Vol. II, pp 508–513; Herkimer County Historical Society site: http://morrisonspensions.org/woodworthsol.html; also, for the British version of the ambush, see Governor Frederick Haldemand Papers, Letters from Colonel Guy Johnson, Add. MSS 21767, British Museum, England, at the Web site above.

15. Willett lost his command in the New York line when the five original regiments in Continental service were reduced to two. Disconsolate and in debt, he petitioned New York's representatives to Congress without results. George Clinton, desperate to combat the punishing raids and disillusioned with Van Rensselaer and Dubois, leaped at the opportunity to employ Willett. For Willett's appraisal of militia, see Lowenthal, p. 59.

16. Lieutenant Doxtader would die at Oneida castle several weeks later from a sickness contracted in his flight through the swamps.

17. Christopher Ward, *The War of the Revolution* (New York: Macmillan, 1952), II, p. 651. This fight occurred at Schellsbush. Other inhabitants of the hamlet had fled.

18. Ward, II, p. 651.

19. Graymont, p. 250.

20. See Revolutionary War Pension Application for Henry Grim, n. 13 above.

21. Willett promised the Oneida warriors a blanket each for participating in the chase. Ten years later he was still pleading with the state to honor his promise to these Indians: Lowenthal, p. 66.

22. Lowenthal, pp. 66–67.

23. St. George's Episcopal is located at 30 North Ferry Street in the Stockade District of Schenectady. The present church dates from 1759 and was built with substantial contributions from Sir William Johnson, among others. Presbyterians also subscribed to the erection of the stone church and shared in its use. A mid-eighteenth-century Masonic lodge met on the church's property. Sir William was an avid Mason. No grave marker is found for Walter Butler, and only one other Butler, Anne, is listed among St. George's eighteenth-century parishioners. Legend holds that Walter's grave was hidden in order to prevent his corpse being disinterred by resentful patriots.

24. Lowenthal, p. 68.

25. See Devendorf: http://www.fortklock.com/Battles.htm for a list and description of skirmishes in 1782 and 1783.

26. Snow, et al., p. 297.

27. Snow, et al., p. 297.

28. Alan Taylor, *The Divided Ground: Indians, Settlers, and the Northern Borderland of the American Revolution* (New York: Alfred A. Knopf, 2006), pp. 118–119. Taylor's is the most comprehensive recent account of the partition of lands and social consequences resulting from the final settlement of the war.

29. Snow, et al., p. 299.

30. Taylor, p. 112.

31. Graymont, pp. 259–262; also quoted in Taylor, p. 112.

32. For the above quotes, see Taylor, pp. 112–113.

33. Graymont, p. 262.

34. Taylor, p. 112.

35. Fort Niagara was not turned over to the United States until 1796.

36. Taylor, p. 156.

37. Taylor, p. 158.

38. Taylor, p. 159.

39. Taylor, p. 164.

40. Clinton was also in no rush at the end of the 1780s to see Congress established on a sound financial footing or in a position to challenge New York's rights. New York was third from the last of states to ratify the Constitution.

41. Taylor, pp. 137–141, chronicles the initial and promising stages of this frontier relationship, its descent into disorder, and the eventual violent crime patterns occurring predominantly among native people.

42. To the Oneida population of 600 or so could also be added 300 from the smaller population of Stockbridge Indians. The Oneida sheltered Brotherton Indians, fragments of the Mohegans, Narranganset, Pequot, Stonington, Farmington, and Montauk tribes driven from their tribal lands to the east. Stockbridge and Mohegan warriors also fought beside the Americans.

43. http://oneida-nation.net/TREATY-KO.html.

44. For the inadequacies of the Articles of Confederation, the Federalist critique of financing under the Articles, and Hamilton's despair at politicians like Clinton, see Ron Chernow, *Alexander Hamilton* (New York: Penguin, 2004), pp. 252–255.

45. Clinton eventually came to personally own the acres on which the Oriskany battle site and Oriske village stood.

46. Graymont, p. 286.

47. Graymont, p. 287.

48. With the Mohawks gone from Tenonanatche to upper Canada, the Onondagas recognized the Oneidas as the keepers of the eastern door and in formal council denominated them leading nation of the Iroquois Confederacy.

49. Graymont, p. 286.

50. Graymont, p. 288.

51. Kirkland, Dean, and Abraham Wemple received about 4,000 acres in individual packets. They converted their gifts into state patents as required by New York, even though by siding with the state they were ignoring the best interests of the Oneidas.

52. Taylor, p. 166. That smaller states rushed to ratify the proposed constitution while Clinton delayed, is explained by the emerging power of New York under the existing Articles of Confederation.

53. http://oneida-nation.net/TREATY-KO.html.

54. For the history of the Grand River settlement and Iroquois affairs in Canada after the Treaty of Paris, see Isabel Kelsay's biography of Joseph Brant, principally Chapters 24–26.

55. Sir John Johnson died in 1830 at the age of eighty-eight. His tomb was bulldozed accidentally in the 1950s and his remains, with those of Mary, were scattered in a construction pit. They have since been retrieved and await a suitable monument. http://www.townshipsheritage.com/Eng/Archives/News/john.johnson.html.

56. http://www.union.edu/About/history.php.

57. W. Pilkington, ed., *The Journal of Samuel Kirkland* (Clinton, N.Y.: Hamilton College, 1980), p. 192.

58. William S. Smith built a stately house a mile and a half south of Hamilton village under University Hill. The house was completed in 1798 and occupied by him until 1808. He died in 1816 and is buried in Sherburne West Hill. Smith fought at Long Island, Harlem Heights, Throg's Neck, White Plains, Trenton, Princeton, Monmouth, Newport, and Yorktown. He was appointed first federal marshal of New York State by President Washington. Diplomatic missions took him to Spain, Portugal, and London.

59. A stone plinth before the chapel on the Colgate quadrangle shows the spot where Payne felled his tree and prayed. But a hundred yards down the hill another plaque stands by a new tree. The plaque announces that this is a *Pinus Strobus* or eastern white pine, the HAUDENOSAUNEE TREE OF PEACE, dedicated by Chief Jake Swamp, Wolf Clan, Mohawk, "in Living Testimony of Friendship Between the Haudenosaunee and the Colgate University Community." In legend the peace tree of *Ayenwatha* and *Dekanawida* sprouted at the founding of the Iroquois League.

60. L. M. Hammond, *History of Madison County, State of New York* (Syracuse N.Y.: 1872), p. 429.

❧ Bibliography ❧

For the French and Indian Wars and Pontiac's Rebellion, I rely heavily on Fred Anderson's *Crucible of War*. For the life of Sir William Johnson, I have found no better book, so far as it extends, than Milton W. Hamilton's *Sir William Johnson: Colonial American, 1715–1763*. Covering the years immediately following the Revolution, the definitive guide to the New York scene is Alan Taylor's *The Divided Ground*. Christopher Ward's *The War of the Revolution* remains the most detailed account of the long, many-sided struggle in upstate, while Kevin Phillips's *The Cousins War: Religion, Politics, & the Triumph of Anglo-America* most completely covers the demographic and psychographic complexion of the New York colony at the outbreak of hostilities. For Joseph Brant and the Iroquoian role in the struggle, two books are essential reading: Isabel Thompson Kelsay's *Joseph Brant 1743–1807: Man of Two Worlds* is magisterial in scope, while Barbara Graymont's *The Iroquois in the American Revolution* remains the most comprehensive guide to the place of the Haudenosaunee in the struggle. I turned to Allan W. Eckert's *Wilderness Empire* and *The Wilderness War* for dramatic detail, and to Snow, Gehring, and Starna's *In Mohawk Country: Early Narratives about a Native People* for important corroborative material.

Abler, Thomas S., ed. *Chainbreaker, The Revolutionary War: Memoirs of Governor Blacksnake as Told to Benjamin Williams*. Lincoln, Neb.: University of Nebraska, 1989.

Addison, Joseph. *The Spectator*, No. 50, Friday, April 27, 1711. New York: Dutton, Everyman's Library, 1964.

Adler, Jeanne Winston, ed. *Chainbreaker's War: A Seneca Chief Remembers the American Revolution*. Hensonville, N.Y.: Black Dome, 2002.

Anderson, Fred. *Crucible of War: The Seven Years War and the Fate of Empire in British North America, 1754–1766*. New York: Alfred A. Knopf, 2000.

Arnold, Isaac N. *The Life of Benedict Arnold*. Chicago: 1880.

Bernstein, Peter L. *Wedding of the Waters*. New York: W. W. Norton, 2005.

Bogaert, H. M. van den. *Journey into Mohawk Country*. New York: First Second, 2006.

Borneman, Walter R. *The French and Indian War: Deciding the Fate of North America.* New York: Harper Perennial, 2006.

Bridenbaugh, Carl. *Cities in Revolt, Urban Life in America, 1743–1776.* New York: Capricorn, 1964.

Brodhead, John Romeyn. *Documents Relative to the Colonial History of the State of New York.* ed. E. B. O'Callaghan. Albany, N.Y.: Weed, Parsons, 1855.

Brumwell, Stephen. *White Devil: A True Story of War, Savagery, and Vengeance in Colonial America.* New York: Da Capo, 2004.

Burleigh, H. C. "A Tale of Loyalist Heroism," *Ontario History,* Vol. 13, No. 2, 1950.

Burns, Rick. *New York: A Documentary Film.* Steeplechase Films, 1999.

Chernow, Ron. *Alexander Hamilton.* New York: Penguin, 2004.

Claus, Daniel. *Narrative of his relations with Sir William Johnson: Documents relative to the colonial history of the State of New York: Documentary History of the State of New York.* Albany: N.Y., 1904.

Clinton, George. *George Clinton to the President of Congress,* February 5, 1780, CC, Item 67, II, 348.

Cobb, Sanford H. *The Story of the Palatines: An Episode in Colonial History.* New York: G. P. Putnam, 1897.

Cooper, James Fenimore. *The Last of the Mohicans.* New York: Bantam Classics, 1982.

———. *The Leather Stocking Tales.* Vol. 1. New York: The Library of America, 1985.

———. *The Pathfinder.* New York: Signet Classic, 1980.

———. *The Pioneers.* New York: Penguin Classics, 1988.

Cuneo, John R. *Robert Rogers of the Rangers.* Ticonderoga, N.Y.: Fort Ticonderoga Museum, 1988.

Dary, David. *Frontier Medicine from the Atlantic to the Pacific 1492–1941.* New York: Alfred A. Knopf, 2008.

De Bougainville, Louis Antoine. *Adventure in the Wilderness: The American Journals, 1756–1760.* trans. Edward P. Hamilton. Norman, Okla.: University of Oklahoma, 1990.

Demos, John. *The Unredeemed Captive: A Family Story from Early America.* New York: Alfred A. Knopf, 1994.

De Peyster, J. Watts. *The Orderly Book of Sir John Johnson.* Albany: Joel Munsell, 1882.

Devendorf, John C. *Battles and Raids in the Province and State of New York, 1609–1814.* http://www.fortklock.com/Battles.htm.

Dieskau, Baron Jean-Armand de. "Dialogue entre le Maréchal de Saxe et le Baron de Dieskau aux Champs Élysées." *Mémoires de Diderot,* I, 1830.

Eckert, Allan W. *The Conquerors.* Boston: Little Brown, 1970.

———. *That Dark and Bloody River.* New York: Bantam, 1996.

———. *Wilderness Empire.* Boston: Little Brown, 1969.

————. *The Wilderness War.* Boston: Little Brown, 1978.

Edmonds, Walter D. *Drums along the Mohawk.* Syracuse, N.Y.: Syracuse University, 1997, original edition 1936.

————. *In the Hands of the Senecas.* Boston: Little Brown, 1947.

Ellis, Joseph J. *After the Revolution: Profiles of Early American Culture.* New York: W. W. Norton, 2002.

Faragher, John Mack. *Daniel Boone: The Life and Legend of an American Pioneer.* New York: Henry Holt, 1992.

Ferling, John. *Almost a Miracle: The American Victory in the War of Independence.* New York: Oxford University, 2007.

————. *The First of Men: A Life of George Washington.* Knoxville, Tenn.: University of Tennessee, 1988.

Fischer, David Hackett, *Albion's Seed: Four British Folkways in America.* New York: Oxford University, 1989.

————. *Washington's Crossing.* New York: Oxford University, 2004.

Fischer, Sidney G. *The Struggle for American Independence.* Philadelphia: 1908.

Fleming, Thomas. *1776: Year of Illusions.* New York: W. W. Norton, 1975.

————. *The Forgotten Victory: The Battle for New Jersey—1780.* New York: Readers' Digest, 1973.

Flexner, James Thomas. *Mohawk Baronet: A Biography of Sir William Johnson.* Syracuse, N.Y.: Syracuse University, 1989.

Foote, Allan D. *Liberty March: The Battle of Oriskany.* Utica, N.Y.: North Country, 1999.

Gallagher, John J. *The Battle of Brooklyn.* New York: Sarpedon, 1995.

Garland, David. *Saratoga: A Novel of the American Revolution.* New York: St. Martin's, 2005.

Gerlach, Don R. *Philip Schuyler and the American Revolution in New York, 1733–1777.* Lincoln, Neb.: University of Nebraska, 1964.

Golway, Terry. *Washington's General: Nathaniel Greene and the Triumph of the American Revolution.* New York: Henry Holt, 2005.

Graymont, Barbara. *The Iroquois in the American Revolution.* Syracuse, N.Y.: Syracuse University, 1972.

Greer, Allan, ed. *The Jesuit Relations: Natives and Missionaries in Seventeenth-Century North America.* Boston and New York: Bedford/St. Martin's, 2000.

Guillett, Edwin. *The Great Migration.* New York: Thomas Nelson, 1937.

Hagan, Edward A. *War in Schoharie.* Schoharie, N.Y.: Schoharie Stone Fort Museum, 1980.

Hamilton, Edward P. *The French and Indian Wars: The Story of Battles and Forts in the Wilderness.* New York: Doubleday, 1962.

Hamilton, Milton. *Sir William Johnson—Colonial American 1715:1763.* Port Washington, N.Y.: Kennikat, 1976.

Hammond, L. M. *History of Madison County, State of New York*. Syracuse, N.Y.: 1872.

Herkimer, Gil. *Roads to Niagara*. Corpus Christi, Tex.: Alfa, 2000.

Hislop, Codman. *The Mohawk*. New York: Rinehart, 1948.

Huey, Lois M., and Bonnie Pulis. *Molly Brant: A Legacy of her Own*. Youngstown, N.Y.: Old Fort Niagara Association, 1997.

Johnson, Guy. *Governor Frederick Haldemand Papers*, Letters from Colonel Guy Johnson. Add. MSS 21767, British Museum facsimile.

Johnson, Sir William. *The Papers of Sir William Johnson*. James Sullivan, ed. Albany, N.Y.: The University of the State of New York, 1921.

Kast, Ida House, and Mildred Kast Conrad. *Mohawk Valley Kasts and Allied Families*. Herkimer, N.Y.: Herkimer County Historical Society, 1985.

Kelsay, Isabel Thompson. *Joseph Brant, 1743–1807: Man of Two Worlds*. Syracuse, N.Y.: Syracuse University, 1986.

Ketchum, Richard M. *Saratoga: Turning Point of America's Revolutionary War*. New York: Henry Holt, 1997.

———. *Victory at Yorktown: the Campaign that Won the Revolution*. New York: Henry Holt, 2004.

———. *The Winter Soldiers*. New York: Doubleday, 1973.

Langguth, A.J. *Patriots: The Men Who Started the American Revolution*. New York: Simon & Schuster, 1988.

Leckie, Robert. *A Few Acres of Snow: The Saga of the French and Indian Wars*. New York: John Wiley, 1999.

Limerick, Patricia Nelson. *Sweet Medicine: Sites of Indian Massacres, Battlefields, and Treaties*. Albuquerque: University of New Mexico, 1995.

Lothrop, Samuel K. "Life of Samuel Kirkland." *The Library of American Biography*. Jared Sparks, ed. Second Series. Vol. XV. Boston: Little Brown, 1855.

Lowenthal, Larry. *Marinus Willett: Defender of the Northern Frontier*. Fleischmanns, N.Y.: Purple Mountain, 2000.

Mann, Charles C. *1491 New Revelations of the Americas before Columbus*. New York: Vintage, 2005.

McCardell, Lee. *Ill-Starred General: Braddock of the Coldstream Guards*. Pittsburgh: University of Pittsburgh, 1958.

McCullough, David. *1776*. New York: Simon & Schuster, 2005.

McMartin, Barbara, Lee M. Brenning, and Peter O'Shea. *The Northwestern Adirondacks: Four-Season Adventures through the Boreal Forest and the Park's Frontier Region*. Woodstock, Vt.: Backcountry, 1990.

Merrell, James H. *The Lancaster Treaty of 1744 with Related Documents*. Boston and New York: Bedford/St. Martin's, 2007.

Middlekauf, Robert. *The Glorious Cause: The American Revolution, 1763–1789*. New York: Oxford University, 1982.

Mittelberger, Gottlieb. *Gottlieb Mittelberger's Journey to Pennsylvania in the Year 1750 and Return to Germany in the Year 1754.* Philadelphia: 1898.

Murray-Miller, Susan. *Five Days in November: The Cherry Valley Massacre.* Cobleskill, N.Y.: Times-Journal, 2003.

Nelson, James L. *Benedict Arnold's Navy.* New York: McGraw-Hill, 2006.

N. Y. Mercury, September 15, 1755.

O'Toole, Fintan. *White Savage: William Johnson and the Invention of America.* New York: Farrar, Straus and Giroux, 2005.

Papers of the Continental Congress. M 247–70 157. "Moses Younglove Declaration," December 1777. Transcribed by William Markland. National Archives & Records Administration.

Parkman, Francis. *France and England in North America.* Vols. 1 & 2. New York: Library of America, 1983.

———. *Montcalm and Wolfe: The French & Indian War.* New York: Da Capo, 1995.

Phillips, Kevin. *The Cousins' Wars: Religion, Politics, & the Triumph of Anglo America.* New York: Basic, 1999.

Pilkington, Walter, ed. *The Journal of Samuel Kirkland.* Clinton, N.Y.: Hamilton College, 1980.

Polk, William R. *The Birth of America.* New York: Harper Perennial, 2006.

Proctor, Lucien Brock. *Historic Memories of the Old Schuyler Mansion.* New York: 1880.

Purcell, L. Edward, and David Burg, eds. *World Almanac of the American Revolution.* New York: World Almanac, 1992.

Reid, W. Max. *The Mohawk Valley: Its Legends and Its History.* New York: G. P. Putnam, 1907.

Richter, Daniel K., and James H. Merrell, eds. *Beyond the Covenant Chain: The Iroquois and Their Neighbors in Indian North America.* University Park, Pa.: Penn State University, 2004.

Roberts, Kenneth. *Arundel.* New York: Doubleday, 1930.

———. *Rabble in Arms.* New York: Doubleday, 1933.

Roosevelt, Theodore. *New York: A Sketch of the City's Social, Political, and Commercial Progress from the First Dutch Settlement to Recent Times.* New York: Charles Scribner, 1906.

Sawyer, John. *History of Cherry Valley from 1740 to 1898.* Cherry Valley, N.Y.: Cherry Valley Historical Association, 1997.

Schaefer, Vincent J. *Vroomans Nose: A Study.* Fleischmanns, N.Y.: Purple Mountain, 1992.

Schama, Simon. *Rough Crossings: The Slaves, the British, and the American Revolution.* New York: Harper Perennial, 2006.

Schecter, Barnet. *The Battle for New York.* New York: Walker, 2002.

Scheer, George, and Hugh Rankin. *Rebels & Redcoats.* New York: Da Capo, 1987.

Schiff, Stacy. *A Great Improvisation: Franklin, France, and the Birth of America.* New

York: Henry Holt, 2005.

Schneider, Paul. *The Adirondacks: A History of America's First Wilderness.* New York: Henry Holt, 1997.

Seaver, James E. *A Narrative of the Life of Mrs. Mary Jemison.* Norman, Okla.: University of Oklahoma, reprint of 1823 account.

Shorto, Russell. *The Island at the Center of the World: The Epic Story of Dutch Manhattan & the Forgotten Colony That Shaped America.* New York: Doubleday, 2004.

Simms, Jeptha R. *The Frontiersmen of New York.* Albany, N.Y.: George C. Riggs, 1883.

Snow, Dean R., Charles T. Gehring, and William A. Starna, eds. *In Mohawk Country: Early Narratives about a Native People.* Syracuse, N.Y.: Syracuse University, 1996.

Stephenson, Michael. *Patriot Battles: How the War of Independence Was Fought.* New York: Harper Collins, 2007.

Stewart, George R. *Names on the Land: A Historical Account of Place-Naming in the United States.* New York: New York Review, 2008.

Stone, William L. *Life of Joseph Brant—Thayendanegea.* Buffalo, N.Y.: Phinney, 1851.

Sullivan, John. *Journals of the Military Expedition of Maj. Gen. John Sullivan against the Six Nations of Indians.* Albany, N.Y.: State of New York, 1887.

Taylor, Alan. *American Colonies: The Settling of North America.* New York: Viking Penguin, 2001.

———. *The Divided Ground: Indians, Settlers, and the Northern Borderland of the American Revolution.* New York: Alfred A. Knopf, 2006.

———. *William Cooper's Town.* New York: Vintage, 1996.

Thomas, Earle. *Sir John Johnson Loyalist Baronet.* Toronto: Dundurn, 1986.

Thomas, Evan. *John Paul Jones: Sailor, Hero, Father of the American Navy.* New York: Simon & Schuster, 2003.

Thomas, Howard. *Joseph Brant: Thayendanegea.* Utica, N.Y.: North Country, 1984.

Thwaites, Reuben Gold. *Early Western Journals: 1748–1765.* Lewisburg, Pa.: Wennawoods, 1998.

Van Buskirk, Judith L. *Generous Enemies: Patriots and Loyalists in Revolutionary New York.* Philadelphia: University of Pennsylvania, 2004.

Wager, Daniel E. "Col. Marinus Willett: The Hero of the Mohawk Valley," an Address before the Oneida Historical Society, Utica, New York, 1891.

Wallace, Paul A. *Conrad Weiser: Friend of Colonist & Mohawk.* Philadelphia: University of Pennsylvania, 1945.

Ward, Christopher. *The War of the Revolution.* New York: Macmillan, 1952.

Watt, Gavin K. *The Burning of the Valleys: Daring Raids from Canada against the New York Frontier in the Fall of 1780.* Toronto: Dundurn, 1997.

———. *Rebellion in the Mohawk Valley.* Toronto: Dundurn, 2002.

Weiser, C. Z. *Conrad Weiser.* Reading, Pa.: 1876.

Willett, William Marinus, ed. *A Narrative of the Military Actions of Colonel Marinus Willett, Taken Chiefly from His Own Manuscript.* New York: G. & C. & H. Carvill, 1831.

Wood, Gordon S. *The Radicalism of the American Revolution*. New York: Vintage, 1993.

———. *Revolutionary Characters: What Made the Founders Different*. New York: Penguin, 2006.

Wood, W. J. *Battles of the Revolutionary War*. New York: Da Capo, 1990.

Yenne, Bill. *The Encyclopedia of North American Indian Tribes*. New York: Random House, 1986.

Young, Alfred F. *Masquerade: The Life and Times of Deborah Sampson, Continental Soldier*. New York: Vintage, 2005.

Zack, Richard, *The Pirate Hunter: The True Story of Captain Kidd*. New York: Hyperion, 2003.

Richard Berleth received his Ph.D. in English literature from Rutgers University in 1970 and is currently professor of communication arts at St. Francis College in Brooklyn Heights, New York. Before returning to college teaching, he worked in marketing and advertising at Time/Life Books, McGraw-Hill, and Simon and Schuster. His other books include *The Twilight Lords: An Irish Chronicle, The Orphan Stone: The Minnesinger Dream of Reich, Samuel's Choice* (children's), and *Mary Patten* (children's). He and his wife, Emily, live in Cobble Hill, Brooklyn.

Index

Page numbers in italics indicate an illustration.